Imagining Development

Imagining
Development

Economic Ideas in Peru's
"Fictitious Prosperity"
of Guano, 1840 –1880

Paul Gootenberg

UNIVERSITY OF CALIFORNIA PRESS

Berkeley / Los Angeles / London

University of California Press
Berkeley and Los Angeles, California

University of California Press, Ltd.
London, England

© 1993 by
The Regents of the University of California

Library of Congress Cataloging-in-Publication Data
Gootenberg, Paul, 1954–
   Imagining development : economic ideas in Peru's "fictitious
prosperity" of guano, 1840–1880 / Paul Gootenberg.
      p.   cm.
   Includes bibliographical references and index.
   ISBN 0-520-07712-1 (alk. paper). — ISBN 0-520-08290-7 (pbk. :
alk. paper)
      1. Guano industry—Peru—History—19th century.   2. Peru—
Economic policy.   3. Liberalism—Peru—History—19th century.
4. Peru—Economic conditions.   5. Peru—Social conditions.
I. Title.
HD9484.G9G66   1993
338.4'76686366'0985—dc20   92–31679
                                                                                CIP

Printed in the United States of America
9 8 7 6 5 4 3 2 1

The paper used in this publication meets the minimum requirements
of American National Standard for Information Sciences—
Permanence of Paper for Printed Library Materials,
ANSI Z39.48–1984. ∞

Contents

Preface

The voice of artisans is like the prophet who preached in the desert—imagining no one to hear or take fruit from such burning desires.   Lima artisan, December 1858

Are we to imagine guano as the staff of Moses, the hoof of Pegasus, that makes water spring from the deserts?!
                                               Free-traders, October 1851

This book is a social history of ideas of the Peruvian elite of the age of guano. It asks a fairly simple question: What were Peru's leaders truly thinking while they took the country down an ill-fated path of export liberalism? What sorts of economic development did they imagine? Simple as it seems, this question is rarely posed by students of Latin American liberalism.

In this book I pursue the developmental notions of ten (or so) of the century's leading statesmen, ministers, lawyers, engineers, liberal theorists, physicians, historians, educators, social scientists, bankers, and industrialists—from Manuel Pardo to Luis Esteves—and find them not so simple after all. Social and political dimensions of their economic thinking loomed larger and larger in charting the course of this complex Peruvian developmentalism. I actually prefer the term "social history of ideas" rather than "intellectual history" since Peruvian social contexts—

including popular thinking—influenced these *pensadores* as much as any abstruse or imported theories did. It also captures ideas that, on the whole, went against the grain of regnant North Atlantic ideologies of development and thus bore little fruit at the time. This, then, was Peru's "imagined" development.

This essay is not a lot of things, too, though one can imagine the *nots* as equally worthy topics for this dimly lit era. It is not an exhaustive, empirical elite study; not a rounded survey of Peruvian thought (for example, of the simpler liberal formulas); not a full social or regional history (though imaginings of masses and nations there were); not a story of the birth pangs of a liberal regime (as was my prior work, *Between Silver and Guano*); and not exactly of the postmodern persuasion (though trying new ways with intellectual culture).

My caveats emptied, why bother at all with such forgotten and frustrated ideas? At the very least, they add to our working knowledge of republican elites, revealing something of the sophistication, diversity, and vitality of nineteenth-century thought. Along the way, as readers may see, their reconstruction reworks much conventional wisdom about Latin American liberalism. These implications, I believe, go well beyond a bizarre Peruvian experience with bird dung.

If I were to trace my own intellectual history, the custom at this point, the roots of this project extend pretty far, too. It sprung while I was studying economic history with Rosemary Thorp in Oxford, in a half-forgotten half-chapter of a master's thesis on the artisans of Lima. After more than a decade, Rosemary's unforgettable concerns with equitable economic development still resonate in these pages. Later, falling under the influence of the Chicago school (of historians), I returned many times to Peru pursuing other projects and periods. The generosity of Fulbright and Social Science Research Council fellowships and the *amistad* of many Peruvian colleagues and archivists helped me to continue scraping up clues on thinking about guano. Late in 1988 I dug up some buried ideas, the century-old Peruvians' and mine, while on grant leave extended by the American Council of Learned Societies. And now in the 1990s the John M. Olin Foundation allows me to turn a prolonged essay into this modest book—though I'm still unsure if it shares their enthusiasm for classical free-market liberalism.

In terms of intellectual contexts, I had the good fortune of first writing at the Harvard University Committee on Latin American and Iberian Studies (CLAIS), amiably directed by Dr. Anne Normann. In social contexts, my landpeople in the great ville of Somerville, Massachusetts, Gary Hawley and Nan Hamilton, made working there all the more livable. As always, JoAnn Kawell's long-distance "flattery line" provided the perfect antidote to writer's cramp, as did Héctor Lindo-Fuentes's brilliant flashes of insight for a readable prose. Total recall of wayward Oxford convictions, I'm sure, comes from a camaraderie shared over the years with my good friends John Santos, James Der Derian, and Deborah Marvel.

Writing this book helped me bridge a difficult transition in my professional life. At its beginnings, I still felt a stranger in a strange land, in a paradoxical place near Boston—though my academic bondage there also became an opportunity to experience firsthand the wonderful collegiality, humor, and support of Latin Americanists and friends everywhere.

And, as the book closed, the opportunity arose for *aliyah* (Hebrew: up-going) to a very different group of scholars—Barbara Weinstein and Brooke Larson among them—at the State University of New York at Stony Brook. This history department—I won't name names—is an intellectual community beyond my sweetest imaginings, my healers of faith. One of the many wonders of Stony Brook are the graduate students, among whom Alec Dawson, Pepe Gordillo, Angélica Sailer, and Nadanja Skrabitz perceptively read this manuscript; complicit in other ways were Pía Alliende, Sergio Serulnikov, Silvana Palermo, Cecilia Méndez (sometime proofer), and, not least, Julie Franks. I owe a temporary sanity to another, Virginia Acevedo, for her intrepid job of indexing, and the beauty of the book to my artful friend, Janet Stein, who designed a cover well worth judging it by. A new family of friends here—Iona, Ira, Kathleen, Matt, Nilufer, and Leonie—have been ever faithful, not the least in reminding me of teaching opportunities forgone while wrapping this all up.

I thank the Latin Americanists and historians Richard Salvucci, Shane Hunt, Steven Topik, Vincent Peloso, John Womack, Jr., Ian Roxborough, Alfonso Quiroz, Stephen Haber, Gene Lebovics; members of the Stony Brook Humanities Institute "Post-Colonial" seminar; and Eileen McWilliam, my terrific editor at the University of California Press, for their thoughtful readings of some raw, half-baked, and over-done first drafts.

Port Jefferson, N.Y., 1993

Peru ca. 1860

1

Introduction
Guano and Its Discontents

Guano in History

Guano is the dried excrement of seabirds. Just off the Pacific coast of Peru, the right mix of natural conditions—the fertile depths of the Humboldt current, the billions of tiny fish it spawns, the millions of gulls on their trail, the arid specks of land called the Chinchas—left, over the millennia, staggering offshore deposits of bird dung. Literal mountains of it. Rich in unleached nitrogen and phosphorus, guano is the best natural fertilizer known to humankind. Ancient Peruvians, masters of American agriculture, recognized the magical properties of the substance known in Quechua as *huanu*—knowledge lost, like much else, under the Spanish Conquest. It was left to another world conquest—the English scientific, agricultural, and commercial revolution—to rediscover guano's value in the early 1840s. Shoveled down chutes by coolies into waiting clipper convoys and spread across the fields of England, France, Australia, and the southern United States, Peruvian bird droppings excited one of the busiest global commodity trades thus seen in history. For republican Peru, the next forty years became its legendary "age of guano."

The guano age (1845–1880) is not much remembered for its fertile ideas, much less for its lasting economic progress. Instead, it has become the historical paradigm for a fleeting "boom and bust" monoexport experience. The penurious and revolving caudillo governments of Peru

soon strictly monopolized world trade in guano; it became their commercial gold mine, though made of baser stuff. Over the full four
decades Peru shipped out some eleven million tons of manure, which
fetched more than $750 million (pesos/dollars) on world markets, a
mind-boggling sum in nineteenth-century terms. For Peru, it was a rags-
to-riches story: stylish living for citified elites, bloated budgets, millions
in fancy imports, a purchased political peace, unlimited access to London credit. In the late 1870s guano reserves inevitably ran down. Saddled with Latin America's largest foreign debt, Peru was unprepared for
the crash. It was riches to rags, with nothing to show in persisting
economic advance. Peru's historian Jorge Basadre, following Cassandras
of the time, aptly dubs the entire episode the "fictitious prosperity."[1]

The Peruvian guano age had caught the fancy of economists in
particular as a font of many lessons or formal models. With rising
interest in Third World development, Jonathan Levin first presented
guano as the classic case of the deleterious "enclave" economy. Guano
was isolated from Peru's domestic development. The trade was financed
and exploited by foreign firms, and the beds were worked by insig-
nificant gangs of imported laborers; any remaining revenues were "re-
mitted" abroad through government malfeasance and the elites' lavish
orgy of importation. Any growth potential bypassed Peru's immobile
quasi-"feudal" society.[2] Several years after Levin, Shane Hunt, in a
trenchant quantitative and conceptual exercise, dispelled this image.
Guano engendered a "rentier" economy, much like that of contemporary oil emirates. The problem with guano was no longer its separation
from Peru; the government (and its native contractors) managed to
retain an impressive 71 percent of final sales and disbursed its benefits in
a fairly rational and dispersed fashion. However, guano still proved a
great "lost opportunity" for development. Exchange rate distortions,
undiscriminating free-trade import policies, and huge, risky state invest-

1. Jorge Basadre, *Historia de la república del Perú*, 5th ed. (Lima, 1963), vols. 2–4, *La
prosperidad falaz, 1845–72:* the name derives from policy critiques of Cisneros and Copello
and Petriconi explored below. Until the 1860s the Peruvian peso and U.S. dollar shared
monetary value and sign; where relevant, they are used interchangeably (i.e., until the
post-1862 *sol* conversion and devaluations).

2. Jonathan V. Levin, *The Export Economies: Their Pattern of Development in Historical
Perspective* (Cambridge, Mass., 1960), ch. 2, "Peru in the Guano Age." For economists,
Levin's was a key developmentalist critique of neoclassical and Keynesian growth formulas, but historians were unduly influenced by his shaky social grasp of nineteenth-
century Peru (e.g., "feudalism," lack of markets, etc.).

ments stymied possibilities for national entrepreneurs, diversification, and gains in domestic productivity.[3]

Other scholars contest time-honored allegations that Peru lost this chance through the sheer perfidy of overseas firms and imperialists. Peru resisted fitful British pressures to open the trade and drove hard bargains with its major foreign consignees, such as Antony Gibbs and Sons, marketing contracts then fully nationalized by the 1860s. Others argue that Peruvian governments, initially wasteful of windfall resources, had acquired a reforming vision and responsibility by the 1860s. The reforms, however, proved futile in the world economic downturn of the 1870s and the crushing Pacific War with Chile (1879–1881). Recent studies also locate scattered signs of diversifying growth in the guano age: investments in modern coastal sugar and cotton plantations, a spread of markets and modernity to the central highlands region, a consolidating legalist bureaucracy and a viable national finance system.[4] No single explanation, in short, accounts for Peru's stalled nineteenth-century development. But with little glitter in guano, and a dismal outcome, it attracts few seekers.

The most cohesive and influential conception of the period, however, is the broader sociological one offered by recent neo-Marxist and dependency historians of Peru. The failures of independent Peru, the failures of

3. Shane J. Hunt, "Growth and Guano in Nineteenth-Century Peru," Discussion Paper 34, RPED, Woodrow Wilson School, Princeton, 1973; an abridged published version appears in R. Cortés Conde and S. Hunt, eds., *The Latin American Economies: Growth and the Export Sector, 1830–1930* (New York, 1985), 255–319 (we cite detailed 1973 version). Hunt's was part of a larger movement correcting "enclave" models of underdevelopment; yet, indicative of sparse research on the guano age, in two decades no one has tested or challenged the new model.

4. W. M. Mathew, *The House of Gibbs and the Peruvian Guano Monopoly* (London, 1981); Mathew, "The Imperialism of Free Trade: Peru, 1820–1870," *Economic History Review* 21 (1968): 562–86; other works by Mathew; Juan Maiguashca, "A Reinterpretation of the Guano Age, 1840–1880," D.Phil. thesis, Oxford University, 1967 (Maiguashca's and Mathew's unpublished writing are widely recycled by later historians); Nelson Manrique, *Mercado interno y región: La sierra central, 1820–1930* (Lima, 1987); Manuel Burga, *De la encomienda a la hacienda capitalista: El valle del Jequetepeque del siglo xvi al xx* (Lima, 1976), ch. 6; Fernando de Trazegnies, *La idea de derecho en el Perú republicano del siglo xix* (Lima, 1980); Alfonso Quiroz, *Domestic and Foreign Finance in Modern Peru, 1850–1950: Financing Visions of Development* (London, 1992), ch. 2. For recent surveys of economic history, Christine Hünefeldt, "Viejos y nuevos temas de la historia económica del siglo xix," in H. Bonilla, ed., *Las crisis económicas en la historia del Perú* (Lima, 1986), 33–60, or Shane Hunt, "Peru: Interpretive Essay," in R. Cortés Conde and S. Stein, eds., *Latin America: A Guide to Economic History, 1830–1930* (Berkeley and Los Angeles, 1977), 547–71.

guano, the failures of the entire "century adrift" became the failures of a class: Peru's would-be ruling class. The *civilistas* (civil elite) raised with guano could not form a coherent "hegemonic" class "project" for the nation. Removed from national realities, wedded to the coastal export oligarchy, and lacking a genuine national-bourgeois consciousness, Peruvian elites failed to transform into an assertive, progressive, or leading "national bourgeoisie."[5]

Instead, the born-again Lima plutocracy of guano looked abroad. Elites slavishly imitated European economic liberalism, with a self-serving free trade in their exporter and consumer interests. Libertarian political ideals proved less utilitarian. A Europeanized appendage on a forgotten hinterland, by the 1840s native elites eagerly had joined British capital as the "intermediary" or "comprador class" in the imperial exploitation of Peru.[6] When the crisis of guano reared itself in the mid 1860s, serious efforts to look inward and socially transform, develop, or involve the larger Peru proved unthinkable. By the 1870s, having assumed fragile power in Lima, civilists seemed oblivious to the dangers of national collapse: band-aid solutions prevailed, ever larger European loans, utopian railroads to extract ever more export revenues. Failing to challenge Peru's foreign dependencies, and failing to address Peru's feeble social cohesion, the truncated project destroyed itself—and Peru—in the conflagrations of the late 1870s.

Clearly, such sociological views evince the profound modern discontent with the age of guano! They also successfully supersede a traditional historiography of liberal ideas and fallen heroes with a biting class and

5. Major works in "new history" include Heraclio Bonilla, *Guano y burguesía en el Perú* (Lima, 1974); Julio Cotler, *Clases, estado y nación en el Perú* (Lima, 1978), ch. 2; Ernesto Yepes del Castillo, *Perú 1820–1920: Un siglo de desarrollo capitalista* (Lima, 1972); Javier Tantaleán Arbulú, *Política económico-financiera y la formación del estado: Siglo xix* (Lima, 1983). "Siglo a la deriva" is Bonilla's image of the century, now pervading even popular perceptions.

6. Luis Pásara, "El rol de derecho en la época del guano," *Derecho* 28 (1970): 11–33; Jean Piel, "The Place of the Peasantry in the National Life of Peru in the Nineteenth Century," *Past and Present* 46 (1970): 108–33; Bonilla, *Guano y burguesía*, ch. 3; Jesús Chavarría, "La desaparación del Perú colonial (1870–1930)," *Aportes* 23 (1972): 121–53; Enrique Bernales, "La instauración del estado liberal en el Perú," in Bernales, ed., *Burguesía y estado liberal* (Lima, 1979), 231–75; Pablo Macera, "Algodón y comercio exterior peruano en el siglo xix," in Macera, *Trabajos de historia* (Lima, 1977) 3:275–96; Efraín Trelles, "Modernidad signo cruel: Curso y discurso de modernizantes peruanos (s. xviii–xix)," in H. Urbano, ed., *Modernidad en los Andes* (Cuzco, 1991), 135–60. Critical versions of concepts are William S. Bollinger, "The Bourgeois Revolution in Peru: A Conception of Peruvian History," *Latin American Perspectives* 4 (1977): 18–57, and Trazegnies, *Idea de derecho*.

global perspective—now our conventional wisdom on guano. As a pioneering new historiography, this view refines elements dominating study of the nineteenth century across Latin America. This interpretation also traverses a specifically Peruvian trail of events and policies, and the forms of class consciousness and formation behind them (though paths through the archives are not yet as developed).[7] What follows, then—to guide the reader through the present study—is a closer chronological and descriptive survey of the decisive developments in the guano age, based on the social interpretation and its recent elaborations. Then we can properly introduce the broader aims, approaches, and aspects of this book, a new social history of Peruvian economic ideas.

Peru's mishandling of its nineteenth-century opportunities now is traceable to its conservative and inadvertent independence from Spain in 1821. Unprepared for nationalism, feeble and factional civilian elites could offer little governing vision for the fragmented ethnic and geographic concoction that suddenly became "Peru." Instead, Peru broke down into "meaningless chaos" as power fell to feuding caudillo bands, military strongmen who ravished the impoverished land for political spoils over the next three decades. During these turbulent times, British interests also slipped into the vacuum of power, all but capturing Peru's rickety national markets with their new industrial wares. Historians are just sorting out the patterns and nationalist politics behind the era of caudillos.[8]

In the mid 1840s one steadier caudillo, General Ramón Castilla, finally won supremacy, and with the flush of guano prosperity Peru's weakened elites at last found cause for unity: in rebuilding themselves in guano and trade enterprises. Their mentors and partners in the new

7. However, much of what new history deems traditionalist (for instance, Basadre's early *ensayista* books) was often quite sociological and interpretive. Our major empirical gap concerns elite formation; the only work is by Engelsen (coastal agrarian elites), Jacobsen (Puno), Quiroz, and Camprubí Alcázar (commercial-financial elites), barely enough to support class generalizations.

8. Heraclio Bonilla and Karen Spalding, "La independencia en el Perú: Las palabras y los hechos," in Bonilla et al., eds., *La independencia en el Perú* (Lima, 1972), 15–65; H. Bonilla, "Continuidad y cambio en la organización política del estado en el Perú independiente," in I. Buisson et al., eds., *Problemas de la formación del estado y de la nación en Hispanoamérica* (Cologne, 1984), 481–98; Alberto Flores Galindo, "El militarismo y la dominación británica (1825–1845)," in C. Araníbar and H. Bonilla, eds., *Nueva historia general del Perú* (Lima, 1979), 107–23. Paul Gootenberg, *Between Silver and Guano: Commercial Policy and the State in Postindependence Peru* (Princeton, 1989), attempts to make sense of early commercial and political turmoil.

laissez-faire were the foreign houses that oversaw guano consignment and import trades—a liberal alliance formalized by the early 1850s with overseas trade treaties, foreign debt settlements, and the sanctification of the radical free-trade tariff in 1852. Reconstituted elites (conceived as an "alliance" of aristocratic Lima merchant families with "feudal" *sierran* landlords) would remain dependent on the Praetorian Castillan state for accumulation.[9] Their formative event was President José Rufino Eche-nique's guano-financed "Consolidation" of the internal debt (1848–1853). In a massively venal process, the now solvent state concertedly placed lost fortunes back in the hands of traditional clans (to the tune of $25 million), padded with a host of other privileged giveaways. Recent research amends this view of the consolidation (major benefits went to emerging cosmopolitan commercial groups), yet it stands as the signifier of guano-age "liberalism"—as if the republican ruling class were born from corruption itself.[10]

By 1860 a true Lima "plutocracy" had blossomed in league with Peru's "order and progress" military. It was, however, a strained alliance, steadily questioned in the era's liberal-conservative polemics. The first step toward civilian hegemony came cloaked in nationalist rhetoric: convincing the state to hand over the chief guano contracts (still held by Gibbs) to the *hijos del país,* the native merchant clan founded in the internal debt. Their basic aim, however, was to transform themselves into fiscal intermediaries for Peru's increasingly indebted government, which required continuing partnership with overseas finance. Centered around Manuel Pardo's National Company of Guano (1862), the swiftly con-

9. This alliance notion (and "feudal" nature of Andean landlords) remains very weak: only Florencia Mallon, *The Defense of Community in Peru's Central Highlands: Peasant Struggle and Capitalist Transition, 1860–1940* (Princeton, 1983), ch. 2, follows relations between a regional elite and the Lima state; see Nils Jacobsen, *Mirages of Transition: The Peruvian Altiplano Between Colonialism and the World Market, 1780–1930* (Berkeley and Los Angeles, 1993), chs. 4–6, for study of Andean social relations under export pressure. See also critique in Jacobsen, "Desarrollo económico y relaciones de clase en el sur andino (1780–1920): Una réplica a Karen Spalding," *Análisis* 5 (1979): 67–82, or Stephen M. Gorman, "The State, Elite, and Export in Nineteenth-Century Peru: Toward an Alternative Reinterpretation of Political Change," *Journal of Interamerican Studies and World Affairs* 21 (1979): 395–418, for political extrapolations.

10. Bonilla, *Guano y burguesía,* ch. 1, Cotler, *Clases, estado y nación,* ch. 2, and Tantaleán, *Política económico-financiera,* ch. 6 (etc.) use consolidation as class-formation centerpiece; see Basadre, *Historia* 3:1301–4, for wise speculations on "plutocracy" concept. Alfonso Quiroz, *La deuda defraudada: Consolidación de 1850 y dominio económico en el Perú* (Lima, 1987), is the empirical revision (and superb social portrait of midcentury elites); a modern commercial nexus (foreign and native) effectively exploited the consolidation.

structed banks of the 1860s reaped speculative fortunes from short-term public lending. The bankers' laissez-faire policy prescriptions wavered between self-serving shelter from public scrutiny (analogous to the hands-off "liberalism" of rural oligarchs) or, as others see it, rational coping with Peru's erratic state.[11] But with the exception of exporting northern plantations, little productive and diversifying investment followed. Peru's budding *dueños del país* were coming of age.

By the mid 1860s this commercial class had sparked a protobourgeois civilist movement. Historians trace its ideological lineage to the 1860 *Revista de Lima,* a literary and political forum that first articulated autonomous elite reformist visions. A change of guard from past theoretical liberals, these "new liberals" remain in most accounts a plutocratic circle of interested exporters. Spearheaded by the banker-politicos Pardo and Luis Benjamín Cisneros, the group's policy goal was to arrest, somehow, the budgetary chaos and economic crisis now discernible with the coming depletion of guano.[12] Cisneros heralded drastic fiscal reforms to diversify Peru's risky dependence and mismanaged military state. Politically, this meant placing stable civil elites firmly in control of their destiny and interests.

Central to the plan, recent historians concur, was Pardo's vision of "turning guano into railroads." A mammoth program of rail construction across the Andes, financed and guaranteed by the mortgage of guano abroad, would usher in a more lasting export prosperity. Railroads were indeed the nineteenth-century world's symbol of modernizing Western progress, but in neocolonial Peru other meanings prevailed. Civilists were not concerned with integrating a fragmented nation and balancing domestic markets for growth. Instead, they hoped to bind Peru even closer to overseas markets and investors with new mineral and agrarian products. Historians regard the scheme as doomed from the

11. Bonilla, *Guano y burguesía,* ch. 1; Yepes, *Perú 1820–1920,* ch. 2; see Mathew, *Gibbs and the Guano Monopoly,* ch. 4, for rounded analysis of contract transfer politics. Such analyses rely on the detailed financial study by Carlos Camprubí Alcázar, *Historia de los bancos en el Perú (1860–1879)* (Lima, 1957); see Quiroz, *Domestic and Foreign Finance,* ch. 2, for revisions.

12. Bonilla, *Guano y burguesía,* 54–64; Yepes, *Perú 1820–1920,* ch. 3; for political outlooks, Margarita Giesecke, *Masas urbanas y rebelión en la historia: Golpe de estado, Lima, 1872* (Lima, 1978), chs. 1–2, focusing on relations with popular groups; the original (and reversed) source on *La Revista de Lima* was Maiguashca, "Reinterpretation of Guano Age," chs. 3–4. See Efraín Kristal, *The Andes Viewed from the City: Literary and Political Discourse on the Indian in Peru, 1848–1930* (New York, 1987), ch. 2, for latest study; the group shows much imaginative concern with greater Peru.

start.[13] Heady projections of Andean exports and fiscal excess aside, Pardo's plutocrats could fathom neither the revolution required in greater Peru's archaic social relations nor the need to mobilize the people in forging viable internal markets and industrial futures. Such visions were unthinkable to narrow-minded leaders bent on economic escapism and entranced by inapt foreign models. Though recent work recovers wider economic and democratic facets of Pardo's thought, *civilismo* meant at best a top-down "traditional modernism."[14]

By the late 1860s manic railroad construction had taken off, farmed out to the deceptively brilliant impresario Henry Meiggs, Peru's Yankee Pizarro. The class project accelerated with the 1866–1867 dictatorship of Coronel Mariano Prado, during which (finance minister) Manuel Pardo and other civil luminaries from the *Revista de Lima* assumed direct charge of economic policy. The price tag soared (to fully one-fifth of all guano monies), and Peru gambled its future on an unprecedented series of loans on European markets. Peru's external debt would quickly climb to £35 million (about 200 million soles)—second largest in the nonindustrial world—even as the mountains of guano dwindled.[15]

In the meantime, however, a dramatic reversal of plutocratic aspirations hit with the Balta-Piérola regime of 1869–1872. Fearful of the Lima finance clique's growing grip on policy and seeking wider funding for the railroads, Coronel José Balta abruptly canceled national guano contracts—awarding all public finance to the better-connected French financier Auguste Dreyfus. A bitter blow to Lima's civil elite, the Drey-

13. Bonilla, *Guano y burguesía*, 57–65, ch. 3; Cotler, *Clases, estado y nación*, 102–4; Guido Pennano, "Desarrollo regional y ferrocarriles en el Perú," *Apuntes* 5 (1979): 131–51; Pablo Macera, "La historia económica como ciencia en el Perú," in Macera, *Trabajos de historia* 2:35; negative views originally codified in Watt Stewart, *Henry Meiggs: Yankee Pizarro* (Durham, 1946).

14. Fernando de Trazegnies, "La genealogía del derecho peruano: Los juegos de trueques y préstamos," in A. Adrianzén, *Pensamiento político peruano* (Lima, 1987), 99–133, expounds (with his *Idea de derecho*) deeper notion of "traditional modernization"—a modernist project constrained by autocratic/aristocratic values—in serious effort to create intellectual history of guano-age state; Carmen MacEvoy, "Manuel Pardo, pensamiento y proyecto político: Aproximación a un intento de modernización en el Perú" (tesis de postgrado, PUCP, 1989), marks subtle extension (unfocused on railways) to Pardo's political thought.

15. Mounting debt is read as perfidious result of national-foreign alliances; for a dispassionate study, see Carlos Palacios Moreyra, *La deuda anglo-peruana, 1822–1890* (Lima, 1983), or Carlos Marichal, *A Century of Debt Crises in Latin America: From Independence to the Great Depression, 1820–1930* (Princeton, 1989), ch. 4, which places Peru's debacle in international contexts.

fus contract thus sparked a political mobilization for direct civilian rule, often looked on as Peru's first full-fledged "bourgeois" bid for power. Pardo personally led the liberal assault on unreliable militarism, involving (or using) the *Limeño* masses at crucial moments of the liberal campaign. The Partido Civil won the 1872 election, ushering in Peru's modern form of plutocratic rule.[16]

Civilist economic ideals, however, did not shift, even in the face of the crunching fiscal and commercial emergency of the 1870s. Dreyfus and Meiggs continued in their posts, and the civilista regime restricted itself to narrow financial reform, unflinching allegiance to free trade, or utopian liberalisms (such as a fiscal decentralization that bolstered rural powerholders). In 1875 the full catastrophe ensued: the first railroads proved unprofitable (halting construction); guano reserves hit bottom; an intervened banking system tottered; and Peru slid into a world-shaking default. The debt-driven formal economy collapsed amid raging inflation and popular distress. Yet bickering civilistas, without a mass base, did little to reverse course. The root cause of paralysis, speculations go, was their autocratic and rigid mentality of development.[17] The final move, President Pardo's "nationalist" expropriation of Atacama desert nitrates—the rising world brand of natural fertilizer—simply echoed Peru's exhausted guano strategy.

This ploy also sparked the apocalyptic 1879 nitrates war with Chile. Bankrupt and divided, Peru stood little chance in the conflict. Chile's powerful land and sea invasion (and liberal British aid) revealed everything the guano-age elite had failed at. Lacking national resolve, Peru's top leaders squabbled and fled. Although some popular resistance regis-

---

16. Yepes, *Perú 1820–1920,* ch. 3; Bonilla, *Guano y burguesía,* ch. 3; for political manipulations, see Giesecke, *Masas urbanas y rebelión,* chs. 5–6—revised in MacEvoy, "Manuel Pardo," ch. 4, by study of civilist popular vision. Bonilla, ch. 2, expounds notion of Dreyfus as foreign robber baron, despite new evidence (e.g., Hunt, "Growth and Guano," 65–67). See Bollinger, "Bourgeois Revolution," 30–33, for civilismo as typical Third World elite movement.

17. Heraclio Bonilla, "La crisis de 1872," in Bonilla, *Crisis económicas,* 167–88; Bonilla, *Guano y burguesía,* ch. 3; Yepes, *Perú 1820–1920,* 96–103; more positive treatment in Maiguashca, "Reinterpretation of Guano Age," ch. 5, views Peru as overcoming the external crisis. Tantaleán, *Política económico-financiera,* ch. 11, speculates on Pardo's new "nationalist" project, an idea stretched to extremes in Enrique Amayo, *La política británica en la guerra del Pacífico* (Lima, 1988), which takes war as free-trade crusade against Peru. See Robert Greenhill and Rory Miller, "The Peruvian Government and the Nitrate Trade, 1873–1879," *Journal of Latin American Studies (JLAS)* 5 (1973): 107–31, for cogent evaluation of crisis responses.

tered, indigenous Peruvian peoples and laborers, bereft of reasons to defend an imaginary *patria,* broke down into chaotic ethnic, class, and caudillo rivalries amid a hopeless war.[18]

Peru's humiliating debacle—and inevitable breakdowns—marked the tragic end of the civilist project. By the 1890s it had led into the new kind of foreign capital dependence—embodied in the 1889 Grace contract—that would gravely limit Peru's twentieth-century possibilities. Thus, Peru squandered the opportunity with guano; indeed, it squandered a century-long possibility of making a viable nation.[19] The fallout continues to scorch, even in Peru's present distress as a national entity.

The historical trajectories just surveyed from sociological-class views evoke the spirit of all dependency syntheses of Latin American national histories and appear largely on target. Obvious criticisms emerge too. For example, this perspective seems intent on incriminating the ideological blinders or blunderings of Peru's ruling class (itself a sign of modern ideational discontent with guano). It poses voluntaristic, "should have done" radical solutions not readily available to nineteenth-century thinkers or bourgeoisies. It perfunctorily considers social-structural constraints (as in the circular notion that Peru's weak internal markets blocked elites from even conceiving them). It follows dependency constructions everywhere in easy reversals of old heroic figures; here, the "modernizing" Pardista martyrs of liberal iconography become Peru's national villains, an interpretation known since the anticivilist polemics of the turn of the century.[20] It surely uses a monolithic brush on elite pensadores.

18. Heraclio Bonilla, "The War of the Pacific and the National and Colonial Problem in Peru," *Past and Present* 81 (1978): 92–119; cf. Mallon, *Defense of Community,* ch. 3, and Nelson Manrique, *Las guerrillas indígenas en la guerra con Chile* (Lima, 1981), which argue for a meaningful nationalist content in wartime social struggles. See Jorge Basadre et al., eds., *Reflexiones en torno a la guerra de 1879* (Lima, 1979) for recent war scholarship, esp. class conclusions in Luis Pásara, "El guano y la penetración inglesa" (15–42), and the more nuanced Margarita Giesecke, "Las clases sociales y los grupos del poder" (43–74).

19. For direct links to the present, see Julio Cotler, *Democracia e integración nacional* (Lima, 1980), or even Alan Riding, "Peru Fights to Overcome Its Past," *New York Times Magazine,* 14 May 1989, 43–44.

20. Scattered critiques exist: Guillermo Rochabrún, "La visión del Perú de Julio Cotler," *Análisis* 4 (1978): 69–85 (fundamentalist view of sociology); Dennis Gilbert, *La oligarquía peruana: Historia de tres familias* (Lima, 1982), 25 (on voluntarism); Paul Gootenberg, "The Social Origins of Protectionism and Free Trade in Nineteenth-Century Lima," *JLAS* 14 (1982): 345–46 ("internal market" analysis); or Marie-Danielle Demelas,

Such shortcomings can be a call for exploring these problems anew as intellectual history. Historians can start by probing deeper at what the era's political elites actually said and thought about development—for example, about the hoped-for uses of guano wealth, the impetus of foreign trade, the mission of railroads, the wider roles of social reforms in national development. Old thinking about guano may reveal new and broader angles on republican development. Building on the advances of sociological history, this book is an effort to restore the intellectual foundations of Peru's problematic yet formative first century.

Scoping the Study

Latin Americanists and students of economic thought may wonder: What wider good is served by a social history of ideas, about such a historically conditioned concept as "development," and of ideas generated by such a historical oddity as Peruvian guano? This historian, reared in old-fashioned (materialist) economics, is not one to argue that ideas per se dictated the possibilities and limits of economic development in nineteenth-century Latin America—notwithstanding the famous dictum of Keynes. Especially as no Peruvian politician rose forth as slave to these defunct local economists.

Then why is this book different from all other books? First, it aims to address a general gap in the history of Western economic thought: nineteenth-century notions of development and their transmission and transformation in Europe's first postcolonial societies of Latin America. Well over a generation ago, the genesis of modern economic growth theory initially inspired discussions of formal antecedents. Classical Smithian and Ricardian Political Economy (and their forerunners) harbored dynamic elements of growth—concerns soon replaced by the allocative, efficiency, and marginalist Economics of the late nineteenth

---

"¿Un libro o un autor a la deriva?" *Allpanchis* 18 (1983): 205–11 (slanted national perspectives).

For earlier codifications, see José Carlos Mariátegui's 1920s notion of deformed liberal mentalities in "Outline of the Economic Evolution," *Seven Interpretive Essays on Peruvian Reality* (Austin, 1971), 3–21, and the remarkable synthesis (during new import substitution) by poet-economist Emilio Castañón, "Esquema de nuestra historia económica en el siglo xix," *El Comercio* (Lima), 28 July 1957.

century. Development resurfaced as a formal field only with postwar preoccupations with macroeconomic management and the modern discovery of Third World underdevelopment, or so our story goes.[21] In this telling, the intervening century gets submerged, along with the dissemination of economic ideas, however improvised or practical, to the rest of the world. Indeed, current studies of transmission processes appear narrowly confined to relations between economists and policymakers rather than addressing relations across geographic, political, and cultural space. Economic historians stand alone in plotting the formidable transformations worked by North Atlantic paradigms on the entire globe since 1800.[22]

Second—to indulge in grander generalizations—the history of economic thought suffers from an enduring divide between the economic and historical professions. Economists remain notoriously wary of intellectual "trespassing." Since the passing of archaic Continental historical economics and the consolidation of modern economics as a positivist quantitative science, the history of economic ideas—unlike the new cliometric economic history—has lost its direct relevance to mainstream theory.[23] To some, economic thought portends the most dismal of

21. E.g., Bert F. Hoselitz, ed., *Theories of Economic Growth* (New York, 1960), esp. essays by Litiche, McKinley, and Hoselitz; John Fei and Gustav Ranis, "Economic Development in Historical Perspective," *American Economic Review* 59, no. 2 (1969): 386–400; Albert O. Hirschman, "The Rise and Decline of Development Economics," in Hirschman, *Essays in Trespassing: Economics to Politics and Beyond* (Cambridge, 1981), 1–24. For political angles, H. W. Arndt, *The Rise and Fall of Economic Growth: A Study in Contemporary Thought* (Melbourne, 1978), esp. ch. 2; J. C. Alcalde, *The Idea of Third-World Development: Emerging Perspectives in the United States and Britain, 1900–1950* (Lanham, 1987)—an aptly Peruvian view of the north.

22. Joseph J. Spengler, "Notes on the International Transmission of Economic Ideas," *History of Political Economy* 2 (1970): 133–51; A. W. Coats and David Colander, eds., *The Spread of Economic Ideas* (Cambridge, 1989), esp. editors' introduction lamenting primitive state of field, even among distinguished economists represented. Also Alexander Gerschenkron, *Economic Backwardness in Historical Perspective* (Cambridge, Mass., 1962), one of the last offshoots of the historical-institutional school. Noneconomists, however, are widening approaches to the transculturation of ideas; see, e.g., vanguard literary analysis in Mary Louise Pratt, *Imperial Eyes: Travel Writing and Transculturation* (London, 1992). Sociological "world-systems" analysis rekindles some interest: see Wallerstein's series "Developmental Theory Before 1945," *Review* 13–14 (1990–1991), esp. Jean-Yves Grenier, "La notion de croissance dans la pensée économique française au 18° siècle (1715–1789)," vol. 13 (1990): 499–550; Bipan Chandra, "Colonial India: British Versus Indian Views of Development," vol. 14 (1991): 81–167; and Dieter Senghaas, "Friedrich List and the Basic Problems of Modern Development," vol. 14 (1991): 451–67.

23. Hirschman, *Trespassing;* Donald Winch, "The Emergence of Economics as a Science, 1750–1870," in C. Cipolla, ed., *Fontana Economic History of Europe* (Glasgow,

sciences, given its implied historical relativism of theory. From the economists' perspective, ideas remain a curiosity field, one hermetically sealed from the social and temporal bearings of most working historians.

Historians, for the most part, stand equally guilty of neglect. The materially oriented practitioners of the last generation—the new social history—routinely dismissed economic thought as "ideology." We comfortably inferred its rationalities from convergence with "interest" and its aims from the most tangible of social and class outcomes. Only popular economic mentalities deserved and won greater historical subtlety, diversity, and respect. And isolated from these trends, traditional varieties of intellectual history withered in their vineyard of rarefied philosophical and political themes.[24]

The recent "turn" of the historical left to cultural and rhetorical analyses holds a rich future for intellectual studies. Yet of all the diverse discourses under deconstruction, economic ideas still seem the least represented or welcome.[25] Born of ancient aversions to scientistic "bourgeois" economics, this neglect also epitomizes today's easy stampede away from any topics smacking of the materialist and structuralist modes.

Before we turn too fast and trip back into old idealisms, a case must be

1973) 3:507–60; Gunnar Myrdal, *The Political Element in the Development of Economic Theory* (1929; rpt. New Brunswick, 1990). Hirschman, Gerschenkron, and Hoselitz were the remarkable refugee cohort, eclectic offspring of German historicism, who basically founded modern development; but cf. Gershenkron's influential address "History of Economic Doctrines and Economic History," *American Economic Review* 59, no. 2 (1969): 1–17, which formalizes split of economic history and economic thought.

Donald N. McClosky, *The Rhetoric of Economics* (Madison, Wis., 1985), is sole serious "postmodern" critique I know of, from this a vigorously Chicago economic historian. Apart from Marxist scholars, bastion of economic thought is group around *History of Political Economy*, a journal whose acronym (*HOPE*) speaks to their professional marginality.

24. For relevant examples, Noel W. Thompson, *The People's Science: The Popular Political Economy of Exploitation and Crisis, 1816–1834* (Cambridge, 1984); Maxine Berg, *The Machinery Question and the Making of Political Economy, 1815–1848* (Cambridge, 1980); and in the new mode, Garth Stedman Jones, *Languages of Class: Studies in English Working Class History, 1832–1982* (Cambridge, 1983). As "ideology," see Louis Dumont, *From Mandeville to Marx: The Genesis and Triumph of Economic Ideology* (Chicago, 1977), or Albert O. Hirschman, "The Concept of Interest: From Euphemism to Tautology," in Hirschman, *Rival Views of Market Society* (New York, 1986), 35–55.

25. See, e.g., Dominick LaCapra and Stephen L. Kaplan, eds., *Modern European Intellectual History: Reappraisals and New Perspectives* (Ithaca, 1982); Lynn Hunt, ed., *The New Cultural History* (Berkeley and Los Angeles, 1989); Roger Chartier, *Cultural History* (Ithaca, 1988)—all notable for absence of economic ideas. Some efforts surface in recent Geertzian wanderings of William Reddy or Pierre Bourdieu's strained transfer of Marxist economic categories to "cultural production."

made for a reintegrative social history of economic ideas. Economic thought makes fertile ground—for bridging our fading determinisms, the indispensable achievements of social history, and the rising culturalist historical mood. Economic thought evokes texts and intertextualities, to be sure, but by nature never strays (too far) from their material and political groundings, contexts, and dilemmas.[26] It crisscrosses classes and cultures and in this case goes well beyond European canons and cores. It actively trespasses on the economists' abandoned realm, without provoking a shooting spree. The history of economic ideas can no longer be orphaned; for at its best, it reconciles our increasingly estranged families of history.

Third, this book may also be a different sort for Latin Americanists. Nowhere is the chasm deeper between mental and structural approaches; nowhere is the study of economic thought both so promising and neglected. In the postwar era, with accelerated import-substituting industrialization and the coeval rise of the Latin American CEPALuist school of structuralist economics, historians turned to the evolution of regional economic thought. This, too, was a brief detour, in search of national routes of development or the overwhelming force of North Atlantic thinking.[27] By the 1960s such concerns had been smothered under the avalanche of Annalesque, neo-Marxist, and dependency studies, both here and there, which swept ideas into antiquarian corners. This massive production of economic and social histories, if exceedingly productive, proved exceedingly broad as well. Little room was left in history for conserving intellectual and political creativity and choice, particularly among maligned historical ruling elites. Since then intellectual culture has been left to our historically mindful but economically

26. For definitions and critiques of social history of ideas, see Robert Darton, "In Search of the Enlightenment: Recent Attempts to Create a Social History of Ideas," *Journal of Modern History* 43 (1971): 113–32; Dominick LaCapra, "Rethinking Intellectual History and Reading Texts," in LaCapra and Kaplan, *Modern Intellectual History*, 47–85; or Roger Chartier, "Intellectual History or Sociocultural History? The French Trajectories," 13–46. Notable applications to economic ideas (with great political range) include Gertrude Himmelfarb, *The Idea of Poverty: England in the Early Industrial Age* (New York, 1985), esp. ch. 1 discussion, and Joan W. Scott, *Gender and the Politics of History* (New York, 1988), pt. 3.

27. E.g., Celso Furtado, *Economic Development of Latin America: A Survey from Colonial Times to the Cuban Revolution* (Cambridge, 1970); Luis Ospina Vásquez's classic *La industria y protección en Colombia 1810–1930* (Medellín, 1955); Luis Roque Gondra et al., eds., *El pensamiento económico latinoamericano* (Mexico, 1945). North American interest was also short-lived, as in Robert S. Smith, "The Wealth of Nations in Spain and Hispanic America, 1780–1930," *Journal of Political Economy* 55 (1957): 104–26; Robert M. Will, "The Introduction of Classical Economics into Chile," *Hispanic American Historical Review* (*HAHR*) 44 (1964): 1–21.

illiterate literary and anthropological specialists.[28] Now, for varied reasons, these boundaries are shifting.

Implicitly, however, ideational arguments always pervaded the region's structuralist historiography, particularly in the dominant dependency synthesis of the formative national era. Economic ideals implicitly served to construct Latin America's "neocolonial" century to 1930. Erratic postcolonial experiments in political and social liberalism, it is now argued, brought few lasting or genuine consequences. But imported economic ideals—the "unifying myth of liberalism"—were another story. The region's nineteenth-century "liberal pause" augured terribly tangible economic legacies: the creation of dependent export and financial structures, capitalist modernization from abroad and above, delayed industrialism—the whole gamut of social and regional disparities bequeathed by the 1850–1930 age of "outward-oriented" growth. Indeed, feverish imitation of Anglo-Saxon free-trade and laissez-faire ideologies made Latin America the purest outpost of liberal orthodoxy in the nineteenth-century world, in this its first true encounter with capitalist modernization.[29] As seen in the sociological interpretation of Peru, determining economic ideas essentialized the neocolonial order.

Few scholars openly confess that conviction: the nineteenth century as economic "culture conflict." One who has done so deems the encoun-

28. See Charles A. Hale, "The Reconstruction of Nineteenth-Century Politics in Spanish America: A Case for the History of Ideas," *Latin American Research Review* (*LARR*) 8 (1973): 53–73, for cogent critique of trend. Yet Hale's own work—the best among intellectual histories—itself reveals a trend against economic ideas: *Mexican Liberalism in the Age of Mora, 1821–1853* (New Haven, 1968) fully integrates economic ideas, which virtually vanish from científico thinking by *The Transformation of Liberalism in Late Nineteenth-Century Mexico* (Princeton, 1989). For rootless idiosyncrasy in recent intellectual history, try Richard M. Morse, *New World Soundings: Culture and Ideology in the Americas* (Baltimore, 1989); a postmodern sign of shifts is Ricardo Salvatorre's "Markets, Social Discipline, and Popular Protest: Latin America from Charles III to the IMF" (paper presented to the SSHA, 1991).

29. This general reading comes from Stanley J. Stein and Barbara Stein, *The Colonial Heritage of Latin America: Essays on Economic Dependence in Perspective* (New York, 1970); Richard Graham, *Independence in Latin America: A Comparative Approach* (New York, 1972); Claudio Véliz, *The Centralist Tradition in Latin America* (Princeton, 1980), chs. 6–7, and ch. 8, "Outward Looking Nationalism and the Liberal Pause"; Fernando Henrique Cardoso and Enzo Faletto, *Dependency and Development in Latin American America* (Berkeley and Los Angeles, 1979): Thomas E. Skidmore and Peter H. Smith, *Modern Latin America* (New York, 1984), ch. 1; David Bushnell and Neill Macaulay, *The Emergence of Latin America in the Nineteenth Century* (New York, 1988), with its more skeptical ch. 13, "The Liberal Legacy and the Quest for Development." Broadly, these views parallel traditional intellectual histories with their shift from romanticism and positivism to more nationalist twentieth-century "isms": e.g., Leopoldo Zea, *The Latin American Mind* (Norman, 1963).

ter as having been as powerful in cause and effect as Latin America's primordial sixteenth-century kind. "Enamoured" with ill-fitting European notions of "modernization," tiny urban elites purposefully pursued free-trade individualism as a weapon for full social hegemony over fading rural oligarchies and their recalcitrant, Americanized "folk." The legacy of this postcolonial culture clash was modern Latin America's baneful "poverty of progress."[30] Triumphal elites, if anything, had shown marked "fears" of genuine national "development."

Such views can also reflect a poverty of research. Our isolated intellectual historians largely bypass economic thinking. Or attention focuses on the obvious Latin vitality of ideas born during the twentieth-century age of inward-directed industrialism—portrayed as the antithesis of the passive, anglicized century behind. In the meantime, studies of Latin American political, literary, nationalist, and popular traditions enjoy increasing sophistication, with all their historical ambiguities, cultural contestations, and multifarious and multinational social origins.[31] Nineteenth-century thinkers could invent nations that barely existed and project constitutions without states; they spun national myths, composed poetic canons, and reified indigenous masses whom they knew nothing about. What did Latin Americans imagine about development? What did they imagine as national futures as they bought and brought themselves into global markets? The discourse could not have been a mindless, materialist, and monomaniacal carbon copy from abroad.[32]

---

30. E. Bradford Burns, *The Poverty of Progress: Latin America in the Nineteenth Century* (Berkeley and Los Angeles, 1980), passim. For timely critique, see Florencia Mallon, "Economic Liberalism: Where We Are and Where We Need to Go," in J. Love and N. Jacobsen, eds., *Guiding the Invisible Hand: Economic Liberalism and the State in Latin American History* (New York, 1988), 177–86—the state-of-the-art collection. For more class-grounded analysis of liberal ideology, see Emília Viotti da Costa, "Liberalism: Theory and Practice," in da Costa, *The Brazilian Empire: Myths and Histories* (Chicago, 1988), 53–72.

31. Joseph L. Love, "Raul Prebisch and the Origins of the Doctrine of Unequal Exchange," *LARR* 15 (1980): 45–72; Albert O. Hirschman, "Ideologies of Economic Development in Latin America," in Hirschman, ed., *Latin American Issues: Essays and Comments* (New York, 1961), 3–42; Tulio Halperín-Donghi, "'Dependency Theory' and Latin American Historiography," *LARR* 17 (1982): 115–30; Fernando Henrique Cardoso, "The Originality of the Copy: The Economic Commission for Latin America and the Idea of Development," in Rothko Chapel Colloquium, *Toward a New Strategy for Development* (New York, 1979), 53–72 (very interesting on innovation during the transmission of ideas).

32. An obvious influence here is the historical sociology of ideas proposed by Benedict Anderson in *Imagined Communities: Reflections on the Origin and Spread of Nationalism* (London, 1983); for examples of strides in other realms, see Nicolas Shumway, *The Invention of Argentina* (Berkeley and Los Angeles, 1991); D. A. Brading, *The Origins of*

Pursuing visions of development is not just an empirical inquiry, for conceptual dualities impede complex understandings. Periodization itself conceals one gigantic and stifling duality: between Latin America's era of "outward-directed" thinking (1830–1930) and the "inward-looking" developmentalist era after 1929. Other dichotomies include persisting Manichaean divides that pitted intellectual against social forces; national against foreign ideologies; nationalist against comprador strategies; external against internal markets; and elite against popular cultures and politics.[33] Such divisions must soften in a rounded social history of ideas. But they are fast dissolving anyway—in Latin America's newest mixed bag of developmental and political possibilisms.

Finally, a few words are needed on the scope of this study and the peculiarities of the Peruvians. The "developmental" visions pursued here focus largely on trade policies, diversification, and technological, industrial, and infrastructural progress or on the roles of the state and popular groups in lasting economic growth. One can imagine very different sets of developmental concerns—demography, entrepreneurialism, capital accumulation, finance, foreign investment, human capital promotion, or agrarian surpluses—issues that infused debates in other national republics.[34]

Mexican Nationalism (Cambridge, 1985); or Alberto Flores Galindo, *Buscando un inca: Identidad y utopía en los Andes* (Lima, 1987).

This orphaned status of Latin American economic ideas is reflected in the latest survey literature: in the *Cambridge History of Latin American* (ed. L. Bethell, vols. 3–4, 1983–85), Frank Safford's and Charles Hale's solid reviews of nineteenth-century social thought barely include economic ideas; yet William Glade's economic survey ignores ideas altogether.

33. For similar historiographic critique, see William B. Taylor, "Between Global Process and Local Knowledge: An Inquiry into Early Latin American Social History, 1500–1900," in O. Zunz, ed., *Reliving the Past: The Worlds of Social History* (Chapel Hill, 1985), 115–90. Despite positive impacts of sociological history, rounded approaches to ideas were arguably advancing before its hegemony; for a relevant overlooked example, see Frank Safford, *The Ideal of the Practical: Colombia's Struggle to Form a Technical Elite* (Austin, 1976).

34. For shifting range of developmental concerns, see Paul Streeten, "Development Ideas in Historical Perspective," in *Toward a New Strategy for Development,* 21–52; Hirschman, "Rise and Decline of Development"; or political analysis in John Sheahan, *Patterns of Development in Latin America: Poverty, Repression, and Economic Strategy* (Princeton, 1987). A recent regional historical survey (biographical, with few nineteenth-century thinkers) is Oreste Popescu, *Estudios en la historia del pensamiento económico latinoamericano* (Bogotá, 1986). For earlier, delimited studies of Peruvian economic ideas, see César Augusto Reinaga, *Esbozo de una historia del pensamiento económico en el Perú* (Cuzco, 1969); Emilio Romero, "Perú," in Roque Gondra, *Pensamiento económico latinoamericano* (1945), 275–324; Macera, "Historia económica como ciencia"; for survey of social thought, Fredrick B. Pike, *The Modern History of Peru* (New York, 1967).

There are many reasons for following these facets of development, which are not all that peculiar. First, the setting of the guano-age economy explains a lot. With the enormous commercial, public, and capital resources released by Peru's bird-dung bonanza, the primordial policy questions of the era were in fact how best to channel opportunities of trade into development. Historically, too, the Andean economy was export driven (by silver mining) and marked by a weighty state sector (as viceregal capital of Spanish South America). But second, major transitions had ensued between silver and guano. These shifts—the dramatic example and impact of the North Atlantic's liberal commercial and industrial "revolutions"—most impressed Peruvian observers and became immediately linked to visions and theories of secular progress. Westernized elites everywhere were similarly struck.[35]

Third, such controversies over trade, diversity, and the state are precisely those isolated in recent dependency visions of the formative nineteenth century. The broad notion here is that free trade forfeited possibilities for diversified development that would have made Latin America part of the industrializing West by 1900. Latin America's historic error, as it were, was taking commercial observer status during the first industrial revolution. By the century's end specialization had transformed colonial backwardness into modern underdevelopment. As a counterfactual, or would-have-been argument, this needs informing with the developmental options genuinely felt at the time.[36] Moreover, today's pyrotechnics around regional "neoliberal" policies put these very issues of diversity and statism on the front burner, though thus far without much history behind them.

Fourth, Peruvian elites were an especially urban-bound group. An overwhelming majority of the country's educated males lived and intellectualized in the capital port city of Lima, culturally and economically

35. Besides Gootenberg, *Between Silver and Guano,* and the general Latin American studies cited above, see Michael Adas, *Machines as the Measure of Men: Science, Technology, and Ideologies of Western Dominance* (Ithaca, 1989), pt. 2, "The Age of Industrialization." See Phyllis Deane, *The State and the Economic System: An Introduction to the History of Political Economy* (Oxford, 1989), for most general argument putting the state at the center of economic thought; see Hunt, "Interpretive Essay," for incisive analysis of Peruvian policy questions.

36. Explicit counterfactual approaches are Gootenberg, *Between Silver and Guano;* Bill Albert, *South America and the World Economy from Independence to 1930* (London, 1983); for state making, Maurice Zeitlin, *The Civil Wars in Chile, or, the Bourgeois Revolutions That Never Were* (Princeton, 1984); or advancing global economic studies, such as Jean Batou, ed., *Between Development and Underdevelopment: The Precocious Attempts at Industrialization on the Periphery, 1800–1870* (Geneva, 1991).

worlds apart from the predominantly agrarian, peasant, and (60 percent) Indian country around them. In worldly, white Lima—whose population of sixty to one hundred and twenty thousand never passed 5 percent of Peru's total—resonated the country's ministries, press, schools, lobbies, and vibrant café-salon society.[37] It proves difficult to pick up genuine provincial accents from the nineteenth century, the tones of thinkers who might have spoken of developmental dilemmas in, say, more agrarian or Andean terms. Yet we will encounter progressively expanding national visions in the nineteenth-century developmental imagination.

Finally, although midcentury Lima already boasted professors and formal courses in European "Political Economy," the country produced no economists of note. Peruvian thinkers emerge literally as wide-ranging pensadores, practical and political men, engaged in building up a new nation as much as raising economic growth. Rather than abstract designs, they imbibed the working examples of overseas statesmen and pundits, though the liberalism they absorbed initially enjoyed a quasi-scientific and religious status. It was precisely their broader state-building concerns—with fiscality, national sovereignty and integration, true citizenries, and social control—that eventually gave their visions an eclectic and thus developmental compass.[38] It also made them typical of nation-building elites across nineteenth-century America.

Rather than oddity, Peru in the guano age posed the developmental challenges of republican Latin America in the sharpest terms imaginable. The stark cultural dualism between urban plutocrats and rural folk, the startling disparities between national wealth and disparate levels of

37. For demographic and ethnic trends, see Paul Gootenberg, "Population and Ethnicity in Early Republican Peru: Some Revisions," *LARR* 26 (1991): 109–57; for insight into intellectual culture, Gertrude M. Yeager, "Women and Intellectual Life in Nineteenth-Century Lima," *InterAmerican Review of Bibliography* 40 (1990): 361–93; I say "male" here, for women writers contributed enormously to literary life (and to indigenismo and educational reform) but rarely broached the gender-segregated realm of economics. Nils Jacobsen, "Free Trade, Regional Elites, and the Internal Market in Southern Peru, 1895–1932," in Love and Jacobsen, *Guiding the Invisible Hand*, 145–76, for an example of regional analysis feasible for later periods; less helpful is the sole regional survey, Héctor Ballon Lozada, *Las ideas sociopolíticas en Arequipa* (Arequipa, 1986).

38. Political limits (and transformation) of liberal "theory" is now standard fare in European historiography: e.g., Arthur J. Taylor, *Laissez-Faire and State Intervention in Nineteenth-Century Britain* (London, 1972); see Steven Topik, *The Political Economy of the Brazilian State, 1889–1930* (Austin, 1987), for fine (but nonideological) study of reasons of state in export economies. For official liberalism, see Tantaleán, *Política económico-financiera,* and its unimaginative officialist policy documentation.

development, and the official enthusiasm for the new liberal exporter creeds—all epitomized the processes in play almost everywhere in the region. A country hardly known for the originality and diversity of its economic policies and ideas, Peru has long served as regional exemplar of growth without development, ill served by its myopic ruling cliques.[39] For all these reasons, Peru merits the close but eminently comparable case study that follows. If Peruvian intellectuals had other visions in mind, the region as a whole likely enjoys a rich but submerged economic tradition.

This book shows that unofficial traditions of "developmentalist" thought infused both elite and popular Peruvian culture, surviving, even thriving, during the country's age of outward-directed growth. Even among highly Westernized dominant classes, active contestation of regnant European practice and theory was commonplace—drawing imaginatively on Peruvian economic experience, nationalist twists of formal theory, serious concerns over export dependence, reasons of state, and a popular-folkloric ethos of productive and distributive justice.

Chapter 2 briefly surveys the influential nationalist thought, aristocratic and artisan, prevalent in Peru before the triumph of free trade at the advent of the guano age. Chapter 3 explores initial guano-age conflicts about diversification—around Juan Norberto Casanova's native industrializing ideology—and how its failure by the 1850s colored liberal orthodoxy and dissenters over the next generation. Chapter 4 is the massive heart of the matter: a reexamination of the 1860s developmentalist schemes of Manuel Pardo and Luis Benjamín Cisneros, the organic intellectuals of guano. Attentive to mounting social costs of liberalism and looming nation-building tasks, their projects for railways, guano, and fiscal reform aspired to broaden domestic development, technology, sovereignty, and participation—the keys, in their minds, to reversing Peru's growing commercial imbalances. Such concerns found audible echoes in nationwide cries for modern communications and economies. Chapter 5, central in other ways, scrutinizes responses to the enveloping crisis of export exhaustion in the 1870s: the reactivation of artisan politics in the era and a new developmental synthesis in the middle-class industrialism of Copello and Petriconi. Chapter 6, a dé-

39. For sterile images of the nineteenth century, see Macera, "Historia económica como ciencia"; for paradigmatic later analysis, Rosemary Thorp and Geoffrey Bertram, *Peru 1890–1977: Growth and Policy in an Open Economy* (London, 1978).

nouement of the 1880s, turns to retrospectives on the national fiasco with export liberalism, as in the integrative industrial *indigenismo* of Peru's first economic historian, Luis Esteves. The conclusions seek to mend the gap between Peruvian ideas and experience and seek implications for study of Latin American social thought. Along the way many other thinkers are met, in what amounts to a genealogy of discontent with fictive prosperities. If little else, Peruvians fervidly imagined their thwarted development.

2

National Heterodox Traditions
The 1820s to the 1840s

From independence in 1821 to the mid 1840s, the Peruvian "republic" slogged through decades of unrelenting caudillo strife and bewildering political and regional disintegrations. Colonial economic foundations collapsed as haciendas, mines, workshops, and trading towns slumped into abandon and disrepair. Plagued by some twenty-four major regime changes in as many years (and countless smaller *golpes* and wider regional wars), Peru's anarchy was enough to blur all initial visions of nationhood. Only the age of guano rescued Peru from its catastrophic age of caudillos—elevating the economic liberalism of the stable export state into a veritable act of national salvation. Yet the new Peru remained awash in the wakes, however muddled, of two prior (even colonial) currents of national economic thought. Along with its caudillo skirmishes, postindependence Peru had just ended a bitter, three-decade battle over protectionism and free trade as the country struggled to define itself in the emerging global order.[1]

Conservative Peru was not then a country born liberal. Volatile but largely forgotten economic-nationalist ideologies, interests, movements, and policies permeated its earliest regimes and first yearnings for development. One strain was eminently elitist, the other profoundly popular, but together they smothered Peru's feeble first generation of theoretical free-traders. Of import here is the influence such crude national ideologies would exert on later developmentalist thinkers of the export

1. For these initial struggles, see Gootenberg, *Between Silver and Guano.*

era, even after being roundly defeated and disgraced in the late 1840s. Unlike purist Peruvian liberals—who could draw on a vast body of formal European theory—Peruvian dissenters had to piece together their own reflections and critiques out of hard economic experience and local ideas. This chapter, for all these reasons, provides a brief overview of Peru's precursory patrician and popular economic traditions and of the reactive and triumphant official liberalism of the 1840s.

A Protection of Elites

The protectionism of elites from 1820 to 1845 was in part a carryover of colonial corporate mentalities and partly a new defensive action wrapped after 1821 in the symbols of Western nationalism. All sectors of the Peruvian upper classes shared in this movement: the Lima commercial *consulado* (merchant guild), shippers, coastal sugar planters, urban millers, finance cliques, provincial traders, landlords, and textile makers, as well as nationalist officers, diplomats, and politicians. Their center of gravity, however, would remain the traditional geopolitical one of viceregal Lima. Stiff tariffs, import prohibitions, exclusions of foreign traders, discriminatory trade treaties, and national monopolies and priv- ileges were among their primitive, homegrown practices.[2] Spokesmen justified such policies out of sheer nativism, the need to promote a "national capitalist class" for an infirm state, compensatory advantages for beleaguered hijo del país entrepreneurs, a complementary "economic independence," integration of far-flung economic sectors, correction of trade imbalances, the conservation of employment and skills, and time- honored notions of social harmony. There was also the historical exam- ple set by the mercantilist rise of Britain and France into great trader and industrial nations—that is, before they began preaching free trade to Peru.

Because Peru's nationalist groundswell came by and large as a defen- sive move against both the novel competition of North Atlantic trades in the region and the first inklings of liberal trade theory, it was not especially coherent or versed in the tenets of emergent classical theory. In

---

2. Gootenberg, *Between Silver and Guano,* ch. 3; this interpretation revises views of initial elites as lacking national resolve. For the range of national pressures, see *Los Clamores del Perú* (Lima), Feb.–Mar. 1827.

streams of pamphlets, petitions, and polemics to generals and ministers, aroused writers drew on glorified notions of self-interest (elevated into reasons of state), espoused mercantilist or physiocratic principles (including a waning bullionism), or mimicked the autarkic mentalities of the archaic Hapsburg colonial state. Sometimes they recited a litany of obscure, eighteenth-century Spanish "economists"—including the ever popular Jovellanos—and remained steadfast admirers of Colbertian achievements or of Argüelles's more contemporary Spanish industrial variant. Even deep in the Andean interior, economic thinking spread, reflected in passionate *Cuzqueño* protectionist pleas or, for a curious example, in a remote Ayacuchan translation of a French text on political economy—annotated with rejoinders to the inapplicable free-trade doctrines of the author (P. H. Suzanne). Lima, as a political port city, enjoyed elaborate cosmopolitan traditions, in intellectual life at least, and literate Limeños devoured in their feisty and varied press a rich menu of economic histories, overseas policy studies, and, with some lag, the latest in European political economy. Yet the newfangled open trade theories of Bastiat, Say, and Smith—voiced by a handful of timid Peruvian liberals and crusading foreign consuls—were routinely dismissed by nationalist spokesmen as "inappropriate," "slavish," "ruinous," "self-interested," "hypocritical," and "unrealistic" for Peru.[3]

Such nationalist negations did not quite add up to a working formula for development, though they often revealed astute criticisms of commercial growth and an unmistakable sense of national self-interest. Nor were Peruvian elites alone, for similar concoctions of nationalist passions and interests swept early economic debates in sister republics such as Mexico, Argentina, and Colombia.[4] But above all they faithfully re-

---

3. See, e.g., José de Larrea y Loredo, *Principios que siguió el ciudadano J. de Larrea en el ministerio de hacienda y sección de negocios eclesiásticos de que estuve encargado* (Lima, pam., 1827), 5–8; Pedro de Rojas y Briones, *Proyectos de economía política que en favor de la república peruana ha formado el ciudadano P. Rojas y Briones, diputado del soberano congreso nombrado por la provincia de Cajamarca* (Lima, pam., 1828); *Observaciones sobre el proyecto de reglamento de comercio presentado al congreso por la comisión de hacienda* (Lima, 1828); A. Garrido, trans., *Principios jenerales de economía política por P. H. Suzanne, traducidos libremente al español y aumentados con notas por A. Garrido, oficio mayor y tesorero interno del departamento de Ayacucho* (Ayacucho, 1832). For initial contact with political economy, see Robert James Shafer, *The Economic Societies in the Spanish World, 1763–1821* (Syracuse, 1958), esp. 157–63.

4. For an exemplary Mexican study, see Guy P. C. Thomson, *Puebla de los Ángeles: Industry and Society in a Mexican City, 1700–1850* (Boulder, 1988), which finds colonial ideologies transmuting into modern economic nationalism; cf. Colombia in Ospina, *Industria y protección*, ch. 2.

flected the crushing economic contractions of the postindependence years and elite anxieties of displacement by interloping foreigners.

Actions spoke louder than words—and to a large degree, interest lapsed in all grand schemes as statesmen coped with the quotidian traumas of meeting imaginary budgets and paying for real wars. Throughout the era the few hundred surviving top national merchants patently resisted openings to freer trade and the material lures of the two dozen or so liberal foreign houses in their midst. Constraints of every sort fell on the port's overseas shippers and retailers. The contrast could not be sharper with the eagerly internationalist Peruvian merchants of the guano age. The organized consulado's timely fiscal and administrative aid to Lima's ephemeral state allowed officials and militarists to deflect incessant foreign free-trade pressures against Peru's web of commercial restrictions and navigation acts.[5] Sugar planters, a faltering but critical commercial force all along the northern coast, championed a sheltered bilateral trade system with Chile, in lieu of still imaginary outlets to the Atlantic. In this long campaign a host of related coastal farmers joined forces against invading foodstuffs: foreign flour, tobacco, rice, lard, wine. These early defenders of regional markets contrast with the agrarian export oligarchy that would dominate Peruvian agriculture by the later half of the guano age.

Andean traders and *hacendados* were mainly out to sustain time-honored interior trade routes or to protect their *obrajes,* the scattered colonial-style wool and cotton manufactories of the highlands. Provincials proved remarkably adept in 1820s political bids to stem the flood of industrial textiles from Britain and the United States, at times weaving complex arguments for the factory cause. To sympathetic congresses, spokesmen wrapped their concern in Peru's burning desire for national "industry," though the inefficient and primitive obrajes were a dying breed. Guano-age politicians became anything but industrial sympathizers. A veritable horde of *Gamarrista* military chiefs (followers of the

5. On (defeated) overseas pressures, see Paul Gootenberg, *Tejidos y harinas, corazones y mentes: El imperialismo norteamericano del libre comercio en el Perú, 1825–1840* (Lima, 1989)—based largely on Despatches of U.S. Consuls in Lima (U.S. Dept. of State, Record Group 59), M154, vols. 1–6, and U.S. Ministers to Peru (T52, vols. 1–16). For merchant politics, Paul Gootenberg, "Merchants, Foreigners, and the State: The Origins of Trade Policies in Post-Independence Peru" (Ph.D. diss., University of Chicago, 1985), chs. 2, 4, 5; vital sources here are consulado "actas" books, in Archivo General de la Nación, AGN, Lima, Sec. H-8, Tribunal del Consulado (Republicano), or Sec. H-4, Libros manuscritos republicanos de la sección hacienda, H-4 1556 (1821–1823); H-4 1584 (1825–1826); H-4 1707 (1829–1835); H-4 1838 (1842–1845).

central conservative figure, Mariscal Agustín Gamarra) sized up pressures from merchants and rural artisans and launched volatile antiforeign crusades that paralyzed overseas initiatives and investments. Even Cerro de Pasco silver miners, the era's one recuperating export group, rejected offers to open mining to foreign capital and expertise (fearing ownership loss) and joined with influential Limeño merchants instead for state-sponsored mine projects.[6]

In such a climate Peru's meager band of liberals remained beleaguered ones until the mid 1840s, though the rhetoric of economic liberalism often resounded, for appearance' sake, in official publications and pronouncements. There were two types of early free-traders in Peru, apart from the ever active (and ever ineffectual) resident U.S., British, and French consuls. The first, a distant regional group, were Arequipan merchants and landed classes, who opposed the centralist north's Chilean trade designs and welcomed British traders into their realm. But notoriously rebellious southerners remained regionally enmeshed and could neither conquer nor influence the Lima state, though try they did. Second, within government circles toiled a small band of intellectuals and bureaucrats, figures such as José María Pando, Manuel de Vidaurre, and Santiago Távara, scions of Bolívar and the expansive Bourbon state tradition. Often linked with the long-suffering Ministry of Finance, they embraced a form of free trade. Their gospel was "internationalism": Peru should integrate directly with Atlantic commerce, transforming Lima's port of Callao into a bustling direct trade import and bullion entrepôt. Peru would reap the fiscal rewards of moderate revenue tariffs and reduced contraband. They could authoritatively quote Turgot, Say, Smith, Malthus, and Bentham and cogently discuss the scary example of monopolistic Spanish policy, using Humboldt's and Juan and Ulloa's renowned histories.[7] Despite such practical aims they remained mere

---

6. "Tratado de comercio entre el Perú y el Chile," *El Redactor Peruano* (Lima), 15 May 1836; J. M. Pando, *Reclamación de los vulnerables derechos de los hacendados de las provincias litorales del departamento de Lima* (Lima, pam., 1833); on obrajes, see esp. "Comercio y Fábricas," *El Telégrafo de Lima*, all May 1828, and debates "Comercio," and "Nuestra patria y el bien de nuestra patria," Feb.–June 1828; or "Política económica," *El Acento de la Justicia* (Cuzco), Sept. 1829; "Los mineros," *Clamores del Perú*, 13 Mar. 1827; for merchant influence (around a formative free-market issue), see Tribunal del Consulado, *Razones poderosas que da el comercio de esta capital por las cuales no deben permitirse los establecimientos de martillo* (Lima, pam., 1834).

7. Paul Gootenberg, "Beleaguered Liberals: The Failed First Generation of Free Traders in Peru," in Love and Jacobsen, *Guiding the Invisible Hand*, 63–97. For internationalist group, see J. M. Pando, *Memoria sobre el estado de la hacienda de la república*

philosophers without a tangible political base, even among like-minded but decentralist regional forces. Tainted by foreign associations (a disgraced Bolívar, meddling Yankee merchants), their plans proved no match for the nationalism of elites. At any rate these topsy-turvy depression years were no time for incubating long-term liberal experiments.

In the early 1840s core Peruvian elites began a wrenching but surprisingly rapid transition to laissez-faire and free trade as cornerstones for the state and economy. Clearly, the 1841 advent of the guano trade gave them some push by providing new arenas for accumulation, public finance, and imported goods. Their conversion also coincided with expanding commerce and shrinking tariffs throughout Latin America and across the North Atlantic economy. But just as critical were Peruvian geopolitical realignments and shifts in the dynamics of national state building, especially in defining this liberalism's special successes, peculiarities, and boundaries. In Peru, free trade became embodied in the larger fabric of national political stabilization and elite formation that swiftly emerged during the first regime of Ramón Castilla (1845–1851)—himself, significantly, a converted Gamarrista nationalist.

In highly complex developments Peru's final and worst round of civil wars in the early 1840s discredited traditional statism by fully associating it with caudillo breakdowns and predation. Between 1841 and 1844 nightmarish army fiscal demands nearly destroyed the national commercial guild and completely sank their varied developmental projects, such as the treasured trade monopoly to Asia. The protection of elites had become its opposite and had failed on every front. In contrast, free trade now offered a financial solution for orderly and progressive state building (guano advances, a professionalized military). It now offered Lima merchants their long-sought recovery as a class, in which the externally funded "consolidation" of defaulted caudillo-era debts would play a notable role. Ideologically, the minimalist design of laissez-faire rule promised relief and shelter from the arbitrary and destructive misrule of statist militarists. In short, desperate Lima elites embraced free trade as a classic form of civilizing *doux commerce*. It was even useful in pacifying

peruana en fin de 1830 presentado al congreso por J. M. Pando (Lima, pam., 1831); Manuel Vidaurre, *Discurso sobre la acta de navegación pronunciado por el diputado M. Vidaurre* (Boston, pam., 1828); [S. Távara], *Análisis y amplificación del manifiesto presentado al congreso del Perú por el honorable sr. ministro J. M. Pando* (Lima, pam., 1831). For refutations and weakness, see "Análisis de las proposiciones del Sr. Vidaurre," *El Eco de la Opinión del Perú* (Lima), Aug.–Sept. 1827, or X. Y. Z., *Reflexiones sobre la ley de prohibiciones reimpresas y aumentadas con notas* (Lima, pam., 1831), actually subsidized by the U.S. legation.

the larger nation. Castilla and his cohorts viewed freer commerce as a way to co-opt and integrate the long rebellious south with Lima and lure similarly devastated provincial oligarchs to their national project, which it shortly did. A final reaction against protectionist politics would come with the frightful miniclass struggles launched by Lima artisans later in the decade. Peru's victorious new breed of post-1850 liberals always reminded their class that any return to exclusionism was tantamount to regress to the anarchic turmoil that had threatened their very class existence in the early republic.[8] The choice between "barbarity or civilization" acquired specific, if exaggerated, meanings in Peru—meanings represented in the state itself.

To be sure, these imperatives coincided with novel and more adroit varieties of free-trade thought, hammered in by a youthful new generation of liberals during the formative political economy debates of 1848–1852. Like Peruvian nationalist thought, this was never just an import. Theoretically, it preached full-blown comparative advantage (though guano made it a natural), new freedoms for consumers and merchants, and a less taxing treasury. Liberals now envisioned more decentralist and capitalist developments; expanding trade would tie together the nation, feed the toiling classes, unleash capitalist spirits, and peaceably revolutionize civil society. "Political Economy" was infallibly capitalized in such writings; the "errors" of the past were now plain to see, as writers ridiculed the usual "monopolists," feudal customs, and ineffectual states. Peruvians became conversant with the latest in radical French free trade (Blanqui, Chevalier), though Bastiat and Say always remained most popular. More easily read, French notions of free trade, that solvent of feudalism and catalyst of class harmony, also seemed more compatible to wary elites than did the Scottish enlightenment's dreary and frightful vision of inevitable class conflicts. But more than fresh thinking, aggressive free-traders invoked new practical heroes; Peel, Huskisson, and Cobden symbolized modern, courageous, and (at last!) consistent foreign state builders.[9] Unabsorbed, by contrast, was the fact that by

8. Gootenberg, *Between Silver and Guano*, ch. 5; for regional angles, see Gootenberg, "North–South: Trade Policy, Regionalism, and *Caudillismo* in Post-Independence Peru," *JLAS* 23 (1991): 1–36. A major firsthand account for 1844–1853 is Manuel de Mendiburu, "Memorias del Gen. Mendiburu" (MS., Biblioteca Denegri Luna); "Rápida ojeada sobre las causas jenerales que han determinado la suerte del Perú," *El Progreso* (Lima), Apr.–May 1850. For "sweet commerce" idea, see Albert O. Hirschman, *The Passions and the Interests: Political Arguments for Capitalism Before Its Triumph* (Princeton, 1977).

9. Turning-point sources are 1848–1852 tariff debates published in *El Comercio*, esp. the perspectives of the political economy youth group Los Cursantes de Economía Polí-

1848 classical liberalism had reached its prime: the national and popu-list Continental reactions, creeping English social intervention, Mill's hundred-and-one exceptions to laissez-faire, including the formal pro-tection of infant industries. Socialist ideas and proletarian revolts were read as good arguments to never industrialize; Peru was a land free of polluting interests, thankfully free to pursue a purer and purifying liber-alism. Though sometimes intellectual name-droppers, Peru's new politi-cal economists now suffered little initial resistance from enthusiastic elite audiences.

As a strictly developmental formula, liberalism became official doc-trine, enshrined in the annual clichés of the fiscal *Memorias de hacienda*. Mired in shadowy negative struggles with "restrictive" illusions, a posi-tive, if unchanging, growth theory is also discernible over the next three decades.[10] Three elements dominate: the primary role of commerce, a comparative-advantage stage theory, and the modest promotional role of the state. A review here will elucidate the backdrop from which distinctive developmental stances would emerge.

Commerce—always and fully unimpeded—was the spur to height-ened consumption, production, and capital formation. Foreign trade, following painful but unavoidable adjustments, was to serve as Peru's market-widening engine of growth. Specialized export-import trades cheapened subsistence, boosted savings, and induced efficiency; more dynamically, trade multiplied new tastes, expectations, technologies, productivity, and mounting merchant capital investments. In social terms, "moral effects" would register in capitalist and market men-talities, the progressive "spirit of association," among entrepreneurs and workers alike. Free traders privileged the visible impact of commerce over "fictitious" productions—in many ways first formalizing a split between external and internal spurs to development. One surmises an unarticulated "vent for surplus" principle at work.

---

tica, 23, 29–30 July, 5, 17–20 Aug. 1851; "Proyecto de reforma del reglamento de comercio y varios otros documentos del consejo de estado," *El Rejistro Oficial* (Lima), 12 Aug. 1850; "Política económica: Leyes restrictivas," *Progreso*, 15, 22 Dec. 1849; "De los peligros del régimen prohibitivo y de la necesidad de remediarlos," 5 Jan. 1850; "Las objecciones hechas en estas últimas tiempos contra el régimen de la concurrencia por C. Dunoyer," Feb.–Mar. 1850.

10. Tantaleán, *Política económico-financiera*, app. table 3 for summaries of such Memo-rias; for originals, see P. Emilio Dancuart, comp., *Anales de la Hacienda Pública del Perú* (Lima, 1902–1904), vols. 1–6; in general, compare ideas with Arthur I. Bloomfield, "British Thought on the Influence of Foreign Trade and Investment on Growth, 1830–1880," *HOPE* 13 (1981): 95–120, or Hoselitz, *Theories of Growth*.

As a young, lagging nation, Peru faced two crippling obstacles to development, lack of private capital and underpopulation, to be superseded in discrete stages. Investments in commerce, mining, and export agriculture would accelerate capital formation and the liberal associative spirit. Peru enjoyed outstanding natural and cost advantages in these activities. (Scientific Ricardian comparative advantage, if hinted at, did not gain currency until the turn of the century.) A Malthusian spirit colored liberal convictions of Peru as a grossly high-wage and sparsely settled land (although peasant populations were in fact briskly expanding throughout the century). Native wage labor was difficult to find, however, and liberals read this shortage as the key reason never to misallocate capital and labor resources in futile and unprofitable manufactures. Instead, populations would grow over time through the beneficent effects of trade on living standards and the wider attraction of liberal policies for foreign workers (or the more visible hand of promoting skilled European—i.e., superior white—immigration). Once Peru amassed its surplus capital, labor, and skills, then and only then might a natural transition occur to more complex and diversifying activities.[11]

The state's simple role was to facilitate these processes. Unfit for entrepreneurial tasks, save in the all-important guano trade, all that was needed from government, following Smith's maxim, was less meddling and lighter taxes. In fact, in Peru this lean state faced some pretty big tasks: lifting the innumerable colonial-era blocks to private property and practice, replacing them with effective capitalist judicial and bureaucratic institutions, balancing bloating budgets, creating much-needed infrastructure in roads, ports, schools, and public safety, and promoting science and immigration. Stability itself—an understandable liberal obsession after deadening caudillismo—required the depoliticization of the state, especially downsizing unproductive political employment, Peru's infamous *empleomanía*. On paper, at least, liberals admitted no conflict between the ideals of export and civil liberalism. However, in their universalism liberals remained remarkably mute on the economic peculiarities of Peru's Andean rural society and the special opportunities and

11. Sources include a seven-part series "Política económica," *Progreso*, July–Aug. 1850; "Legislación mercantil," all Aug. 1849, "Estranjeros," 29 Aug. 1849, "Inmigración," 8 Sept. 1849; "Rápida ojeada sobre la suerte del Perú," Apr.–May 1850; or the "cursantes" writings from *Comercio* cited above; esp. "Consejo de estado," 22 July 1850. By the 1860s, views codified in a series of national economics textbooks, e.g., Felipe Masías, *Curso elemental de economía política* (Lima, 1860), or Pedro M. Rodríguez, *Elementos de economía política* (Lima, 1876).

dilemmas afforded by the enclavish public management of guano. In any case, by 1850 this official developmentalism of the export age was set.

Two fundamental continuities from fading elite nationalism, nonetheless, would mark or distort the export liberalism of the guano age. Foremost was the state's guano monopoly itself, rapidly organized amid caudillo turmoil in 1841 and inspired by the passing military-consulado nexus and its traditional fiscal *estancos*. Guano-age Peru's brand of commercial and fiscal liberalism remained fueled by a uniquely statist, even nationalist institution, an irony never lost on vociferous overseas critics. At first necessarily reliant on British and French carriers and finance, the Peruvian government basically owned and worked the country's entire export sector. They pursued price-setting policies abroad; bargained hard for contractor profit shares reaching 60 percent; and deployed these funds for a lavish expansion of state activities (some eight to tenfold between 1850 and 1870).[12] Moreover, officials implemented increasingly nationalist policy goals, such as the Peruvianization of the trade for native merchants and bankers in the early 1860s.

Second, for elites themselves, particularly those commercial clans that arose from the ashes of the consulado, export growth fueled continuing public privileges, promotions, and prebends, from lucrative service contracts, slave manumission prizes, and tax breaks to massive giveaways like the inflated $25 million settlement of the internal debt.[13] This inner circle of merchants, professionals, and politicians, though slowly expanding, never surpassed a few thousand well-connected families in the nineteenth century. Peru's elitist free trade, like protection before, hinged largely on a symbiotic relationship between capital elites and the central treasury, now transformed into a ménage à trois with their lusty seduction of foreign financiers. The costs of laissez-faire—namely, unbridled import competition, de facto centralization, and paltry welfare and development measures—were borne mainly by the artisans, petty retailers, workers, regional societies, and forgotten peasant majorities of Peru. Needless to say, the material impact of Peru's export liberalism was not always congruent with the libertarian and republican ideals that accompanied its march elsewhere in the Western world.

12. Gootenberg, *Between Silver and Guano*, ch. 5 (origins and peculiarities of monopoly); Hunt, "Growth and Guano," tables 6, 10, 11 (state profits and expansion).
13. Gootenberg, *Between Silver and Guano*, 132–37; Quiroz, *Deuda defraudada*, chs. 4–7, for a detailed portrait of this liberal sociology of guano; there were about two thousand initial beneficiaries of the consolidation, though most benefits went to the top 125.

Popular Mechanics

Peru's second economic tradition, the popular, informal one that lost out by the 1850s, was that voiced by Lima's artisan community. As a legacy of its colonial heyday, Lima boasted a diverse crafts sector, overwhelmingly devoted to finished luxuries for its Europeanized bureaucratic and merchant aristocracy. In the late 1820s such light manufacturing still encompassed some seven hundred to nine hundred modest workshops (a quarter of the city's incorporated establishments), produced a fourth of taxed municipal business incomes, and employed perhaps three thousand to five thousand skilled apprentices, dayworkers, and black slaves. Organized into forty or so traditional guilds, most crafts specialized in ornate goods such as fine furniture, jewelry, dresses, saddlery, lace, buttons, carriages, watches, lamps, and such exotic Lima specialties as the *saya y manto* woman's cape; others plied motley smith and repair trades or processed foodstuffs (from liquors to lards) for the urban market. All these producers intertwined with the hundreds of petty creole shopkeepers and hawkers dominating the city plazas and streets. Strategically located in Peru's port capital, and constituting a corporately organized and literate lobby, Limeño artisans became a vibrant political presence after 1821. In this respect urban craftsmen were worlds apart from Peru's much larger and more diffuse rural artisanry, the tens of thousands of Andean-style peasant weavers and hewers of crude household necessities who stayed well out of political sight and range. As social distances shrank in Lima during the postindependence depression, guilds became useful to urban notables in varied forms of political mobilization, such as staged elections, caudillo standoffs, and standing militias, and in such vital municipal services as policing runaway slaves and rabid dogs.[14] It makes sense, then, to regard guild masters as one of Peru's rare "middle sectors." Guilds stood sandwiched between white elites and a frightfully dark-skinned *populacho*,

14. For detailed analysis of artisan sector, see Paul Gootenberg, "Artisans and Merchants: The Making of an Open Economy in Lima, Peru, 1830 to 1860" (M.Phil. thesis, Oxford University, 1981), chs. 3–5; major quantitative source is Lima's "Matrículas de Patentes" tax register, found for 1826–1860 amid AGN sections H-1 and H-4. On colonial roots, see Emilio Harth-Terré and Alberto Márquez Abanto, "Las bellas artes en el virreinato del Perú: Perspectiva social y económica del artesano virreinal en Lima," *Revista del Archivo Nacional del Perú* 26 (1962): 352–446; for social fears of the era, Christine Hünefeldt, "Los negros de Lima: 1800–1830," *Histórica* 3 (1979): 17–51.

whom they helped to contain and discipline through work routines and regulations. Moreover, the intricate protectionism of artisans converged with that of early elites.

Guild protectionism, too, was eminently defensive. Artisans sought to shelter, through high tariffs and outright prohibitions, their light craft manufactures. Their prime concern lay in promotion of skilled labor and employment, not in improved technology, efficiency, scale, or industrialism (Lima still had no factories to speak of). At the same time, to many, artisans colorfully and convincingly wrapped their aims in the national interest, epitomizing the flesh-and-blood hijos del país. To the guilds, foreign merchants and crafts—such as the novel, mass-produced, up-market imports that flooded Lima in the late 1820s—were unnecessary, ruinous, unfair, and downright unpatriotic. Such competition was forcing Peru's long-suffering model citizens into lives of vagrancy, vice, and political mayhem—a most frequent and threatening motif. Craft leaders invoked the standard of the "honorable," "humble," and "democratic" artisan. They vaunted republicanism and popular education. Their earnest work ethic and simple skills were assets to the nation, and their political and fiscal health a prop to republicanism, which obviously had to heed the needs of "the people."[15] Vague notions of a fixed "just price" infused this quasi-market mentality, immediately turned against new external competitors, too. Autodidactic craft leaders could also list their favorite Spanish economists, but mostly they railed against "imitative systems," "theories applied to other countries"—but just not right for conditions in Peru. As in elite discourse, countless special "exceptions" took precedence over the finer dictates of free trade. Hardly radicals— their very existence hinged on upper-class patrons—artisans profusely apologized for their "affronts to the lights of the century." Still, they boldly warned that if Peru lost its sparse indigenous skills, it would become "tributary of whoever approaches our shores to trade."[16]

15. For bits of artisan thinking, see J. M. García, "Representación que han elebado los gremios antes las cámaras," *Comercio,* 17 Oct. 1849; *Comercio,* 27 Feb., 21 July, 13 Aug., 23 Sept. 1843; "Reglamento de comercio—los artesanos," 1 Aug. 1850; "Los artesanos," 3 Jan. 1859; "Los artesanos," *Clamores del Perú,* 13 Mar. 1827; later pamphlets, e.g., *Artesanos* (Lima, pam., 1859); archival sources include guild-master missives in Matrículas de Patentes, e.g., AGN H-4 1517, Lima, 1834, 230–36; or AGN H-4 0227, Lima, 1842–1843, 348–49.

16. García, "Representación que han elebado los gremios antes las cámaras," *Comercio,* 17 Oct. 1849; see also political poetry, "Triunfo de los artesanos, Perú libre en su progreso, viva el nombre de García y las leyes del congreso," Colección de Volantes (Biblioteca Nacional del Perú), 1849.

If virtually an instinctual mode of thinking, craft political economy closely resembled that of better-read Continental artisans, who occasionally enriched their ranks, and of counterparts in every Latin American town with colonial guild survivals—Bogotá, Santiago, Puebla. Besides stiff craft tariffs, popular welfare would also be advanced by lower-cost mass necessities (for instance, imported foodstuffs, tools, and typical manufacturing inputs such as foreign cloth). Peru's responsive tariff structure thus provided artisans with the advantages of what is now termed effective protection. It was the state's "duty" to support native "industry," as aptly expressed in frequent military supply contracts for fancy uniforms and the like. Because craftsmanship centered on quality items for a remnant colonial aristocracy, artisans continued to be obsessed with taste considerations rather than cost. They boasted the superior quality of home goods over flimsy, cut-rate imports. Hierarchic guild masters tried, without much success, to carry on as well with restrictive guild statutes, which supposedly regulated quality, training, and entry, but they warmly welcomed the trickle of new European craft immigrants to Lima. "Teachers" and "models," their tasteful creations and techniques would spill over to ill-trained native artisans and shopkeepers.[17]

As a protectionism, artisan political economy proved absolute, since labor efficiency and final cost were hardly its central concerns. To portray such popular philosophy as a consistent, much less viable, conception of "development" would be an exaggeration. Much like elite nationalism, it basically thrived on hard times.

Still, this amalgam of petit bourgeois notions proved highly workable in early republican politics. Peddling their ideas with timely petitions and protests, Lima guilds had won tariffs of 50 to 90 percent by the late 1820s, followed by a host of full import prohibitions during Peru's "prohibitions era" of 1828–1840. In their campaigns guild leaders could exploit their business and political connections to elite merchants and suppliers. Other aspects of their program found their way into policy (such as pro-artisan immigration law), and even after textile and

17. *Comercio*, 23 Sept. 1840, 23 Aug., 27 Nov. 1849; for immigrants, see newspaper ads and esp. Matrículas de Patentes, AGN H-1 OL 342/1339, "Razón de los estranjeros que pagan patentes de industria," 1848; and "Estado de los artesanos de Lima," *El Intérprete del Pueblo* (Lima), 3–9 Apr. 1852. Richest comparative work is Luis A. Romero, *La Sociedad de Igualdad: Los artesanos de Santiago de Chile y sus primeras experiencias políticas* (Buenos Aires, 1978); on regulations, Paul Gootenberg, "Guilty Guilds? Artisans and the 'Monopoly' Problem in Nineteenth-Century Peru," typescript, SUNY–Stony Brook, 1992.

other tariffs fell by the wayside in the 1840s, urban crafts remained under special protective duties. Throughout the era their impassioned pleas rang in the Lima press and eloquent memorials (such as that of the cigar maker José María García before the full 1849 congress). Guilds cut deals with caudillos, candidates, and political clubs and packed the chambers to cheer or jeer congressional delegates.[18] What artisan appeal lacked in economic theory, or sense, it made up by embodying heartfelt desires for national dignity and popular progress.

However, by the mid 1840s—amid Peru's emerging import prosperity and solidifying elite state—artisan influence had begun to wane. By 1852 it lay totally shattered in the victory of a strict Manchesterian free-trade tariff and its legislated containment of artisan initiatives. Defeat came after Lima's guilds launched a dramatic 1849–1850 campaign to impose last-ditch protectionism on the guano economy's recovering consumer class. Following long, fiery, and shifting debates and initial concessions to the guilds, the struggle ended in a striking and lasting backlash against all artisan protectionism.[19]

Artisan losses reflected in part the inevitable result of the guano bonanza, but they also mirrored the weaknesses of popular economic thinking. Peru's revitalized import capacity allowed urban consumers access to a new range of luxuries, and such Europeanized elites naturally preferred the imported variety denied over three decades. Over the long haul, traditional artisan dependence on an upscale clientele had thus turned self-defeating. Emphasis on fine taste was easily turned on its head by liberals into loud public derision of the "miserable," "backward," and "crude" styles of Lima crafts. New liberals also exposed artisan claims to represent the true "national" interest. For example, by the late 1840s French, Italian, and English craftsmen had become a visible force in Lima, running about a fifth (122) of the city's most prominent and prospering workshops—as decrepit national crafts fell to under a fifth of Lima's total business economy.[20] Guilds supplied few

18. For early artisan pressures, see Libros de Cabildos/Actas de la Municipalidad (bks. 45–49), 1831–1839, Archivo Municipal de Lima; see also *Telégrafo*, 14 June, 20 July 1827, 26 Aug. 1829; *Comercio*, 21 July, 18 Aug. 1840; 17 Oct., 7–8 Nov., 20, 27 Sept. 1849; "Reglamento de comercio," *El Amigo del Pueblo* (Lima), 14 May 1840; Matrículas de Patentes, AGN H-1 OL 279/903, "Memoria de los síndicos procuradores," Oct. 1840.

19. Gootenberg, "Social Origins of Protection and Free Trade," esp. 351–58; key sources are tariff debates in *Comercio*, Dec. 1849, July–Aug. 1850, Sept. 1851.

20. Esp. "Reglamento de comercio—unos cursantes de economía política," *Comercio*, 23 July 1850; "Reglamento de comercio—srs. artesanos," 5 Aug. 1850; "Consejo de estado—reglamento de comercio," 14 Aug. 1850; "Representación del comercio de Arequipa al gobierno," 15 Aug. 1850; "Comisión de hacienda," 3 July 1851 (etc.).

necessities to greater Peru and had little to say about national development (much less about the provinces, who began protesting their inappropriate and privileged tariffs). Artisan democratic pretensions were belied by their enthusiasm for guild stratification and market restrictions, now deemed atavistic and "oppressive" in a burgeoning metropolis beset by price inflation. Preserving rote native skills appeared increasingly anachronistic as awareness spread about the North Atlantic revolution in machinery and modern factory production. Inert guilds, in fact, had never moved to produce in mass for the low-cost markets, a bias enshrined by pro-artisan tariff structures. When they began to rail publicly against Lima's first factory experiments in 1850, nostalgic artisans exposed themselves as out of step with the nineteenth century.[21] It is not strange that Lima's artisans, suffering vigorous free-trader tirades and defections of powerful supporters, could barely respond.

Most important, artisan political economy now looked like a concoction of narrow, ad hoc interests. Unable to set productive priorities, it simply led to squabbling, beggar-thy-neighbor demands rather than any coherent growth strategy. This familiar politicizing spiral was dramatized for elites during the 1849–1852 tariff struggles, when initial artisan protests sparked an escalating and conflicting competition for support by every imaginable group jeopardized by the emergent export economy. Liberals claimed that this process, if not contained, would lead Peru to a closed economy—a veritable "China" or "Paraguay." To principled liberals, a uniform and consciously inflexible free trade could rationalize policy and forever prevent such populist contagions.[22] This argument sealed the 1852 tariff.

But the last straw, in early 1850, had been an unseemly radical artisan political outburst. Sensing their growing isolation, and seizing the Jacobin slogans of Europe's 1848, renegade guild leaders smeared the Lima "idle aristocracy" of wealth and the hostile new liberals. Others called on artisans to elect their own "popular" governments and do away with all unresponsive politicians: "We want a republican government that watches over the country's industry, that provides guarantees to the guilds. . . . We are the majority and power resides in us." Controversy

21. E.g., "Comunicados—los artesanos que continuarán," *Comercio,* 25 July 1850; Gootenberg, "Artisans and Merchants," chs. 3–5, explores overall fragility of artisan political economy.

22. "Reglamento de comercio," *Comercio,* 23 July 1850; editorial (*El Comercio*), 4 July 1851; "El reglamento de comercio en el senado," 5 Aug. 1851; for one dramatic personal conversion, see speech of Sen. Seone, 19 Aug. 1851.

erupted over artisan elector lists and politicos still pandering to the guilds.[23] All this unsettling rhetoric added a powerful and decisive new imperative of class fear to economic policy-making. Last sympathies for artisans evaporated among Lima's guano nouveaux riches. The task was to keep dangerous artisans out of their plutocratic republic.

The 1850s thus began with a rapid marginalization of artisans from economic policy, civil politics, and the fruits of recovery. True, guilds received concessions for subsistence costs, some residual protection, and (eventually) such welfare measures as a school of arts. And artisans would also fare better with prosperity than would impoverished native retailers pushed aside by expanding foreign shops. But guilds clearly perceived how the coalescing civil institutions of Lima were out to bypass them; they lamented how the liberal age was to belong exclusively to merchants, well-heeled consumers, and the propertied classes. They felt expendable—and indeed they were.[24] Consequently, artisan ideology lost its original vitality in the 1850s and moved underground, where it barely and stubbornly survived. Guilds retreated into a consciously depoliticized and inward-looking politics of mutual aid—or exploded in desperate acts of Luddite despair, such as Lima and Callao's fiery protectionist riots of 1858.

Yet their plight, their failures, their aspirations, and even bits of popular folk protectionism would come to haunt Peru as the guano age progressed—when Peru's fiscal crisis unfolded amid a revitalized artisan politics of the 1860s. Then, a new generation of elite skeptics, moved like the first by politics, national interest, and perilous trades, would at least meet the artisans halfway.

23. For radicalism, see *Comercio,* "Srs. echeniques—los artesanos," 14 Nov. 1849, "Un maestro de artesano," 12 Dec. 1849, "Reunión de artesanos convocada por D. F. Grillo," 27 Dec. 1849; for electoral controversies (during the Vivanco-Echenique presidential contest), *Comercio,* all Jan.–Feb. 1850; on hostility toward liberals, "Editores del Progreso—leyes restrictivas," 5 Jan. 1850.

24. E.g., "Unos artesanos," *Comercio,* 29 Nov. 1851 or "Estado de los artesanos en Lima," *Correo de Lima,* 16 Oct. 1851. These themes are explored much further in ch. 5, below.

3
Diversifying with Guano
Casanova, 1845–1853

In the mid 1840s Peru—or at least Lima—was frenetically transformed. Lima, waning center of colonialism, had seen only
further disasters after independence: the ordeals of rampant militarism,
political disintegration, bankruptcy, and economic despair. Factional-
ized and conservative elites expressed at best a confused national purpose; Peruvians remained distanced or hostile about an uncertain connection to the world outside. By 1840 the old imperial capital of Lima
seemed a ghost of its former splendor, still slipping in population (under
55,000) as well as wealth, glory, and power. But fortunes changed
completely in 1841—with the European rediscovery of guano. The
easily mined mountains of bird dung on the nearby Chincha Islands lay
right within Lima's grasp. Peru's perceptive generals swiftly declared the
fertilizer a national monopoly and in a few years reconsolidated their
state at Lima. By 1845 the fabulous age of guano had arrived.

Guano riches worked many wonders in the first decade. Exports
soared from less than $700,000 in 1845 (24,701 metric tons) to more
than $6 million in 1853 (316,116 tons)—fully three-quarters of all ex-
ports, the rest largely Cerro de Pasco silver. Prosperity granted an end to
the fighting in 1845; under the resolute General Castilla the semblance
of a national state was born, with working congresses, codes, bureaus,
and budgets—the latter, doubling to over $10 million by 1853, based
chiefly on the flow of guano and renewed foreign credits. Scores of once-
wary foreign merchants now flocked to Lima and the open arms of the
consulado; manufactured imports to Callao alone more than doubled to
the $6 million range between 1845 and 1850. Peru began respecting her

foreign and domestic debts, long in arrears. All this was good news to Lima's suffering elites. Under Castilla's steady tutelage, they could dress like good Europeans, rebuild fallen family fortunes, demand proper deference, and properly debate their national future. Only artisan malcontents clung to misgivings. Mentalities and practice revolutionized as the latest currents of European thought also flooded the Limeño milieu. In direct and sublime ways Peru opened itself to the world. By 1852 its traditionally isolated stance had been fully superseded by the most vigorous liberal commercial order of the region.[1] Peru would rely on its unlimited guano riches and laissez-faire to forge a modern economy and society.

This chapter, however, focuses on early dissenters in these transformations—those who from the start questioned the type of diversity and prosperity imagined by exports alone. Failing to slow the march to liberal hegemony, they still left a mark. The most striking of these developmental schemes was Juan Norberto Casanova's *Ensayo económico-político sobre el porvenir de la industria algodonera fabril del Perú* (1849).[2] On the surface this book seems a mere publicity vehicle for the huge new textile mill that Casanova founded and managed, but in its core it unveils an ambitious project to tap guano revenues for industrial diversification, at this the start of Peru's era of export specialization. Brief experiments with this idea from 1845 to 1853 profoundly affected liberal and dissenting thinkers over the next generation. The interest swept Lima in two contradictory waves: first, in widespread fascination with industrialism as integral to Peru's newfound progress; second, in a dogmatic and phobic class reaction to elite industrial possibilities.

Industrial Movements

Peru had endured its share of promanufacturing policies in the decades since independence, but these had been directed at light urban crafts or the equally backward rural obrajes, neither of which held

1. On free-trade transformations, see Gootenberg, *Between Silver and Guano*, ch. 5; for initial guano exporting, W. M. Mathew, "Antony Gibbs and Sons, the Guano Trade, and the Peruvian Government, 1841–1861," in D. C. M. Platt, ed., *Business Imperialism, 1840–1930: An Inquiry Based on British Experience in Latin America* (Oxford, 1977), 337–70.

2. See also the reprint edition, (1972), with a prologue by Pablo Macera, Biblioteca Peruana de Historia Económica, 1972.

true productive or technological promise. By the late 1830s emphatic provincial campaigns to revive colonial-style factories (or country weavers) had failed. Not a single manufactory of Cuzco, Ayacucho, or La Libertad survived; they had been felled, it appears, by imports of industrial cottons (legal or otherwise), incessant civil turmoil, labor flight, and the broader regional depressions of the postindependence era.[3] Urban craftsmen, on the other hand, plodded along in familiar ways and numbers. But the year 1845, tail end of Peru's turbulent caudillismo, also marked a turning point in industrial perspectives, projects, and possibilities.

The precarious social peace forged by Castilla's national pacification, sped along by new regional alliances and guano, allowed Peru a fresh start at civil politics: the little-studied "first civilismo." For the first time in a decade, from July to October 1845 congressional delegates swarmed into the capital from all corners of Peru. Amid lively revived debates on how to stabilize and organize the nation, another polemic broke out over timeworn issues of industrial promotion.[4] This vast but forgotten controversy was not so much between protectionists and liberals, although free traders were gaining ground; rather, it revolved around sierran versus coastal perspectives and colonial versus modern notions of economic diversity.

Ayacuchan and Cuzqueñan delegations to the 1845 congress, led by their deputies Cabero and Ponce, sparked the polemics by lambasting the Lima government's failure to save their defunct manufacturers. That failure had left the Peruvian countryside "agonizing" in poverty, vagrancy, vice, and unrest—even in the dreaded "fear of matrimony." Charged speeches graphically recounted the demise of rural clothmakers and the squalor in their homelands and relayed to congress humble cries for aid from displaced weavers at home.[5] "There is no nation in the world," ran one refrain, "that allows its industry to be destroyed, that conspires against its own existence"—not even Spain! A desperate if eloquent nostalgia pervades these pleas, harking back to an imagined golden age of colonial artisanry. In Huamanga "from its capital to its

<hr/>

3. Gootenberg, *Between Silver and Guano*, 46–48; there is still no adequate study of final obrajes.

4. Basadre, *Historia* 2:740—even this barely notices Peru's first peacetime congress. Outstanding source is *Extracto de las sesiones de la cámara de diputados publicados en el "Comercio" de Lima* (Lima, 1845); full transcripts (with senate debates) also in *Comercio*, all July–Oct. 1845.

5. E.g., *Comercio*, 8 July, 8, 23 Aug., 15 Sept. 1845; the most detailed plea is Cabero's (23 Aug.), in *Extracto de las sesiones*, 108–10.

most miserable hamlet, their spinning wheels and looms once presented such a happy and flattering picture," filtering some $600,000 of benefits throughout the region. All was lost in Peru's "unlimited freedom of commerce."[6] The interior's proposals were just as nostalgic: for strict regress to bans on all cloth imports into Peru or even banishment of the foreign peddlers who plied them up the Andes.

But by 1845 this approach could not wash with a worldly congress. Instead, throughout the debates two issues seemed to raise wider concerns. First, delegates voiced the notion that industrial employment might extinguish the social malaise that had long inflamed Peru's smoldering caudillo struggles. Prospering industries would bolster the fragile peace. This was to become a recurrent political connection in the next generation. Second, delegates keenly perceived that Peru's newfound calm itself raised prospects for all sorts of economic ventures, as decades of chaos had sabotaged all previous hopes of reviving industries and agriculture.[7] In short, some elites viewed manufacturing as crucial to consolidating a progressive civil politics. Liberty, stability, and industry marched together.

To be sure, a handful of deputies, among them Cuadros and Urrutia, hurled classical free-trade arguments against the agitated Andean traditionalists. They paraded pragmatic principles of natural or cost advantage, though, in a sense, these also had long been a commonsense understanding of Peru's specialized colonial heritage. Peru, they claimed, was destined to be a mining and agricultural nation—"un país minero y agrícola." (Paradoxically, such calls also provoked a new wave of agrarian protectionism with the peace.) The lesson of fading colonial artisanries and futile crusades to save them was that in Peru manufacturing could simply never "work."[8] Restrictions worked only to produce contraband. Yet in 1845 this still remained the minority response; many outspoken deputies and senators confidently rejected the liberal recipe. Liberty was not yet synonymous with commerce.

Amid this debate, in late August an influential group of coastal delegates (led by Tirado and Vega) suddenly countered both traditional

6. Speech of Dep. Cabero, *Comercio*, 23 Aug. 1845.

7. *Comercio*, 15 July, 9 Aug., 25–27 Aug. 1845.

8. *Extracto de las sesiones*, 81, 111–15, 139; there are head-on debates of Smith's "brilliant" or "exaggerated" theory, but most positions derive from economic examples such as the United States. For new agrarian nationalists, see Francisco de Ribero, *Memoria o sea apuntamientos sobre la industria agrícola del Perú y sobre algunos medios que pudieran adoptarse para remediar su decadencia* (Lima, 1845), 7, 24–28, 34; Carlos Ledos, *Consideraciones sobre la agricultura* (Lima, 1847), 12, 167.

stances with a wholly new concept. Instead of engaging in fruitless efforts to revive archaic manufactories or to return to narrow dependence, Peru needed to develop the same kind of modern factories now transforming England and the United States. Infatuation with the machine had just gripped the Peruvian imagination. Such revolutionary industries should be based on the latest imported plants and located in the coastal consumer heartland. Though this argument signaled shifts to Lima interests, it was also cogent; transport costs were a daunting obstacle to any form of sierran development, the theme codified by later civilist writers. Limeño discourse revealed a flexible mind-set, a breaking out of dyadic liberal-protectionist categories. The intrinsic power of machinery, peace, and capital was infinitely greater than ineffectual restrictive laws. Free trade, that "beautiful theory," needed to be applied, but in gradual ways, safeguarding the "health of the people."[9]

Enthusiasm gained rapidly for this compromise modernizing plan. In effect, this debate also marked the end of Peruvian hopes in colonial obrajes and rural industry generally. Their last promotional props (some unfulfilled military contracts) disappeared with little protest the following year. A final regional voice, that of the maverick Puneño radical Juan Bustamante, warned of shipping out Andean "gold" and wools "only to serve the tastes and grandeur of European industry"—but the caveat fell on deaf ears.[10] Until the 1860s no Limeño would evince interest in regional manufacturing, and then under different duress. But equally striking, in 1845 no one bothered to regard rising guano prosperity as a new hindrance to Peruvian diversity or industrialism; on the contrary, it represented a technologic threshold. By October 1845 congress had hammered out its draft law to promote modern factories in Lima. It included generous awards to factory pioneers and for immigrant technicians and workers, such as technology and market privileges, duty-free inputs, and long-term tax breaks.[11]

9. *Comercio*, 15 July, 9, and esp. 27 Aug. 1845.

10. "Ministerio de guerra," *Comercio*, 19–21 Nov. 1846. Juan Bustamante, *Apuntes y observaciones civiles, políticas y religiosas con las noticias adquiridas en este segundo viaje a la Europa* (Paris, 1849), 34; off to witness the events of 1848, Bustamante makes offers—all ignored—to contract European technicians to retrain sierran artisans (82). Best known for his later, ill-fated indigenismo (Huancané, 1867), Bustamante was a wide-ranging radical, for example, mobilizing populist artisans in 1850 (*Comercio*, Jan.–Feb. 1850). Ch. 6, below, explores the return of sierran traditions in the 1880s.

11. *Comercio*, 24 Sept. 1845; "Cámara de diputados," 4 Feb. 1848 (the fate of this law remains unclear). For era's conflictual industrial concessions policy, see Gootenberg, "Artisans and Merchants," 101–6.

Lima entrepreneurs responded immediately, and by 1848 a full-fledged industrial experiment was rising in the capital. Businessmen grasped the opportunities afforded by peace, the consumer revival, and such highly publicized privileges and support. An eminently elite enterprise, in many ways this movement was counterposed to traditional artisan and weaver protectionism. For five years Peru's self-proclaimed "infant industrialists" were to garner the wholehearted backing of all top officials and even prominent free-traders.

In glasswares and utensils the merchant Jorge Moreto had already established his protected factory by 1841. In 1847 the Bossio brothers revived it, moved it to Callao, and greatly expanded its product range while offering new shares and bringing in skilled European managers. In silks José de Sarratea, a landowner and independence war hero, multiplied his mulberry plantings and pressed ahead with imports of specialized steam machinery for a wide range of silk novelties. Both projects received government monopolies and subsidies, Sarratea, for example, in his spacious, rent-free factory. A sparkling water-driven paper mill was established by Amunátegui and Villota, the merchant-owners of *El Comercio*, Peru's most influential (and most free-trader) daily. They sank $50,000 into imported machinery alone; the factory would provide not only reliable and cheap newsprint for the national press but scores of jobs to the poorest of the poor, busily recycling rags throughout the city. Eugenio Rosell, another trader, opened a factory for candles and a wide array of whale oil by-products. The government itself invested heavily in its naval foundry at Bellavista, established in 1846. Part technical academy, Bellavista was to train mechanics (forty-three annually) for private business and to earn its keep through private contracts for making and repairing sophisticated machinery.[12] The most impressive project of all, however, was the cotton textile mill Los Tres Amigos.

Using a mechanized plant shipped in from Paterson, New Jersey, the owners envisioned a factory with a capacity of one hundred looms and twenty thread machines. They would soon move to employ five hundred workers with an annual production of ten million yards—that is, virtually all of Peru's cloth import bill. Juan Norberto Casanova, the founder and director, found a willing partner in José de Santiago, scion of

12. Published descriptions of factories in Eduardo Carrasco, *Calendario y guía de forasteros de la república peruana para el año de 1849* (Lima, 1848), 82–83; Manuel A. Fuentes, *Estadística general de Lima* (Lima, 1858), 719–28; or Alberto Regal, *Castilla constructor* (Lima, 1967), ch. 6; and manifold press accounts.

one of Lima's oldest merchant clans and then chief of the prestigious merchant consulado. (The third amigo, the less well known Cagigao, was soon replaced by the importer Modesto Herce.) Pedro Gonzales Candamo, Peru's wealthiest and best-connected financier, supplied a soft loan of $85,000 to the factory from his abundant consolidation funds; Domingo Elías, the country's leading "capitalist" (and its most aspiring civil politician), was to supply ample cotton from his flourishing Ica plantations. Along with the official daily *El Peruano* (which ran florid descriptions of the factory) and *El Comercio* (the merchant mouthpiece), Elías's new ultraliberal *El Progreso* (precursor of 1870s civilismo) exalted these "intrepid and patriotic capitalists" and Lima's burgeoning climate of "industrial progress." "The machines of Lima" beckoned the future.[13] The government awarded the group its usual array of industrial privileges and, after hearing their nationalist arguments, a special 40 percent textile tariff in 1848, despite the sacrifice of public revenues. The three-story, water-driven mill, located in the heart of the city (in the legendary colonial Casa de la Perricholi), was well underway by 1848. Initial investments came to more than $200,000, no small sum in Peru. Some 162 workers, mainly destitute women and children, commanded the bustling machines.

What clearly was shaping here by 1848 was a concerted effort to legitimize an elite industrial lobby at the advent of the guano age. The press campaign, particularly the effusions from Peru's official gazette, was far out of proportion to the handful of factories underway. It was as if modern industry were the foremost symbol of a progressing Peru— and, at last, a respectable alternative to its increasingly disreputable artisans. A still active senator Cabero preached about the "national factories of paper and cottons having a hand to not fail in the cradle." Foreign tourists to Lima went away impressed with "the support" for and "successes" of the "first Conquest of industry in Peru." Castilla himself toured the plants. News and endorsements rapidly spread to Cuzco, which called for "many imitators," especially in the interior; Peruvian students abroad analyzed the factories in their theses.[14]

13. Casanova, *Ensayo económico-político*, passim; see also series in *El Peruano* (Lima), "Industria," 13 Sept. 1848; "Nueva fábrica de tejidos de algodón," *Peruano*, 21–25 Oct. 1848; "Industria nacional—protección a las máquinas de Lima," *Progreso*, 24 Nov. 1849; "Elaboración del papel en el Perú," *Peruano*, 22 July 1848; *Comercio*, 16 May, 24 July 1850; loan data in Quiroz, *Deuda defraudada*, 192.

14. "Fábrica de papel en Lima," *Los Intereses del País* (Cuzco), 19 July 1848, 19 Nov. 1848—a paper dedicated to "material and social progress with the end of revolts";

A sterling example of this campaign registered in October 1848. At a solemn ceremony the factory owners gathered to present the exuberant President Castilla with the following gift: Lima's first cotton sheet, wrapped in Lima paper, tied with a Limeño silk ribbon. The packet was placed in the refurbished Museo Nacional—where future generations would surely flock to admire the founders of industrial Peru. "The question," ran one state editorial, "is not just of benevolence to the impresarios, who truly deserve it, but of the general interest—of the progress, wealth, and power of the nation."[15] Textile production rose on schedule; announcements appeared for factory expansions and newer ventures.

Guano into Factories?

Juan Norberto Casanova's hopeful 127-page tract was a formal expression of this moment and interest. The *Ensayo económico-político sobre el porvenir de la industria algodonera fabril del Perú* comprises as well an original "infant industry" argument, offered in a broad program of what is now called "import-substituting industrialization." Casanova's immediate aim was to publicize his textile factory and gain even stronger government backing. Indeed, portions of the book first appeared in the government press. A larger agenda, set out in the preface, was to encourage other national capitalists to join in the industrial movement, in cottons and many other lines. The audience—Lima's men of capital and influence—was obvious; the mystery was how they would read Casanova.[16]

Bustamante, *Apuntes y observaciones,* 121; Cabero speech, *Comercio,* 4 Oct. 1849. Max Radiguet, *Lima y la sociedad peruana* (1856; rpt. Lima, 1971), 149–50; José V. Lastrarría, "Lima en 1850," in A. Tauro, ed., *Viajeros en el Perú republicano* (Lima, 1967), 96–97. Toribio Pacheco, *Dissertation sur les instruments qui concourent à la formation de la richesse* (a published law thesis; Brussels, 1852), 79. Pacheco, later a key civilist legal thinker, presents even-handed discussions of trade theories (Colbert to Ricardo); the thesis makes an exemplary source on transmission of economic ideas.

    15. Carrasco, *Guía de Lima,* 83; "Industria," *Peruano,* 13 Sept. 1848—calling for new industries and investments for the era of peace.

    16. Casanova, *Ensayo económico-político,* Advertencia preliminar—Introducción, 59; he dedicates the book to "Representatives of the Nation—who have always promoted industry with enthusiasm." Little is found on Casanova's biography; not a prominent merchant, in some accounts he appears as "Dr." Casanova.

The book reflects a hodgepodge of influences. It brims with the United States's recent experience, which Casanova recounts from his three visits in the mid 1840s to New Jersey firms—a fascination that would echo in many emerging voices. He also hails Spanish industrial promotion, along with Mexico's famed early industrial experiments; indeed, Casanova's closest regional counterpart was Puebla's incredibly prolific textile promoter of the 1830s and 1840s, Estevan de Antuñano, who penned dozens of pamphlets and books for the industrial cause.[17] Casanova seems less infatuated with theory. No hints are found of the coeval infant-industry ideology of Friedrich List (or, for that matter, of Hamilton), though his work more or less replicates the argument, minus European statism. Typically, Casanova barrages us with economic lights in the introduction: Smith, Ganilh, Say, Florez Estrada, Chevalier, Mill, the counts of Villanueve and Bargemont, later even Sismondi. The main text, however, gleans liberally from "the celebrated *español* Andrés Borrego"—an obscure fellow industrial promoter (and politician) uncelebrated by economic history. So, despite the title, Casanova's *Ensayo económico-político* is more significant for its timing and purpose—"to show Peruvians their true interests"—than for its political economy. As with most dissidents from regnant liberal theory, Casanova necessarily embraces relativism and improvisation. Political economy "is subject to such a grand diversity of contexts, countries, customs, habits, laws, and necessities, that we must modify principle—there are so very few absolutely true theories."[18]

In fact, the bulk of the *Ensayo económico-político* is a detailed descriptive tour of the budding factory, a paean to its rosy prospects. Yet a programmatic (even psychological) message runs through this long technical and cost survey: strong rejoinders to traditional and local claims that Peru lacks the basic "elements" for industrialization. Casanova must awaken Peru's dormant and discouraged industrial entrepreneurs. Many surmise that Peru cannot efficiently muster the requisite cheap labor, raw materials, expertise, power, internal markets, surplus capital, and so on. But in Casanova's uplifting vision, Peru raises finer cotton than the United

---

17. Robert A. Potash, *The Mexican Government and Industrial Development in the Early Republic: The Banco de Avío* (Amherst, 1983), 111–12, 142–43; Thomson, *Puebla de los Ángeles.*

18. Casanova, *Ensayo económico-político,* Advertencia preliminar, 3, 71, 89; Borrego's protectionist *Principios de economía política* (1844) is so obscure that no references are found in standard histories of economic ideas; see Raymond Carr, *Spain 1808–1939* (Oxford, 1966), 244–45, on political activism; or Evarista Correo Calderón, *Registro de arbitristas, economistas y reformistas españoles (1500–1936)* (Madrid, 1981), 373.

States does; Lima's abundant waterpower just awaits harnessing; good wages can attract hundreds of willing and malleable workers (especially indigent women and children); contracted foreign technicians will train competent local replacements; his imported machinery is top-notch and most apt for Peru's labor-short economy; local cloth is superior to most imports; and popular demand for coarse cottons is massive and rising.[19] Dozens of calculations are mustered to convey this gung-ho Peruvian entrepreneurialism, flinging statistics from *Parliamentary Papers* to the U.S. cotton belt. A subsidiary theme, worked out in lengthy reviews of machine innovations, is the transformative power of modern technology, another fascination of later writers. It is as if the mechanical marvels of the industrial revolution alone have now superseded traditionally fixed cost calculations of trade. Moreover, after balancing raging European debates on the working class, Casanova endorses the "moral" force of machinery on popular society.[20] Liberal trade was not the only moralizer around.

Casanova repeatedly spins another appealing politic theme: how virtually all national groups—agriculturalists, the poor, capitalists, the state—will harmoniously benefit from integrated national industries. He broadcasts, for instance, "the advantages that agriculture reaps by selling its products in the same soil where cultivated, manufactured, and consumed"—predicting opulence for the southern planter-politico Elías. He even imagines the day when Peru, "so abundant in mines," will construct industrial plants on its own, a wishful notion of later writers. He personally encourages other Peruvian businessmen to compete with his textile concern, "six or seven more factories." Other factories will emulate in "infinite localities" outside Lima, "at the foot of plantations," powered by mighty Andean currents dropping to the sea.[21] Protection need not spell "monopoly"; its goal is to bolster entrepreneurial "confianza" and the liberal "spirit of *empresa* and association."

Finally, there is a patently sociopolitical side to Casanova's industrialism, in the spirit of the 1845 congress—and beyond. The country remains anxious with memories of incurable discontent, revolt, civil wars. Industrialization, through its massive and disciplining employment, secures order. "The history of nations offers no more certain and clear truth. Individual well-being is the great guarantor of conduct. . . .

---

19. Initial chapter topics followed this survey: (1) primary materials, (2) motor power, (3) cost of primary materials, (4) salaries, (5) machinery, and (6) "difficulties."

20. Casanova, *Ensayo económico-político*, chs. 2, 5.

21. Casanova, *Ensayo económico-político*, 5, 87.

He who can live does not sell himself; when constantly occupied, he does not intrigue; he who improves and prospers from work lives contently, loves his patria, and blesses his rulers."[22] So along with his other inverted free-trader motifs, Casanova proffers Peru a sweetly civilizing industry.

Despite such propitious industrial conditions in Peru, Casanova must underline the need for sustained government support, the object of his crusade. He finds working and legal precedents in Peru's past efforts to promote obrajes, guilds, and colonial agriculture. But public support for modern factories that cheaply supply growing markets, argues Casanova, is worthy beyond comparison. The obrajes and handweavers made a "miserable" form of industry, and Casanova suggests that local tailors may well suffer harm from factories, given the artisans' penchant for using cheaper imported cloth.[23] As required for Peru's nationalist writers, the book recites in its defense the long history of protectionism in Britain, France, Spain, and North America (and exemplary China!), skirting the controversial shoals of the North Atlantic's newfangled free trade. To mocking Casanova, free trade is rank hypocrisy from nations whose very greatness stems from past promotional policies: "Nothing is odder than to watch today peoples who prospered with grave impositions and monopolies argue for free trade—after being the worst of prohibitionists."[24]

Eventually, a dispassionate case for infant-industry tariffs gets clarified in a direct, specific, even compelling way. Casanova posits that with any industry substituting imports, home markets inevitably start out saturated with competing goods. Textile prices may remain so low throughout Peru that no factory can freely compete, at least not until it works up to its full and thereby efficient utilization of capacity. His is a sensible appeal to temporary efficiency, learning, and scale factors—akin to contemporaneous Continental arguments, but fitted to an underdeveloped context affected by advanced trade. Once working capacity and average costs are achieved, tariffs can be phased out.[25] More muddled is his theoretical conception of duties as an "anticipation of capital created" (in lieu of a hideous "consumption tax"); tariffs aim to channel created capitals into national industry. Nor are restrictions the sole

22. Casanova, *Ensayo económico-político*, 89.
23. Casanova, *Ensayo económico-político*, ch. 9, "Porvenir."
24. Casanova, *Ensayo económico-político*, 86, 96.
25. Casanova, *Ensayo económico-político*, ch. 8, "Fomento," ch. 9, "Futuro," esp. 89–98; the appendix reproduces government concessions to date. For (supportive) congressional tariff debates on the factory, see *Comercio*, 29 Jan., 4–5 Feb. 1848.

solution; in the interim, proposals are specified against contraband and for the subsidies discussed below.

The *Ensayo económico-político* ends on a more ominous note: its foreman's handbook of powers (backed by four armed guards) for inducing competitive worker productivity, as well as such paternalistic schemes as a worker savings bank, chapel, prizes, and hygienic program.[26] Earlier in the book Casanova rejected the miseries of the European working class in favor of the benevolent uplifting imagined in the formation of the North American kind. Still, attuned to creole class fears, Casanova places enormous weight on popular order and discipline; Lima's "immoral" workers are enjoined from talking, playing, and even singing in the plant, not to mention fined for drinking, smoking, and pilfering. Los Tres Amigos must have felt like a dreary bit of Waltham along the Rímac.

Beyond such practical plans and policies, Casanova's most striking idea is a broad proposal for subsidizing factories. Like many economists, Casanova contends that direct public subsidies, rather than tariffs, would make the optimal targeted means of transitional support—a "protección efectiva," as he dubs it, "a true and legitimate protection." With capital subsidies alone, factories could "beat back the attacks of foreign rivals." Here he delves deeply into Spanish and French precedent.

Where would such funding come from? The guano of the three Chincha Islands alone amounts to, in Casanova's suggestive metaphor, a "Banco Nacional," retaining by his estimate $289 million in "deposits." Someone other than the Peruvian public made those deposits, of course, which in a wider calculation reach $700 million—remarkably close to the historic returns of the trade. More important, Casanova's outlook on guano was not far removed from that of the Peruvian state, which regarded its fertilizer monopoly as a public good and development resource, an idea resounding from initial pamphlet wars on the shape of the trade.[27] If driven by desires to avoid conflictual tariff fights, this

---

26. Casanova, *Ensayo económico-político*, 49, ch. 10, Fábrica de Lima.
27. In fact, few writers in the ongoing debates on management of the trade ever focused on the direct developmental benefits of guano. Nationalist (i.e., hijos de país) *Estudios sobre el huano, o historia de los contratos celebrados por el gobierno para su expendio exterior* (Lima, pam., 1851) vaguely depicts guano as a "powerful instrument for the social betterment of coming generations"; Francisco de Ribero, *Memoria sobre las huaneras de la república* (Lima, pam., 1846), 10–12, discusses uses in southern and rising cane and wine agriculture; Alejandro Cochet, *Disertación sobre el origen del huano de Iquique* (Lima, pam., 1841), actually about nitrates, most forcibly argues for domestic use over "waste" for foreign profits: "Are not these true treasures in deposit?" (32–33). In all his writings Castilla simply affirms the state's "duty" to administer the trade, despite contravening liberalism: A. Tauro, ed., Ramón Castilla, *Ideología* (Lima, 1948), 33.

notion of a guano development fund found parallels, for example, in Mexico's industrial Banco de Avío; it also echoes in later reformist projects, such as Cisneros's "fomento" fund of the 1860s.

Specifically, Casanova proposes that for all of the projected Lima factories, modest guano subsidies should cover the cost of invested risk capital—and act as the major incentive to spreading industrial investments.[28] In all his thinking, movement of capital is Casanova's utmost concern. Another key innovation (picked up by later fiscal planners) is his call to strictly separate ordinary budget expenditures—the civil and military lists—from guano revenues. Peruvian officials, Casanova knew, were already predicting budgetary abuses, shortfalls, even austerities. If rationally conserved, guano could be devoted wholly to "the aggrandizement of the pueblos in all of their material and intellectual improvements; building their roads, protecting their industry." After bloating guano treasures to a billion pesos, Casanova asks: "Is this the impoverished country our model financiers lament? This is the lamentable state of Peruvian finance? Hic patet ingeniis campus."[29]

This is no modest proposal. At the start of the guano age, when Peru enjoyed options at hand, a portion of the elite was significantly expressing diversification ideals rooted in exploitation of export-induced capital and demand. Peru's temporary bonanza could be harnessed to a wider and longer modernization and development. With foresight, the over-specializing dangers of commercial prosperity could be averted—just as later critics, including most economic historians, wish had happened.

Critics, Now and Then

Casanova's opus has been analyzed before. The advent of modern dependency ideas resurrected the *Ensayo económico-político* as a classic of Peruvian economic history. Yet the work's redemptors still read Casanova's plan as "utopian"—a doomed and unworthy alternative, particularly as its author lacked the proper appreciation of "imperialist" contexts. More generally, historians deem industry implausible for nineteenth-century Peru, on many grounds, the most pervasive being

28. Casanova, *Ensayo económico-político,* 80–84, and ch. 8, Concurrencia Indígena; for subsequent public debates, see *Comercio,* Feb. 1848, 19, 29 Oct. 1849, 25 July 1850, 4–5 Oct. 1851.

29. Casanova, *Ensayo económico-político,* 82–83.

the country's lack of viable "internal markets." Yet at the same time willful neglect of industrial possibilities verifies the national incapacity of Peru's would-be bourgeoisie.[30]

Redolent of the prejudiced projections of republican free-traders, such arguments remain unconvincing. Full-scale industrialization seems unlikely in nineteenth-century Latin America, which lacked the militarist resolve and social preconditions of catch-up countries such as Germany and Japan. But more incremental technological gains could have registered from select import substitution, if countries had opted to forego some consumption for long-term goals of steadier development.[31] And Casanova in particular was a highly pragmatic, even empirical thinker, who arose at an opportune time to push for the country's diversification. His mission was precisely to spark an entrepreneurial élan against anti-industrial prejudice.

If free-trade imperialism is the issue, it is generally a tricky one to verify. Casanova, at least, was sensitive to the dangers of unhindered trade with Britain. In fact, he discusses at length (some ten pages) futile English threats to stem Spanish industrialism. If such "hostile" dumping came down on Peru, that "terrible measure" of prohibitions would be needed, or Peru would respond with the productive flexibility of the early United States. He deems such a campaign unlikely, however, given Peru's relatively modest market. Short of extremes, Casanova's effort to present a workable and diplomatic form of protection speaks to his concern, and the initial support from Peru's highest commercial and political classes reveals his political acumen—notably the "truly patriotic enthusiasm of President Castilla." Indeed, the factory and tariff merit but passing mention in British consular reports, with no intention to oppose them directly; by 1840 most of the early free-trade pressures on Peru had subsided.[32] Peru's strict national management of the guano monopoly

30. Macera, "Algodón y comercio exterior": originally a pessimistic prologue to his 1972 edition of Casanova; cf. Bonilla, *Guano y burguesía*, ch. 3, esp. 151–53, and odder Tantaleán, *Política económico-financiera*, ch. 8.

31. For global issues, Batou, *Between Development and Underdevelopment*; P. Higonnet, D. S. Landes, and H. Rosovsky, eds., *Favorites of Fortune: Technology, Growth, and Economic Development Since the Industrial Revolution* (Cambridge, Mass., 1991); or regional survey, Frederick S. Weaver, *Class, State, and Industrial Structure: The Historical Process of South American Industrial Growth* (Westport, Conn. 1980), chs. 4–5.

32. Casanova, *Ensayo económico-político*, 53–58, 112, based on Sr. Borrego's account. On free-trade imperialism in Peru, see Mathew, "Imperialism of Free Trade," and Gootenberg, *Tejidos, harinas, corazones y mentes*. For foreign perceptions of factories, see British Foreign Office (PRO) FO61/117, Adams to Palmerston, 12 June 1848, and FO61/126, 12 Jan. 1850; or U.S., T52/8, Clay to Buchanan, 12 June 1848.

had demonstrated an effective will to counter the dogma (and hearty pressures) of the era's liberal superpowers. If national resolve stopped at tariffs and imports, this was a policy matter of political choice, not of external force and inevitability.

Most saliently, Casanova firmly grasped the nature of Peru's economic opportunity. First, his type of enterprise, geared to mass markets and using competitive technology, was the appropriate kind. Profit and growth opportunities could emerge here in an era of burgeoning consumer demand, as the guano age soon became. The earlier wave of North Atlantic import competition, since the 1820s, had forged a market for modern manufactures in Peru as well as enhanced labor mobility. Such conditions are intrinsic to any process of import substitution; if the market covered by the import bill is large enough to sustain factories of efficient size, which it certainly was by 1848 for simple textiles, local production becomes an economic alternative.[33]

Second, the nineteenth century was also an opportune, if not optimal time for countries such as Peru at least to initiate modern industries. Prior to the capital-intensive "second" industrial revolution of the 1870s, the technological demands, capital requirements, and economies of scale needed for viable international competition were actually quite modest. "Learning by doing" and self-financing remained the norm in European consumer industries. By the late nineteenth century, however, this opportunity had passed, and by then most of Latin America had fallen irrevocably behind the industrializers. Modern productivity and technology gaps developed in the half century 1820–1870. These lags had little to do with Latin American incapacity (much less vacant ideas) and much to do with larger economic contexts and national policy choices.[34]

Third, even Casanova's specific proposals lay within the realm of the possible. In October 1849, for example, the Peruvian congress voted the suggested subsidies to the textile and paper mills—directly in the form of guano! Los Tres Amigos was to receive 3,000 tons annually over the

33. Albert O. Hirschman, "The Political Economy of Import-Substituting Industrialization in Latin America," *Quarterly Journal of Economics* 82 (1968): 2–32; on new demand, Hunt, "Growth and Guano," 97–107. In ch. 6, Casanova carefully calculates the market; a 10 million yard import market could have hosted "5–10" contemporary plants.

34. Paul Baroch, "Agriculture and the Industrial Revolution," in Cipolla, *Fontana Economic History* 3:496–97; my argument parallels José Gabriel Palma, "Growth and Structure of Chilean Manufacturing Industry from 1830–1935: Origins and Development of a Process of Industrialization in an Export Economy" (D.Phil. thesis, Oxford University, 1979), chs. 1–3; and Stephen Haber, "Assessing the Obstacles to Industrialization: The Mexican Economy, 1830–1940," *JLAS* 24 (1992): 1–33.

next six years, similar to the deal for the merchants at the paper mill. The retail value of this pledged subsidy approached half a million pesos. Obviously, a government that, in the same years, gave away many millions in transfers to elites during the internal debt resolution was capable of supporting such a fiscal program, had it chosen to do so.[35] But events intervened.

Fourth, in hindsight Casanova's diversifying ideal seems to have been a rational road for Peru to have followed, even as favorable terms of trade promised some tough import competition. As current economic analysis of the guano age shows, by the 1850s export-boom inflation and currency overvaluation meant that most export-generated demand was getting lost in unproductive import leakage. A rentier economy was cooking; the outcome was set unless Peru adopted preferential tariffs for more promising industries or engaged in massive public domestic spending. Instead, Peru embraced uniform ad valorem tariffs at the start of the decade, and guano-induced demand worked to dediversify the Peruvian economy and stifle its entrepreneurial and employment potentials. Peru became a classic case of the economist's "Dutch disease"—a simplified dependent economy harmed by its abundant imports.[36]

Finally, even Casanova's particular factory was a practical project, as later events affirm. After the mill folded in August 1852, its machinery lay rusting in a Lima warehouse for virtually two decades. In 1869, with scant hope for government support, Carlos López Aldana (the repressive former foreman of the original factory) moved the equipment upstream to establish Peru's first modern cotton mill at Vitarte. Even based on by then very outdated technology, the Vitarte mill performed spectacularly well, swiftly cutting into Peru's cloth import bill—and forming the cornerstone of Peru's modern industrial base of the 1890s.[37] Similar events might have transpired in the 1850s, with developmental "demonstration effects"—had Casanova succeeded. Despite his prescience, he did not.

What Casanova and his peers did not foresee in 1848—given the

35. Quiroz, *Deuda defraudada,* chs. 6–7; for debates on industrial guano subsidies, see *Peruano,* "Ministerio de hacienda," 27 Oct., 10 Nov. 1849; *Comercio,* 19, 29 Oct. 1849, 4–5 Oct. 1851; some reports put subsidy at eight thousand tons total.

36. Economic analysis from Hunt, "Growth and Guano," 97–113, though Hunt is less specific on which industries Peru failed to promote. See also W. M. Corden, "Booming Sector and Dutch Disease Economics: Survey and Consolidation," *Oxford Economic Papers* 36 (1984): 359–80.

37. Basadre, *Historia* 4:1813, 5:2045; my linking of López Aldana to Casanova is from C. Damián de Schutz and J. Moller, *Guía de domicilios de Lima y del Callao para el año de 1853* (Lima, 1854).

universal acclaim for elite factory experiments—was any sudden and sharp reversal in government policy. That was precisely to occur in 1851. This involved political story is retold elsewhere, but in short, caught in the maelstrom of Peru's last protectionist struggle of 1849–1852, Casanova's factory pioneers became sacrificial victims of Lima's emerging liberal interests.[38] Peru's newest free-traders, moving against the radicalizing artisan offensive of 1850 (and mounting demands by national shippers, planters, and millers), opted to crush all strains of Peru's protectionist contagion. Lima's self-styled "cursantes de economía política"—graduates of Peru's first formal political economy class—proved remarkably effective, even with notables and politicos who had shunned blanket free-trader recipes only months before. The driving idea was simple; that a simplified, fixed, and flat Manchesterian tariff would settle once and for all Peru's political problem of chaotic, chronic protectionism. Class issues, too, drove this conversion to free trade, the new political imperative to smother pesky artisans and define the sybaritic life-style of the emergent urban plutocracy. That disunited artisans and factory owners publicly bickered about tariffs, as Casanova had predicted, only dramatized the liberal indictment.

During this struggle the flight to anti-industrialism was striking. Lima's most progressive civil groupings (such as the "progressive club" around impresario Elías) made a volte-face against the factories. Periodicals that had run editorials lauding Lima's industrial pioneers suddenly invented new ones condemning the efforts. Even *El Comercio,* lumping itself with tailors, lambasted its own paper mill!

> The mercury of Huancavelica, cotton thread, linens, paper, etc.: they are all in the same case as furniture, handmade clothing, etc.—all claim equal rights to be protected. . . . Industry whose products cannot compete with foreigners ought to disappear. . . . If paper or cottons cannot be manufactured in this country cheaper or better than what foreigners bring us, then we're not going to make paper or cottons.[39]

The government rapidly rescinded its industrial privileges and specific

38. Gootenberg, "Social Origins of Protection and Free Trade," esp. 351–58; invaluable sources congress debates in *Comercio,* all Dec. 1849, July–Aug. 1850, Sept. 1851, and "Los cursantes de economía política," *Comercio* 22–23, 30 July, 17 Aug. 1850.

39. Editorial, *Comercio,* 4 July 1851—tellingly, this is their first ever editorial; also "El reglamento de comercio en el senado," 5 Aug. 1851. *Progreso*'s conversion in "Política económica" series, July–Aug. 1850; on group's importance, see Juan Luis Orrego Penagos, "Domingo Elías y el club progresista: Los civiles y el poder hacia 1850," *Histórica* 14 (1990): 317–53.

duty rights, even harassing the factories with deadly bureaucratic hassles. The old "great *padrino*" of the factories, congressional president Joaquín de la Osma, worked overtime to repeal the promised guano subsidies. Officials studiously ignored the cries of betrayal from Casanova and the others: "*Así es el Perú:* that's the way all things go here. Today measures of progress and protection, and *mañana.* . . . We hope the Society of Cottons won't suffer the same fate as other businesses that couldn't develop, with such wise obstacles put in their way."[40] Finally, in late 1851 congress voted to overturn its own recent import laws and instituted instead the liberals' uniform tariff—the one that was to define Peruvian commercial policy over the next three decades. The legislation, so telling of its politicized origins, openly forbade all political tampering with tariffs, such as the executive decrees required by the factories.[41] Tottering guilds had prompted this crisis, and Lima's youthful free-traders drove it to the extreme; the hopeful factory owners became its prime victims.

Faced with these compounding difficulties and then squabbles among partners, Casanova's factory quietly shut its doors by early 1853, when the silenced promoter himself also passed away. All of the other Lima factories went under in these same few years. (Later, the paper mill would reopen at extreme cost.) Their proximate cause of death was stiff import competition in a new booming import economy.[42] Overall, the textile mill, for example, had been able to employ only some 5 percent of its installed capacity, as cheapening cotton imports doubled, saturating Peruvian markets in the years 1848–1852. The broadest process in play was the rapid sociological consolidation of Lima's capitalist elite in these very years. Revived in the import boom (and enriched by export-revenue giveaways), its emergent mental reflex became anti-industry, though it needn't have been so extreme.[43] Free-traders had success-

---

40. "Industria del país protejida por el sr. ministro de hacienda," *Comercio,* 25 July 1850; paper factory complaints, 4–5 Oct. 1851.

41. *Comercio,* 14 Aug. 1851, and final revision, all Dec. 1851; "Reforma de reglamento de comercio expedida por el congreso," arts. 4–5 (Biblioteca Nacional del Perú, MS. collection, D2182, 13 Oct. 1851). This was also a policy-making struggle between Castilla and Echenique.

42. Failures are rarely documented: see Fuentes, *Estadística de Lima,* 719–23; *Peruano,* 18 Jan. 1851; *Comercio,* 14–15 Jan., 30 June 1852; import flood specified in "Proyecto de reforma del reglamento de comercio y otros documentos," notas, *Rejistro Oficial,* 1851. Only Rosell's factory made it into consulado bankruptcy proceedings; AGN sec. H-8, Concursos, 1851.

43. Quiroz, *Deuda defraudada,* chs. 6–7, esp. sociological portraits of business elite.

fully stamped export growth as the antithesis of domestic markets and industry.

The most tangible impact was the negative message conveyed to Peru's potential entrepreneurs and investors. Why should capital-mobile merchants pursue such risky projects, with initial losses, when the Castilla and Echenique regimes of the 1850s were vigorously promoting surer profits in the liberalized import sector? Entrepreneurial reaction was predictable, and not a single respectable businessman would invest in factories for the rest of the guano age, at least not in the exposed economic climate of Lima. By the mid 1850s Lima had become South America's proverbial capital of imports. For the duration of the export age it missed benefits of technological and occupational diversity.

Free-traders actually won twice with their 1852 triumph. Through incessant liberal propaganda, the modest failures of this handful of factories became legendary to later Limeños. Although European trade theory seemed to dictate that Peru should specialize in its bird crap, mines, and plantations, Peruvians were not a theoretically minded people. Few actually read Smith and Say, though the names dropped around. Endless preaching about Peru's god-given destiny as a país minero y agrícola, and against the hellish temptations of protectionism, made for good gospel. But liberal prophets always had to cite hard local facts to make their point. Thus, a negative argument about industry infused liberal tracts throughout the guano age, for they were forever wrestling with the phantom of manufacturing, which had once beckoned to a Peruvian public. For liberals, no alternative existed to all-out primary specialization—because these contemplated factories had failed.

Two examples from a full decade later will suffice. Trained as a student *cursante* against Casanova and the guilds, the legal theorist José Silva Santisteban became Peru's most ubiquitous free-trade pundit of the guano age. Declares Silva Santisteban in one antitariff pamphlet:

Instead of teaching our workers a precarious skill, let us consecrate them to cultivate cotton, indigo, cochineal, and to the building of ports and roads. Let the foreigners skillfully bring us the fashions in shoes and clothing—which if nice to know how to make, are always better to be able to pay for. The glass factory and textile mill proved with their sad outcome, for all to see, that we are just not suited for manufacturing.[44]

44. José Silva Santisteban, *Breves reflexiones sobre los sucesos ocurridos en Lima y el Callao con motivo de la importación de artefactos* (Lima, pam., 1859), 41, 47; like other classics of the genre, this pamphlet deftly combines European theory with local history.

From this modest moral Silva Santisteban draws an even more modest proposal: a forced march of disgruntled city artisans into healthier rural pursuits. A congressional panel of 1859, deflecting desperate guild pleas for vocational training and tariffs, similarly declared, "The still recent history of what happened among us with the cottons factory, is eloquent testimony . . . [of results] if the same system used with cottons were to be used in promoting the arts."[45] Like mausoleums of industrial failure, the deserted factories would serve liberal memories over the next three decades. Casanova's homespun saga became as famous in Lima as those of Smith and Peel, a fable known from the cream of society to the untutorable artisan in the street. This was not the demonstration effect Casanova had pined for. But not everyone would buy the easy lessons.

45. Perú, Cámara de Diputados, *Dictamen de la comisión de hacienda de la cámara de diputados sobre las representaciones de los gremios de Lima y Callao* (Lima, pam., 1859), 15— and further examples in 1860s congress debates and finance memorials. One leading liberal ideologue, Francisco García Calderón, *Estudios sobre el banco de crédito hipotecario y las leyes de hipotecas* (Lima, 1868), 17–18, uses failures (now *two* decades past) as central argument for Peru's concerted promotion of export agriculture for the 1870s.

4

Impending Crises
Fuentes, Pardo, and Cisneros, 1854–1868

Liberal Scenes

The mid 1850s to early 1860s in Peru became the decade of triumphant export liberalism for the elites—and of deepening despair for popular Lima. In time this combustible mixture, and the first burning doubts about the future of guano, would kindle a new generation of critical policy thinkers. The new projects coming out of Lima—above all, railways across the Andes and fiscal rationing of guano—would color the remainder of the export age.

By the late 1850s the affluent classes of Lima had much to celebrate in their newfound commercial order. Between 1852 and 1857 guano exports jumped from $4.3 to $12.5 million annually before settling in the $20 million range of the 1860s. The ready availability of ever larger merchant advances and London credits made Peru, in effect, the richest regime of South America. Rarely had a change from rags to riches occurred so swiftly. Under the Gibbs contract alone the Peruvian state garnered over $57 million in profits between 1849 and 1861, inaugurating Peru's heady *afluencia fiscal*. Budgets, built overwhelmingly on guano (three-quarters of funds), also tripled to $20 million levels by 1860.[1] With their public fortune officials laid foundations of a modern bu-

---

1. Hunt, "Growth and Guano," tables 6, 8—Peru's profit on guano was a high 65 percent; Basadre, *Historia*, vols. 2–3, coins period as "La afluencia fiscal."

reaucracy and constructed the codes and constitutions suitable for the capital's rising capitalist norms.

Although little of this prosperity yet filtered out of Lima, there it revolutionized the life-styles of Peru's directing classes. Public works and private prebends remade the city into a livable and fashionable metropolis, with stately museums, parks, plazas, academies, boulevards, mansions, and theaters, not to mention the latest in potable water systems and Italian opera. Imports—everything from workaday textiles to lavish accessories and vintage French wines—officially reached the $15 million mark, and perhaps much more, by decade's end. Peru's leading merchants, now relishing their close ties with foreign houses, watched commercial revenues soar nearly threefold above those of the mid 1840s. More blatant gifts to the fortunate few—the outright transfer in the early 1850s of more than $20 million for their internal debt consolidation—more than made up for the prior travails it supposedly paid for. By 1860 Lima's commercial classes had recast themselves into a veritable national plutocracy, branching into newly capitalized banks, urban real estate, coastal plantations, and international trading companies.[2] By 1862 business confidence had so swelled that Peruvians, the celebrated "hijos del país" group, took direct management of the guano trade itself from foreign firms, a move to fulfill even grander entrepreneurial aspirations. Although political conflicts continued to smolder (the civil war of 1854 between Echenique and Castilla, struggles over the modernizing 1857 constitution, rumblings from the ignored provinces), the strong arm of President Castilla dominated the age, allowing no rerun of the caudillo anarchy of the past. All could grasp that his order and progress marched in tandem. Stability enabled Peru's awakening intellectuals and regularized congresses to conceive, discuss, and move toward a more durable and national future. Such material and political successes pointedly validated Peru's opening to the world—on which all this progress hinged.

The other side of the guano coin was its distressing social effects on Lima's working masses. (Outside the coastal-capital region, export capitalism still sparked little perceptible change.) Urban social distances widened dramatically in the 1850s. A boom-led inflation erupted in the mid 1850s (price levels rose nearly 70 percent by 1865), pushing down real wages of urban folk by one quarter during the first half of export

2. For elite portraits, see Quiroz, *Deuda defraudada*, chs. 5–7; Gootenberg, "Artisans and Merchants," ch. 2, commercial growth figures.

prosperity. Price hikes seemed strongest in staple foodstuffs, stirring popular passions. Among other verifiable developments, small service occupations actually receded in the 1850s, a surprising shift brought on as large firms enveloped much of the city's traditional street-corner retail sector. Facing now a true deluge of low-cost imports, skilled craftsmen fared little better; the number of workshops stagnated throughout the 1850s, and their revenues barely returned to stable 1830 levels. Lima was becoming a city dominated by a hundred or so large merchant firms assuming more than half the city's business earnings. Over half of these leading shops and warehouses belonged to Europeans. Entire old-style guilds, catering to vanishing Limeño tastes, disappeared. An alarming 17 percent or more of Lima's male workers stood permanently idled by the end of the decade.[3]

Pessimistic popular groups also suffered more intangible political losses. By the early 1850s politicians were handily ignoring their wants in Lima's reviving elitist political forums. Estrangements became mutual as weakened older guild leaders withdrew from the business of politics. No new spokesmen or ideas emerged to protect and project their inter-ests (though, as seen in the next chapter, some would after the mid 1860s). Instead, signs of desperation intensified. In 1851 Luddite work-ers, in evening raids, took to sabotaging foundations for Lima's first railway line; in 1855, following the liberal revolt against the disgraced president Echenique, popular crowds sacked the shops and mansions of "consolidados"—the wealthiest and most visible members of the guano elite. Rampages against foreigners began to accompany every change of regime.[4]

Shortly before Christmas 1858 frustrations came to a head. Agitated by duty-free imports granted for city construction projects (run by Lima's renowned millionaire Gonzales Candamo), the carpenters' guild took to the streets after being turned away in their peaceful protest march on the congress. A ragamuffin army of craftsmen, unemployed laborers, vagrants, and political radicals joined forces, sending Lima and

---

3. Gootenberg, "Artisans and Merchants," chs. 2–3, based on patentes registers; native unemployment, calculated from Fuentes, *Estadística de Lima*, 630, reached as high as 28.5 percent. On inflation, see Paul Gootenberg, "*Carneros y Chuño:* Price Levels in Nineteenth-Century Peru," *HAHR* 70 (1990): 1–56, esp. social analysis, 38–42.

4. Quiroz, *Deuda defraudada*, ch. 5; Giesecke, *Masas urbanas y rebelión*, 96–101, and passim. The visible popular politics of the 1850s was explicitly inward "mutual aid": e.g., "Unos artesanos," *Comercio*, 29 Nov. 1851. For one popular antiforeign rampage, see José Dean, *Cuestión saqueo de 6 de noviembre de 1865 en el Callao ante la opinión pública* (Lima, pam., 1866); none of thirty firms sacked was Peruvian.

Callao into three furious days of popular riots. Artisan snipers appeared in the main squares; a dozen casualties fell; destitute looters sacked the best of French boutiques. Enraged carpenters ended up by burning to the ground the new train to suburban Chorrillos, Lima's cherished symbol of elite progress. General Castilla, personally leading his crack cavalry and artillery against marauding artisans, was able to break the rebellion, following up with severe repressive reprisals.[5] This mayhem was popular desperation enshrined, though officials talked instead of foreign conspiracies and "subversives." For months Lima's press went on about the "horror" and meaning of the events.

After the riots, responses to the artisans epitomized official Peru's unbending faith in export liberalism. The guilds had not asked for much, a few modest and "patriotic" measures to relieve unemployment. "Civilized governments," ran their formal petition, "are engaged in fomenting national industry, the basis of a state's wealth . . . and if such protection is born from the pressing necessity to inspire work habits and better society, it is so very imperative in societies where occupations remain limited for the men who form the social majority."[6] In a studied response to the guilds the congress conceded that artisans seemed "incapable of sustaining a true contest with free competition" and feel rightly gripped by "black terror about their future." But any return to protection was simply out of the question: "Economic Science has proven its errors." Sheltered industries wither as "contagious parasitic plants"; only full exposure to "liberty" produces hearty employment—though "it requires great efforts and sharp sufferings to bear its fruits." "The days when duties made an instrument of industrial promotion are lost in the annals of the centuries, never to reappear. . . . In Peru's guano fields lie more than enough means to spur labor and development—without recourse to taxes condemned by civilization and its conscience."[7] As if science weren't enough, the deputies kept invoking a free-trader God at

5. On still understudied uprising, see Gootenberg, "Artisans and Merchants," 1–10; Francisco Quiroz Chueca, *La protesta de los artesanos: Lima-Callao, 1858* (Lima, 1988), a document collection; Cecilia Méndez, "Importaciones de lujo y clases populares: Un motín limeño," *Cielo abierto* 29 (1984); or coverage in *Comercio*, Dec. 1858–Feb. 1859.

6. *Artesanos*, 5, 7; based on petition of tailor Juan Guevara—among requests were control of contraband, a school of arts, lower food costs, and a few craft prohibitions.

7. Cámara de Diputados, *Dictamen sobre las representaciones de gremios*, 2, 5, 8, 15–18, 23 (quote); in its amalgam of Catholic predeterminism, naturalism, and free trade, the commission claims that the "Legislador del Universo" even created contraband to keep his flock from "aberraciones" such as tariffs (p. 11); see Myrdal, *Political Element of Economics*, ch. 2, on teleological strain of liberalism.

the helm; how He would transmute guano into honorable work was left up to faith. Meanwhile, congress promised some cheaper foodstuffs, a technical school, industrial prizes—and charitable "courses in the liberal economic teachings." The backlash of the 1840s lived on.

Liberal spokesmen such as José Silva Santisteban redoubled their efforts to "complete the pacification with healthy political economy." But Silva Santisteban also sought to dramatize the depth of challenge to Peru's power groups. "For the first time, the peaceful populations of Lima and Callao have become a struggling scene, mixed with blood and destruction; for the first time the popular rage has exploded in the Peruvian capital; for the first time, the masses have risen in the name of work and protection of national industry."[8] Limeños knew enough about European events to understand the specters suggested, and denunciations of "communists" and "anarchists" began to supplement customary attacks on protectionists. Although Silva Santisteban also marshals a lucid economic logic for liberal orthodoxy (focused on relative cost factors and monopoly distortions), his tract was blatantly punitive to dissenters—as if free trade were the final solution to the artisan problem. In such bristling defenses of free trade, Limeños absorbed calls to stick without quarter to the liberalism of guano. Besides—insisted all—Peru could never be a "manufacturing nation."

Yet even the doctrinaire minister of finance Juan José Salcedo had to concede that something was awry in the business of guano. In his 1860 ministerial report he confesses, "I judge as highest priority trying to open new spheres of activity for the people of Lima," all the while detailing their afflictions of unemployment, rising living costs, usury, and the uneven concentration of commercial wealth.[9] Just as remarkable is his simultaneous rejection of any hint of change in official thinking and policy:

It is commonly felt that for a country to be rich it needs to produce

---

8. Silva Santisteban, *Breve reflexiones sobre los sucesos con la importación*, 5–6, passim; his sixty-three-page tract is anything but "brief"; Alberto Regal, *Historia de los ferrocarriles de Lima* (Lima, 1965), 96, shows Silva as no innocent, having been the judge distributing Chorrillos lands. Trazegnies, *Idea de derecho*, 100–117, analyzes Silva's sophisticated work in legal theory (state action to forge liberal norms), which fits repressive economics; see response "Los artesanos: Folleto del Sr. Silva Santisteban," *La Zamacueca Política* (Lima), 29 Jan.–12 Feb. 1859; the official text of 1870s, P. Rodríguez, *Elementos de economía*, ch. 1, still conflated protection and "communism."

9. Juan José Salcedo, *Memoria que presenta al congreso de 1860 el ministro de hacienda y comercio* (Lima, pam., 1860), 18, 31–34.

everything; and with such pinings, they imagine that a cheapness of consumption can enervate a people. With this goal, they try to acclimate what nature does not spontaneously harbor, and try to give a fictitious existence to forced industry—thereby weakening a nation's truly productive forces.

In the state of development now achieved by changing world commerce, the country that can economically—with just one production—obtain and supply all the rest of its needs is in the best position. Better than if it tried to produce them, using prohibitions, millions of workers, limitless capitals.[10]

Salcedo's official faith in a singular product, his yearning for a "nation of consumers," his fixation on the "fictitious," his terror of contraband above all social ills—these remained the era's conventional wisdom in a peculiarly Peruvian translation of the classical theory of trade. Its incessant trivializing of diversification and protective thought silenced sympathetic voices. In 1859 only the oddly crapulent revolutionist writers of Lima's *Zamacueca Política* dared to embrace any artisan ideas, and they soon paid Castilla's repressive price.[11] Peru's protectionist holdouts had been pushed to the bottom and fringes of respectable society. Any skeptics would have to overcome such political anxieties, associations, and absolutes.

Once the heady optimism of the 1850s wore thin, however, a more palatable line of elite questioning emerged: what would happen if that one miraculous product ran out, or if it inspired Peru's expansive treasury to wild excess? Everything would go. By 1860 such jitters could already be felt. The liberal publicist José Casimiro Ulloa, noting Peru's deepening trade imbalances and government's mounting recourse to merchant advances, warned that "guano exports on the present scale can persist only for some fifteen years. Then impends the crisis—if in the meantime, Peru has not vastly diversified its economy and augmented its production and export of other goods."[12] Less than two years after Salcedo, the next finance chief, José Gálvez, officially broke some bad news: with recent swings in guano prices Peru was technically bankrupt. He sought still larger loans. In 1864, during Peru's costly war with Spain (in which Spain briefly captured the guano islands), deficits and loan

10. Salcedo, *Memoria de hacienda de 1860*, 9–10, 32; note concept of "fictitious"; contraband, a major theme, was put at 30 percent of import value.

11. For *Zamacueca Política* writers and revival of artisan legitimacy in 1860s, see ch. 5, below.

12. J. C. Ulloa, "La hacienda pública," *La Revista de Lima* 8 (15 Jan. 1860); conditions covered in Pike, *Modern History*, 111–13; for relevant fiscal reports, Dancuart, *Anales de hacienda*, vol. 7; Basadre, *Historia* 3:1058, finds an even earlier warning (by Elías) in 1854.

burdens became more than technicalities. The first stage of Peru's crisis had arrived, sparking a decade of frantic diversification schemes.

This chapter explores the evolving critical-liberal thought of three outstanding intellectuals and statesmen of the 1850s and 1860s—Manuel Anastasio Fuentes, Manuel Pardo y Lavalle, and Luis Benjamín Cisneros. It pursues their discontents with guano and the paths taken as each worked his way out of the blinders of sacrosanct economic theory. Fuentes was moved by concerted study of Lima's social realities; Pardo, by the callings of a larger Peru; Cisneros, by the urgencies of firming the state's fiscal moorings. These concerns echoed in a regional decentralist movement, conjured up around national communications and a new liberal scientism of engineers, that drove the frenetic railway construction of the late 1860s. Diversification was back on the agenda—or so each would argue.

Manuel A. Fuentes: Social Realities

The Lima of the 1850s and 1860s was the compact world nurturing the outlooks of Peru's fledgling plutocrats—apart from de rigueur Parisian excursions and schooling. Not all could ignore signs of crisis, felt in daily brushes with riches and penury, ferment and despair. But better-off Limeños also absorbed a formal intellectual portrait of their rapidly changing capital. The key figure in these urban social studies was Manuel Anastasio Fuentes, Lima's remarkably prolific and versatile census taker, journalist, medical and legal expert, social commentator, administrator, satirist, historian, and folklorist. Fuentes's studies of midcentury Lima remain the starting point for all historians of the age. At the time they constructed the self-perceptions of the country's literate classes.

An audience thirsting for works such as Fuentes's was growing in size and sophistication in the guano age. As cosmopolitan port and capital, Lima had always boasted a vibrant literary and political scene. Lima hosted Peru's recognizable civil society—with several thousand well-read lawyers, teachers, literati, doctors, clerics, officials, artists, and motley other professionals and public employees. By the late 1850s at least fourteen thousand men met the literacy and property requisites to serve as political electors; some eight thousand citizens met the even stricter criteria for holding public office. Educated women mixed in innovative literary circles and charitable societies. Even before guano affluence, observers were struck by the city's lively press (four or five major dailies, propagating the latest in international, commercial, and political news); its informal political and literary gatherings (*tertulias*); its *colegios* and universities (the rival San Carlos and Guadalupe Academies, or San Marcos University, the oldest continuous institution in the Americas); and myriad political clubs and motley pamphleteers. The complexity and range of elite culture expanded markedly after 1850. State offices, immigration and travel, libraries, science institutes, theater, a Club Nacional, literary monthlies, and private societies spread to suit every taste and need. In 1858 Lima employed 744 public school teachers alone, enjoyed 419 self-described "artists," and drew some 21,000 foreigners from around the globe, representing over a fifth of the city's inhabitants.[13] By the 1870s civil politics had become formalized in major lobbies (such as a Sociedad Nacional de Agricultura), professional guilds, immigrant societies, workers' and women's circles, and the galvanizing party politics of civilismo. An English-style jockey club catered to oligarchic amusements, competing with the customary watering holes of Chorrillos; Eiffel visited to draw up new monuments. Yet, however multifaceted Lima's intellectual milieu, much of its reference and style lay abroad. Thinkers were apt to have more feel for European trends than for those at home—much less for the exotic Andean land beyond. The impact of a Fuentes, along with the popular national *costumbrista* writers, was to shift consciousness inward.[14] The social discovery of Lima (and later, expanding visions of Peru) was also a step to new forms of national economic thought.

Inspired by the French statistical school, Fuentes embarked between 1858 and 1878 on a series of painstakingly researched studies of Lima society and life-styles of the guano age. In 1858 Fuentes published his first and greatest tome, the 774-page *Estadística general de Lima,* based on extensive personal surveys of population, occupation, business, commerce, government, institutions, architecture, customs—or just about anything anyone wanted to know about the Peruvian capital. Updated

13. Fuentes, *Estadística de Lima,* 620–24, passim; Radiguet, *Lima y sociedad peruana;* Basadre, *Historia,* vols. 3–5, for fine overviews of intellectual and cultural developments; Yeager, "Women and Intellectual Life," for inside view.

14. Maida Isabel Watson, *El cuadro de costumbres en el Perú decimonónico* (Lima, 1979). To sense the vitality of Lima's intellectual weight and variety, compare to lesser intellectual capitals: Héctor Lindo-Fuentes, *Weak Foundations: The Economy of El Salvador in the Nineteenth Century, 1821–1898* (Berkeley and Los Angeles, 1990), 1, insightfully suggests limited horizons of a nation starting with a "professional" class of four lawyers, four doctors, twelve surgeons, and seven druggists; cf. Véliz, *Centralist Tradition,* ch. 10, for possible deleterious impact of overdeveloped urban-intellectual culture.

versions followed in 1862, 1866, and 1869, and lavishly illustrated French and English editions, as well as numerous neighborhood street guides and official almanacs.[15] A prominent journalist since the 1840s, Fuentes gathered his political-satirical prose in 1863 as the three-volume *Aletazos del murciélago,* from his newspaper of the same ironic title ("The Flappings of the Bat"). In it Fuentes codified the everyday life of Lima's folk in the costumbrista genre later exemplified by Ricardo Palma's classic *Tradiciones peruanas.* (At the time, Palma was a youthful writer with the *Revista de Lima;* he also conspired with the ornery radicals of the *Zamacueca Política.*) Fuentes pioneered in blending the genre with the people of the street.[16]

One of Peru's premier scientific historians, Fuentes collected and published documents that underscored historic republican change. Fuentes also translated and edited key works of French political economy (such as those by the social-sciency Pradier-Foderé, who came to Lima as an adviser), dabbled in legal theory, and in 1877 was charged with producing Peru's official economics textbook—presumably to finish the pacification work that Silva Santisteban could never quite complete. In the mid 1870s Fuentes organized Pardo's new faculty of Political Science and Administration, directed Peru's first scientific national census (1876), and put together seven volumes of results and spin-off studies, such as his own scholarly monograph on Lima's "floating population" (vagrants). Aside from such literary and scientific pursuits, Fuentes was a bona fide member of Peru's economic plutocracy. He was, for example, a founder (and then "chief consultant") to the 1862 La Providencia bank, the first of the oligarchic finance institutions that were to shape the latter half of the guano age.[17] Fuentes was not just in touch with Peruvian reality—he was its major student and propagator.

15. Fuentes, *Estadística de Lima* (1858); a nonexhaustive list of analogous works includes *Guía histórico-descriptiva, administrativa, judicial y de domicilios de Lima* (Lima, 1860); *Lima: Apuntes históricos, descriptivos, estadísticos y de costumbres* (Paris, 1866–1867); *Lima, or Sketches of the Capital of Peru, Historical, Statistical, Administrative* (Paris, 1867; rpt. 1925); *Guía industrial y mercantil de Lima y el Callao* (Lima, 1869); and various guides of late 1870s, when Fuentes headed department of statistics.

16. M. A. Fuentes, *Aletazos del murciélago: Colección de artículos publicados en varios periódicos* (Paris, 1866), 3 vols. Watson, *Cuadro de costumbres,* ch. 8, "M. A. Fuentes: el Cuadro como reflejo del pensamiento científico"; Trazegnies, *Idea de derecho,* 130–35, 221–25; Basadre, *Historia* 3:1362–76.

17. Carlos Milla Batres, ed., *Diccionario histórico y biográfico del Perú: Siglos xv–xx* (Barcelona, 1986) 5:91–92; Camprubí, *Historia de bancos,* 39. Perú, Dirección de Estadística, *Resumen del censo general de habitantes del Perú hecho en 1876* (Lima, 1878), 7 vols; Manuel Fuentes, *Estadística del movimiento de la poblacion de la provincia de Lima en un periódo de cinco años y en el año de 1877* (Lima, 1878).

Known for his traditional elitism (even monarchism) in political thought, Fuentes reveals throughout his *obra* an acute sensitivity to social dilemmas and a skeptical slant on official variants of liberal progress. Above all Fuentes would graphically, even didactically, convey the emerging "social question" of liberalism to his readers—its manifest impact on the shape and people of Lima. The 1858 *Estadística general de Lima* exemplified these concerns. As it went about quantifying and sketching recent transformations of Limeño life and economy, it never brushed over the underside of guano prosperity.

Spurred by its commercial windfall, Lima had burgeoned from a sluggish postindependence town of some 55,000 to an overcrowded city of 94,195 inhabitants by 1857, more than a third of them solid white citizens. Initial census chapters of the *Estadística de Lima,* posed in the objective form of exhaustive occupational surveys, soon began focusing on urban dilemmas and above all on Lima's chronic underclass "vagrancy." Fuentes identifies more than 5,500 Limeños—one-fifth of adult males—"without profession." This number exceeded the 4,152 men gainfully employed in all commercial pursuits. As Fuentes warns, "Nobody can deny, however great their patriotism, that Lima is among the world's cities hosting the largest proportions of vagrants and corrupted men." No doubt such corruption loomed greatest among the city's 10,000 blacks and 13,000 mestizos. Adopting the tone of scientific moralist, he moves on to dissect the peculiar vices of Lima's mass idleness—gambling, begging, drunkenness, crime, social diseases, prostitution. Somehow Fuentes identifies 640 full-time prostitutes, 316 "perpetual drunks," and 490 chronic beggars—of whom "439 seem rather healthy in appearance."[18] Closer analyses of hospital, court, charity, and prison populations illustrate the challenges facing the city's civic elite. Even the vaunted diversion of guano funds to Lima's huge control-conscious model penitentiary (with its panopticon-style workshops) cannot attenuate these lurking dangers.

Further into his work, Fuentes scrutinizes the city's remaining artisan workshops, exposing such social difficulties as poor nutrition, substandard housing, and rising rents. Lima still employed 10,497 "artesanos y obreros"—if true, this was Lima's largest occupational category after the elites' personal army of domestic servants, cooks, and maids. Artisans

18. Fuentes, *Estadística de Lima,* pt. 1, Población y censo; 164–68, 209–11, 609–11, 660 (quotes, 74, 608); Giesecke, *Masas urbanas y rebelión,* chs. 3–4, an analysis of urban social relations based on Fuentes's surveys; cf. Himmelfarb, *Idea of Poverty,* for core perceptions.

were scattered among the city's 1,093 formally recognized master work-shops, with the largest numbers in tailoring (193 shops), shoemaking (192 shops), and woodworking (153). Fuentes found disproportion-ately few apprentices here (480 overall), a sure sign of contracting prospects for work. Obviously, all such numbers need to be carefully treated by historians with so many "artisans," for example, shifting in and out of building trades and other services.[19] Here strong criticisms rang out against the new practice of contracting foreign workers and businessmen to perform urban services, amid so many native unem-ployed. A telling anecdote concerns the repaving of city streets in 1847, which imported not only workers but even the more prestigious Euro-pean stones. After absorbing these portraits of enforced idleness, could liberals still cling to alleged "lack of arms" (labor shortage) as the cen-tral explanation for the country's hobbled development? But the elitist Fuentes was equally wary, at times openly contemptuous, of the artisans themselves: labor and discipline must "moralize" a sluggish people. He assails guild market restrictions, the crude work habits of Peruvian craftsmen, and productive energies lost on objects of luxury.[20] All in all, the *Estadística de Lima* might have augured the disturbances erupting the year it appeared.

Fuentes's *Estadística de Lima* devotes a full chapter to Lima's "indus-tria fabril y manufacturera." Only one of the 1840s industrial projects survived through 1858; yet Fuentes significantly pauses in studied de-scriptions of each factory's plan, plant, and sad saga. It is as if he was mulling over the frustrated modernization of his city and one foreclosed solution to its social malaise. Fuentes takes readers on a tour of the abandoned Tres Amigos plant and of Sarratea's barely consummated silk works. He admiringly dubs them "the industrial factories that began to root in our soil with such happy results—under the protection of our independent government."[21] The paper mill (which alone made it

19. Fuentes, *Estadística de Lima*, "Cuadro de las profesiones de todos los habitantes de la capital," 621–22; 702; "Cuadro de las personas empleadas en las fábricas y talleres de la capital," 724–25. Fuentes's sources (mainly tax registers) and methods often remain vague; for distinct set of tax-based calculations (and broad problems thereof), see Gooten-berg, "Artisans and Merchants," app. 1; for general critique, Rory Miller, "The Population Problem of Late Nineteenth-Century Lima" (paper presented to the International Con-gress of Americanists, Amsterdam, 1988).

20. Fuentes, *Estadística de Lima*, 74, 621–22, 655, 673–79, 679–705, 724; see Fuentes, *Guía histórico-descriptiva* (1860), ch. 3, for even greater detail on artisan pursuits.

21. Fuentes, *Estadística de Lima*, 719–24; quote, 720; Fuentes is fullest of contempo-rary factory histories, with some (like Sarratea's story) from personal communication.

through "every sort of obstacle") wins praise for providing work to scores of paupers, who scrounge for raw material in the city's discarded rags.

How does Fuentes account for Lima's imposing monuments of industrial failure? Fuentes seemingly downplays stock class slogans: those framing the factory debacle as proof of Peru's natural "incapacity" for modern industry or listing the inevitable and innumerable obstacles at work. Instead, Fuentes reminds Peruvians of grave "humiliations" suffered by the entrepreneurs from the state: "These establishments needed strong capital, but would offer at the start certain losses and had to sustain the stiff competition of European manufactures. They needed strong and resolute protection by the government, to start producing those advantages the country should have enjoyed from them."[22] The paper mill, adds Fuentes, managed to pick up the pieces only by ignoring the "disincentives" and "disillusions" of erratic officials, hanging on without protection. In keeping alive positive memories of industrialism, Fuentes pointedly recalled the withdrawal of government support the decade before.

The *Estadística de Lima* is also an exegesis of commerce. Limeños learn that the city consumed more than $7.8 million in every conceivable type of foreign imports, up $1.8 million in only a few years. Pages of descriptions and statistics of varied marketplaces and products reveal the cornucopia of Lima's new consumption habits. By 1858 more than half of the top 264 merchants in the consulado were Europeans. Fuentes laments what was already becoming a local developmental cliché: "The scarcity or, better put, total dearth of factories has made it necessary to import almost everything needed for a comfortable life." Further on Fuentes labels the "sultanic despotism" of resident foreigners, who sense no "social obligations" to Peru, save their "own interests," depriving locals in city contracts and commercial speculations.[23] Such misgivings about overseas influence seem in line with studies of Fuentes's more literary works, which reveal a profound *criollo* ambivalence about rising foreign cultural sway and protonationalist middle-class morals—drawn to show that Peruvians can and should advance on their own.

Similar motifs sound throughout Fuentes's later publications of the 1860s—amounting to a drawn-out critique of social ills of Peru's liberal-

22. Fuentes, *Estadística de Lima*, 699, 720–23.
23. Fuentes, *Estadística de Lima*, 665–66, "Industria mercantil," 705–15; Watson, *Cuadro de costumbres*, 127–28, 134, for literary analysis of criollo nationalism.

ism of excess. With his scientistic realism Fuentes remains closely attuned to the condition of artisans, their new mutual aid societies, their
modest productive advances and their plight with overseas competition,
as illustrated, for example, throughout his 1860 *Guía histórico-descriptiva
administrativa, judicial y de domicilios de Lima*. In fact, Fuentes was
involved, if marginally, with artisan causes. As early as 1850 he published a report on elections (during the guilds' last meaningful mobilizations) critical of exclusion and exploitation of popular—that is, dark-
skinned—electors; in 1858, in the aftermath of the artisan riots, his
signature graced the guilds' protectionist petition to congress.[24] The
Aletazos del murciélago brims with uncompromising barbs of venal high
politics, particularly manipulation of the masses, and many a challenge
to liberal icons, albeit conservatively inspired. For example, liberal writers from José Simeón Tejeda (1852) to Silva Santisteban (1859) custom-
arily attacked guild pleas for tariff protection by denouncing in turn
guild monopoly and privileges. This was a disingenuous posture since
by 1850 guild market restrictions existed only on paper at best. In
raising "freedom of industry" as the most hallowed slogan of Peruvian
laissez-faire, liberals could blame artisans for their own plight.[25] Fuentes
turns empty slogans and liberal-protectionist polemics on their head, for
example, in the satirical verse "La libertad de industria":

> Poor Industry! In Peru there is no industry
> And why are there no *industriosos?*
> Because we lack industriosos
>   And furthermore why not?
> 'Cause the government doesn't protect it.[26]

Fuentes was by no means a romantic, unlettered, or even consistent
antiliberal. His knowledge and translations of, and his devotion to,
Continental political economy bear this out. He was, for example, an
architect of Peru's modernizing commercial codes; his 1877 school text,
Catecismo de economía política, is based on the thought of Jean Gustave

24. Fuentes, *Guía histórico-descriptiva*, ch. 3, "Artesanos y obreros," passim; M. A.
Fuentes, *Relación sucinta de los principales hechos ocurridos en algunos pueblos del Perú, con
motivo de la ingerencia de los funcionarios políticos en la renovación de los colegios electorales*
(Lima, pam., 1850); *Artesanos*, 2: guilds (and their opponents of 1859) already refer to
Fuentes for vital statistics.
    25. José Simeón Tejeda, *Emancipación de la industria* (Arequipa, pam., 1852); Silva
Santisteban, *Breves reflexiones sobre los sucesos con la importación*, 11, 21–25 (from Fuentes
figures); for analysis of "freedom of industry," see Gootenberg, "Guilty Guilds?"
    26. Fuentes, *Aletazos del murciélago* 1:160.

Courcelle-Senueil, one of the most radical French free-traders of the century (and the region's earliest maligned "foreign adviser"). His was to Fuentes "a science that, today more than ever, should be propagated in Peru." Yet in 1879, amid the full-blown export crisis, Fuentes, in his survey *Movimiento de la poblacion,* could suggest a concerted state job-creation program to head off urban unrest, a conclusion verging on the most interventionist critiques of the time.[27] In short, Fuentes, fully cognizant of liberal imperatives, developed and spread a studied ambivalence to theoretical systems from a firsthand feel for their consequences. Not just widely consumed, Fuentes was literally the social constructor of Limeño reality.

Don Manuel Pardo: Railroads to Industry

If Fuentes seems a mere intellectual skeptic with no personal following, the same could never be said about Don Manuel Pardo (or Luis Benjamín Cisneros, to follow). Pardo was the most active, influential, and frequently cited figure of Peru's emerging 1860s civil elite. If Fuentes divulged the real Lima, Pardo revealed a greater Peru—an imagined patria to be consummated by railways, markets, and industries.

The career and legacy of Manuel Pardo y Lavalle are well known.[28] Born in 1834 into a venerable political and literary family, European-bred Pardo epitomized Peru's new self-made millionaires of the 1860s in his personal transmutation from youthful aristocrat to capitalist spirit. Rapidly rising as an importer and financier (founder of the 1862 Banco del Perú and pioneer of commercial insurance in La Paternal), Pardo soon became the nation's pivotal native guano merchant. As the assertive

27. Manuel Fuentes, *Catecismo de economía política* (Lima, 1877), intro.: state had ordered economics taught even in all grade schools; cf. disciple Masías, *Curso de economía* (1860); Fuentes, *Movimiento de la poblacion,* prologue. Albert O. Hirschman, "A Prototypical Economic Adviser: Jean Gustave Courcelle-Seneuil," in Hirschman, *Rival Views of Market Society and Other Recent Essays* (New York, 1986), 183–86; see "Sociedad de economía política," *Comercio,* 16 May, 14 June 1856—where Peruvian policies debated by these radical Parisian economists.

28. For extensive (procivilist) biographies, see, e.g., Jacinto López, *Manuel Pardo* (Lima, 1947), containing Pardo's major writings; Evaristo San Cristóval, *Manuel Pardo y Lavalle: Su vida y su obra* (Lima, 1945); Alejandro Revoredo, "La obra nacionalista y democrática del partido civil," in *Centenario de Manuel Pardo, 1834–1934* (Lima, 1931), 79–127.

president of the National Company of Guano in the 1860s, Pardo organized the "hijos del país" network that supplanted foreign contractors in 1862 and underwrote the treasury over the next decade. Needless to say, the Pardos represented one of the country's wealthiest and wide-ranging economic clans. Of greater import, Pardo blazed the bourgeois trail of translating Peru's elite interests into political action.[29] An eclectic thinker and prolific writer, Pardo helped found the seminal 1860–1862 *Revista de Lima;* from there he served as both guiding light and moving force that in the next decade carried into power the nation's plutocracy as embodied in the Partido Civil, the liberal civilian party that would shape modern Peru over the next half century. In this regard, Pardo exemplified the "new generation" liberals of the 1860s, reacting against the Castillan caudillos' perceived spoliation of Peru's export riches in transfers, debt, and militarism—even though these strongmen had arguably raised Pardo's business class in the first place.

By the mid 1860s Pardo had taken his place as the country's outstanding political figure. In 1866, with other celebrated national liberals, he jumped into heady collaboration with the short-lived Prado reform dictatorship. As its energetic finance minister, Pardo launched the "guano into railroads" scheme and other reforms originally spelled out in the *Revista de Lima*—before resigning in disgust at congressional blocks to his (and Cisneros's) attempted fiscal overhaul. In the late 1860s Pardo took charge of revitalizing Lima's highbrow paternal welfare agency, the Beneficencia Pública de Lima, and instituting deeper approaches to the city's seething distress, such as popular education and housing drives. From 1869 to 1872 Pardo served as Lima's immensely popular mayor, approaching the new ferment of working classes as an opportunity to widen his network and concerns. All the while he threw himself into organizing his civil business allies against the Balta-Piérola military regime—which in 1869, under Finance Minister Nicolás de Piérola, had traded in national guano contracts (controlled by men like Pardo) for the overseas management and finance of Dreyfus.

After building from scratch Peru's first modern political party and launching an unheard-of nationwide campaign, Pardo's Partido Civil sailed to victory in 1872. With the aid of informal people's militias Pardo put down a bloody, last-minute coup attempt, becoming Peru's first civilian president. Lima's liberal elites had at last assumed power, with

---

29. Basadre, *Historia,* vol. 5, esp. 2167–70; and MacEvoy, "Manuel Pardo," the most recent and sophisticated (intellectual-political) biography.

Manuel Pardo their reformist spokesman and symbol. Over the next four years the party moved to implement its program for bolstering civilian institutions, rationalizing the state, educating the masses, and decentralizing administration—all part of the attempt to construct the envisaged civic culture of Pardo's "practical republic." These were trying times for anyone in power, given relentless military and conservative roadblocks to reform and the unrelenting crisis of guano. In the late 1870s Pardo returned to politics as senate chief in a personal effort to heal the country's then-shattering conflicts. In 1878 an assassin's bullet elevated Pardo into the eternal martyr of Peruvian liberalism.[30]

As the object of hagiographic coverage since then, Pardo's career and achievements, though not his moving ideas, are well documented. The new generation of structural and dependency historians of Peru, if fixed on outcomes more than ideas, has provided critical correctives. Pardo, still towering as the century's decisive figure, stands out as the "organic intellectual" of the nascent ruling class. His, their, project was a Peruvian *desarrollo hacia afuera*, articulated in the name of a modernizing coastal elite. Pardo's hallmark contribution was his conception of the railroads, which would be thrown across the Andes in response to the impending exhaustion of guano and would bring into play a new generation of marketable exports from the interior. However, Pardo emerges as a deeply flawed architect of bourgeois Peru. When addressing the country's ills, he misread its fundamental social realities and pressing alternatives, national integration, diversification, mobilization among them. Pardo's "deep liberalism expounded in the *Revista de Lima*" remained a superficial, and thus doomed, neocolonial mentality and solution. The collapse brought on by Pardo's railway mania sealed Peru's fate in the nineteenth century.[31] More recent studies, turning inward to intellectual culture, capture civilist ideology as a "traditional modernism": a genuine attempt at nation making, it was nevertheless confined by traditional top-down structures of domination. For example, the latest intellectual

---

30. See, e.g., López, *Pardo;* or prompt hagiography in Andrés A. Aramburú, *El asesinato de Manuel Pardo, presidente del senado* (Lima, pam., 1878).

31. A version of Pardo found in every history since 1970: see Bonilla, *Guano y burguesía,* esp. 54–63 (quotes and analysis); Macera, "Historia económica como ciencia," 35–37; Cotler, *Clases, estado y nación,* 100–108; Yepes, *Perú 1820–1920,* 80–96 (quote, 105); Giesecke, *Masas urbanas y rebelión,* ch. 2; Hugo Garavito Amézaga, *El Perú liberal: Partidos e ideas de la ilustración a la república aristocrática* (Lima, 1989), pt. 3; Chavarría, "Desaparación del Perú colonial," 125–28. Modified versions in Tantaleán, *Política económico-financiera,* 228–29, a theorized civilist "nationalist project"; Amayo, *Política británica;* and Bollinger, "Bourgeois Revolution," 32–33, as truer bourgeois movement.

and political biography of Pardo finds subtlety in his evolving civic philosophy and praxis—his lucid notions of modernized state capacities—though that philosophy fell short of true modernism in its antiindustrial economic slant.[32]

The origins of Pardo's economic thinking remain open to debate. Not only was Pardo the first Peruvian executive trained in political economy, but he also absorbed manifold perspectives. Scion of the prominent conservative thinker Felipe Pardo y Aliaga, the young Pardo attended a Chilean commercial academy and later studied in Lima's San Carlos Academy (with Bartolomé Herrera, Peru's zealous Hispanic conservative); he then undertook advanced work in Spain and tackled formal political economy at the Collège de France (under the radical liberal Michel Chevalier, heir to both the Say and Saint-Simon schools). He returned to Peru during the heady free-trader days at the advent of the guano age. Older biographers point out activist tendencies in Pardo's thinking and work (as one might expect with Hispanic and Saint-Simonian influences).[33] Recent historians underline the sway of Chevalier and Continental laissez-faire, their importance gleaned from Pardo's mid-1860s campaign to ensure noninterventionist banking legislation (for banks in which Pardo held a healthy stake); from stated antipathy to state monopolies; and from antiprotectionist slogans as minister of finance. The railroad projects themselves speak to his export orientation.[34] But alone this seems patchy evidence. For example, in countries such as Peru, compelling reasons existed to embrace liberal banking (well-founded fears of capricious state intervention); as president, Pardo himself led the regulation of the banks (over the protests of his financial peers) and introduced national monopolies, as in the nitrates nationalization of 1875. Pardo's conservative political rivals of the 1870s, the Piérolists, wielded in opposition a far purer form of classical laissez-faire—branding civilista policies dangerously statist and protectionist.[35]

32. Trazegnies, *Idea de derecho;* MacEvoy, "Manuel Pardo," esp. conclusions, 250–52—revisionism excelling in political ideas (and less focused on railways). Renewed interest likely reflects civic culture concerns among today's Peruvian intellectuals.

33. For example, Pike, *Modern History,* ch. 5; Reinaga, *Pensamiento económico,* ch. 3, on Saint-Simonian edge; MacEvoy, "Manuel Pardo," ch. 1, for range of influences.

34. Views gleaned mainly from Camprubí, *Historia de bancos,* 21, 30, esp. ch. 2, "La absoluta libertad bancaria"; e.g., used in Yepes, *Perú 1820–1920* (105–6), and others cited in n. 31, above. Reinaga, *Pensamiento económico,* ch. 3, titled "Manuel Pardo: Un neoliberal del siglo xix"; Romero, "Perú," 306–8, favors as "mestizo liberal."

35. See Quiroz, *Domestic and Foreign Finance,* ch. 2, for finance revisionism; Alberto Ulloa, *Don Nicolás de Piérola: Una época en la historia del Perú* (Lima, 1949), a serious biographical study on opposition thinking.

But most important, we have just a foggy sense of Pardo's long-range vision of development.

In June 1860 a circle of aspiring young writers, businessmen, and politicians founded *La Revista de Lima*—now regarded as the seminal policy organ of the nineteenth century. Lasting three years, the journal appeared in the aftermath of the city's artisan riots and amid a gathering storm of liberal disillusion with Castilla's heavy-handed treatment of the 1857 and 1859 congresses. Troubling regional and political unrest were resurfacing, as were signs that Peru's heavy reliance on guano revenues (and related debt and trade imbalances) had entered a newly perilous stage, soon confirmed by the government financiers of the early 1860s. Elite political worries, especially distrust of the military, was revealed by the scholarship that first recovered the ideological role of the *Revista de Lima*.[36]

Deeper meanings ascribed to the *Revista de Lima* vary. Some historians grasp the groups' reformist outlook on guano as cloaking export-class greed, part of coeval native merchant campaigns to nationalize the trade and of their growing operations in public finance. Others read the group discourse as that of Peru's new coastal capitalist elite, defining themselves in a deeper ideological contest with Peru's precapitalist landlords of the interior—a position exemplified in the journal's literary indigenismo. Some perceive a straightforward "generational" shift at work—a change of guard from Peru's aging theoretical liberals so traumatized by caudillo instability. Younger liberals strove for a durable civil order in Peru, based on a thoroughgoing civilian rationalization of the state.[37] Such orienting notions of class and political culture can be placed in tangible social contexts. The writers of the *Revista de Lima* lived amid the shifting social malaise of Lima—the early 1860s urban scene driven home by Fuentes, a noteworthy contributor. Furthermore, shriller voices had just broken out on the political scene—the *Zamacueca Política* iconoclasts (explored below)—firing direct assaults on guano and plutocratic complacence. The *Revista de Lima* appears as a timely class organ, but a moderating one responding to these omnipresent Limeño tensions.

Many essays in the *Revista de Lima* indeed appear to be the work of an aspiring managerial elite, hoping to cool ideological passions and polar-

36. Maiguashca, "Reinterpretation of Guano Age," chs. 3–5.

37. Maiguashca, "Reinterpretation of Guano Age" (generational reform); Bonilla, *Guano y burguesía* (comprador elite); Kristal, *Andes from the City*, ch. 2, "The Export Oligarchy" blends in original analysis of *Revista de Lima* writings on Indians.

izations with effective reform. The inaugural issue boldly announces their pragmatic and eclectic approach: "The *Revista de Lima* is not a periodical with a flag or a system; nor is it conservative, liberal, romantic, positivist, protectionist, or abolitionist."[38] What was it, then? The majority of its writings were poems, stories, and novellas with little overt (but much hidden) political content; it was the starting place for outstanding artists such as Ricardo Palma, José Arnaldo Márquez, Luciano Cisneros, and the feminist Juana Manuela Gorriti. There were also clearly enunciated political messages by would-be políticos such as Espinoza, Laso, Luis Cisneros, Noboa, Pacheco, Lorente—and Manuel Pardo. In contrast, the journal published many a numbing technical report on this or that economic proposal. A cultivated readership also caught up on the world's latest social trends in, for example, an essay on positivism or a favorable series on "feminism" by the reputably stodgy Fuentes.[39] Travelogues—geographic and literary excursions into the uncharted territory, and possibilities, of Peru—were also popular feature articles, reminiscent of the salon scientific and cultural genre of the late-colonial *Mercurio peruano*. Antonio Raimondi's reportage on Amazonia was first savored here.

Lead policy articles stuck to the announced independent political stance. President Castilla, the father of the plutocracy, is roundly scolded for ignoring the "social question" as well as fundamentals of democracy. Other writers vaunt popular education, for "the school is a great workshop"—a theme of coming resonance. A June 1860 series entitled "Foreigners" tackles diplomatic accusations that Peru was not doing enough to protect and advance foreign property. On the contrary, argues the anonymous author, Peru has afforded every privilege imaginable to Europeans, even at the expense of "indigenous industry." The country was literally inundated with foreign trinkets—"from our hats to shoes, and from the mirrors and gilded furniture of the salon, to the pots and pans of the kitchen." Foreigners had claimed all the benefits of Peru's liberality.[40] This old refrain in artisan discourse here stands as an indict-

38. *La Revista de Lima*, no. 1 (15 June 1860).

39. Kristal, *Andes from the City* for literary-social role; the *Revista de Lima* linked to the later journals of Palma, Ulloa, Pérez, and Gorriti, esp. the 1870s *Correo del Perú*. Fuentes in vol. 4 (1861); Pardo left an important (economic) travelogue, "El partido de Saña, o Lambayeque, en el siglo pasado," *Revista de Lima* 2 (1860).

40. "Extranjeros," *Revista de Lima*, 15 June 1860; cf. Luis B. Cisneros, "El Perú en el aniversario de su independencia" 2 (July 1860); Tomás Dávila, "Instrucción primaria," 2 (1860).

ment of Peru as a plutocratic, consuming household. The same year, Luis Benjamín Cisneros (not so pleasing a poet as his brother) proffers nationalist verse excoriating the "egotistic pamphleteers selling us Europe." An 1860 analysis of guano commercialization was among the more interesting of such surveys. The author, the liberal journalist and pioneer medical figure J. C. Ulloa, was soon accused of *rojo* tendencies and later became an anticivilist critic with his free-trader daily, *La Patria*. Ulloa proposed the most nationalist solution of all: direct state administration abroad, a rejection of all foreign consignees that would conserve "two millions annually." In a later piece Ulloa warns of the impending "Anglo-Saxon invasion and conquest of Latin America"; the United States, with its incorrigible "contempt for the *raza latina*" and its Monroe Doctrine, was particularly dangerous.[41] In short, motley opinions were heard by what were no doubt equally diverse and curious Limeño audiences.

The most decisive—and currently noted—proposal from the *Revista de Lima* was surely Manuel Pardo's 1860 series "Estudios sobre la Provincia de Jauja," swiftly republished in a sixty-six-page booklet.[42] It was one of six economic essays that Pardo, at the ripe age of twenty-five, contributed to the journal. *Estudios sobre Jauja* won immediate acclaim as the first formalized warning that Peru's guano wealth might lead into national catastrophe. Pardo demanded resolute action to employ the country's remaining deposits productively, to reverse the wasteful expenditures of the past, and to avert Peru's impending crisis of export depletion. The 1860s thus opened in Peru with a new and many-sided watchword, "productivity." Pardo's crucial policy reform—the productive transformation of guano into trans-Andean railroads—followed from his detailed analysis of the possible impact of modern communications on the sleepy valley of Jauja, in the central highlands. How was Pardo to convince his readers, the policymakers, his class?

Few of his readers should have taken *Estudios sobre Jauja* as a clarion call for further export bonanzas. Pardo's proposal here is, in fact, a

41. J. C. Ulloa, "Huano (o examen comparativo entre los diversos sistemas ensayado o propuestos para la administración del huano)," *Revista de Lima* 2 (1860): 773–90; Ulloa, "La Reconquista" 4 (1861): 9. Basadre, *Historia*, vol. 3, for Ulloa's maverick (nacionalist) activities; Ulloa earlier authored *El Perú en 1853: Un año de su historia contemporánea* (Paris, pam., 1854), a scathing antifeudal attack on Echenique—based on Proudhon.

42. *Revista de Lima* 1 (June–July 1860); Manuel Pardo, *Estudios sobre la provincia de Jauja* (Lima, 1862); rpt. in López, *Pardo*, 211–72.

measured and cogent scheme for enhancing the productive diversity of Peru's potential regional and domestic markets. It includes a surprising and detailed project of import substitution, as part and parcel of Peru's productive revolution.[43] Three influences or themes stand out, none of which falls into the binaries of export/national development or laissez-faire/interventionist thought.

First, though Pardo's scheme is reminiscent of Casanova's (unnoted) diversification ideals, a key difference emerges too. Pardo shifts concern away from the productive potential of Lima, where factories faltered amid the capital's Europeanized consumption elite. The alternative, which assumes clarity in the work of subsequent writers, is a pristine national countryside brimming with productive possibilities. An imagined economic decentralism preceded the civilist political decentralism of the next decade. Second, Pardo relies on no standard European theorists in his developmentalism, referring perfunctorily only to his own French mentor, whose touted models are roundly ignored. Apart from a new positivist tinge, the unspoken influence appears to be the utopian Saint-Simon—in his indictment of idle consumption, obsession with productive "work," and forms of people's industrialism.[44] But in the main, local dilemmas, economic history, and specific country cases (especially an undreaded United States) guide Pardo's thinking.

If Casanova kept his own experience in mind, Pardo's model was likely new experiments in rural manufacturing. In 1859 the venerable Cuzqueño landowner, merchant, and prefect Francisco Garmendia revived the long-defunct Lucre obraje as a modern woolens factory; his tortuous haul of imported machinery over the Andes became a legend in its time and spotlighted again the obstacles posed by Peru's primitive transport. In 1862 another *hacendado,* Jacinto Terry, performed a similar feat in the northern mountains of Ancash, after the recipe offered by Pardo. (Neither man was a country bumpkin; after Garmendia's successful manufacturing venture, for example, he reappeared in Lima as Pardo's 1872 civilista vice president!)[45] In *Estudios sobre Jauja* Pardo

43. Curiously overlooked in writers citing *Estudios sobre Jauja,* who depend on Maiguashca's 1967 "Reinterpretation of Guano Age"—focused on guano and finance reform (pp. 100–104 briefly cover Pardo's hopes for "domestic" economy).

44. Chevalier merits one introductory mention—for activist posture towards "vías de comunicación"; see Hale, *Transformation of Liberalism,* ch. 2, for Saint-Simon influence on Mexican científicos' "fomento."

45. Basadre, *Historia* 3:1293–95, for rich (family history) account of Garmendia efforts; or obituary in *La Patria* (Lima), 20 Mar. 1873.

championed similar developmentalist efforts for Junín, predicated on the spread of modern communications. But the background experiences remained the flawed one of Limeño protectionism and an equally flawed official liberalism of the 1860s—which would admit no form of diversification in Peru.

Pardo opens his *Estudios sobre Jauja* in a famous definition of Peru's national dilemma. Over the past fifteen years guano had provided the country some $150 million of revenues, but that wealth was "already lost" to development: "The honor of Peru has so very little to report." Pardo reviews for readers Peru's mounting difficulties in public debt finance, unmanageable import burdens (now over $20 million annually), and the specter of rapidly depleting guano reserves. Peru's entire wobbly edifice rests on guano. The central theme appears: "Peru is consuming far more than it can naturally produce"—a theme that was soon to be a cliché of the 1860s guano-reform movement.[46] But Pardo departs in fundamentals from countless calls of the 1850s for revamping the ways of guano trade and finance, plans for squeezing just a little more out for Peru's state. The deeper issue is Peru's need to "produce." Threats of "bankruptcy," Pardo forewarns, are no longer "metaphor." Peru now has left perhaps ten or twelve years of prime guano deposits. But if guano were used correctly, genuine, lasting, and transforming productive benefits can register. The chief use and stimulus must be national railroads.

One of myriad lines already under consideration in 1860 was to highland Jauja. Adjoining the old central Cerro de Pasco silver mining district, the export epicenter of late-colonial Peru, the Mantaro region now stood isolated from both capital and coast. Pardo had studied the province firsthand in the mid 1850s, when doctors sent him there for his asthma. (He was accompanied by his old teacher, Herrera. The attachment was lasting: in the late 1870s Pardo would be the region's man in the senate.) Junín was a temperate and diverse zone, rich in natural

---

46. Pardo, *Estudios sobre Jauja*, 4–5, 41–44; see Mathew, *Gibbs and the Guano Monopoly*, ch. 4, and Maiguashca, "Reinterpretation of Guano Age," ch. 3, on guano reform movement; Ulloa's 1860 "Huano" was far out in left field. For Pardo's fundamental departure from mainstream ideas of time, compare, e.g., with Carlos Barroilhet, *Ojeada sobre la crisis política y financiera del Perú* (Paris, pam., 1859). "Peru consumes more than it produces, and without doubt the prolongation of this state will lead in a direct line to a disaster. Reducing consumption and augmenting production—those would be, for any other country, the only adequate measures to prevent the catastrophe" (14). But Barroilhet assures readers that Peru is "exceptional" because of its "incomparable guano riches" and thus need only reform consignment systems.

resources, though mining had decreased markedly since the advent of guano. Jauja's outstanding social feature (which Pardo clearly grasped) was a wide dispersal of small property. Instead of a typical Andean latifundia or Indian zone, Pardo settled on a society in which deep-rooted and resistant mestizos (and scattered native communities) dominated farming, herding, and overland commerce.[47] The choice was not coincidental. To Pardo, Jauja had clearly demonstrated a natural entrepreneurial style, for example, in the rapid rebound of wool estates after every civil commotion. Furthermore, given the region's strategic location above and adjacent to the capital, Jauja was of military importance as a center for staging and harboring revolts during the course of the caudillo era.

How would effective connections with Lima help the region and the nation? "If the locomotive, in other countries, facilitates production and commerce, in ours its mission is much higher: to create what today does not exist; to fertilize and give life to the elements of wealth, that today lie in an embryonic, latent state."[48] Though posed in vague and very general terms, this recipe for building ahead of demand takes graphic form. Pardo proves both more and less the dreamer usually portrayed.

To be sure, communications might galvanize the region's wool and precious metals, but traditional provincial exports actually get slighted in the essay. First of all, Pardo emphasized potential "foodstuffs for the consumption of Lima." He hardly needed to remind readers of the "alarming problem" of food shortages in the capital: the inflation and subsistence crisis had just been dramatized by destitute artisans in the 1858 riots (and later by Mayor Pardo, the activist head of a late 1860s commission on urban prices). But price inflation was more than a spark to worrying unrest: taking off with the guano boom, it was aggravating Peru's unsteady trade balances as well, cheapening imports relative to national agriculture.[49] Pardo emphatically opposes the costly public

---

47. Pardo, *Estudios sobre Jauja*, 14–24; Pardo's interest in smallholders also clear in "Inmigración vascongada," *Revista de Lima* 1 (July 1860): 101–8—against coastal planter coolie trade, in favor of Basque colonization (who share the "amor al trabajo" of Anglo-Saxons). See MacEvoy, "Manuel Pardo," 187–94, for less sympathetic attitudes to Indian. For now well-studied Mantaro society, see Mallon, *Defense of Community*, pt. 1; Nelson Manrique, *Mercado y región*, using Pardo; or Carlos Contreras, *Mineros y campesinos en los Andes: Mercado laboral y economía campesina en la sierra central, siglo xix* (Lima, 1987).

48. Pardo, *Estudios sobre Jauja*, 24; cf. Bonilla, *Guano y burguesía*, 57–65.

49. Pardo, *Estudios sobre Jauja*, 26–27. [M. Pardo], Lima, Consejo Provincial, *Datos e informes sobre las causas que han producido el alza de precios de los artículos de primera necesidad que se consumen en la capital* (Lima, 1869); for inflation shortages and impact, see Gooten-

recourse to duty-free subsistence imports—a favorite populist ploy of 1850s free-traders—which he would later oppose again as finance minister. Why, he insists, does Peru import 300,000 *fanegas* of Chilean wheat when with reduced transport costs, fertile regions such as Jauja could supply consumers their grains, cattle, sugar, and salt with "magnificent" national savings? Agriculture, then as now, was a major element of Pardo's productive and integrative import substitution.

In this emphasis, *Estudios sobre Jauja* also echoes timeworn polemics of aristocratic agrarian protectionists of the early republic. However, Pardo's plan differs from past agrarian nationalisms both in its context and in the class of potential farmers that it imagines.[50] By 1860 Peru's recuperating coastal planters (including Pardo's family in Lambayeque) were turning decisively to overseas sugar and cotton exports, plowing under their former fields of rice, wheat, and beans. For the most part, they were also turning into a potent oligarchic free-trader interest—the backbone, in most views, of the civilist rise itself. But here Pardo lauded the agrarian promise and home markets of predominantly peasant-farmer producers of the sierra. In 1867 Pardo would boldly challenge planter export "interests" in his ministerial fiscal package. Such autonomy of interest marked the reveries of many of Peru's urban thinkers.

What else could efficient internal transport trim from Peru's precarious import bill? Coal. Fossil fuel had recently become an essential new input for machinery and even home heating. By the 1860s galloping urban demand had denuded Peru's traditionally exploited coastal woodlands. Given freight costs from Newcastle, coal imports were already a pressing burden on the balance of payments, approaching $2 million annually. With railroads on line, coal imports were bound to skyrocket. But Pardo's technological revolution was designed above all to be an exchange-saving one. Pardo probably drew on the coal development studies of Mariano de Rivero—the republic's premier mining engineer (and the Junín prefect during Pardo's sojourn)—who, in vari-

---

berg, "Price Levels in Peru," or Vincent Peloso, "Succulence and Sustenance: Region, Class, and Diet in Nineteenth-Century Peru," in J. Super and T. Wright, eds. *Food, Politics, and Society in Latin America*, (Lincoln, 1985), 46–64.

50. Pardo, *Estudios sobre Jauja*, 26–27; M. Pardo, "Memoria que el ex-secretario de estado en despacho de hacienda y comercio presenta al jefe supremo provisorio de la república" (1867), López, *Pardo*, 363. On early agrarian protectionists, see Gootenberg, *Between Silver and Guano*, ch. 3, or Ledos and Rivero tracts cited above; Juan Rolf Engelsen, "Social Aspects of Agricultural Expansion in Coastal Peru, 1825–1878" (Ph.D. diss., UCLA, 1977), chs. 3–5, 7, on rising exporters, including Pardos (423).

ous surveys published during the mid 1850s, vaunted exploitation of central highlands deposits.[51]

The *Estudios sobre Jauja* hardly stops at primary products. Pardo turns next to a discussion of Peru's nascent wool trades: the briskly growing business of shipping sierran wools to England in return for industrial woolens. In the four decades since independence alert Peruvians had grasped how this trade had finished off Peru's colonial obrajes and country weavers and must have sensed the dominance of textile imports (some 70 percent) in Peruvian foreign trade.[52] Pardo refuses to endorse expanding fiber exports to close the gap. Instead, he implores Jauja, via railways, to reverse the export-import trend:

What? That a factory of coarse cloth for the consumption of the people cannot be established in a province that possesses the primary materials, that has the workers, where wages are so cheap, where there are all sorts of dyes? And above all, the region is protected from foreign competition not by high customs duties, but by another protection, which nature puts on everything this province wants to import. Can we hope for more favorable conditions for the establishment of any industry? But what do these conditions serve, when the transport of raw material for a great factory—supplying some forty leagues of Peru—costs double the value of the material. Can it then be done? Make roads and all will grow from the soil; without them, all efforts are useless![53]

Pardo's profound Peru was not "naturally" unsuited to industry. His precocious (if muddled) application of the modern concept of "natural protection" turned liberal slogans on their head. Now the interior, so remote from competitive markets, appears naturally amenable to manufacturing.

From one angle, Pardo was seemingly evading tired protectionist–free-trader polemics. Tariffs, ever controversial in Peru, merit only passing mention as a "sad deception for promoting manufactures." Speaking

51. Pardo, *Estudios sobre Jauja*, 28–29, 59; Mariano Eduardo de Rivero, "Minas de carbón de piedra del Perú" (1855) in Rivero, *Colección de memorias científicas, agrícolas e industriales publicadas en distintas épocas*, 2 vols. (Brussels, 1857) 2:211–17 (with substitution idea); and "Apuntes histórico-estadísticos sobre el departamento peruano de Junín en los años que lo administró como prefecto" (1855), 186–210.

52. Pardo, *Estudios sobre Jauja*, 30; cf. export-favoring M. E. de Rivero, "Memoria sobre las lanas del Perú" (1855), in Rivero, *Colección de memorias científicas e industriales* 2:240–58; Rivero, e.g., discusses vanishing colonial "telares employing thousands" (243). Heraclio Bonilla, "La expansión comercial británica en el Perú," *Revista del Museo Nacional* 40 (1974): table 3, for textile import shares.

53. Pardo, *Estudios sobre Jauja*, 30.

to urban coastal elites, Pardo believed in neither their workability nor their political advantage. As finance minister in 1867 Pardo dubs tariffs the "mistaken protectionist idea"—albeit in an ironic (and misunderstood) passage ridiculing planter fiscal resistance—all in the name of "protecting national agriculture."[54] Others, notably Cisneros, would directly readdress the bogey of state protection. But Pardo's overoptimistic thinking is indicated by his notion of "productivity" advancing so "naturally"—in a sort of bucolic vent-for-surplus—demanding few of the sacrifices or trade-offs needed in large-scale and long-term investments. This was a utopian strain in much Peruvian thinking to come, though Pardo the civilist corrected himself with his later dedication to educational—that is, gradual human capital—investments.

From another angle, Pardo was right to pinpoint dismal transport as the prime obstacle to the start-up and productivity of all highlands enterprise—including his envisioned factories. Peru suffers the most fissiparous geography of all American states; transport costs had soared with the severe dislocation of national muleteer communications in the postindependence years, in part as mules (but less so llamas) became a coveted prize of military bands. Whole internal exchange networks vanished, withdrawing from monetary society, becoming, in a word, "Indian." In complex senses, deteriorating communications melded with larger issues of Andean "feudalism," though not always in the ways imagined by city liberals, indigenistas, or historians.[55]

To economists, lower transport costs (and, closely related, reduced transaction costs) would make a most efficient means to foster growth in such an economy and would work more directly than tariffs or even monetary subsidies would. This, for example, is what happened in

---

54. Pardo, *Estudios sobre Jauja*, 41; Pardo, "Memoria de hacienda y comercio" (1867), in López, *Pardo*, 350–51, 363; readers can judge Pardo's irony here: "Las ideas proteccionistas probado con este motivo [sugar tax resistance] que tiene raíces profundas aun en las inteligencias más claras y más familiarizadas con los sanos principios de la ciencia" (350).

W. A. Lewis, of course, hailed the modern (allegedly costless) theory of industrialization by "unlimited supplies" of rural labor; however, Pardo does not discuss labor markets enough to warrant this interpretation. On Pardo's later educational drive, see David Cornejo Foronda, *Don Manuel Pardo y la educación nacional* (Lima, 1953).

55. On extant transport sector, see Nelson Manrique, "Los arrieros de la sierra central durante el siglo xix," *Allpanchis* 18 (1983): 27–46 (and adjacent studies by Urrutia and Valderrama and Escalante). Gootenberg, "Population and Ethnicity," 141–52, for social conceptions of indigenous feudalism. I am taking issue here with Bonilla, *Guano y burguesía*, 151–53 (notion of constricted "internal market"), which does not truly explain why railroads were a misplaced priority for market widening.

comparable Mexican industries with the coming of railroads, when factories fared better with wider national markets than had their heavily protected counterparts of an earlier era.[56] Throughout this essay Pardo pushes for a more integrated national economy, with wider markets that contrast with but do not clash with the country's dominant export economy. The shift of scene to Peru's rural sector—in the narrow cost sense more promising than inflationary Lima for development—also attests to the emerging national outlook. Inspiration for railway mania, at least in Pardo's canonical text, seems both rational and national.

The depth of Pardo's manufacturing proposal becomes evident in his critical rundown of prospective rural industries. Pardo explains that "what is happening in the Peruvian interior with wools will happen with all our primary materials when exported. But most of them can be put to use there in manufacture, for which there is no lack of elements."[57] Besides revealing those "elements" denied by free-traders, *Estudios sobre Jauja* reflects Peru's previous frustrations with attempted diversification. Pardo preaches that Peru should not hope for "huge factories" devoted to making such luxuries as fine cloth, silks, porcelain, or glass. Instead, with

cheaper wages and foodstuffs, primary materials, ready coals and better yet—powerful waterfalls—why can't Peru establish factories for coarse cloth, rough cottons, and linens, or those for ordinary pottery, for leather goods, and a host of potassium and chemical products. In contrast, these are the industries within reach of the secondary classes, and those that best advance the welfare of the people and progress of the nation.[58]

Pardo goes on to criticize the classic (and revenue-eating) French models of luxury workshop promotion. Colbert, long the protectionist idol in Peru, was out—though Pardo, among others, still found much to admire in the broader French activist state of his times.[59]

---

56. See John H. Coatsworth, "Obstacles to Economic Growth in Nineteenth-Century Mexico," *American Historical Review* 83 (1978): 91–92; and Haber, "Obstacles to Industrialization."

57. Pardo, *Estudios sobre Jauja*, 31.

58. Pardo, *Estudios sobre Jauja*, 31.

59. See, e.g., preference for French developmental activism in M. Pardo, "El crédito hipotecario en Francia y Chile en 1859 y 1860," in López, *Pardo*, 312–18 (*Revista de Lima*, 1861) and "Inmigración vascongada" (1860), which praises French agrarian promotion in railways, irrigation, and mortgage banks in support of private accumulation: "The Peruvian state is the richest operating in the world—yet we still complain we lack private capital."

In part, Pardo's realistic assessment of appropriate industries seems inspired by the fate of Lima's luxury craft guilds, which, despite decades of promotion after 1821, had made little headway. As Casanova had before, Pardo envisaged Peru's prospects in simpler mass markets, those easiest to master in technique and those (apart from the highly visible elite trinkets) that could actually reduce Peru's worrisome import bill. For such an eminent figure, Pardo's developmental vision was eminently small-scale and "popular"—by and for those "secondary classes." It exudes the spirit of Saint-Simonian industrial *trabajo*. The best investments, Pardo contends, are those that

spawn modest dividends for their owners and contribute modestly to the welfare of the populations that sustain them. The city of Cincinnati, erected only yesterday in a wilderness, has achieved with its leatherworks, slaughterhouses, crude furniture factories, and its eight-piece wooden clocks such prosperity and growth that it is now the western capital of the United States—if not the leading manufacturing capital of the Union.[60]

Here one finds—much as in Casanova—the blatantly imitative model: the incremental, decentralized, and popular industrialization of what Pardo playfully calls "l'enfant colosse." Pardo's exemplar verifies an intellectual trend among Peruvian writers of the 1860s—disillusionment with long-admired Continental models (whether statist or liberal), which are being superseded by the "barbarous" example of North American frontier development.[61] It makes sense, too, for the formerly colonial United States represented the world's premier newly industrializing nation. Yet few writers, Pardo included, grasped essential differences with their internally "discovered" frontiers: Peru was a nation of entrenched Andean peasant populations, who, until the 1880s, remained unimaginable as an element of progress.

Still another inspiration stems from Pardo's reading of Peruvian economic history—his resuscitation of the Spanish colonial regime as a model of benign and balanced intervention. This reading was probably a tradition continued by civilist state builders of the 1870s. Pardo's fascination with the viceregal state rings clearest in a concurrent regional

60. Pardo, *Estudios sobre Jauja*, 32.
61. Pardo, *Estudios sobre Jauja*, 33, 45. Britain, by contrast, was rarely a development model for Peruvian writers (except in tariff debates, that is in the actions of Peel and Huskinson). Beyond language barriers, Britain may have seemed too interested a status quo party in Peruvian eyes. See discussion of imperialism in Copello and Petriconi and in Esteves, below.

foray of the *Revista de Lima,* his 1860 essay "El partido de Saña o Lambayeque en el siglo pasado"—a pioneering stab at Peruvian economic history and surely the first to deploy "modern statistics."[62] This northern coastal plain, home to Pardo's own budding sugar plantation, felt the stirrings of commercial revival after 1850. In Pardo's search for the coast's prior development, historical diversity and promotion policies merit special attention.

Pardo laments, as all liberals reflexively did, Spain's harmful monopolies, in the spirit of "Colbert and Sully." But advantages were to be had, too:

They regulated production yet could favor it at the same time. Local authorities protected the laborer and *industriosos* and prevented their depredation. They fostered every new crop and new industry, made roads and built bridges. It contrasts to the economic system today in place—called by some "liberty"—and that with our excessive respect for the word, we would never call "abandonment." Today, to be sure, we don't regulate production or direct industry. But neither do we protect or promote it, safeguard the artisan from robbers, found new industries, or construct bridges and roads.[63]

Thus, Pardo believed that the liberal state, with its obsessive individualism, had lost valuable social functions, developmental ones worth national recovery. Pardo's assessment was a long way from instinctive liberal curses of Spain—as source of every baneful habit of Peruvian sociology. From the century's foremost modernizer, this perspective is novel; perhaps Pardo's conservative father (or stay in Spain) left this surprising outlook.

After formal criticism of mercantilist theory, Pardo dwells on the specially favored colonial productions—industry—in a strained revision of imperial "industrial" policy. At a time when proposals abounded to revamp the coast for specialized cotton exporting—Duval's, for example, in the same *Revista de Lima* issues—Pardo sounds ambivalent. Cotton cultivation for local weavers

was specially favored under the auspices of colonial officials, as if they divined the role this shrub was called to play a century hence in the general riches of the world. Without abstracting Spanish authorities from the era's dominant economic ideas, their productive efforts went more into weaving

---

62. Pardo, "Partido de Saña," *Revista de Lima* 2 (1860): 688–96; MacEvoy, "Manuel Pardo," 143–45, notes this colonial influence as well; we explore (similar) economic history—of Esteves—in ch. 6, below.
63. Pardo, "Partido de Saña," in López, *Pardo,* 282.

industry than into agriculture—as if promotion were creating in the colonies (as in the *madre patria*) their own elements of production, emancipating them from foreign trade. Not so strange—since only in our century has reciprocal commerce between civilized nations demonstrated all its advantages. But the fruit of such textile promotion was the zone's immense workshops.[64]

In his historical relativism Pardo seemed strangely impressed by the diversity and level of colonial production, though he could not openly endorse the "protectionist policy" that he found responsible. Colonial revisionism would crop up again in Peruvian critical writings, notably in Esteves's economic history of the 1880s. Pardo's historical fascination with diversity, direction, and manufactures spilled over to Jauja— though there mainly as an automatic result of powerful railways.

In neither economics nor politics is it correct to read Pardo's work as some Andean "Notes on the State of Jauja." The political inspiration was, at best, ambiguously democratic, harking to the orderly peace of the colonial era. *Estudios sobre Jauja* could just as well be read as an urban scheme to reassert sovereignty over, and renewed exploitation of, Lima's then distanced and discontented agrarian domains. Stock liberal concerns about Indian "lethargy," the violence of rustic caudillos, and the specter of urban breakdown colored Pardo's vision of a national "moral uplifting" through railroads. To Pardo, productive "work" disciplines and forges modern citizenries, as well as disciplining an unruly balance of payments. Railways would accelerate rural mobility, cultural contact, and thus enlightment among peasants:

By merely bettering their moral condition, we can give them those principles of personal dignity and independence without which they can never amount to anything but miserable helots, commoners attached to the soil—and blind instruments of everyone who cuts a cudgel to order them about. By improving the material condition of our people, we shall erect the most effective barricade against the advances of tyranny, on the one hand, and on the other, against the forces of the anarchists.[65]

Pardo is not terribly specific on just who represent Peru's tyrants and anarchists, though his Athenian gibe at Spartan oppressors suggests a

---

64. Pardo, "Partido de Saña," in López, *Pardo*, 284; cf. Alfredo Duval, "Memoria sobre algodones" and "Algo sobre algodones," *Revista de Lima* 3 (1861). Pardo, though, was not against cotton exports, which he once praised as "the replacement" for guano in "Inmigración vascongada" (152–53).

65. Pardo, *Estudios sobre Jauja*, 47.

lot. It is not hard to guess whom he imagined in 1860 Lima as liberal reformers went about carving out a civic space between strongman Castilla and the restless plebes. Balder repressive and strategic arguments followed, for railroads, lifting federal troops swiftly to the scene, would forever neutralize the central highlands as a staging ground for caudillo revolts. The heart of the message, however, seems to be neither Pardo's patent liberal paternalism toward natives, nor his revulsion toward locomotive-bashing artisans in the streets, nor his pointed aversion to Castilla's autocracy. It was the long-term civilist political mission itself. Railroads were to work a national social transformation, the *república práctica* as voiced in later party ideals.[66] National communications, national technology, and national development would slowly lay cornerstones for solid civil rule—national and popular bedrock for civilist politics. Pardo was much more the Juárez than the Díaz of Peru, and not just in their precocious shared visions of integration by rail.

To be sure, the involved *Estudios sobre Jauja* touches many other points besides the unexpected option of regional manufacturing—for example, varied railroad finance schemes, enabling fiscal reforms, imagined resource discoveries, or Amazonian colonization from Jauja (that recurrent pipe dream of Limeños anxious over city "vagrants"). As it began, though, the book ends with guano.

As it was for Casanova, the pressing issue for Pardo is not whether but how to direct the extraordinary gift of export wealth. By 1860, Pardo warns, Peru was consuming from abroad "three times" what it could "naturally" produce: "This cannot be eternal." When guano fades, Lima-style incomes will abruptly collapse by three-quarters—throwing Peru from "civilization back to *barbarie*." A positivist Pardo was reminding his class here of the traumas of caudillismo and penury haltingly reversed by Peru's successful brand of centralist free trade.[67] Yet despite

66. See Manuel Pardo, "Algo sobre el proyecto de código penal (vagancia)," *Revista de Lima* 4 (1861): 103–10, which chides a libertarian congress for not harshly punishing vagrancy—as "a collective crime," akin to "sedition and revolt," especially among "inferior races." "A state, especially a republic, must form citizens, not Lazzaroni."

See Maiguashca, "Reinterpretation of Guano Age," ch. 3, for reformist order concerns; Kristal, *Andes from the City*, ch. 2, on civilist "Indians"; and esp. MacEvoy, "Manuel Pardo," as "traditional modernizer"—but with deepening social analysis and popular mobilization towards the 1870s.

Pardo was not humorless: a relevant example is his call for Peruvians "to become a nation and not migratory birds"—one of the few memorable guano puns of the age ("Memoria de hacienda y comercio" [1867], in López, *Pardo*, 301).

67. Pardo, *Estudios sobre Jauja*, 39–50. Anticaudillismo was vital in initial 1850s victory of free trade; see Gootenberg, "Beleaguered Liberals," 79–89.

dire warnings, the *Estudios sobre Jauja* ultimately brims with optimism. Pointing again to the North American romance with canals and iron horses, Pardo conjures up "a magic change," a totalizing "moral revolution." The imagined transport revolution will revolutionize Peruvian economics, fiscality, politics, and values—themes embraced and embroidered across the Peru of the 1860s. The *Estudios sobre Jauja* was not yet a document of crisis.

On a Railroad to Nowhere?

Rereading the *Estudios sobre Jauja* suggests that the origins of Peru's manic railway development of the 1860s and 1870s are not adequately explored—despite the many verdicts on the process. In 1861 the Peruvian congress, moved by Pardo's panegyric, approved the country's first major trunk line to Jauja. That same year Pardo composed another policy essay on railroads for the *Revista de Lima*, his "Ley general sobre ferrocarriles." In it Pardo, in the cause of development, took to task the narrow fiscal and security concerns of Castilla's stolid regime: "Peru wants public works instead of fifteen thousand soldiers—the spirit of the nineteenth century has finally seized the people and congress." But this was largely a technical consideration of financing schemes. Pardo cautiously endorsed state profit guarantees to lure foreign capital and contractors into Peru's politically risky construction climate—the solution effectively required throughout Latin America. Phrases here (such as liberal fiscal incentives "to attract foreign capital") can mislead historians to truncate Pardo's original conception, as if railroads were meant to open Peru to a new age of foreign capital.[68]

Pardo's diversifying vision in *Estudios sobre Jauja* was no fluke, neither in his own intellectual and public trajectory nor in Peru's energetic

68. Manuel Pardo, "Medidas económicas del congreso de 1860: Ley general sobre ferrocarriles," *Revista de Lima* 3, 3 pts.; López, *Pardo*, 299. For verdict on export railroads, see Bonilla, *Guano y burguesía*, 55–63; Cotler, *Clases, estado y nación*, 102–7; and Pennano, "Desarrollo regional y ferrocarriles." Standard (unanalytic) text is Stewart, *Meiggs;* Maiguashca, "Reinterpretation of Guano Age," ch. 5, "Turning Guano into Railroads," is most attuned to development schemes; for modern evaluation, Rory Miller, "Railways and Economic Development in Central Peru, 1885–1930," in R. Miller et al., eds., *Social and Economic Change in Modern Peru* (Liverpool, 1975), 27–52; propositioned in Heraclio Bonilla, "El impacto de los ferrocarriles: Algunas proposiciones," *Historia y Cultura* 6 (1972): 93–120.

national and official response to railroad ideals. Just where were Peruvian railways going? Was the lofty destination something like Pardo's nebulous "moral" revolution?

In 1851 Peru opened the first functioning railroad in South America (the short Callao–Lima line). Its commercial success in rationalizing port communications underscored the need for modern transport in the country with the most daunting geography of the Western hemisphere.[69] Slow and scarce mule trains could no longer suffice. By the late 1850s, as every awakening regional oligarchy pined for its own outlet to the sea, formal railroad proposals became a kind of techno-literary genre in Peru. The *Revista de Lima* alone, in less than three years of existence, published three other projects: a highly liberal financing plan by the noted free-trade professor Felipe Masías; an engineering and industrial survey by Federico Blume, later the crony of Henry Meiggs; and a "proyecto" for an Arequipa–Islay line by Toribio Pacheco (a European-trained legal theorist who in the 1840s wrote glowingly of Lima's factories), who also called for reversing export formulas. A railroad through the south would allow guano to pass inland to Arequipa's granary, employing tradable fertilizers at home to multiply food production for domestic markets.[70] Dozens of such proposals—such as the 1867 report by Cisneros (under Pardo's Ministry of Finance)—suggest the genuine spirit and direction of the rail frenzy that came to dominate the final decade of the guano age.

Most of these feasibility studies indeed share Pardo's developmental, social, and political concerns and fall into three discernible categories: prognoses, regionalist responses, and technological spin-offs. A logical place to begin is Peru's first formal governmental communications report, an 1856 compilation of engineering studies, which Pardo himself cites, stressing spurs to internal commerce and industry. The chief surveyor, one Ernesto Malinowski (the Polish émigré who later oversaw Pardo's trans-Andean line), expressed high hopes that railroads for Peru

69. Regal, *Historia de ferrocarriles*—with fine detail on early involvement of Lima commercial elites.

70. *Revista de Lima*—Toribio Pacheco, "Proyecto de ferrocarril de Arequipa a Islay" (Nov. 1860); Federico Blume, "Breves observaciones sobre el establecimiento y economía de ferrocarriles considerados como empresas industriales" (Nov. 1860); Felipe Masías, "El gobierno y las empresas de ferro-carril en el Perú" (Nov. 1861); Luis Benjamín Cisneros, "Memoria sobre ferrocarriles" (1868), rpt. in L. B. Cisneros, *Obras completas* (Lima, 1939) 3:141–86; a compendium of studies is Cuerpo de Ingenieros y Arquitectos del Estado, *Anales del cuerpo de ingenieros del Perú* (Lima, 1874), 2 vols.

"will be the resolution of *all* social problems." Two-thirds of the country had yet to be made "Peruvian," according to this Central European's nation-integrating ideal. Malinowski's memorial also underscored special benefits that would accrue to national producers grappling with import competition. He argued that with reliable rapid transport, nationals "should be able to compete with analogous goods from other countries. And not just in foreign markets, but even in this country, as wheat, coffee, cacao, and so on prove, which for the coastal consumer now come largely from abroad—even when interior growers can supply them in sufficient quantity, even superior quality."[71] He, too, wrote of opening coal mines and of honing local engineering skills (with a national "school of engineers"), all the while invoking the apt precedent of railroads across the Alps. More than a decade later, Malinowski (fully assimilated into national elite circles) recalled his original nation-building ideals in an 1869 memorial on the trans-Andean project: the aim, he reminded a flagging congress, is to unite the Amazon with the Pacific, bringing into play the national wealth foreseen by Pardo in 1860.[72] A pertinent question, explored below, is the cultural lens such immensely influential foreign engineers brought to the Peruvian scene.

An even more striking project evaluation appeared in 1868—just when Manuel Pardo's economic team was pushing to accelerate Andean rail construction. (By the early 1870s Peru had nearly fifty different lines underway, public and private, financed under the Balta-Piérola scheme of mortgaging all remaining guano deposits on European markets.) John William ("Juan Guillermo") Nystrom, another prominent foreign engineer and adviser, reported a more ambitious vision than Pardo's, heralding potential backward (as well as forward) linkages from railways. His vision focused on Cuzco, ancient and decrepit pole of Andean economy. Nystrom, the state engineer, predicted that the Cuzco railhead would

attract the most important manufacturers to come there, principally with machines to cut wood, to make doors and windows, and to build and finish the carts, roads, and steamboats that will locate in the valley. In addition,

71. Peru, Convención Nacional, *Documentos legislativos sobre el establecimiento y la mejora de las vías de comunicación en el Perú* (Lima, pam., 1856)—primarily enclosed Malinowski "Memoria," 16, 24; E. Malinowski, *Ferrocarril central transandino: Informe del ingeniero en jefe d. Ernesto Malinowski* (Lima, pam., 1869); see Stewart, *Meiggs*, 44–45, for role.

72. Malinowski, *Ferrocarril central transandino*, 7.

there will be manufacturers of glass, porcelain, rubber articles; and machines to weave wools and cotton and to obtain the articles that chemistry demands.[73]

Nystrom's case for more complex railway capital goods was just as emphatic. Nowhere in Latin America was this feat contemplated or achieved on a significant scale (though in the 1880s Chile was making sophisticated copies of cars and locomotives, and in southern Peru, a British foundry tried the same).[74] But writing in 1868, Nystrom envisioned constructing rails and engines in such remote and primitive zones as the valleys of La Convención and Urubamba. A crony of Malinowski, he proposed a "Sociedad Metalúrgica del Cuzco" to organize the area's new foundries, which would surround locally developed iron and coal deposits. "When one makes motors at home," Nystrom insisted, "the peculiar experience of each locality grows in the measure that each operation advances. Such local capital goods might cost, at first, double the imported ones; but at least the funds and outlays would remain there to benefit the interior."[75] The precedent hailed here—industrializing St. Petersburg (rather than Cincinnati)—is sociologically intriguing, as that city was planned and placed on the Russian frontier. Traditional peasant Cuzco had been, of course, a major colonial center of obraje manufacturing and had suffered terrible economic losses through the first half of the nineteenth century, virtually withdrawing from the national economy. To promote regional revival, Nystrom suggested the immediate formation of state workshops, backed up by an equally ambitious provincial "Institute of Science." The peculiar mind-set of tinkering engineers doubtless spawned such wide visions of "learning by doing" and indigenous technology.[76] Like Pardo's industrialism, none of this—particularly the use of domestic inputs in railroad building—ever got off the

73. Juan Guillermo Nystrom, *Informe al supremo gobierno del Perú sobre una espedición al interior de la república* (Lima, pam., 1868), 7, 11.

74. Palma, "Growth and Structure of Chilean Industry," ch. 3, explains special market for capital goods; Ballon, *Ideas en Arequipa*, 177–79.

75. Nystrom, *Informe al gobierno*, 20–27, 77; Magnus Mörner, *Notas sobre el comercio y los comerciantes del Cusco desde fines de la colonia hasta 1930* (Lima, 1979), 9–15, for regional decline.

76. Among studies of foreign perceptions of nineteenth-century Peru (Macera, Tauro), none shares Safford's *Ideal of Practical* (ch. 4) focus on technical elites; an attempt is Jorge Grieve, "El desarrollo de las industrias mecánicas en el Perú entre 1800 y 1880," *Historia y Cultura* 15 (1982): 23–69. No contemporaries positively mention Paraguay's metallurgic industries; see Thomas L. Whigham, "The Iron Works of Ibycui: Paraguayan Industrial Development in the Mid-Nineteenth Century," *Americas* 35 (1978): 201–18.

ground. But men like Nystrom knew what would pique the imagination of their Peruvian hosts. Another Nystrom report of 1869 (on opening the Chanchamayo jungle region) insisted on the inhumanity of reducing its famously recalcitrant natives by force; instead, trade and transport should peaceably assimilate Indians to "comercio y industria."[77] Here was another motif of railway writings: modern communications as liberal "discovery-conquest" of a mysterious greater Peru.

With models such as these, a rhetoric of railroads echoed throughout the Peru of the 1860s. Overlooked regional rail proposals are easily pursued, for along with varied critiques of guano sales policies, they make the ubiquitous genre of the decade's economic pamphleteers. Sampling the scores of regional proposals and progress reports reveals two overriding themes. First, as a forum for the convergent thinking of regional, political, and technical elites, the schemes reveal lofty dreams of national integration and stability—broad noneconomic ideals, able to hold diverse material aims. Hidden agendas were more economic: provincial public works as means of decentralizing Lima's guano wealth, a dissembled policy of national fiscal redistribution. The second element was technological dynamism: the railroad as nineteenth-century civilizing agent—a fascination with transforming science, under the influence of engineers and explorers streaming into the Andes. Both facets expressed discovery principles: the capital's conquest (in Cisneros's memorable phrase) of the "real Peru."[78]

One sterling regional proposal—the 1864 *Ferrocarril de Arequipa: Informe de los empresarios*—harked from Peru's second city and Lima's chronic republican political rival, Arequipa.[79] Backed by the solemn *actas* of scores of Arequipan notables (and then from upland Cuzco, Puno, and Lampa), the project was presented by migrant promoters "Patricio" Gibson and "José" Pickering, the former of the important southern merchant clan. Apart from usual technical and financing considerations, the group promised four outstanding benefits from a $10–20 million link from the sea through the southern Andes: economic diversity, machine culture, Indian incorporation, and regional political stability.

First, the developmental prospects of Arequipa's coming railroad

77. J. G. Nystrom, *Informe al supremo gobierno sobre la espedición de Chanchamayo por J. G. Nystrom* (Lima, pam., 1869), esp. "Programa para el fomento del progreso."

78. Luis Benjamín Cisneros, *Proyecto de ley presentado por el diputado por Jauja L. B. Cisneros y memoria sobre los ferrocarriles peruanos* (Lima, pam., 1868).

79. *Ferrocarril de Arequipa: Informe de los empresarios* (Arequipa, pam., 1864).

were couched in terms of a diversified regional revival. With Arequipa's efficient outlet to the sea, the city's withered agrarian *campiña* would bloom anew. Until postindependence turmoil and invasive Chilean food imports, the zone had traditionally supplied a wide selection of wines, cereals, and vegetables for the urban and Andean trades. Linked by rail, new internal markets, lively labor mobility, and the latest farm implements would erase the legacies of foodstuffs competition. "What disgrace," lamented the report, "to see in Peru, on the outskirts of its main cities, thousands of uncultivated 'topos' of land, forcing us to buy from Chile even the flour of our daily bread. Thus, it will be feasible to raise the proper products of our fields—abandoned for inability to compete overseas."[80] Echoing Pardo's breadbasket call for Jauja, such notions had obvious appeal for Arequipa's dominant landed classes. Rather than focusing on the area's fallow mines of silver and copper, the proposal privileged wheat, cotton, and alfalfa.

Powerful locomotives steaming across deserts and mountains make an impressive symbol of nineteenth-century progress. Here the powerful import was a demonstration effect. The railroad would foreshadow the viability and spread of modern "machines" throughout the sierra. "Equally," the report imagined, "the railroad, allowing the introduction of machinery, will promote new factories of many classes. Peru exports many articles of constant value and demand in a rudimentary state— when in the country itself we could fabricate them, at least in first preparations, thus facilitating their transport and augmenting their values."[81] The south thus replicated Pardo's vision of import-substituting railways, though here it was conceived mainly in a value-added sense. But why should transport-cost reductions lend themselves to local processing of wools, cottons, and minerals when, in economic terms, savings would just as likely favor bulk exports? The answer seemed to center on unusual backward linkages expected from Andean technology imports—a contagious social "admiration for machines and the arts." In this mission, muleteers were hardly competition.

80. *Ferrocarril de Arequipa*, 3–4; see Tomás Dávila, *Medios que se proponen al actual congreso constitucional del Perú y al gobierno supremo, para salvar de su total destrucción la casi-arruinada agricultura de la importante provincia de Moquegua* (Arequipa, pam., 1853), for protective agrarian interests and transport difficulties (52–53); one of greatest civil war losses was precisely mules. John Frederick Wibel, "The Evolution of a Regional Community Within the Spanish Empire and Peruvian Nation: Arequipa, 1780–1845" (Ph.D. diss., Stanford University, 1975), for regional background.

81. *Ferrocarril de Arequipa*, 5; see Jacobsen, *Mirages of Transition*, ch. 2, 5, for area crafts and later rail impact.

The Arequipeños were equally mindful of rural mass markets: "Many articles of home manufacturing, principally for Indian use, could be had so easily and economically with the help of simple machines. And the time saved by Indians in their fabrication could be employed advantageously in indispensable manual labors."[82] Arequipeños envisioned two specific productivity advances from labor-saving devices: first, the revival of formerly widespread part-time household weavers of the sierra, a revival that in turn would enhance their availability for critical labor—presumably for seasonal work on elite haciendas. It is hard to grasp why more efficiently employed peasants would seek outside wages, but this was a tortured logic of landed classes, suffering through an era of contracted native labor markets.

The third theme of *Ferrocarril de Arequipa* concerned the Indians themselves. Arequipa constituted a white and mestizo beachhead in a sea of native community hinterlands, and its Europeanized spokespersons contemplated a wider technological regeneration of Indian workers—at first glance a strange association with trains. This analysis was also among the first open discussions of the Indian problem since the 1840s talk of native welfare and vanishing obrajes. The project stressed, "When we study the possible advancement of Peru, and especially the south, it is absolutely necessary to consider the condition of the Indian." "Well known" are the Indians' paltry "wants" and disincentive to betterment, ran their familiar neocolonial refrain. But after five years of steam engines "he won't be the same Indian of today! We don't need so-called useful European immigration"—the usual despairing whitening recipe in Peru—when "apt" Indian workers abound.[83] "Frequent communications of this race with the whites will help to mix them; thus the railroad will be the most efficacious means for creating the healthy and intelligent proletariat that, content as the English *peón*, his place fit in the world, will make the base of a democratic republic—moderated to law and friend of national progress."[84]

As a revelation of the imagined "moral" and "civilizing" mission of steam, this vision supersedes Pardo's classless mestizo reveries, though

82. *Ferrocarril de Arequipa*, 5, 19.

83. *Ferrocarril de Arequipa*, 6; see Pardo, "Inmigración vascongada" for more typical whitening views; Charles Walker, "Rhetorical Power: Early Republican Discourse on the Indian in Cusco" (paper presented at the AHA, Chicago, 1991), for consolidating racialism; Gootenberg, "Population and Ethnicity," table 8, shows Arequipa department about 50 percent Indian, hinterland Puno over 90 percent.

84. *Ferrocarril de Arequipa*, 6.

Pardo hinted at similar effects from rail mobility. Fixed to its nineteenth-century moorings, the ideology is both unmistakably racist (Indian sloth and withdrawal as genetic) and imaginative in its improving, flexible, and socially defined mestizo ideal. *Mestizaje* equals the commercialization and proletarianization of Peru's self-sufficient native, now a salvageable being. With heightened contact and inevitable miscegenation, peasants might even surpass their coveted utility as laborers and consumers and become real citizens, bedrock of the republic. If we follow recent studies of nineteenth-century technology, colonialism, and caste and ignore Peru's peculiar racialist context, this was an incorporative modernization worthy of a Rostow—or, indeed, a Marx.[85] To southern elites and their advisers, the railroad amounts to a machine to civilize their own colonized peoples. By omission and confession, much of Peru's gathering technological fascination suggests such neocolonial undercurrents.

Finally, Arequipa's promoters heralded the long-term political stabilization project of railroads: that confluence of "order, law, entrepreneurial élan, peace"—and machinery. In part, this association serves as a veiled regional threat to Lima state makers, albeit with payoffs in the wings. Liberal Arequipa, Peru's legendary "pueblo caudillo," had staged four decades of destabilizing revolts against the northern centrist state, as leaders such as Castilla, Pardo, and Cisneros knew all too well. By the 1860s Peru was moving toward a tense national compromise, but memories remained fresh. Arequipans reminded their Lima audience how much they remained "feared in the north of the republic."[86]

The argument begins by repeating that old mental linkage between poverty, unemployment, *empleomanía,* and caudillismo. The "natural" contentiousness of "energetic" Arequipeños stemmed from their greater historical need for "work." Only the railroad would stop forever the

85. Adas, *Machines as Measure of Men,* "Epilogue," analyzes lost origins of 1950s modernization theory. Adas quotes a similarly minded nineteenth-century thinker on colonial technology; this thinker believed not only that railroads would "dissolve" all caste divisions but that "when you have introduced machinery into the locomotion of a country, you are unable to withhold it from its fabrication . . . without introducing all those industrial processes necessary. . . . The railway system will therefore become, in India, truly the forerunner of modern industry" (K. Marx, "The Future Results of British Rule in India" [1853], 240). Kristal, *Andes from the City,* chs. 2–3, for civilist indigenismo as "proletarianization" ideology.

86. *Ferrocarril de Arequipa,* 7; classic account is Juan Gualberto Valdivia, *Memorias sobre las revoluciones de Arequipa desde 1834 hasta 1866* (Lima, 1874); Wibel, "Arequipa," chs. 4–5, for political integration.

"revolutions," as commercially "regenerating" Arequipa "is called on to become the center of civilization for a colossal portion of the globe."[87] They imagined themselves the coming Pacific entrepôt of the Andes, and indeed, Arequipan commercial sway had at least spread toward Cuzco since 1821. In a less grandiose economics of stability, the pamphlet then promised Lima savings of $1 million annually—the current expenditures for stationing the 2,000-man (occupation) garrison in the south.

These were other ways of speaking of national integration, ultimately posed as the great unfinished task left by Spanish colonialism: "When the day comes uniting north and south by railroads and other common interests, the last vestiges of provincialism will vanish, that favorite plant of the colonial system, cultivated and harvested by despots ever since."[88] To extend their agrarian metaphor, rail lines would wither the deep-rooted southern caudillo. The promoters aptly pointed to Italy as a new nation united and consummated by rail.

Finally, although Pardo receives no credits here, the proposal closes on his realpolitik jeremiad. Peru is at the crossroads. "The day is coming, and not terribly long, when the earnings of guano cease. Then, Arequipa and the resources of its interior will be the stuff of southern industry— that which Peru will rely on to exist among the nations." Will Peru relapse into regional turmoil and "barbarism"? In guano's end of days, "confusion and anarchy will drag Peru into the abyss—unless that forward-looking spirit in our legislative body takes advantage now of their profitable resources, to establish industry and individual wealth, as bulwarks for the country's salvation. The Arequipan railway must be the first step."[89] Here was an offer few politicos could refuse.

So many other tracts parallel these Arequipan lines of national integration, political security, and regional development. One very public confirmation comes from Luciano B. Cisneros—the noted poet brother of Luis Benjamín, fellow *Revista de Lima* figure, and in 1868 Minister of Beneficencia (public welfare) in the liberal coterie around the Prado junta. Following the devastating 1867 southern earthquake, Cisneros headed a Lima mission to the region to assess reconstruction needs. His official report reads like the developmentalist counterinsurgency pro-

87. *Ferrocarril de Arequipa*, 7, 17; Alberto Flores Galindo, *Arequipa y el sur andino: Ensayo de historia regional, siglos xviii–xx* (Lima, 1977), ch. 2, for emergent regional hegemonies.
88. *Ferrocarril de Arequipa*, 22.
89. *Ferrocarril de Arequipa*, 8, 22.

grams that officially entered Latin America a century later with the Alliance for Progress.[90]

After calculating short-term damages, Cisneros quickly turned to his long-range program for southern "paz y trabajo": large state investments in irrigation and land reclamation, a regional mortgage-reconstruction bank, technical assistance and schooling, and, of course, swift development of area railroads, "that noble aspiration of modern societies." In unpoetically blunt prose Cisneros warned: "Even political advantages accrue here—for it is clear to all that lack of useful work is the source of *empleomanía,* and thus of revolutions. The best means to nip them in the bud, stealing every pretext from rabble-rousers, is to provide southern dwellers the productive tasks of agriculture."[91]

Cisneros's program zeroed in on specific regional security issues and benefits, not unlike those of Peru's progressive officers of the 1960s. "Under economic aspects, does Peru need foreign grains, with such fertile valleys capable of astonishing fertility? As far as political aspects, would these Arequipeños always live agitated by revolutionary ideas and political passions—if they could draw from the land a cheap existence?"[92] Capital intellectuals and policymakers were clearly picking up on southern warnings and hopes. Too late this time, for the Prado regime fell the very next year to the southern-based (and pro-railway) uprising of Coronel José Balta. With his sensitivity to food production, Cisneros captured both angles—domestic subsistence and external autonomy—in future national "food security" doctrines.

That same year, Luis Benjamín Cisneros (brother of Luciano Benjamín) presented his lengthy 1868 message to congress on the evolving railroad mania, now encompassing nineteen lines. Cisneros's emergency plan: divert by 1872 all German guano profits directly into Meiggs's construction, something Balta's southerners would parrot (with Cisneros's blessings) in the grander form of the French Dreyfus contract. Cisneros reminded congress of the overarching mission of railways: "Especially to unite the Pacific shore with the trans-Andean regions, putting the *true Peru* into easy communication with the rest of the world."[93] This was a telling Limeño word choice, which Peru's great

90. Luciano Benjamín Cisneros, *Apuntes sobre la comisión al sur por el ex-ministro de beneficencia* (Lima, pam., 1868).

91. Luciano Cisneros, *Apuntes sobre el sur,* 50.

92. Luciano Cisneros, *Apuntes sobre el sur,* 50; see Víctor Villanueva, *El CAEM y la revolución de las fuerzas armadas* (Lima, 1974), for modern social developmentalism, still focused on southern agriculture (the giant Majes project) as security zone.

93. Luis Cisneros, *Memoria sobre ferrocarriles,* 37.

historian Jorge Basadre would put so evocatively in the enduring notion of "el Perú profundo"—Peru's imagined real country. Here Cisneros attributed Peru's national disparateness to being a nation that imports "so much" from abroad, the flip side of the emerging ideals of market integration. Even at this late date Cisneros conceived the projects as a form of "national exploration," as city bureaucrats, from the railroad surveys, encountered the social geography of their "lightly populated country." In this discovery mode Cisneros decreed distinctly domestic criteria for selecting rival routes: first, know where real villages thrive and commercial traffic already flows.[94]

In the most general analysis, railroad proposals mark a midpoint in a larger but dimly understood nineteenth-century genealogy of regional political awareness. In the late 1840s Peru's "regions" (principally the uppity south) became a linchpin in the new liberal hegemonies of the Castillan state and free trade. The passing of postindependence north-south trade wars, initial caudillistic separatism, and autarkic interior protectionism was seized by Lima liberals as an opportunity for national integration. Their political regime, however, remained shackled to the unitary designs of Gamarra's constitution of 1839.[95] But it was the guano revenue of the 1850s that rapidly resurrected Peru's de facto economic centralism—as the nearby monopoly's profits flowed overwhelmingly into the coffers of the Lima state, its merchants, its urban consolidation and rentier classes. Retired caudillos and motley regional talents converged on Peru's burgeoning capital, when, despite initial hopes, comparable opportunities long lagged in the provinces. By the mid 1850s regional rumblings had resurfaced against the new centralism of guano, though Arequipa stayed relatively dormant, erupting only at high points of liberal-conservative strife.

Pardo's *Estudios sobre Jauja* signaled a reactive and reformist rhetoric of decentralism, framed with a possible Lima hinterland in mind. In the 1860s Peru's national scientific-discovery literature, among other factors, deepened integrationist desires. (Perhaps most important was Raimondi's two-decade *obra*, culminating in *El Perú* of 1874.) On its own the economy of guano had spilled over only into littoral plantation fever. But it was the railroad proposals, written in their exaggerated regional scripts, and the revanchist political pressures around them that truly

94. Luis Cisneros, *Memoria sobre ferrocarriles*, 45.
95. Gootenberg, "North–South"; Jorge Basadre, *Elecciones y centralismo en el Perú: Apuntes para un esquema histórico* (Lima, 1980), ch. 1; Quiroz, *Deuda defraudada*, ch. 5, on 1850s unrest; Víctor Villanueva, *Ejército peruano: Del caudillaje anárquico al militarismo reformista* (Lima, 1973), chs. 1–2, on political migration.

rekindled and rallied a resurgent regional politics. At heart, Peru's generous railroad investments became a form of national redistribution of export wealth, posed in the name of regional developmentalism (irresistible in the provincial politics of congress) and amenable to farsighted Lima state makers for their long-term promise of political peace.[96] This seemed a safer form of national politics than the open centralist-decentralist warfare of the initial republic.

These developments moved apace into the 1870s—as rail construction itself became an active medium of national discovery (seen, for example, in the countless dispatches devoured in the Lima press); as national economic prospectors and census takers fanned out into the sierra (Fuentes was again a major figure); and as provincial notables aligned to meet the new agencies, demarcations, and possibilities of the slowly spreading central state. In murky ways, these shifts laid the groundwork for the drastic fiscal-political decentralization mounted by President Pardo in office, following the first truly national (and "electrifying") campaign in the republic's history.[97] As civilism tried to connect Peru in new fashions, such nationalism would reflect (as we will see) in the wider scope of economic thinkers of the 1870s (Copello and Petriconi), culminating in a proto-indigenista rejection of Lima of the 1880s (Esteves). Railroad pressures stood halfway, in the meeting of capital and regional minds.

Other reports and essays mimic and extend the pivotal themes. A splendid statement of regional "revindication" came together in an 1864 essay, "Los ferrocarriles y su influencia sobre la economía nacional."[98] The author, one "Tomás" Miles, posed the railroad mission as a reversal of provincial decline and grievances, a typical perception. He opened with stock nineteenth-century slogans: without "commerce and wealth, nations, communities, individuals regress"—that is, slide back into barbarism. The Incas, even the retrograde Spanish, had maintained superior interior links across the Andes. In the common conflation of science and industrialism, Miles wrote that "in the present age when other nations

96. Pennano, "Desarrollo regional y ferrocarriles," for pressures; for discovery works, consult countless examples in Carlos Moreyra y Paz Soldán, *Bibliografía regional peruana* (Lima, 1976).

97. MacEvoy, "Manuel Pardo," ch. 3; Basadre, *Historia* 4:1919–22; Mallon, *Defense of Community*, ch. 2, for incipient state expansion; we follow these larger themes in chs. 5 and 6, below.

98. Tomás Miles, "Los ferrocarriles y su influencia sobre la economía nacional," *El Tiempo* (Lima), 15 Oct. 1864; placed as a series, continuations were unfortunately not found.

are seeking the potent help of science and the motor force of steam, . . .
the arts, factories, and manufactures flourish."
What had happened in Peru? In this overview, Andean Peru, as late as
the 1840s, remained bustling in self-sufficiency, producing all varieties
of weavings, foodstuffs, and artifacts "spread out through all pueblos of
the interior." Now, after decades of guano, Peru was saddled under $16
million in imports; agriculture had "expired" under the weight of food
imports (some $5 million of these); outsiders were invading sierran
shops and occupations.[99] Railroads, in these commonsense understandings, were the solution for reversing harmful foreign trade patterns,
halting interior decline, revitalizing internal markets and exchange.

Few spoke of additional exports—which Peru (unlike, say, Mexico)
hardly needed anyway. The exceptions were overtures for short private
lines to specific haciendas or mines. Even in such obvious export zones as
southern Iquique—stark desert save for its mule-traversed nitrates and
copper oases—other themes beckoned. The southern impresario Carlos
Basadre, who publicized Tacna in the *Revista de Lima,* spoke in terms of
"national" material gains, for example, the "hundreds to be employed in
a national enterprise."[100] With a railway, an infectious "spirit of association" (J. M. Químper's 1850s liberal code word for capitalist enterprise)
would bury notions of Peruvians fit only for bureaucratic and military
posts, that "we display activity and energy only for ripping out the
entrails of our patria." In short, a railway would stem the chronic
"revolutions" of Tarapacá—an attractive enough proposal for Castilla's
own birthplace. The "Commerce of Iquique" appended the petition in
their own idiom of "moral and political" uplift; communications revealed "degrees of civilization." In Peru, pacifying sweet commerce rode
an iron horse.

Foreign railroad contractors spoke the same civilizing tongue, ampli-
fied for audience effect. Henry Meiggs's speeches at each subsequent
railway opening approached hyperbolic absurdities. At the extravagant
1871 inauguration ceremony for the long-sought Mollendo–Arequipa

99. Miles, "Ferrocarriles y su influencia."
100. Carlos Basadre, *El ferrocarril de Iquique: Observaciones jenerales sobre los benéficos
resultados que esta empresa producirá en favor de las industrias salitreras y minerales de la
provincia de Tarapacá* (Lima, pam., 1860), 22–24, "Informe del comercio de Iquique,"
which appends copy of Chevalier's "Curso de economía política," endorsing guarantees
for private construction. C. Basadre, "Apuntes sobre la provincia de Tacna," *Revista de
Lima* 6 (1862). Also, José Antonio García y García, *Ferro-carril de Eten a Montsefú,
Chiclayo, Lambayeque, Ferreñafe* (Lima, pam., 1867).

line, the Yankee Pizarro preached, among other theological injunctions, that "this railway converts the divine precept of work into sweet occupation." Hundreds—the cream of Limeño society—were shipped and railroaded in to imbibe speeches celebrating this arranged regional political marriage. Before enthralled crowds at the completion of Pardo's Lima–Jauja line, Meiggs anointed the railroad as "social revolution," "battering-ram of modern civilization, whose whistle will awaken the native race from slumber." Parroting Pardo, he adds, "Today, Peru as a nation has its beginning."[101]

Compared to such grandiosities, the ongoing congressional railroad debates of the 1860s stuck closer to practical matters, usually the intricacies of financing schemes and settling the scores of rivalrous regional pleas thrown at their feet. It is hard to find export mania in the congress, either. In 1862 proposal-smothered politicians confessed they could not "deny this kind of request," particularly, one might add, given their putative representation of the regions. A later commission on the Jauja project fell into the usual social hyperbole: "We are convinced that the only cause of public misery, the sole obstacle to progress in this society— in every sense—is the lack of facilities for transit and transport."[102] An October 1864 debate on funding the Arequipa line saw ultraliberal Silva Santisteban leading a noneconomic charge: as a revolutionary hotbed, Arequipa has proved too defensible. With rail links, the central government would always prevail (and save millions) by swiftly mobilizing and dispatching troops only when necessary—an excellent Porfirian twist on the southern security argument. In a prior debate Silva Santisteban had extolled the mines, woods, wheat, and coal of northern Cajamarca— especially those on his own family estancia—as good reason to expect a decided "influencia social" from a proposed line. No invisible hand here. Mainly, however, projects won priority on the basis of existing traffic (i.e., merchant reports) and signs of possible agricultural diversity, as clarified in one mid-1860s debate over a hastily drawn rival Tacna– Arequipa line.[103] The moral, material, and national expectations of railroads were never on the table: by now, these were too ingrained in the minds of Peruvian elites.

In sum, this foray suggests a larger national discourse around rail-

101. *Inauguración del ferro-carril de Mollendo a Arequipa por A. U. G.* (Lima, pam., 1871), 44; Stewart, *Meiggs*, 61–64, passim.

102. *Diarios de los debates: Congresos ordinarios, Cámara de Diputados* (Lima, 1862– 70), Oct., Nov. 1862.

103. *Diarios de debates*, Sept. 1863, Oct. 1864.

roads markedly similar to Pardo's in *Estudios sobre Jauja*. The awaited moral revolution of railroads symbolized diversification, regional rejuvenation, social peace, stability, and national, Indian, and market integrations. In political terms, such writings presented a form of fiscal regionalization of guano wealth, one easily digested by anxious Lima state builders. One last element—the mechanical imagination—was gaining ground over time, as exemplified in the thinking of one Héctor Davelouis.

Davelouis, a French chemist employed at the Lima mint, penned an 1863 memo analyzing the probable impact of roads and rails on a modernizing Huancavelica mine—the legendary colonial mercury source in disrepair since Spanish times.[104] In Davelouis's thinking, a railhead there would quickly displace onerous California quicksilver imports (thus raising silver output everywhere); lead imports would cease as well as Peru came to supply emerging industrial metals "to the entire globe"; woolens works would spring up around reviving mines. Peru, in short, would "join the ranks of great powers." "It is a principle universally admitted in political economy," averred Davelouis, "that from one industry springs others, so that an enlightened and prudent government should sustain one, even if unprofitable, to promote others." Huancavelica was of doubtful profitability, he confessed—as should have many of the rail pamphleteers. But all seemed drawn to what modern economists term positive "external economies" in the development process, or even the "unbalanced" stimuli to growth suggested by other theorists.[105] And they were mesmerized by something else.

One doubts that chemist Davelouis really read political economy; more likely, his multiplier effects came as natural to him as the clockwork mechanisms of the Newtonian universe. Moreover, his costly rail scheme was woven in his mind with broader technification notions. The state-run Huancavelica mine would become "a true school, a stimulating fount for all who are idle." Literally, Davelouis's railway would lead to a new school of mines. This idea of public works as technical tutelage would reach its apogee in the manic building spree of the Balta regime. In one presidential address of 1870 Balta sold his shaky, debt-run pro-

104. Héctor Davelouis, *Informe que el suscribe eleva a la consideración de los poderes legislativo y ejecutivo sobre el estado actual de la minería en el Perú* (Lima, pam., 1863), 7–9, 15.

105. Davelouis, *Informe sobre minería*, 15. See Tibor Scitovsky, "Two Concepts of External Economies," *Journal of Political Economy* 52 (1954): 143–52; Albert O. Hirschman, *The Strategy of Economic Development* (New York, 1958).

gram as "the happy dream of the people—it mobilizes work, stems joblessness, creates industry, engenders the spirit of business, renews credit, and is the root of public tranquillity." The goal: "convert the entire republic into an immense workshop [*taller*], in which we construct the fortunate future of the nation."[106] This was technification from above writ large.

In the 1840s free-traders had peddled commerce as the multiplicative mother of invention; by the 1860s, however, it was European science and industry sweeping the imagination of Peruvian elites. This was a mentality of technicians and tinkerers suddenly loaded with cash. In representations at least, the railroad arose in the Andes as a technical messiah, as a gargantuan, positivist Christ child. Railroads would magically resurrect, convert, and tutor Peru in the scientific marvels and capacities of the nineteenth century. It implied utopian social engineering, too, that uncanny power to "always" resolve "all" social problems at hand. Clearly, much of this hyperbole was the product of sales pitches, political and otherwise, but it was also a larger cultural movement of Westernizing elites. (The next chapter looks at technification from below, when popular participatory voices also embraced these scientistic ideals.)

The high priests, or missionaries, of this movement were the dozens of European engineers, surveyors, geographers, advisers, archaeologists, scientists, and machine tenders who swarmed to Peru after midcentury. Some—eclectics such as Malinowski, Blume, Nystrom, Pickering, Raimondi, and Davelouis—continued to sink roots. Their flock multiplied—Thorndike, Sada, Duval, Backus, Bibinski, Jaworski, Lembcke, Middendorf, Wiseman, Johnston, Martinet, Habich, and so on—as Meiggs's empire expanded in earnest after 1869. Even Garmendia lured in European technicians to run his Lucre woolens mill. The foreign emissaries of science had first appeared in the midcentury Andean and Amazonian exploration-travel literatures. In their "capitalist vanguard" eyes, technology-poor Peru became Midas-like: in Raimondi's words, that "beggar sitting on a mountain of gold." Men like Pardo transculturated these ideas, producing their own Peru—just in time for the arrival of the *técnicos* in the 1860s.[107] These men brought with them not

106. P. Ugarte and E. San Cristóval, comps., *Mensajes de los presidentes del Perú* (Lima, 1943), vol. 1, 28 July 1870; and messages of Pardo years (1872–1876).

107. Stewart, *Meiggs*, is among best sources; see Pratt, *Imperial Eyes*, for "transculturation" of science notions.

so much economic ideas (of the political economists) but can-do technical capacities and optimistic transforming attitudes that Peruvian officials were eager to adopt. A few, notably Malinowski and Raimondi, as political refugees of 1848, surely brought a distinctive social baggage to their jobs. Some, Meiggs included, were rumored "Israelitas"—a secret source, no doubt, of their biblical discourse and prophetic inspiration. Often the esteemed engineers became promptly confused with economic experts as well: how else to explain Malinowski's blueprint for Peru's monetary reform of 1862, or Blume's influential ideas for banking reform in the mid 1870s?[108]

    To be sure, Peru had long cultivated its own modest national scientific tradition, exemplified in the late-colonial spirit of Hipólito Unánue; the republican life and works of the geologist and naturalist Mariano Eduardo de Rivero; the chemists' debates in the 1840s over the uses and nature of guano (was it animal, mineral, or vegetable?); the inventive naval engineers of the new Bellavista foundry; or guano-age tinker-thinkers such as the clockmaker Pedro Ruiz Gallo or the inventor José Arnaldo Márquez (discussed below).[109] But in contrast to other Latin American republics—Colombia is the best-known case—few Peruvians traveled abroad to imbibe modern science and technology in the nineteenth century. European literary or political sojourns were the norm. Instead, science landed in Peru, especially during the climactic railroading years of 1869–1872, in the persons of technological advisers and mechanical carpetbaggers; they naturalized Western science, scouted the country (with a distinct lens from former commercially minded travelers), or literally set up shop, including small industries. Under such mentors Peruvian students soon eagerly learned on the job. As with several thousand other white, middle-class immigrants of the late guano age, fair skin and European mind-sets favored their easy entry into the Lima elite. Many engineers naturalized into patriotic Peruvians whose names still grace Lima high-school academies. (For example, Malinowski, in addition to fiscal services, also played a hero's role designing

    108. Meiggs was one rumored Anglo "marrano," for having helped establish the Jewish cemetery in Lima! E. M. [Malinowski], *La moneda en el Perú* (Lima, pam., 1859); Federico Blume, *Observaciones sobre el proyecto del banco central* (Lima, pam., 1876); Luis Alberto Sánchez, *Historia de una industria peruana: Cervecería Backus y Johnston S.A.* (Lima, 1978), chs. 1–2, analyzes an engineer's industrial role (and finance roles, 55).
    109. Mariano Eduardo de Rivero, *Colección de memorias científicas e industriales* (1857), 2 vols., for some idea of his eclectic career; for incipient liberal interest, see "Ventajas de la tecnología," *Progreso*, 8 Aug. 1849; ch. 5, below, for Márquez. We still need a history of republican science.

Callao's successful defenses against Spanish invasion in 1866; Blume, besides monetary policy, concocted his legendary anti-Chilean submarine for national service in 1879.)[110] Their lineage and cult affected the establishment of mechanical sciences in Peruvian universities, the creation of Pardo's agricultural normal school, experimental farms, the faculty of political science and administration, the census bureau, the school of mines, artisan schools of arts, and *Cuerpo civil de ingenieros*—institutions of the 1870s that best embodied civilismo's vision of building a "practical republic." Pardo imported a coterie of Poles to start his impressive network of normal schools, cornerstone of civilist educational expansionism. The Cuerpo de Ingenieros, headed by another Pole, "Eduardo Juan" de Habich, emerged, after a slow start, as civilismo's most lasting achievement. With more than three hundred graduates in the decades after 1880, engineers became the country's largest new professional class, erecting Piérola's 1895 Ministry of Development (*Fomento*), spearheaded by the next civilista president of Peru (López de Romaña, 1899–1904).[111] New-style educational nationalists emerged, vaunting the sciences in national reform: "The glories that the sciences are producing only exist in England," argued impetuous Mariano Amézaga, "but among us, scions of Spaniards, only politics! Science does not possess a patria, and we have to use it to scale the heights of civilization."[112] By the 1870s technological determinism came wrapped in the social evolutionism of Comtean positivism.

A remarkable sign of this naturalizing mechanic mentality appears in the founding pamphlet of the private 1871 Asociación de Ingenieros del Perú. Here technology has acquired unmistakable Peruvian accents.[113]

110. Safford, *Ideal of Practical* (Colombia), esp. ch. 4; Basadre, *Historia* 4:1583; 5:2084, 2103, 2473; Pardo's push to "middle-class" immigration seen in ch. 5, below. Recall that in 1856 Malinowski ("Memoria") called for an engineering academy; on his commission were the formidable liberal Gálvez brothers.

111. Macera, "Historia económica como ciencia," 50–51; Basadre, *Historia* 5:2099, 2103, 2121, 2125–27; Pike, *Modern History,* 186–90; Cuerpo de Ingenieros, *Anales del cuerpo de ingenieros; Anales universitarios del Perú* (Lima, 1862–69).

112. Mariano Amézaga, *Problemas de la educación peruana,* A. Tauro, comp. (Lima, 1952), 8, and "La facultad de ciencia," sec. 20; among earliest critiques was Manuel Pardo, "Sociedad de beneficencia de Lima," *Revista de Lima* (1860), in López, *Pardo,* 405–11; we follow Amézaga populist group in ch. 5, below.

113. *La asociación de ingenieros del Perú* (Lima, pam., 1871), 4; the frontispiece displays a seductive muse of "science and progress," who reappears in similar publications; I suspect the group centered around Felipe Arancibia, national engineer active in founding of civilismo (MacEvoy, "Manuel Pardo," 255).

"Industry and work," the manifesto begins, "are the branches that foster the life of societies"; science explains how "nineteenth-century civilization has surpassed all others." Similar grandiose claims follow. The application of science in Peru, however, was long hampered by "political fratricide." But with peace and guano had arrived this "unique moment of tranquility—and progress in all directions is being woven from below, in a web of iron."[114] Their transparent rail metaphor seems hardly accidental. Bit by bit, the quality of new scientific methods in mining and agriculture was improving. In the closing section, "What Is Left to Do," the association's aim, their engineering vision, expands—unconstrained by the ordinary scarcities and sobrieties of economics.

Like the arguments of Nystrom and fellow tinkerers, this was a call for science to nationalize—by doing—and by placing science at the heart of the economic process. "Progress and industry have not been represented among us because it has been purchased abroad to simply apply here." In short, Peru had eluded true technological development by importing it wholesale, a perspective shared in more recent agendas of technological autonomy and appropriate technology. The association's solution was direct enough: "Now, it seems, is the time to consider fabricating ourselves what should supply our necessities . . . , *fábrica nacional,* adequate to our own uses."[115] Their projects varied but leaned toward domestic capital goods production: "Railroads, bridges, docks, boats, machinery, we could easily construct, if we dedicated ourselves to try our work. It should not be said we are at the beginners stage; aptitudes we have, plus energy and sufficient knowledge. One day we must stop living in this odious wardship; we must make industry attain a national character."[116] This recommendation contrasts with Pardo's simpler import-substitution ideal and in some sense was timely. By the early 1870s capital goods (for railways, mechanizing plantations, mines, and small shops) had risen perceptibly in the Peruvian import bill. Some engineers, as railroads laid them off in the crisis of the mid 1870s, would drift into establishing machine shops, foundries, and pioneer factories.[117]

114. *Asociación de ingenieros,* 11.
115. *Asociación de ingenieros,* 20.
116. *Asociación de ingenieros,* 20.
117. William S. Bollinger, "The Rise of United States Influence in the Peruvian Economy, 1869–1921" (M.A. thesis, UCLA, 1971), ch. 1; Grieve, "Artes mecánicas"; Bonilla, "Expansión comercial británica," table 3. During 1870s, capital goods climbed to 8–10 percent of imports, higher in U.S. bill. We explore 1870s "microindustrialism" in ch. 5, below.

Beyond their banner of nationalist capacity (that "odious wardship"), Peru's engineers insisted on its clear economic sense: "We have exported huge capitals in exchange for industry and progress, and these capitals could have been employed in the country with greater profit and economy." The society spelled out its objectives: "promote the fabrication of all types of machinery, adaptable to agriculture, mining, and manufactures," as well as launch a private technical academy, a large model machine shop, and sundry little projects.[118]

Lima's engineering association left little visible imprint in the 1870s in its hope of capturing and transforming a modest share of Peru's huge public works' expenditures. Nor did their thinking approach the form of peoples' science embodied in the era's coeval craft renaissance, explored below. However, the association faithfully reflected novel mentalities of technical nationalism and the improving "civilizing" mission at the very heart of Peru's railway mania.

A few closing comments are needed on the ultimate outcomes of the subsequent Peruvian railroad boom. How do such ideas tally with the results or with lasting images in Peru's political imagination? This analysis surely suggests that Peruvian leaders had more in mind than go-for-broke export promotion when they embarked on the massive railroad projects of the 1860s and 1870s. How to balance such visions with the ultimate cost of the scheme, which ended so disastrously for Peru, is another question. One wonders about laying blame exclusively on the civilist elite (much less on narrow ideas), for many factors were at work. Paradoxically, the breadth of driving ideas makes a more likely suspect.

One factor was the choice of the flamboyant Yankee Meiggs as chief contractor, who, along with Dreyfus, was charged with spawning the subsequent financial imbroglios. But Meiggs's unrestrained building activity (and by extension, Peru's hefty foreign debt of £35 million) collided head-on with the London market's panic in the early 1870s and with the ensuing world depression. Essentially unforeseeable events, these were the proximate cause of Peru's bankruptcy in 1875, which, among other consequences, doomed most of the railways underway.[119] Clearly, railroads had always been (in Hunt's modest phrase) a "risky overinvestment" in one project. Still, this gamble should not negate the

118. *Asociación de ingenieros,* 25–27; see Adas, *Machines as Measure of Men,* 221–30, for comparable railroad (mental) associations elsewhere.

119. Maiguashca, "Reinterpretation of Guano Age," ch. 5; Marichal, *Century of Debt Crises,* ch. 4; Bonilla, *Guano y burguesía,* for one dismal evaluation.

fact that large-scale public works were among the few effective means for Peru to benefit directly from guano wealth. State spending was one rational way (given unmanageable exchange rates) to keep export income working in domestic markets.[120]

Historians often fault widespread elite corruption, extravagance, and ineptitude (not to mention foreign perfidy) as the fatal blows to Peru's public works program. But rarely can a school of scandals explain much of scale; even in today's Latin America, corruption remains a convenient factional shibboleth, with, in relative terms, modest economic costs. For the guano age, this ad hominem imagery is traceable to Fernando Casós's caustic anti-oligarchic (and highly political) 1870s novel *Los hombres de bien*—which also exemplifies the critical bent of prominent liberal writers.[121]

Swindlers and dreamers no doubt had their day, but impersonal forces and compelling ideals were also at work. At base, Peru faced the same difficulties suffered by all Latin American countries in railroad development—and even more so. Because of extraordinary geographic challenges and an extremist strategy of building ahead of demand, Peru's railroads, most notably the line way up to Jauja, became mile for mile the most expensive in history. Meiggs was a talented promoter, and as engineering (and touristic) feats his vertiginous railroads remain a marvel. But as critics point out, these were basically "railroads to nowhere," a lunatic passage to "the moon." As such, they took years to turn profits and stimulate the sorts of commercial payoffs and development imagined at the onset; some never did. The first lines of the mid 1870s were clearly operating at a loss and came quickly under fire. Somehow the uninspiring mules survived the competition![122]

The why of this dismal economic result remains obscure, even in a strict accounting sense. Financial tomfoolery aside, Peru's losses suggest some powerful noneconomic motives at work. On the face of it, the notion of modern communications appears rational enough—though Candide-like extreme rationalities often run the risk of lunacy. Railroad unprofitability is not explicable by simply projecting a Fogelesque North

120. Hunt, "Growth and Guano," 107–9.

121. Stewart, *Meiggs*, passim; see Basadre, *Historia* 5:2153–56, on Casós's impact (prominent, with anticivilist González Prada, in Stewart's old formulation).

122. Stewart, *Meiggs;* Bonilla, *Guano y burguesía,* ch. 1; Miller, "Railways and Economic Development," only economic study; Juan Ignacio Elguera, *Memoria presentada por el ministro de hacienda y comercio a la legislatura ordinaria de 1874* (Lima, pam., 1874), for early recognition.

American thesis onto Peru (the idea that nineteenth-century railroads represented unnecessary social investments). It was precisely in underdeveloped mountainous regions, as John Coatsworth persuasively proved for Mexico, that the railroads' social savings and boost to productivity were unmistakable, since no alternative transport innovations sufficed. This is not to mention the intrinsic difficulties, anywhere, in measuring the many external economies of transport.[123] For Peru, clarifying profitability issues gets even thornier. The physical devastation, financial collapse, political turmoil, and two-decade depression that followed the Pacific War made all types of economic expansion improbable, directly impinging on both the forward impact and book profitability of the railways. By the time Peru fully recovered, the automotive truck was becoming an efficient alternative and effectively finished national integration during Leguía's road-building drive of the 1920s. Nor are the sociological counterfactuals—the notion that Andean "feudalisms" somehow blocked the dynamic impulse of railroads—very convincing ground, since most recent studies of rural society reject that immobile image of Andean social structure.[124]

Above all, the evidence of railway unprofitability itself belies notions that railroads were born from monomaniacal desires to capitalize on Peru's potential export resources. In that scenario Peru would have built railroads to somewhere, as so clearly occurred in profiting Mexico, Argentina, and Brazil. The major factor behind Peru's fiasco—and global default—was that railroads did not link as yet economically significant zones and thus did not bring new exports into line, dilemmas recognized at the time from London to Lima and in Meiggs's last-ditch exporting schemes. Silver, for example, Peru's most marketable Andean export, hardly required railways to prosper, as it was such a high-value-to-weight item.[125]

123. John. H. Coatsworth, *Growth Against Development: The Economic Impact of Railroads in Porfirian Mexico* (De Kalb, 1981).

124. On roads, see Fiona Wilson, "The Conflict Between Indigenous and Immigrant Commercial Systems in the Peruvian Central Sierra, 1900–1940," in R. Miller, ed., *Region and Class in Modern Peruvian History* (Liverpool, 1987), 125–61; or Mallon, *Defense of Community*, chs. 6–9. Gootenberg, "Population and Ethnicity," for new rural research; Bonilla, *Guano y burguesía*, epilogue, for thesis of precapitalist block and civilist failure; only Bollinger, "Bourgeois Revolution," 32–33, suggests a successful forging of rural proletariat.

125. Julio Revilla, "Loan Frenzy and Sovereign Default: The Case of Peru in the Nineteenth Century" (typescript, Boston, 1990), concurs in economics; William Clarke, *Peru and Its Creditors* (London, 1877), 61–71, for Meiggs's critique of "beautiful theo-

In Peru other considerations—noneconomic idealisms of regional integration, diversifying development, social and civil stability, technological tutelage—were brewing in the minds of those who directed the lines into obscure and primitive corners of the country. Ultimately, railways might best be judged by those idealist standards, even if problematic on their own integrationist terms. Such utopias rarely run on short-term accounts. Utopias are always "nowhere."

With a long lag, in some zones, Peru's railroads did stir commercial life and even a degree of capitalist modernization, as some have shown precisely for Junín. But such gains were obscured by other unintended outcomes, well past the disasters of the Pacific War. Because of Peru's massive default, the finished trunk lines became largely foreign-owned after 1890 (as part of the Grace contract settling Peru's delinquent external debt). Peru thus lost the one concrete legacy of its guano age, a nationally owned communications network.[126] Subsequently, in the early twentieth century, foreign firms manipulated the lines to advance their new export enclaves, as occurred quite scandalously with the U.S. Cerro de Pasco Copper Corporation in Junín. Strong nationalist sentiments ensued against the railroads in general, now clearly associated with imperial enclaves; among other factors, this politics colored lasting perceptions of their origins. A dispassionate history of Peruvian railroads has yet to be written. But post facto reasoning from painful legacies of the civilist project barely conveys the original intent of thinkers such as Pardo.

Luis Benjamín Cisneros: Neoprotectionist Turn

For Pardo and countless rail pamphleteers, rural manufacturing was imagined as one beneficial, if natural, side effect of national

---

ries" and own efforts to redirect rails to Cerro exports; by then, Meiggs felt guano had hurt Peruvian productivity; Topik, *Political Economy of Brazilian State,* ch. 4, on integrative and political aims of even coffee railroads.

126. See Samuel Velarde, *Deuda externa y ferrocarriles del Perú* (Lima, pam., 1886); Rory Miller, "The Making of the Grace Contract: British Bondholders and the Peruvian Government, 1885–1890," *JLAS* 8 (1976): 73–100; Miller, "Railways and Economic Development"; Mallon, *Defense of Community,* ch. 5; Peter Klarén, *Modernization, Dislocation, and Aprismo: Origins of the Peruvian Aprista Party, 1870–1932* (Austin, 1973), 71, 125. By 1915 rail renationalization became a formal anti-imperialist (and later APRA) cause, yet even free-traders (like Gubbins in 1900) attacked foreign transport monopoly.

integration and a productive use of guano. A more concerted, intricate, and striking industrial proposal appeared in 1866: Luis Benjamín Cisneros's landmark study, *Ensayo sobre varias cuestiones económicas del Perú*, usually heard as a clarion call for fiscal reform.[127] Apart from its profound impact on the fiscal restructurings of the late guano age, Cisneros's 150-page book marks three innovations in Peruvian diversification thought. First, in a novel "structural" analysis of Peru's rapidly gathering crisis, Cisneros brings the state back in—to save it from its own self-destruction. This was a broad plan for forced and accelerated diversification, which could no longer be left to the magic of markets or railways. Second, Cisneros does not blithely pass over thorny issues of consumption trade-offs or tariffs; he critically reformulates protection as a key component in Peru's diversifying development. Third, Cisneros departs by championing manufacturing as a direct solution to Peru's impending crisis, backed by a new and wider set of institutional supports. In short, the *Ensayo sobre cuestiones económicas* was an unmistakable work of the external crisis, whose urgency had become unmistakably clear in the six years since Pardo's warnings. Though this was still not as comprehensive (or political) a response as would come in the 1870s, Cisneros came to critical thought through local dilemmas, apparent in the very form of his neoprotectionist argument. Why did Cisneros push to overhaul Peruvian fiscality? Was his the narrow technocratic answer usually supposed?

A well-traveled and well-versed intellectual and activist, Luis Benjamín Cisneros and Pardo shared remarkably similar careers, social standings, and legacies. Through most of their lives the two budding statesmen relished close personal and business ties, ties finally cut by their political differences of the 1870s. Born in the late 1830s, as a youth Cisneros (like Fuentes) absorbed the last burst of artisan politics; his brother served as legal adviser to the Lima guilds in their troubled year of 1850. By the late 1850s Cisneros had emerged as a leading civil reform thinker, first disseminating his ideas from the platform of the *Revista de Lima*. A lawyer, senator, and European-based diplomat (his 1866 book was written and published while he was commercial attaché in France), Cisneros went on to become a leading civil ideologue, best known for his contributions to constitutional theory. He also pioneered the romantic novel in Peru: *Julia* (1860), a scathing critique of Limeño

127. Luis Benjamín Cisneros, *Ensayo sobre varias cuestiones económicas del Perú* (Le Havre, 1866), rpt. in Cisneros, *Obras completas* 3:16–140.

materialism, published serially in the *Revista de Lima,* and *Edgardo* (1864), an ambivalent portrait of the volatile caudillo figure.[128]

Cisneros was also a wealthy banker, among the most active stockholders in Pardo's Banco del Perú and in the late 1870s director of the prominent Banco de Lima. With Pardo, Cisneros crusaded for railroads and public works, heading up the emergency 1867 commission that put Peruvian railway construction on the fast track, as part of the civil team around the Prado regime.[129] Only in the 1870s did Cisneros and Pardo part political ways, though not so far as to prevent Cisneros from serving as vice president for Pardo in 1872 and on prestigious educational posts. The dissension began in 1869 with Cisneros's outspoken role as principal national defender of the Dreyfus contract—which Pardo hammered against as spokesman for spurned national guano contractors. (To end the controversy, the regime finally ignored the supreme court's verdict against Dreyfus.) Apart from being one of Dreyfus's main Peruvian business partners, Cisneros hoped that the European contract would help rationalize the state (by distancing it from the demands, frauds, and bunglings of national financiers) and thus best expand funding for the development projects all parties were banking on. It was a stance consistent with Cisneros's fiscal reforming zeal, and posed in equally patriotic terms. Later Cisneros embraced the oppositional liberalism of Piérola, leading congressional charges of "socialism" against Pardo's presidential banking regulation.[130] One of Meiggs's closest associates and friends in Lima, Cisneros in the late 1870s became founder and director of the Peruvian Nitrate Company—Pardo's state-sponsored corporation for extending the fertilizer bonanza. Cisneros's entrepreneurial and political life, obviously, took many turns. Following the Pacific War, Cisneros, like his poet brother Luciano, retreated into his lifelong literary pursuits.

Economic history remembers Luis Benjamín Cisneros best as archi-

---

128. Basadre, *Historia* 3:1742, 1886–87; *Revista de Lima* (1860); *Comercio,* 20 Aug. 1850, for brother's artisan involvement (defending against Echenique merchant contracts); *Edgardo,* in Basadre's reading, was a call for "peace, order, and social and national solidarity."

129. Milla Batres, *Diccionario biográfico,* vol. 1; Camprubí, *Historia de bancos,* 188, 208, 249, 289, 346; Cisneros, *Memoria sobre ferrocarriles* (1868).

130. See Luis B. Cisneros, "El negociado Dreyfus 1870," in *Obras completas* 3:187–227; and later (1874) policy critique of his "joven y ilustrado presidente" in "¿Que no hay remedio?" 3:358–69. *Diario de debates,* Sept. 1876 (and 1870 for Dreyfus controversy); Stewart, *Meiggs.* Ulloa, *Piérola,* is about the only modern book to defend Piérola strategy; but Hunt, "Growth and Guano," 66–67, shows that at the least Peru even raised its profit margins with Dreyfus—to over 100 percent, excluding unknown costs.

tect of Peru's fiscal reform of the 1860s—a Limantour of the guano age. In Peru, unlike *científico* Mexico, lucid and stringent budgets were not drawn to entice foreign capital in a concerted bid for a stable international "investment climate." The country enjoyed an ample investible export surplus and copious capital flows—from 11 to 20 percent of national product in recent estimates.[131] Peru's dilemma was how best to manage, absorb, and invest its available funds.

Along this line, scholarship tracing the reform movement that grew into civilismo points to Cisneros, on a par with Pardo, as its ideological mentor. The *Ensayo sobre cuestiones económicas* served as a precision model for Peru's fiscal and budgetary reforms of the late 1860s. Exploiting the praetorian powers and platform of the anti-Castilla Prado regime of 1866–1867, Cisneros and Pardo began the task of rebuilding Peru's domestic tax systems (liberally and foolishly abandoned in the mid 1850s) and of putting an end to the chaotic guano consignment systems.[132] The general thrust of export and budgetary reformism, promulgated in varied ways by varied regimes over the next decade, was to transform guano into a strictly managed and predictable regularized income, with significant portions earmarked for diversion into public works. The short-term goal was to reverse the fiscal deficits, overseas stopgap borrowing, and financial disarray that had become so destabilizing during the mid-1860s conflict with Spain. Coronel Prado's project was joined by virtually every leading liberal of the age (the two Gálvezes, Lissón, Pacheco, Casós, Químper, and Tejeda among them), despite their militarist aversions; such advisers added a pinch of liberal constitutionalism to the caldron of top-down economic reform. Cisneros's stamp also marked the emergency measures of the Balta-Piérola years (1869–1872); this regime, with its burgeoning ties to Dreyfus and European developmental loans, has been too easily depicted as a clearcut example of *entreguismo*. Piérola's movement, too, encompassed important reforming elements, as seen in Cisneros's many defenses.[133]

131. Hunt, "Growth and Guano," 93–96. Peru's capital surplus (apart from absorption problems) is one reason why Peruvian thinkers and statesmen prove far more flexible with and critical of foreign capital and investment, than say, Mexican counterparts. On Mexican climate, see Alexander Dawson, "Mexico—The Treasure House of the World: Perceptions of Economic Development in Porfirian Mexico" (M.A. thesis, University of Calgary, 1991).
132. Maiguashca, "Reinterpretation of Guano Age," chs. 3–4—which integrates Cisneros's literary and fiscal concerns.
133. On Piérola and Dreyfus, see n. 130, above. See fine analysis of Prado group in Basadre, *Historia*, vol. 4, chs. 63–64; critical historiography in Bonilla, *Guano y burguesía*,

From 1872 to 1876 Cisneros's fiscal blueprint continued to serve Pardo's party, the new civil militants of budget organization and retrenchment. And just as in Pardo's case, Cisneros's original developmental visions remain lost, perhaps in his flurry of public activism and positions. Historians charge that liberal fiscal reform, ignoring the country's structural and social flaws, was as escapist a reform valve as were the civilist railroads. But what was, to Cisneros, the grand purpose of Peruvian fiscal reform? What might a firm hand on export monies achieve?

On the surface, the *Ensayo sobre cuestiones económicas* reads as another call to avert the looming commercial and fiscal crisis of guano exhaustion. Cisneros dedicates his package to Prado's closest circle of advisers—notably the beleaguered "Secretary of Hacienda and Commerce, Manuel Pardo"—with hopes of winning their immediate approval.[134] It seems neither the ultraliberal nor "neomercantilist" plan variously depicted by historians. It proved a workable policy document—and much more than that in its imagined development.

Characteristically, the *Ensayo sobre cuestiones económicas* opens with a sweeping diagnosis of Peru's commercial boom since the 1850s. It was guano alone that has allowed Peru's two-decade binge of consumption, as most other exports faded. Tapping his own sources and methods, Cisneros reestimates the true Peruvian import bill in 1865 at more than $34 million—double the official figure (of $15 million) and probably an exaggeration. Flattering reader sensitivities, Cisneros takes pains to laud the "progress" worked by this commercial revolution. Guano affluence revived Peru's languishing coastal cities and heralded a new capitalist spirit, remarkably so among merchant activities joined to world trade.[135] But now, in 1866, this whole style of development has reached its limits—and directly imperils the Peruvian future.

Recalling Pardo's rhetorical query, Cisneros asks, "What will happen when guano is depleted or artificial fertilizers made?" (The latter prob-

---

54, ("[Pardo] y más tarde Luis Benjamín Cisneros, son los principales inspiradores de la política económica de la emergente elite económica"), 70–116; Cotler, *Clases, estado y nación*, 104–7; Yepes, *Peru 1820–1920*, 68–75.

134. Cisneros, *Ensayo sobre cuestiones económicas*, dedication, 30. The "neomercantilist" label is (liberal-orthodox) Romero's, "Perú" (310–12), seeing Cisneros as regression from Pardo liberal modernism—a "grosería mercantalismo monetista," obsessed with colonial-style "trade balance." This, too, is a reading corrected by analyzing Cisneros's developmental and budgetary aims.

135. Cisneros, *Ensayo sobre cuestiones económicas*, 1–27; presumably, Cisneros's insider trade data came from his duties as commercial agent in France.

lem was already emerging in Europe.) All of Peru's midcentury advance "is due to this accidental wealth of the fertilizer of Chincha"—framing guano as the most artificial of Peruvian "industries." As his critique shifts into full gear, Cisneros dubs commercial prosperity as merely superficial: "If we employed all the productive forces of Peru to buy foreign manufactures, as some insist, just how will our cities continue to progress?"[136]

For a fiscal thinker, Cisneros's boldest move was, in fact, to shift discussion away from technical fiscal recipes to a deeper commercial and structural analysis of balance-of-payment dilemmas. Peru's import mania was the root cause of the country's external crisis. So far, Cisneros cogently points out, only $6 million of guano revenues go to meet foreign debt payments, despite the bad publicity around them. Current budget deficits are even less demanding. What needs much sharper attention, then, are the many millions more—Cisneros's $34 million—needlessly "wasted" on unproductive imports. If Peru wants government to underwrite railways and nationhood, then it must first address those losses. Peru's national dilemma is not how to pay off debts and consume French luxuries but how to reduce drastically its commercial dependence. Cisneros's answer is a rigorous and permanent cut in imports.

Cisneros's critical eye on guano consumption was not so uncommon by the mid 1860s, and it was not the prerogative only of miserly and jealous artisans. For example, Carlos Lissón (a leading liberal educator, Prado adviser, pioneer sociologist, and later civilista founder) wrote scathingly of fictive prosperities in his 1865 *La república en el Perú,* a social study steeped in the anti-Spanish nationalism of the day. Lissón decried Peru as a truly "poor" country, dangerously deluded by illusions of export wealth, lacking in true and progressive entrepreneurs. Its "Indians, agriculturalists, mestizos, tailors, and shoemakers" are all choking in the lap of others' passive luxury. More generally still: "A country's wealth is not some easy deduction of its soil. That can be very poor and its inhabitants very rich, and vice versa. Just look what happened to Potosí and Pasco. What will be left in time from guano?"[137] Instead of a "lottery" of giveaways to the country's "nobility," Lissón calls on Peru to

136. Cisneros, *Ensayo sobre cuestiones económicas,* 26, 29–31.

137. Carlos Lissón, *La república en el Perú y la cuestión peruano-española* (Lima, 1865), 73–74; we explore anti-Spanish nationalism with artisan politics in ch. 5, below. Lissón, a volunteer artisan teacher, explores issues further as positivist in Carlos Lissón, *Breves apuntes sobre la sociología del Perú en 1886* (Lima, 1887), 69. Basadre, *Historia,* vol. 3, chs. 52–54. Cisneros shared in anti-imperial movements: see poem "Al Perú" (1864), rpt. in *Obras completas* 1:121–22.

educate and produce a productive citizenry. Cisneros codified these growing misgivings into a concerted government program. Pardo had evinced idealisms of productive diversification; Cisneros demanded that the state make them happen.

The core chapter 2 of *Ensayo sobre cuestiones económicas* is titled simply "Industria"—that nineteenth-century catchall term for all kinds of productive work. Here Cisneros covers the usual array of formulas to foster Peruvian "industry": stable public peace, less urban welfare *empleomanía,* irrigation schemes (like his brother's for the south), public investment banks, scientific schools and experimental stations for regional agriculture and mining, chartered companies for resource development—and, of course, Andean railroads. Regarding the latter, Cisneros proves as devoted to the creed as Pardo: "The wealth that railways are destined to create and develop in the interior of the republic will be sudden and beyond our wildest expectations."[138] Yet Cisneros knows that mere faith in the good works of railways no longer suffices.

Along with these projects runs a retrospect critique of letting commercial progress run an unguided course. Cisneros's synopsis of the first half of the export age could have awakened Peru's Casanovas from oblivion: "And had we devoted the huge revenues of guano to create new industries, to foster those we have, or to help exploit the overflowing commercial resources that nature gave us—in this way, we would have opened in the country a thousand spheres of industrial activity, in which every man and family would have found their elements of subsistence—and future."[139] To Cisneros, undisciplined commercial growth was not just behind Peru's macroeconomic instabilities but, as artisans would have it, was the root of the country's unsettling social problem. The pervading social theme of *Ensayo sobre cuestiones económicas* is this struggle against "empleo-necesidad." Cisneros invents this term for bloated public employment to emphasize diminishing possibilities in the private sector—idleness caused by Peru's rentier economy.[140] Public employment not only drains the national treasury but is politically

138. Cisneros, *Ensayo sobre cuestiones económicas,* ch. 11, "Industria," 29–37 (quote p. 34). Cisneros's *Memoria sobre ferrocarriles* (1868), discussed above, was largely technical, not developmental, study.

139. Cisneros, *Ensayo sobre cuestiones económicas,* 31.

140. Maiguascha, "Reinterpretation of Guano Age," chs. 3–5, analyzes this theme. Hunt, "Growth and Guano," 80–83, however, dispels the notion of public employment itself as a wasteful cause; not only were real salaries and expenditures decreasing, but much of this spending was "developmental"—in education, health, public works.

explosive for the state, the calling card of restless caudillos and clients everywhere. *Industria* for the masses is the sole guarantee of civil rule, regional peace, and development, by now a ubiquitous standard. Paradoxically, in Cisneros, building an autonomous and stable state—his ultimate aim—requires its productive activism.

Having isolated Peru's social and fiscal quandary, the *Ensayo sobre cuestiones económicas* abruptly turns to more specific "Industrias de fábrica y manufactura." Over the next pages Cisneros presents, as the centerpiece of reform, a plan for state-sponsored industrialization—or as he puts it, "the road to an industrial future." The journey begins, however, by turning back to Peruvian historical experience. Like others, Cisneros knows his European theory (the book was composed and published there), but he grounds his analysis in Peruvian realities, in what we would now consider a structural argument. The shortage of native manufacturers was driving Peru's import overload—reaching the breaking point with the 1860s hike in world industrial prices. The roots go deeper, however, into the historic market orientations of would-be native import substituters.

Everyone knows that the scarcity or, better put, total absence of factories and grand manufactories has made it necessary for Peru to import virtually everything needed for a comfortable life. Sure, our artisans work with some regularity on shoes, clothing, and furniture. But naturally they have never achieved the level of perfection of the Europeans—which is why the majority of such goods consumed throughout the republic fare from foreign lands.[141]

Quoting Fuentes to establish his points on consumption, guilds, and factory failures, Cisneros paints that conventional image of a guano-age Peru clothed "from head to foot" by foreigners.[142] This "shortage" of national goods has a cause, but it is not the liberals' imagined shortage of native labor. Cisneros's analysis zeroes in on the misdirected luxury orientation of urban artisan production; local crafts stood little chance of competing with overseas goods in refined, Westernizing elite markets. This conundrum originated in deeper historical-commercial trends—intensified since Peru's 1820s opening to Atlantic trade—which ingrained

141. Cisneros, *Ensayo sobre cuestiones económicas*, 29.

142. Cisneros also uses Fuentes, *Estadística de Lima*, on tariff needs; sole study mentioning Cisneros's industrial idea is Maiguashca, "Reinterpretation of Guano Age," 131, 157.

the "taste, need, and economy for European imports throughout Spanish America . . . and which has made us realize the low quality, vulgarity, or primitiveness of all our industries."[143] In other words, Cisneros is not talking about cost factors, as Casanova and Pardo had in their different ways; indeed, he has little to say on comparative advantage or even terms of trade. Colonially forged tastes and colonially structured crafts could not survive Peru's critical nineteenth-century moment of incorporation into the Atlantic world—leaving discontinuities and gaps in indigenous production. Cisneros's diagnosis approaches modern structural analyses of lagging industrialism in the commercially and culturally created Third World.[144]

Cisneros cannot romanticize Peru's backward ("vulgar") artisans, who remain just as hooked on imported styles as urban elites. For example, he discusses at length the bustling Limeño tailoring trade requiring reams of costly European cloth. But Cisneros seems to be reacting mainly against the plutocratic version of "civilization," code word for their colonized, imported life-styles. For industrial efforts to succeed in balancing trade, local taste and productive orientations would have to be matched. From Cisneros's pen, this becomes justification for a new type of Peruvian protectionism. To distinguish it from the traditional sorts easily debunked by free traders, Cisneros dubs his "the *intelligently* applied system of protectionism."[145] Cisneros takes his protectionist turn.

There are four elements in intelligently applied protectionism, but these "all reduce to one: consolidate the exceptional wealth of guano in order to make it infinitely productive." First, Cisneros comes out for industrial subsidy incentives to cover start-up costs of new factories. Dubbed the "system of direct protection," such guano subsidies bring to mind Casanova's early scheme or the tradition of Continental state workshops. But the state, insists Cisneros, should award monies only to factories that use raw materials abundant in Peru and that enjoy efficient scale. Cisneros thus rules out the "artificial," import-dependent, and petty production of guilds—which neither display dynamism nor con-

143. Cisneros, *Ensayo sobre cuestiones económicas,* 41–42.

144. See similar concerns in Celso Furtado, "Subdesarrollo y dependencia: Las conexiones fundamentales," in Furtado, *El desarrollo económico: Un mito* (Mexico, 1978), 92–114, or David Felix, "De Gustibus Disputandum Est: Changing Consumer Preferences in Economic Growth," *Explorations in Economic History* 16 (1979): 260–96.

145. Cisneros, *Ensayo sobre cuestiones económicas,* 37–38, 57.

serve precious foreign exchange. Later Cisneros illustrates the subsidy plan by examples, showing how far a modest annual fund of $200,000 could go in incipient factory enterprises.[146]

Second, Cisneros extolls the "intelligently applied" use of customs duties—which means applying them only where indispensable, only for industries that can truly be established and multiply, only on a temporary basis, and only with careful foresight and selection. Such strict criteria were informed by Peru's fruitless prior attempts at industrial tariffs and privileges. Cisneros also factors in what is now known as "effective protection"—lower duties for industrial tools and inputs—with its potent protectionist incentives (though at another point he speaks of special subsidies for factories supplying national inputs). Interestingly, with so many criteria to settle Cisneros never specifies Peru's required tariff levels. But his vision is clearly not of a closed economy. He is too sophisticated to pose protection as the liberals' zero-sum choice between related external and internal markets. But his is an explicit plan to reorient Peruvian trade and consumption—the issues that Pardo found too hot to handle.

In part, Cisneros's "intelligent" protection simply affirms a productive and balance-of-payments priority on mass-consumption lines, as others had before. But he is also taking on the free-trader bugbear of "artificial" industries, seemingly confirmed by indiscriminate craft tariffs and factory failures. Cisneros's insistence that guano is the most "artificial" and fleeting "industry" looms central here. Guano revenues must be diverted into productive lines to "free us from the tyranny of foreign markets and procure an element of our own life. The benefits they lend the country are everlasting and thus inestimable."[147]

What remains murky is why tariffs become the policy tool—if taste preferences (rather than cost) had driven consumers abroad. One suspects that Cisneros, in his budgetary zeal, was simultaneously looking toward revenue raising. The focus on articles of everyday use is decisive, though, for in mass necessities tastes need not pose an insuperable obstacle. Consumer preference might be shifted with temporary tariffs, equal to any premium placed on overseas origin, until buyers learned the insignificance of quality difference. Cisneros opines:

It would be absurd to try to establish now in Peru factories for certain luxury

---

146. Cisneros, *Ensayo sobre cuestiones económicas*, 37, 44.

147. Cisneros, *Ensayo sobre cuestiones económicas*, 44; recall Basadre's "fictitious prosperity" periodization—allegedly from Copello and Petriconi (1876)—and more important, the rhetorical and conceptual reversal here of free-trader "fictitious" industries.

goods, for fine cloth for instance, for which we enjoy neither the elements nor advanced industrial skills. But we can create industries for less difficult and widely consumed products. Factories for coarse cottons and woolens, for eating utensils for the poor, for farming tools, and for building materials merit the preferred protection of public power.[148]

In short, Cisneros wanted to push the style of development previously only fantasized by Pardo—doing so in product lines with decent chances of survival, in lines weighing down the import bill, in lines with wide employment spin-offs, in lines of basic technology. He heralds the successful precedents of Garmendia's Cuzco woolens mill and the sparkling new home-market sugar refinery in nearby Callao. Later Cisneros avers that import quotas would make the most direct instrument for project selection and foreign exchange savings.[149] If confusions remain, at least Cisneros had the clarity (or courage) to confront needed trade-offs of present consumption for long-term productive investments—issues obscured by those evading tariffs in their plans.

A third element of "intelligent protection" is rejection of all exclusive industrial privileges—a condition harking back to the controversial (and failed) technology monopolies of the half century since independence. This stance also accentuates the liberal spirit and expansive scale of Cisneros's developmental vision, which shares in the wider technological mission of civilist railroad writers.[150] Finally, returning to Peru's miserable artisans, Cisneros demands "unlimited protection" for the just-opened Lima School of Arts (which we explore later). Such schools will improve their techniques and style, the only way for viable craft competition in upscale markets. And Cisneros, echoing the new regionalist imperatives, is adamant that analogous schools be placed in "every province of Peru" (something civilistas would try). Cisneros thus actively pursues technological innovation and spread, which, significantly, he joins to "intelligent" protection. Ultimately, rural manufacturing will offer steady "work and salary" to poor families, including the debased "indigenous" ones.[151] Alone, none of these ideas seem startling, having floated around since the advent of the export age. The novelty lay in

148. Cisneros, *Ensayo sobre cuestiones económicas,* 40–41.

149. Cisneros, *Ensayo sobre cuestiones económicas,* 37, 41, 76; in 1872 Garmendia and Cisneros would serve as Pardo vice presidents.

150. Cisneros, *Ensayo sobre cuestiones económicas,* 37; for analysis of monopoly policies, see Gootenberg, "Artisans and Merchants," 101–7; or Salcedo, *Memoria de hacienda de 1860,* pt. 14, for vast contemporary criticism.

151. Cisneros, *Ensayo sobre cuestiones económicas,* 37, 40; influence of school seen in ch. 5, below.

Cisneros's integration of these elements into an urgent, encompassing, and activist program.

Peru's last elite protectionist ideas had issued from Casanova virtually two decades before. Cisneros's "intelligently" applied tariffs were a more critical and conditioned variety and came embedded in a new array of positive social supports. His critical edge was sharpened in contrasts with outmoded artisans and with the cutting critiques of a liberal generation. In anticipating potential drawbacks to protection, the *Ensayo sobre cuestiones económicas* exudes a modern flavor (akin to current Latin American and neoliberal critiques of twentieth-century import substitution). Cisneros was concerned that industry genuinely relieve external imbalances, foster appropriate and dynamic technology, and break through monopoly or retrogressive patterns of consumption and distribution—not exacerbate them.[152]

It is crucial to observe how Cisneros, one of Peru's most cosmopolitan intellectuals, addresses the critics of protectionism, at this the height of free trade's international prestige. At first Cisneros denies his colors: "We are not partisans of the protectionist system; on the contrary, we are zealous for an unlimited liberty of commerce. But in the present economic situation of Spanish America there are exceptional circumstances that make it imperative to grasp the terms of this grave issue."[153] The disclaimer is not fully disingenuous, for the *Ensayo sobre cuestiones económicas* does embrace expansive tenets of contemporary liberalism.

To define the "exceptional" contexts, Cisneros turns to history, of the proximate nineteenth century, in his defense. His are not just the age-old potshots at Europe's "hypocritical" past. Lagging Latin America won its independence, Cisneros points out, just when Europe was making its greatest strides in industry and marine transport. Overseas goods and examples quickly antiquated Latin American skills, yet they paradoxically inspired desires for national emulation and development.

Now once one grasps these conditions, what system should be employed to create and develop the industries for which we are suited? When the economists discuss the principles of protectionism and free trade, no doubt they have not placed themselves in the perspective of countries without roads and

---

152. See, e.g., survey by Catherine Conaghan, James Malloy, and Luis Abugattás, "Business and the 'Boys': The Politics of Neoliberalism in the Central Andes," *LARR* 25 (1990): 3–30.

153. Cisneros, *Ensayo sobre cuestiones económicas*, 41; from Casanova on, critics emphasized "exceptional circumstances."

dense populations, and deprived of all types of factories and manufactures. Their doctrines are based on the industrial systems of the European states, more or less rich in workshops and factories. Their own partisans defend the doctrines under the principle of the reciprocal convenience of states, referring only to themselves, and without ever thinking of the situation of the new, small, and distant republics of Spanish America.[154]

It is not a bad reading of Smith's original realpolitik, though it comes closest to List's national economic system, posed in an "Americanist" idiom. (Cisneros partook of the pan-American movement against mid-century Spanish and French regional imperialism.) Several ideas are packed in here. One is identification of a pressing national development gap: could trade alone bridge it? Another is historical relativism: political economy had indeed ignored non-European lands (save for its orientalist brush on Asia). Were its universalist assumptions of factor mobility, for example, correct here, or did new states have to take a leading role in forging market conditions? At the least, Cisneros contests that natural-selection version of static comparative advantage that had filtered to free-traders in the Americas, so amenable to colonial-physiocratic partisans of a país minero y agrícola. Cisneros focuses a nationalist lens on a pivotal juncture in world economic history. Peru must struggle, in its national interest, against being relegated to the lower rungs of economic specialization. Other writers would follow up, in a kind of local, nineteenth-century dependency thought. Analogies aside, Cisneros genuinely argues against all "imitative" systems, as, for example, when taking swipes at statist French models. Each "constellation of states"—Spanish America in his case—must decide its own preference, and if it be protection, it must follow the "general interests of the nation."[155]

Of greater historical import is why protectionist thought revived in the Peru of the mid 1860s. Two speculations, ideological and political, help make sense of Cisneros and relate to his mission of bolstering the Peruvian state. The first concerns the ideological power of free trade among the guano-age elite, an appeal that had outlived its usefulness to emerging state builders.

At its apex in the early 1860s, free trade was largely an ingrained

---

154. Cisneros, *Ensayo sobre cuestiones económicas,* 42; mention of transport bottlenecks, of course, is not accidental.

155. Cisneros, *Ensayo sobre cuestiones económicas,* 42–43; see analogy in Senghass, "List and Problem of Development," or Will, "Classical Economics in Chile." Esteves and Copello and Petriconi, below, for "dependency" notions.

legacy of the successful liberal state building of the previous generation (i.e., its coeval rise with elite political stability and capitalization of the 1850s). It was a congratulatory ideology synonymous with elite order and progress.[156] But by the 1860s free trade had assumed a stultifying rigidity. In 1864 Peru's minister of finance was still busy extirpating ghostly "ideas of the protective system, mistaken in theory, absurd in practice"; Peru needed only its "natural industry" of agriculture and mining, "which are recognized by science over fabrication, which still can't root in our soil." Congress took similar extremes, for example, rejecting any supports for national foodstuffs farmers in 1862 on the grounds that contagious "protection is all illusion." In 1864 even the military's plans to build a reliable national armory (on the Springfield system) in the secure Jauja valley were thrown out, as Deputy Silva Santisteban put it, "because manufactures are not for all countries"— gleefully reciting the fate of Casanova's cottons![157] In liberal Peru not even national security made a tenable exception to laissez-faire, not even as Spanish fleets besieged Callao. Official liberalism took its starkest form in that classic, guano-soaked slogan of Silva Santisteban: "'Tis better to pay for all manufactures than know how to make 'em."

Cisneros stood this slogan on its head. To concerned statesmen, such ignorance was no longer better. Clearly, it would soon be impossible to pay for lavish imports—as drilled home in the 1860s by topsy-turvy terms of trade brought about by the U.S. Civil War, the cotton famine, swinging guano revenues, and the frightful experience of the Spanish war, which exposed the almost lethal frailty of public finance. The state needed the flexibility now to set priorities regarding import consumption, fiscal and military survival, expansion of services, and national development. Peruvians were even resisting the modicum of domestic taxation as a confiscatory market infringement. As Peru's fiscal breakdown became imminent, unbending allegiance to free trade was becoming an anachronistic threat to the viability of the state—and the state was the life force of Peruvian liberalism and its Limeño constituency.[158]

156. Gootenberg, "Beleaguered Liberals," 79–89. For sample contemporary ultra-liberal view, see *El Perú y la influencia europea* (Paris, 1862), 13, 23, 27—a virtual call for liberal neocolonization of the country.

157. Ignacio Noboa, *Memoria que el ministro de hacienda y comercio presenta al congreso de 1864 en los distintos ramos de su despacho* (Lima, pam., 1864), 27–28; *Diarios de debates*, Oct.–Dec. 1862, July 1864. Silva argues: "It is necessary to grasp that not all pueblos are fit for all things—look at the results obtained when the cottons factory was tried, full of illusions, then disillusions. Manufactures are not for every country" (171).

158. Pardo, *Memoria de hacienda y comercio* (1867); Cisneros always argued with state "autonomy" in mind, as in "Negociado Dreyfus" (1870), which defends (211) contract as

Cisneros (despite his later assaults on Pardo's fiscality) is interesting for the ideational flexibility he reveals among high financial, official, or commercial circles. Men such as Cisneros and Pardo did not have to regard an export economy as a zero-sum game with domestic development, nor did they necessarily fear elevated tariffs. To them, policy was not religion but a political, practical, and protean reason of state.

Second, Cisneros was also likely grappling with the rise of a more rigid and genuine class (not just ideological) interest in free trade— though we still know precious little of these elite configurations. By the early 1860s a new Peruvian planter export group was rapidly taking root along Peru's central and northern coast. The planters' progress leapfrogged with the decade's remarkable world cotton and sugar prices (the result, again, of the U.S. and Cuban civil wars), with more than 250 modernized plantations dominating nonfertilizer exports by the mid 1870s. Millions of soles of guano revenues recycled through Lima's new agrarian mortgage bank, the Banco Hipotecario Territorial, infused the coast, in one of the few diversifying developments of the decade. The nouveaux riches, such as the Aspíllaga clan of Pisco and Saña or the agrarian banker Aráoz, quickly positioned themselves in politics, organizing their neighbors and clients into a unique lobby on Lima and intertwining with the country's top commercial and financial circles. To Peruvian planters, unlike erstwhile merchant and political elites, free trade and laissez-faire were indeed bald economic imperatives: for securing low-cost imported machinery, for competitively placing their products abroad, for preventing dreaded export levies, and for halting the diversion of scarce labor into alternative activities.[159] The sugar planters were the germ of the rigidly liberal Peruvian ruling group that would plague crisis-prevention efforts such as Cisneros's, placing constraints on the notable autonomy of the guano-age state. By 1867 they had already forced Minister Pardo's resignation over his fiscal plan

---

the "2 de mayo de nuestra hacienda pública"—date of Peru's triumphant 1866 victory over Spain. See Topik, *Political Economy of Brazilian State*, for general model of export-led polities assuming interventionism for reasons of state; or Ronald Berg and Frederick Weaver, "Toward a Reinterpretation of Political Change in Peru During the First Century of Independence," *Journal of Interamerican Studies and World Affairs* 20 (1978): 69–84, for (ambiguous) Peruvian political class autonomy.

159. Engelsen, "Social Aspects of Agricultural Expansion," ch. 5, and esp. ch. 7; Pablo Macera, "Las plantaciones azucareras andinas (1821–1875)," in Macera, *Trabajos de historia* 4:116–50; MacEvoy, "Manuel Pardo," 221–22; or Vincent Peloso, "Entrepreneurs and Survivors in Rural Peru: Planters, Peasants, and Cotton in the Pisco Valley, 1840–1940" (typescript, Howard University, 1991), ch. 2, on export development and emergent planter politics.

(based on *Ensayo sobre cuestiones económicas*) to enact a trifling 3 percent export tax. (Pardo later confessed, "It collided with a great number of interests, from the most elevated sectors of our society.") In the early 1870s planters joined the civilists in droves, organized regional Juntas de Agricultura, and set themselves up in a potent Sociedad Nacional de Agricultura, further complicating or neutralizing autonomous policy initiatives. In part, sugar was becoming king because it was producing royal amounts of foreign exchange (over 12 million soles in 1876, three-quarters of agrarian exports)—most of it out of the state's needy reach. Neoliberalism was as contagious as protection.[160] By then Cisneros himself had turned antistatist, in the congress defending bankers against Pardo's tyrannical "socialism" (i.e., efforts to stabilize unbacked bill emissions and establish a workable national currency).

In the mid 1860s Cisneros, of the wide-ranging and literary urban elite, was exposing the dangers of a structurally embedded liberalism. His scant detail on recommended levels of taxation and tariffs may well have reflected this general political purpose. Still missing, however, was a political strategy for gathering a national developmental coalition to push through his imagined reforms. That would have to wait until the new actors of the 1870s, notably Copello and Petriconi. In any case, the timely interventionist thought of the 1860s hardly arose from thin air.

A host of other detailed and heterodox proposals permeate the *Ensayo sobre cuestiones económicas*. There are plans for apt agroindustries, such as silks and dyes, and here Cisneros speaks obliquely of a colonization "land reform." Quinine ("Peru-bark") collection in the southern Andean rain forest must advance to a "fabrication stage" before export. A full chapter explores the long-controversial issue of a merchant marine, which Cisneros hopes to "Peruvianize" (a term echoed by much later reform-

160. Despite literature just cited, we lack elite studies precise enough to determine if debates themselves reflected discrete elite economic factions. See Cisneros, "¿Que no hay remedio?" (1874) for his own conversion; quote, Manuel Pardo, *Memoria que el ex-secretario de estado en el despacho de hacienda y comercio presenta al jefe supreme provisorio de la república* (Lima, pam., 1867), 350.

See García Calderón, *Estudios sobre el banco hipotecario* (1868), for striking example of new agrarian laissez-faire. (He calls for full specialization in coastal exports, partially on the grounds that "Peru can't be a fabricating nation. . . . The Lima factories of silk, cottons, and glass absorbed huge capitals, dying right after birth" [17].) Linked with Piérola's anti-Pardo group, Francisco García Calderón was among the most influential thinkers of the 1870s; e.g., his codifying *Diccionario de la legislación peruana* (Lima, 1879) brims with invectives against "gremios," "industria," "privilegio," etc. See also agrarianist Fernando Casós, *La minería y la agricultura al punto de vista del progreso* (Lima, pam., 1876).

ists) in state-sponsored shipyards, though to the benefit of all "America." This question galvanized protectionist-liberal polemics of the mid 1860s, with Pardo coming down on the other side.[161] All sorts of industries must "nationalize" in Peru, claims Cisneros.

Another chapter confronts difficulties at customs, where free-traders always found potent ammunition in the state's fiscal reliance on customs duties and the costly smuggling spurred on by tariffs. In painstaking detail Cisneros forwards administrative reforms to thwart contraband. In an innovative twist he ultimately attributes pandemic contraband to Peru's global structure of commercial dependence; saddled with such an unwieldy variety and complexity of imports, bureaucratic procedures are tough to rationalize and easy to evade. Cisneros also assails government subservience to free-trader merchants as the deeper cause for declining customs revenues.[162] Tax reform proposals—to counter the fit of liberal generosity in the mid 1850s that left Peru bereft of nonguano revenues—include novel upper-class consumption and export duties, those that Pardo found so hard to realize.

There is the better-known plan for rationalizing the guano trade itself, which found instant and effective partisans in the state. The reform ended long-standing merchant advances, cost-leaky consignments, and international pricing irregularities, not only to raise public profit shares but, equally important, to free guano funds from the pressures of ordinary (and political) expenditures. Its ultimate aim was fiscal austerity not for its own sake but for liberating both the state and ample funds for developmental projects. From a rationalized budget of 25 million soles, some 7 million could then be devoted to "roads, public works, and industries."[163] In context, "Guano," the final chapter of the book, had been prefaced by five sections laying out the coveted developmental projects. Export and railway reforms, as history tells, proved the easiest to assimilate by Peru's civil elite—because effective political constituencies were already in place and, one suspects, because they could be had without deferred prosperity.

161. Cisneros, *Ensayo sobre cuestiones económicas,* chs. 3–4; quinine ideas from M. E. de Rivero studies. See Perú, Congreso, *La protección y la libertad: Debates del senado y otros documentos* (Lima, pam., 1868), for polemics following Prado purchase of three boats for a "Compañía Nacional de Navegación," after Cisneros's notion. Congressional free-traders killed the project, for "there can be no vacillation. Liberty is alone our cult—for she resolves all social problems" (89)—invoking a bit of liberal social utopianism, too.

162. Cisneros, *Ensayo sobre cuestiones económicas,* ch. 4, esp. 78–80.

163. Cisneros, *Ensayo sobre cuestiones económicas,* "Huano" and conclusions; see Maiguashca, "Reinterpretation of Guano Age," chs. 3–5, for reform movements.

Finally, Cisneros's perspective on the popular classes deserves a fresh look as well, for it proves more elusive than a starkly defined divide between elite and the masses. The technocratic *Ensayo sobre cuestiones económicas* was not openly an essay on the social question. The most obvious social message, from beginning to end, is the forging of social peace through employment—never a revolutionary insight in Peru— and Cisneros's idiosyncratic worries about the pressures of political employment ("empleo-necesidad") on the workings of the state—an exaggerated concern, as modern studies show.[164] Fiscal reform was sold as a way to ensure "twenty years without anarchy and civil war," the time needed to place Peru on a steady growth path. Throughout Cisneros brandishes a national standard, along with blatant criticism of oligarchic mismanagement and rentier values. The more concealed message is that to progress, Peru must somehow involve its people in production. Surely the mounting urban social unrest of the mid 1860s was on his mind (with xenophobic and bread riots now an inescapable fixture of the urban scene), intensifying his generational obsession with orderly and civil political process. But few of Cisneros's specific proposals reveal a particularly popular bent: at his most radical he calls for enhanced technical training (for decades a guild aspiration) and some lower duties on goods and inputs for popular sustenance and production.

Above all looms Cisneros's larger conception of development itself as the antithesis to fleeting guano abundance and unbridled consumption. Executives and congress must promote "an industrial future" because it is "human work, not minerals, that makes the measure of real wealth."[165] This was neither the value notion of classical economy nor the industrial ethic of Saint-Simon, nor the capitalist civilizing dreams of nineteenth-century liberals. It was also a concept that many a local artisan could relate to, as it shared in their own customary ethos of "honorable" and "skilled" *trabajo*.

Yet at the same time Cisneros firmly rejects the artisan protectionist standard and was clearly not trying to develop or cater to a popular following. The guilds, he claims, cannot be trusted, on their own, to

164. I.e., Hunt, "Growth and Guano," 80–83, showing declining real welfare transfers and (Cisneros-like) rising developmental funding. Cisneros, *Ensayo sobre cuestiones económicas,* conclusions; see also Cisneros, "Consideraciones sobre el contrato de 17 de aug. de 1869" (*Obras completas* 3:225–35), where he promotes Dreyfus contract as a blow against an upper-class "banker-merchant monopoly" and as "solving forever" "the thirst for material progress."

165. Cisneros, *Ensayo sobre cuestiones económicas,* 57.

promote productive industry. Such skepticism was understandable after the initial trials of republican trade policy, when guilds still wielded influence. Cisneros knew of the last haphazard artisan campaign of 1849, when each craft promiscuously demanded ever higher tariffs, with scant thought to Peru's fiscal or developmental horizons. The *Ensayo sobre cuestiones económicas* thus cuts directly to deep-seated (and essentially political) dilemmas of applying protection intelligently. Rather than dismiss artisans out of hand (a free-trader reflex of the 1850s), Cisneros proposes here an institutionalized process of industrial and protective project selection. This he conjures as a sort of state control board to avert the irrational sway of popular and parochial group interest:

The government should, for the first time, conduct a serious, careful and effective survey, taking in the views of the guilds of industries in all corners of the republic. In this way, we can discover their true necessities and clearly recognize which industries are those that require a just protection; which would harm the consumer without benefit; and which are ready for even lower duties. This is how protection must be formed, rather than letting them demand of the government. In the latter case, all industries will simply plead for "protection"—without the data and opinions that must be collected by a commission of illustrious and practical men.[166]

Cisneros, like Fuentes, Pardo, and the railway promoters, was not a democrat in the popular sense of the word. The best turn for policy-making was depoliticizing the state—hardly an inclusive move in a society that naturally excluded most everyone in the streets, villages, and fields. His stance exuded a suspicious class bias and a top-down technocratic sensibility, along with the sensible aversion to the traditional passions of liberal and protectionist politics. In another national context Cisneros would have made a good fiscal *científico*, working toward a more independent and still exclusionary state.[167] Later writers, whom we turn to next, would pick up on and extend the dilemmas of popular participation in development. For Cisneros and others of the reformist elite, neither his fellow elites nor the people alone could save Peru from its impending crisis.

166. Cisneros, *Ensayo sobre cuestiones económicas*, 76, 74–75.
167. Cf. Hale, *Transformation of Liberalism;* or Trazegnies, *Idea de derecho* (but which omits legal corpus of this "traditional modernizer").

5

The Return of Popular Industrialism
Copello and Petriconi, the 1870s

The Arriving Crisis

The crisis of guano dependence burst in full force by the mid 1860s—and would persist, without relief, over the next decade and a half. It unfolded amid the political maturation of Lima's reformist civilian forces—Pardo's Partido Civil of 1872—whose flurry of responses would fail to stem the collapse in time.

Peru's first signs of emergency showed up as simple budgetary imbalances of the early 1860s, alarming enough in a state assuming ever more administrative scope. By the mid 1870s this gap had transformed into an insuperable external crisis—with Peru's foreign debt of £35 million matched only by that of the Ottoman Empire—after a desperate race against the exhaustion of the Chincha Islands. In 1869 Peru earmarked a quarter of its £4 million of guano exports for debt service; by 1876, the year of its shattering default on the London market, all of Peru's evaporating £2.6 million in guano sales poured into interest alone.

The crisis unfolded in twists and turns to avert it. In the early 1860s the bolstering of national finance became the principal policy: the transfer of guano contracts to leading Peruvian merchants (after derogation of the last Gibbs monopoly) and their creation of a profitable modern financial system to meet Peru's chronic fiscal shortfalls. However, the costly defense against Spain's attempted invasion (1864–1866) starkly revealed the inadequacies of public finance—rescued by a Pardo-arranged £7 million war loan—just as it prompted a nationalism demanding stronger initiatives from the state. (Spain, on the pretext of 1863 incidents with citizens in northern Talambo, had first occupied the guano isles and, after drawn-out diplomatic maneuvers, blockaded and attacked Callao in 1866.) In reaction to these political and economic events the ephemeral Prado regime (1866–1867) pursued a stringent national fiscal reform (restored taxation, rationalized guano lending) while moving headlong into diversification through railroads—toward realization of the fiscal and developmental programs heralded by Cisneros and Pardo. But in 1868 the treasury still fell short by a third and owed the increasingly distrusted hijos del país bankers more than 15 million soles. The following Balta regime (1869–1872) disavowed the nationals, as Finance Minister Nicolás de Piérola, in a controversial about-face, turned over the entire guano enterprise to the French financier Auguste Dreyfus. Dreyfus was given full charge of managing Peru's fiscal straits abroad, based on his ability to quickly raise massive capital (on dwindling guano reserves) to underwrite Meiggs's railroads, now frenetically heading toward Cuzco and Junín. This was Peru's euphoric era of public works. The first major issue—of £11.9 million—succeeded; the second loan of 1872, for £36 million, crashed on takeoff, as rumors spread of Peruvian insolvency. Whatever the intent, Dreyfus succeeded primarily in multiplying Peru's external debt ten times in three years.[1]

In part, the Partido Civil gained power in 1872 as a national reaction to the Balta-Piérola strategy, yet Pardo necessarily remained attached to both Dreyfus and Meiggs. Peru turned toward austerity. Pardo offered a comprehensive program of economic and fiscal stabilization and a gradualist vision of national modernization, but his plan was shaken by chaotic events. By 1873 the national banking network and all the businesses jerry-built around it were tottering; government moves to control emissions only aggravated the liquidity crunch. On ordinary expenditures alone, budget deficits reached 8 million soles, nearly 50 percent. In 1875 Pardo engineered a bold statist takeover of southern nitrate fields, with the help of national banks, as a makeshift solution. But nitrate revenues and galloping sugar exports could not make do. By January 1876 Peru had defaulted on European markets; the national railroads

---

1. Basic sources on crisis (and reforms) include Maiguashca, "Reinterpretation of Guano Age," chs. 5–6; Yepes, *Perú 1820–1920*, chs. 2–3; Quiroz, *Domestic and Foreign Finance*, 58–70; Marichal, *Century of Debt Crises*, ch. 4.

halted after seven hundred kilometers (leaving twenty thousand workers wandering the countryside); major banks closed doors; credit-starved planters stopped sowing seed. And foreign interests were infuriated with Peru.[2] Pardo's compromise successor, civil-military Prado, inherited the ravages of unbacked paper money, world depression, deepening unemployment, and a £40 million debt. Calamity soon hit harder, in the form of the Chilean invaders of 1879.

The rise of civilismo was surely a trial by fire. It also occurred amid a mystifying renewal of national political instability (eight military regimes in the 1860s followed by a decade of bitter civil-military strife). By 1864 the age of Castillan strongmen had passed, the victim of the general's alienation of erstwhile liberal allies, his myopic economic vision, and paralytic response to the Spanish invasion threat. To be sure, political fault lines still erupted around timeworn liberal-conservative constitutional issues (in 1860 and 1867), yet civil aversion to militarism now was taking on a life of its own. This drive to full civilian rule is often associated with a rising generation of pragmatic liberals and a *grupo de poder* from the maturing national merchant, banking, and planter classes of the 1860s. After embracing the Prado dictatorship, reformists ran their first candidate, Manuel Ureta, in 1868 and intensified their mobilization against "militarists" Balta and Piérola in their 1871 campaign, now reaching out to disaffected urban and provincial groups with their new-style political party. After heading off Gutiérrez's golpe in July 1872, Pardo suffered four stormy years as Peru's first civilian elected president. The civilistas attempted, amid grave circumstances, to move forward on broad administrative, educational, military, democratic, and decentralist reforms, against an intransigent church, army, and conservatives rallying around the cult of caudillo Piérola.[3] General Prado's uninspiring compromise succession in 1876 and deepening elite factionalism revealed the limits to Peru's nascent republican politics.

By the late 1860s Peru's economic transformations were finally spilling over from Lima. "Capitalism" was beginning to infiltrate the profounder Peru. Postindependence population had doubled to 2.7 million by 1876; markets spread into the reaches of the central and southern

2. Clarke, *Peru and Creditors;* for recovery program, Pardo addresses, 21 Sept. 1872, 28 Apr. 1873, 3 Feb. 1875, 28 July 1876, Ugarteche and San Cristóval, *Mensajes de presidentes;* or Bonilla, "Crisis de 1872."

3. Balancing survey in Pike, *Modern History,* ch. 5; critical analysis in Bonilla, *Guano y burguesía;* Giesecke, *Masas urbanas y rebelión,* chs. 1–2; MacEvoy "Manuel Pardo," ch. 3, for revised political history.

sierra, awakening their landed elites to new possibilities. Diversification and guano investment occurred: in southern wool and alpaca exports, very rapidly in northern, coastal sugar and cotton plantations (via agrarian mortgage banks and the import of fifty thousand indentured Asian workers), in austral Atacama nitrates, and in the occupational, physical, and institutional complexities of Lima. The state began to touch the lives of Peruvians. New interests and new national configurations brewed. Little of this change, however, affected the daily lives of Peru's submerged social majority—the 60 percent who struggled on as "Indian" peasants of the Andes—or at least not positively.[4]

This chapter pursues intellectual responses to the gathering national crisis of the 1860s and 1870s, of publicists and activists who wished to look (and push) beyond the fiscal straits and solutions of governments. This time, thinkers steeped in the fervor of rising civil politics began to grope for an imagined "people" (of Lima) as a social and political force in development. This shift began in ambiguous liberal notions about artisans of the 1850s; took shape with the real-life revival of popular-nationalist politics of the 1860s; won credence in a new socially oriented technical education and work ethic of the civilista 1870s; and gained a foothold in the budding sociology of immigrant small industrialists. These influences spawned novel thinkers of the mid 1870s—such as Juan Copello and Luis Petriconi—whose middle-class industrialism this chapter places in their long-term social and intellectual contexts. No one, seemingly, could avert the crisis, but some at least hoped to learn from it.

Artisans as Liberal Challenge, 1852–1858

By the mid 1860s a contagious new strain of "populism" gripped many Lima thinkers, converging with, and ultimately enriching, their fiscal and economic concerns. Its social seeds remain buried in what we still don't know about nineteenth-century Lima, but this populism was already affecting 1860s writers such as Cisneros, who felt compelled to address, in roundabout ways, an artisan challenge. As the revival of popular protection advanced, major pro-industrial prophets of the

---

4. Mallon, *Defense of Community,* ch. 2; Burga, *Encomienda a hacienda capitalista,* ch. 6; Manrique, *Mercado y región,* chs. 2–3; Jacobsen, *Mirages of Transition,* chs. 5–6; Gootenberg, "Population and Ethnicity," esp. 148–52, on Indians.

1870s went straight to the people in a transformed climate of activated urban politics. Such writers, to some degree, were manipulating the marginalized old artisan politics for political gain or hoping to channel Lima's new forms of social unrest into new sluices of "social control."[5] Yet above all homespun industrial ideologies reveal that developmentalist thinking was not confined to oligarchic dreamers such as Pardo and Cisneros; it had spilled over into a "politics" of development, sharing in the delayed republican aspirations of Lima's artisan class, however reified by elites. By the time Peru's predicted export crisis hit with full force in the mid 1870s, a synthetic middle-class industrialism had appeared, blending long-standing elite and artisan standards. The celebrated 1876 nationalist manifesto by Copello and Petriconi, *Estudio sobre la independencia económica del Perú*, embodied these social developments, its roots stretching back to the early 1850s.

The last stand of traditional Lima guilds was their 1849 campaign to foist on congress the Ley de Artesanos—a last-ditch appeal against Peru's nascent import economy, defeated by the liberal tariff of 1852. At first guilds appeared to be closing in on victory, with early political "clubs" and caudillos catering to artisan clientele. But Peru's new liberals swiftly rebounded and crushed the drive. Old-style guilds were caught in a reactive class mobilization against craftsmen (especially those hoisting the radical anti-aristocratic banners of 1848); against a customary unfocused artisan protectionism; against industrialism writ large; and against the fluid politics of the 1850 election, which finally brought the free-trader conservative Echenique to power. Policy was set for the guano age.[6] In part, the guilds lost for lack of a credible developmental perspective.

Guilds felt intensely "betrayed" by their traditional patrons and by the political system. As one craftsman bemoaned, "Equality is unknown among us; prosperity calls to its breast only the owners of money. The worker is condemned to be victim of the whims of metallic power. No measure is felt to raise the people from the misery in which they are

---

5. For varied models, see Steve Stein, *Populism in Peru: The Emergence of the Masses and the Politics of Social Control* (Madison, 1980) (urban populism as social control); June Hahner, *Poverty and Politics: The Urban Poor in Brazil, 1870–1920* (Albuquerque, 1986) (rare look at origins of "clientelism"); Giesecke, *Masas urbanas y rebelión* (Hobsbawmian "primitive" popular politics); MacEvoy, "Manuel Pardo," ch. 3 (civilist citizenry search). Rather than shibbolethic social control of prepolitical masses, I seek convergent political concerns—an approach closest to MacEvoy's analysis.

6. Gootenberg, "Social Origins of Protection and Free Trade," 347–58.

sunk . . . and the indifference of the rich." Denigrated and pushed aside
by Peru's official liberalism, Limeño artisans all but withdrew from
formal political activity. Republicanism seemed a sham: "Sure, around
us there are democrats, but not democrats of the heart! For they only live
to gulp down guano. . . . Viva la libertad! Ha, poor artisans!" By late
1851, instead, beleaguered and disillusioned artisans organized the first
of their republican mutual aid societies in hopes of weathering their
crises far from a disappointing liberal politics of elites.[7]

Not much was heard from the submerged guilds over the next decade, their worst on record as luxury imports and inflation kept workshops from sharing in the glitter of commercial recovery. Evidence
suggests material changes as well; for example, customary guild masters
were losing their grip on workers and apprentices as unemployment,
and a generally more fluid labor market, accompanied Lima's demographic expansion. The abolition of black slavery in 1854, and the rapid
influx of fine European craftsmen to the city, also undermined traditional guilds. In high politics the 1850s became the congratulatory, if
bickering, time of elite liberal dominance. Only a handful of political
mavericks still voiced overtures to artisans, among them Juan Bustamante, the Puno deputy long dear to protectionist and other lost causes
and eventual martyr in the bizarre southern peasant uprisings of 1867.[8]
Such calls remained exceedingly vague—isolated reminders for government to heed the forgotten "arts." For the most part, outcast artisans
quietly endured assaults from rising liberals, relentless attempts, it would
seem, to bury popular memory under a shroud of laissez-faire.

José Simeón Tejeda's 1852 antiguild polemic, *Emancipación de la
industria,* penned with his native Arequipa in mind, was prominently
displayed and quoted in Lima dailies. Tejeda's message, like Silva Santisteban's, was unabashedly repressive: a blast against restrictive guild
institutions, influence, and ideas. Inscribed in the "industrial" liberation
idiom of Saint-Simon, guilds came across here as the bastion of Peru's

7. "Unos artesanos," *Comercio,* 29 Nov. 1851; M. F. de Mendiola, "Estado de los
artesanos en Lima," *Correo de Lima,* 16 Oct. 1851; or Basadre, *Historia* 5:2045–47, on
early (unlinked) mutual aid.

8. Gootenberg, "Artisans and Merchants," chs. 1, 4 (artisan decay); Giesecke, *Masas
urbanas y rebelión,* ch. 4 (proletarianization); Bustamante, *Apuntes y observaciones,* 31–32,
82–83 (protection and school of arts calls); *Comercio,* 7–12 Jan. 1850 (as guild partisan);
see Nils Jacobsen, "Civilization and Its Barbarism: The Inevitability of Juan Bustamante's
Failure," in J. Ewell and W. Beezley, eds. *The Human Tradition in Latin America: The
Nineteenth Century* (Wilmington, Del., 1989), 82–102.

most archaic illiberal values—rank medieval "monopolists." "Industrial power" was shackled by feudal bonds to the state. And if artisans could not fully accept free markets and free trade—one and the same cause— they had no one but themselves to blame for their poor performance and political plight.[9] Tejeda was on track to becoming a leading civil politi- cian (eventual chair of the civilist congress), and his work, though a gross exaggeration of residual guild powers, codified the elites' negative representation of native crafts. Liberal-democratic spokesmen forever pictured artisans as hopelessly lazy, insolent, trivial, and untalented. In the writings of the 1850s guilds appeared to be a major obstacle to economic or moral change, never a potential wellspring of progress.

By 1862 the state had formally rescinded its last sanctions to guild prerogatives, though by then Lima's motley mix of craftsmen, putting- out workers, building trades, and servicers of import luxuries seemed better represented by their mutual aid movements than by impotent guild masters. Rooted in a covert politics of the 1850s, in 1858 artisans chartered the Sociedad Democrática de Callao—on the eve of the year's protectionist rampage. In 1860 the Sociedad de Artesanos Auxilios Mutuos emerged (as did a murkier sympathetic Sociedad Amiga de las Artes), with an explicitly and fully apolitical mission, followed by a myriad of analogous self-help, educational, savings, burial, and cultural fraternities. These associations seemed to spread in tandem with each failed quest to affect government policy. Their politicking bans, to be sure, were meant to safeguard artisans from internal dissension and exploitation from above.[10] And because mutual aid posed no direct challenge to Limeño high society and economy, it was smoothly ab- sorbed as part of the city's modernizing scene, touted, for example, by observers such as Fuentes. On tariff issues, however, the stock response remained Silva Santisteban's. Free-trader faith was simple toward ar- tisans: no quarter to their quaint but seemingly incorrigible protection- ist beliefs, which eventually would be "eradicated" through heavy doses

9. Tejeda, *Emancipación de la industria*, melding Jovellanosian, Benthamite, and Saint- Simonian liberalism; Ballon, *Ideas en Arequipa*, 96–102; reproduced in Lima's *Intérprete del Pueblo*, Mar. 1852; or J. Espinoza, "Artesanos, gremios y maestros mayores," *Comercio*, 20 Oct. 1852. The imported "antifeudal" discourse of such works affects historians' perceptions of Peruvian elites, too.

10. Sketchy survey of mutual aid and covert politics in Basadre, *Historia* 5:2045–47, "El mutualismo obrero," and covert politics. For typical apolitical stance, see *Reglamento de la sociedad tipográfica de auxilios mutuos* (Lima, pam., 1868), art. 73: "Es prohibido en las reuniones tratar asuntos ajenos de su institución, a menos que alguno amago internacional amenace nuestra existencia política"—a reference to Spanish invasion experience.

of "sane" political economy. No opportunity was lost to delegitimize guild privilege, politics, and protectionism. If educational tactics failed to root out monopolistic thoughts, liberals suggested the abolition in toto of Lima's urban artisan question—by their forced (or economic) march into rural export pursuits, where labor was needed.[11]

Apart from frontal assaults, however, genuine and more promising attempts were made to convert artisans to laissez-faire. Most often these campaigns revealed the political cracks and contradictions in the facade of Peru's liberal-democratic purists. This was a romantic Jacobin alternative, if bereft of popular base. One example of utopian laissez-faire was Francisco Bilbao's *El gobierno de la libertad* (1855). Bilbao, the famed Chilean radical, had fled for safety to Lima after organizing Santiago artisans in an abortive 1851 democratic-liberal revolt—going well beyond the popular economic discontent brewing in Peru. In Lima the pan-Americanist Bilbao hooked up with Enrique Álvarez, the precocious (and short-lived) social revolutionary; together they aspired and conspired to carry the popular fervor of the 1854–1855 anti-Echenique rebellion into deeper realms: to bring "el pueblo al poder." Such urban tumult seemed catchy across the Andes in the period 1845–1855: the tragic "socialist mirage" of revolutionist-liberal artisans in Bogotá (which ended up in a true starvation march of vanquished artisans into the countryside); the anti-aristocratic and protectionist panderings (1848–1855) of the Bolivian caudillo Manuel Belzú, husband of the Peruvian feminist critic Manuela Gorriti; the crushed Chilean Jacobin rebellion of Bilbao's own Sociedad de Igualdad; and the final offensive of protectionist *gremios* in Lima. (Hobsbawm once classified such events as the most delayed and distant wave of Europe's ideological upwelling of 1848, and the same ideas, and even some refugee artisans, were occasionally at work.) But the losing outcomes for Andean artisan politics stemmed as much from the coeval wave of European manufactured exports, which made artisan democratic alliances so precariously problematic.[12]

11. Silva Santisteban, *Breves reflexiones sobre los sucesos con la importación,* 1–10; for typical anti-"monopoly" rhetoric, see Baldomero Menéndez, *Manuel de geografía y estadística del Perú* (Paris, 1861), 145: "El Perú no es ni podría ser nunca, a nuestro juicio, un pueblo industrial. Los que desconocen esta verdad y no les importa que se grave notoriamente a la mayoría de la población para favorecer unos pocos y sostener un monopolio perjuicialismo a los intereses públicos."

12. Romero, *Sociedad de Igualdad,* with many Chilean parallels to Lima artisan thought; Robert Gilmore, "Nueva Granada's Socialist Mirage," *HAHR* 36 (1956): 190–

Everywhere, in short, beleaguered traditional artisans wavered between the attractions of liberals' libertarian prospects and the fading corporatist prestige of conservatives. Ultimately, both sides in liberal-conservative conflicts abandoned inconvenient artisans. The artisans' organic-democratic aspirations did not neatly fit into the dichotomies of liberal-conservative discourse, which, if anything, defined a multivalent "culture clash" between elite and folk. Bilbao, who reputedly swayed budding rojos such as Ulloa and Cisneros before Castilla kicked him out, illustrates the disjuncture. Bilbao's role, like that of other Chilean exiles in Peru, was to pioneer certain Continental categories in Peruvian democratic discourse (such as "czarismo o el populismo") and a populist program of universal education, free association, progressive pan-Americanism, and "the people to power" (a romantic notion of direct representation). Along with Bilbao came fresh translations of Fourier and Proudhon. But part and parcel of Bilbao's universalism was a hopelessly utopian, internationalist, and popular version of free trade: "Commercial liberty is solidarity with the land, fraternity with the climate, the reciprocity of production in alliance with nature."[13] "In the government of liberty," Bilbao promised, "the freedom of commerce is a fact, by which the country ensures its production geared to what nature, topography, and climate decree." Few of Lima's urban and nativistic artisans bought this bucolic naturalistic scenario, which sounded suspiciously similar to Silva Santisteban's ravings about the country life.

About the same time, the future bohemian gadfly Fernando Casós, the most visible liberal spokesman of the 1854 revolution, listed artisans among the dispossessed. The war did enjoy a popular-democratic backing in its civil armies and mass revulsion against Echenique's venal guano "consolidados" clique. Casós, in his galvanizing manifesto, singled out the country's meager efforts to save its degraded artisan class: "The arts, in such a fashion, have been caught in the rapid flight that depletes them. The government has not founded a single school, a single workshop, or taken any measures of improvement." But Casós's primary stress was on the primacy of commerce, "whose *élan vital* stems but from liberty." Casós's partner in agitation, J. C. Ulloa, in his antimilitarist broadside,

210; Burns, *Poverty of Progress,* 106–10 (Belzú sympathizer); E. J. Hobsbawm, *The Age of Capital, 1848–1875* (New York, 1975), 4. For Peru, see Jorge G. Leguía, "Las ideas de 1848 en el Perú," in Leguía, *Estudios históricos* (Santiago, 1939), 113–54, finding a lot of "socialists" among liberals; Amézaga, *Perú liberal* pt. 2, chs. 6–7.

13. Francisco Bilbao, *El gobierno de la libertad* (Lima, 1855), v, vii, 32–33: for generational contexts, see Raúl Ferrero Rebagliati, *El liberalismo peruano: Contribución a una historia de las ideas* (Lima, 1958), 23–32.

condemned not just Echenique but also (with a little help from Proudhon), a congenital corruption of elites. In Peru, Ulloa reports, "commercial questions" unfortunately had smothered other pressing economic and political debates, though he hastened to celebrate loudly the free-trade triumph: "the commercial code of Peru is more liberal than that of the most civilized nations of Europe." Even the accused and deposed president Echenique could express more (or more vague) concerns for artisans in his own war pronouncements—notwithstanding the fact that more than anyone else, Echenique had played the free-trader nemesis of the guilds during their tariff debacle of 1851. Soon liberal manifestoes questioned Castilla's military buildup, suggesting that these funds would be better put into popular education and "fomento."[14] (Casós's career illuminates some later liberal paths and deviations; as the purest of Peru's civil libertarians, he tried with Cisneros to impeach Castilla during the congress of 1859 and led the national propaganda barrage against the Dreyfus contract; in 1872 Casós, as titular head of the military junta against Pardo's ascension, turned on the insufficiently pure civilistas and later exposed plutocratic sins in *Los hombres de bien*. Ulloa had the constancy to stay with libertarian free trade, except in the business of guano, for the rest of his career.)

Perhaps Juan Espinoza's populist *Diccionario para el pueblo: Republicano democrático, moral, político y filosófico* (1855) best exemplifies the confounding messages being sent to artisans. Espinoza, a former Uruguayan soldier (and later *Revista de Lima* essayist, mid-1860s nationalist, and civilista founder) exalted property-owning artisans in the political arena.

[Artisans] form the middle class of society between the proletarian and the rich; in republics, they support on their robust shoulders the rich landlord, the military man, the official, and everyone who wants to place themselves on top; the artisan of Paris, as in Lima, is the one who dresses and shoes the people, builds the houses . . . , and defends the country. But they don't form associations to make their force and value felt.[15]

14. Fernando Casós, *Para la historia del Perú: Revolución de 1854* (Cuzco, 1854), 91; J. R. Echenique, *El General José Rufino Echenique a sus compatriotas* (Lima, pam., 1858), 20, 110; Ulloa, *Perú en 1853*, 16; *La Actualidad: Periódico Político y Literario* (Lima), 1855, p. 7. Basadre, *Historia* 3:1047–55, 1100, and ch. 66, "La revolución popular y liberal de 1854."

15. Juan Espinoza, *Diccionario para el pueblo: Republicano democrático, moral, político y filosófico* (Lima, 1855), 66 (artesanos), 26–27 (aduanas), 330 (concurrencia industrial), 447 (fábricas), 783 (protección a la industria). For political activity concerning artisans, see J. Espinoza, *Comentarios a la constitución anónima de la sociedad del orden electoral* (Lima, pam., 1853), and 1860s "Hijo del pueblo" group, below.

But apart from assaults on autocracy, the mainstay of Espinoza's self-help entries were incessantly paternalistic (and exceedingly abstract) lectures on the elementary evils of guild restriction and the horrors of protection: "that ignorance of the people in not understanding their true interests." "Patriotism resents it," ran another definition, "but experience and economic principle teaches that not all peoples who want to can become manufacturers." In an earlier incarnation Espinoza had been busy exposing the peoples' real interests, penning public diatribes (cribbed from Tejeda) against the "antique and barbaric routine of guild organization," and calling on the lowest strata of artisans (and the police) to overthrow this class oppression.[16] There were few takers, as artisans had no other protectors left to speak of.

Liberal understandings of economic "monopoly," so central in these writings, were wholly at odds with the artisan one. Craftsmen, rather than demonize tariffs, railed against foreign imports, startling wealth concentrations, and dwindling national opportunities as the "monopolistic" threat to their livelihoods and liberties. "Foreign" was the artisan adjective instinctively linked to monopoly, in a semantic struggle seen since the 1820s.[17] Peru's radical liberals engaged in much wishful thinking about artisans. But both sides seemed stuck on the reefs of popular protectionism.

Another key political contradiction in the budding democratic thought of the 1850s was between the romantics' glorification of civic voluntary associations and a "middle class" (the operative anti-authoritarian concepts in José María Químper's initial writings on *El principio de libertad*). Yet liberals simultaneously needed to exclude even voluntary guild association from their progressive recipe, as in Químper's assertion that "workers' associations were, in effect, no other than the ancient corporations." "Nada de gremios" was his pat slogan, and Químper was already adding socialism to imagined threats to free markets.[18] Such disassociations left liberal representation of the artisan uncannily abstract, an import category of social theory, with no flesh-and-blood working hijos del país worthy of the name. Only in the mid 1860s would some begin finding usefully progressive associations in Lima's apolitical mutual aid societies, and later even in some mobilizing

16. Espinoza, *Diccionario para el pueblo,* 477; Juan Espinoza, "Artesanos, gremios y maestros mayores," *Comercio,* 20 Oct. 1852.

17. See Gootenberg, "Artisans and Merchants," ch. 4, for deeper long-term analysis.

18. José María Químper, *El principio de libertad* (Lima, 1856), A. Tauro, ed., 1948, 63, 67–68, 71–77 ("Libertad de industria y de comercio"), 82.

ones. As elite constitutional, religious, and liberal-conservative struggles heated up in the late 1850s, led by the liberals of *El Constitucional*, Francisco de Paula González Vigil, in his two 1858 classics (*Importancia de las asociaciones* and *Importancia de la educación popular*), abstractly tried to heal this breach with a new utopian socialist twist, although he was still troubled by guilds.[19] In the main, however, these works were legalistic calls for free political parties against despotic caudillos, for a bourgeois business ethic, for broadened education, for the love of work against "laziness." All such theorizing avoided specifying why Peru's hypothesized "middle class" found such paltry work and lowly civil status in the export society of the 1850s. (Química was another liberal who went to work for the Prado regime; by 1872 he was resisting the civilist movement, and in the 1880s he spearheaded efforts to block the Grace contract as an imperial—and civilist—humiliation for Peru.)

We know little about these thinkers' direct relations, if any, to the artisan class. They generally appear in their writings as an honorable category of social theory, fit for conversion to the liberal republican cause, when properly cleansed of their market deviations. But craftsmen and shopkeepers, who always clung to their humble democratic beginnings, seemed—at least in their few extant public writings—unable to shake off their modest protective and nationalist notions. The brothers José and Pedro Gálvez talked to artisans from the 1850 Club Progresista and would organize them in the 1860s; Espinoza tried to win electoral partisans in 1853 (and would also try later); Vigil actually advised mutual aid societies on proper associative principles and recruited guild leaders (such as Mariano Salazar y Zapata) to fight for Castilla's 1857 constitution against reactionary attacks.[20] But the general conclusion holds that Peru's most progressive liberals of the 1850s were more concerned with establishing elite civil institutions than with extending citizenship and opportunity to lower orders. They were at most top-down "traditional modernizers."

19. Francisco de Paula González Vigil, *Importancia de las asociaciones* and *Importancia de la educación popular* (both 1858; rpt. Lima, 1948); see *El Constitucional* (Lima), 1858, and role of J. G. Paz Soldán. Basadre, *Historia*, vol. 3, ch. 49; 6:2857 (González Vigil); 7:2755 (Química).

20. "Programa del sr. Domingo Elías, para cuando suba a la presidencia," *Comercio*, 15 Oct., "Desarrollo del programa del club progresista," 6 Nov. 1850—with stress on "associations" and school of arts; Espinoza, *Sociedad del orden electoral*; *El Hijo del Pueblo* (Lima), 22 Feb. 1864; Basadre, *Historia* 6:2857; see Trazegnies, "Genealogía del derecho peruano," on traditional modernizers.

Conservative thinkers, by contrast, were not interested in republican, protectionist artisans at all; in this regard they were unlike traditionalists elsewhere in the Americas (notably Mexican nationalists such as Lucas Alamán) or Peru's bygone Gamarrista caudillos. Peru's classic antirepublican statement by "Pruvonena" (a.k.a. José de la Riva Agüero, 1858) was unrepentant in its contempt for the "colored people," "plebes," and "anarchists" who had "inverted the social order" since 1821 and despised volatile Gamarra-style sierran populism. It made no issue at all of commercial change. Fuentes, a less hysterical sort, could at least rigorously present artisans, quantitatively and colorfully, as part of Peruvian reality, though he hardly partook of their political feelings. The archconservative Bartolomé Herrera, the most active midcentury ideologue, negated "popular sovereignty" in terms at least as philosophical as the liberals' rarefied "people" and directed his struggles into ever narrower religious realms, Peru's obsessive conservative cause (though in relative terms the Peruvian church was barely besieged). In economics he only hinted at a divine interventionism.[21]

Conservatives thus presented but a shadow of a corporatist project from which to attract antiliberal resentments. When their thoughts did turn to commerce, they seemed to embrace free trade with little hesitation—on the grounds that without European influence and aid (and, in the mid 1860s, without undivine intervention), Peru would sink into a native barbarism worse than that before Pizarro's salvation in 1532. Their unbridled Hispanicist worship of Europe inhibited economic nationalist thinking. Not incidently, and in striking paradox, Peru's major conservative caudillos proved more blatantly liberal on trade and laissez-faire than did their strong-state liberal political adversaries, though this was also a vestige of their stronghold in the socially conservative south. This pairing worked itself out from the Echenique-Castilla rivalry of the 1850s through the Piérola-Pardo conflicts of the 1870s, with the conservatives blasting utopian *rojos*, liberals, and protectionists in the same breath. Openings to artisans would develop instead out of liberal currents and civilist practice and from a shared patriotic revulsion to reactionaries willing to turn Peru back to Spain in the mid 1860s.[22] In

---

21. José de la Riva Agüero [Pruvonena, pseud.], *Memorias y documentos para la historia de la independencia del Perú y causas del mal éxito que ha tenido ésta* (Paris, 1858), 2 vols., passim, 602; Bartolomé Herrera, *Escritos y discursos*, comp. J. Leguía (Lima, 1929), 2 vols.; Trazegnies, *Idea de derecho*, 90–99, 130–35; Amézaga, *Perú liberal*, ch. 5; Jeffrey Klaiber, *La iglesia en el Perú: Su historia social desde la independencia* (Lima, 1988), esp. ch. 3; on Mexican economic conservatives, see Potash, *Mexican Government and Industry*.

22. E.g., *Perú y la influencia europea* (1862); for conflation of difference, see Gonzalo

any case, the artisans themselves, still pining for their substantive republican equality, evinced little interest in hierarchic conservative causes. By and large, then, the artisans of the 1850s were simply lectured to about wayward habits, never grasped in concrete terms (Fuentes aside), and demobilized in republican politics. If they expressed ideas of their own, these rang out in the prepolitical—or perhaps antipolitical—form of mob actions, such as the 1855 rampage against aristocratic property or the protectionist riots of 1858. There was, indeed, a "culture conflict," even between sympathetic elites and the folk.

The Renascence of Artisan Politics, 1859–1876

Yet attitudes began to shift perceptibly toward recognition of the flesh-and-blood national artisan after the 1858 riots. Apart from a shock wave against liberal complacencies, the protest revealed that Castilla's liberal order had a harsh, repressive underside, until then limited to the general's immediate or constitutionalist rivals. To be sure, most comfortable Limeños likely concurred with the bitter free-trade polemics of Silva Santisteban and the congress. And the only immediate impact on thinking was a rush to fill San Carlos academy's Public Chair of Economics and Industrial Legislation. (The *cátedra* was awarded not to Silva Santisteban but to Felipe Masías, whose exceedingly abstract free-trader economics text of 1860 became the standard.) A few years later a government prize was announced for an essay on the unignorable "social problem." The winner, an anti-industrial tract called "Means to Stimulate the Peruvians to Useful Work According to the Current State of Society and Conducive to Public Order," says a mouthful about Peruvian elite sociology in its title alone—though the author conceded that his proposed education drive might at least propel a demand for nationally made pencils.[23]

Portocarrero, "Conservadurismo, liberalismo y democracia en el Perú del siglo xix," in Adrianzén, *Pensamiento político*, 85–98; Ulloa, *Piérola;* see Daniel Gleason, "Ideological Cleavages in Early Republican Peru, 1821–1872," Ph.D. diss., University of Notre Dame, 1974, for clerical focus; Ballon, *Ideas en Arequipa,* 277, for first Catholic (and, logically, southern) artisan clubs (1880s).

23. Tomás L. Saanpperé, *Memoria sobre los medios de estimular a los peruanos según la situación actual de la sociedad al trabajo provechoso y más conducente al orden público* (Lima, pam., 1867), sec. viii: predictably, "La industria fabril, en la casi totalidad de sus ramificaciones, no sólo no existe al presente, sino que, con mucha dificultad se aclimatara entre

But other voices came forth, too, infiltrating broader elite concerns about the extravagant use of guano by Peru's militarist regimes and their fitful pace to full civil rule. By the end of the decade a form of industrial populism was in gear, born from liberal disenchantment with Castilla, electoral organization, anti-Spanish patriotism, a revived artisan politics, and new peoples' notions of technification. The first audible salvo was the radical satire of the *La Zamacueca Política* (a "Periódico político, popular y joco-serio"), whose premier issue, not by coincidence, hit the streets a week after the artisan jacquerie. Intermittently repressed by the authorities, the conspiratorial *Zamacueca* was organized by a shady group of dissidents under José Lecaros (and the artisan organizer Salazar y Zapata), men who broached no limits in their antagonism to the Castillan order. But it also seems to have lured liberal purists dismayed with Castilla's harassments of congress; Ricardo Palma, the budding costumbrista writer, secretly honed his talents composing political portraits for the *Zamacueca* (which took its name from an infamously plebeian Afroperuvian dance).[24] In an obvious move to spur a popular following, the paper wholeheartedly embraced the artisan cause.

Here, too, the craftsmen appeared as Peru's progressive but degraded "middle class"—but they were now portrayed with none of the studied ambivalence and abstraction of earlier liberal theorizers. The *Zamacueca* openly defended artisan violence, seconded their calls for tariffs and prohibitions, and publicized the plight of "political prisoners" held since the riots. It condemned state contracts to foreigners, demanded the long-promised school of arts and guild reorganization, damned Castilla for guano giveaways (such as the Gibbs contract), and distributed artisan pamphlets. Column after column bristled with sharp and irreverent barbs against free-traders such as Silva Santisteban, whose particular corpus was summarized in a critical review as "pedantic, trivial, false, in

nosotros, en términos de impedir cuando menos, la importación de productos extranjeros" (29). Masías, *Curso de economía* (1860), in very abstract (antiphysiocratic) vein, does argue that "industria fabril" produces value (chs. 3–4); ch. 5, "Industria fabril en grande y en pequeño: Cual de estas dos formas es preferible," hypothetically deals with reformist priority theme.

   24. *La Zamacueca Política*, Jan. 1859–Aug. 1859; Basadre, *Historia* 5:2045, for (unlinked) career of Lecaros; 4:1775, Palma role. With guild leaders, Lecaros had formed militias for Castilla in 1854 and 1857; with his 1858 Sociedad Filantrópica Democrática, he was implicated in artisan riots but rehabilitated by San Román in 1862. *Zamacueca* was unceasing in charging Castilla with "betrayal" of 1854 liberalism; artisans wrote of supporting "Dr. L." in elections ("Artesanos," *Comercio*, 22 Dec. 1858).

poor taste—and simply an excuse for repression."[25] On the political style of Castilla, the paper offered, for instance, this lively protest song:

On the eve of elections
to the pueblo he promised
that their industry would be respected
And with his lances and battalions
these were the obligations
now left broken
    Let's say today, *Cacha-bota* [untranslatable pun],[26]
    satiated and conceited
    when dealing with guano
    his soul gets so excited.[27]

This was not the most graphic of the guano-oriented social verse of the times, a form pioneered in José Sanz's 1856 mock epic "La Huaneida."[28] Another *Zamacueca* poem, called simply "The People," made guano liberalism, greedy foreigners, a parasitic aristocracy, and militarism the amalgamated foes of the masses:

And what to do, if this is industry
what's it left for us?
Paris, London, and Brussels
in exchange for our guano
send us a thousand trifles
of poorly gilded copper,
gloves, perfumes, laces
make-up, false jewels [etc.],
and twenty thousand other pieces of junk
that goad on our pathetic women.
    On this road we follow
    and the pass we traverse;

25. See esp. "Los artesanos: Folleto del sr. Silva Santisteban," *Zamacueca*, 29 Jan.– 12 Feb. 1858 (his pamphlet was published simultaneously in *El Comercio*); "Los artesanos," 8 Jan. 1858, "Presos políticos," 19 Feb. 1859, "Progreso del Perú," 2 Apr. 1859, "Artesanos," 9 Apr. 1859.

26. This Peruvian slang actually carries a sexual connotation; it may be roughly translated as "boot-fucker" (pers. com., E. Falco, Stony Brook, May 1992).

27. Untitled, *Zamacueca*, 16 Feb. 1859; these weren't only ones disturbed with Castilla's words to guilds; "Promesas hechas a los artesanos," *Comercio*, 18 Jan. 1859, by chiefs of Lima political "clubs."

28. Basadre, *Historia* 4:1889–91, discussed guano as poetic social genre; among works, Felipe Pardo's "Pueblo que no trabaja y come huano" and "La huaneida" criticized "el porvenir lejano contemple en el bulto colosal de huano."

with this sort of government
we're on the short path to hell.[29]

One gets the "joco-serio" flavor here. (By the 1870s bombastic satirical journals would become a lasting hallmark of Limeño political culture.) But the mercurial *Zamacueca* is a serious source for assaying the attitudes of a disaffected portion of the elite, its iconoclastic followers, and their special new romance with restless, flesh-and-blood democratic artisans. Their most frequent target was a sort of opportunistic and *entreguista* militarism, which radicals blamed for Peru's economic uncertainties and for the predicament of national industry and artisans. During the years of the republic, "sixty-one thousand" had died for the sins of the militarists, eighteen thousand under Castilla alone. Castilla had only made a "mockery of republicanism." The *Zamacueca* shows the direct imprimatur of Lima artisans (in their *comunicados*, for example), no longer at the mercy of other's hopeful interpretations. The *Zamacueca* fired away at corrupt oligarchy three decades before González Prada codified his similar vein of defiant working-class nationalism in the 1880s. By August 1859, when the *Zamacueca* declared itself in open rebellion against the state, Castilla ordered the subversives out of business for good.[30] In this climate, legalistic purists in the congress were expelled the next year after plotting Castilla's overthrow; Luciano Cisneros, Palma, Vigil, and Ulloa stood among them.[31] Surely not by coincidence, a far more sober but parallel elite critique of high guano society and militarism began appearing in the *Revista de Lima*, which shared some of the cast.

Was there any new economic argument here? Theirs was a highly partisan one, a literal gut translation of artisan views. It posed a fundamental sociopolitical argument: Peru's blind adoration of foreign products had spawned a skewed distribution of wealth and power, protected by the oppressions of a squandering, self-serving militarism. In their formal riposte to Silva Santisteban's take on the artisan problem, the *Zamacueca* defended the high quality and ample quantity of local labor, estimating guild membership at an optimistic twenty thousand; they

29. "El pueblo," *Zamacueca*, 27 July 1859. "Viva el pueblo" was a common refrain in paper (as in the 1858 riots).
30. "Los catorce gobiernos son la causa verdadera del malestar permanente," *Zamacueca*, 14 May 1859; and 18 June 1859, 3 Aug. 1859.
31. Basadre, *Historia*, vol. 3, ch. 49; the paper often mentioned and clearly identified with this liberal group; *Comercio*, 17 Jan. 1859 (first repression), Aug. 1859.

mocked the notion of independent craftsmen marching off to rural exports (lands were already owned by the rich, and real men cannot painlessly abdicate their skills and memories); they read political economy and European economic history as a protectionist parable. The reasoning was so artisanal that the *Zamacueca* rejected even modern industries in favor of craft revival:

In vain does Sr. Santisteban try to prove that the country cannot establish grand factories, large-scale manufacturing. For no one asks for textile factories or the prohibition of foreign cloth; so why muddle the issues? The import of handicrafts [*obras de mano*] is the unwanted one. For unable to compete here with foreigners, with expensive labor, it is clear that our artisans are perishing. . . . There are a thousand ways a rich nation can promote the arts and industry.

If Sr. Santisteban misses in our writings technology and science, it's because we speak so that the people can understand us.[32]

This, then, was not comparable to the full-scale developmentalism of Casanova, Pardo, or Cisneros. Rather than an economic discovery, the *Zamacueca* marked the first political rediscovery of Lima's simple artisan, plus a fresh kind of social critique of the regime. Yet by the end of the decade it would be hard to dismiss a progressive and popular role for liberal "technology and science."

The 1860s saw increasing efforts to legitimize or exploit from above the artisan cause, though this populist turn (and its relations to topsy-turvy elite politics) is hard to untangle. These began with the return of banished liberals under San Román (1862) and would culminate in the civilista election in 1872. By then the elite image of the hopeless artisan had been thoroughly replaced by the artisan as cornerstone of productive civil progress. One should not overstate the elite democratic impulse, for the "artisans" who acquired new meanings remained reified; few in number and close to creole urban culture, artisans made a convenient stand-in for an imaginary "people."

One early and recognized literary example was Trinidad Manuel Pérez's 1862 "proletarian theater" piece, *La industria y el poder,* which was profusely dedicated to the now combined Society of Artisans of Lima and Callao. (Pérez, a well-known figure in Limeño literary circles, was founder of the 1870s *El Correo del Perú,* a journal in the lineage of the *Revista de Lima* and a forum for Palma, Gorriti, and the young

---

32. "Los artesanos: folleto del sr. Silva Santisteban," *Zamacueca,* 5 Feb. 1859 (and all Feb.–Mar.); for parallel radical view, "Los artesanos," *Comercio,* 3 Jan. 1859.

González Prada, among others.) The play unabashedly romanticizes the virtues of a suffering working class, offering simple artisan characters who protect "liberty" against the endless transgressions of corrupt "opulent society." Interestingly—in the aftermath of security roundups after the 1858 riots—the plot involves unfair charges of "conspiracy" against the young "hijo del pueblo" Andrés. Pérez earnestly deals with Limeño guilds as they were, not as fanciful "industries." In a hopeful final scene a "minister" (secretly related to an artisan) emerges as their "defender," saying something about artisan aspirations for political familiarity and legitimacy. In short, the play formally embodied the guilds' old "honorable artisan," though it was obviously influenced by contemporary European social drama. Unappealing to Lima's critics, *La industria y el poder* nevertheless went through two more editions and pleased sympathetic audiences well into the 1870s. After one documented 1865 performance of "political significance," the author was "crowned" by artisan leaders.[33] This transformation from the 1850s liberal representation of retrograde artisans was more than a turn in literary fashion.

More portentous still were tangible efforts to revive moribund artisan politics and recruit craftsmen to emerging civil causes—efforts linked to the nationalism engendered by the Spanish war and to liberal activists in the Prado regime. The newspaper *El Hijo del Pueblo* (1864–1868), one such forgotten attempt, was actually directed by shining liberal lights such as Espinoza, Vigil, and even Silva Santisteban himself. Its prospectus was dedicated to "the moral progress and enlightenment of the masses." The paper was linked to Colonel Francisco Bolognesi's new mutual aid society of the same name, specializing in peoples' education, rule of law, workers' savings, and popular moralization (for example, guild juntas to hunt out artisan wife-beaters).[34] Here one no longer detects the customary guild-bashing and not a single lecture on free trade. Instead, the pages of the *Hijo del Pueblo* featured patriotic exhortations (quite effective during the emerging conflict with Spain) and

33. Trinidad Manuel Pérez, *La industria y el poder* (Lima, 3d ed., 1876); *Comercio*, 11 Dec. 1865; analyzed as "proletarian theater" in Basadre, *Historia* 3:1385–86, 4:1891. For Castilla's post-riot jailing of "foreign" elements in artisan "conspiracy," *Comercio*, 27 Dec. 1858.

34. "Prospecto," *El Hijo del Pueblo* (Lima), 22 Feb. 1864, and Juan Espinoza, "¿Qué son los hijos del pueblo?" 20 Feb. 1868; unfortunately, the sole extant copy (BNP) is in deplorable condition; also *La República: Revista Seminal Política y Literaria* (Lima), Ulloa's nationalist paper aligned with "Hijos del pueblo," 20 Mar. 1864; *Constitución reglamentaria de la sociedad los hijos del pueblo* (Lima, pam., 1864). For Bolognesi, Jorge Basadre, *Peruanos del siglo xix* (Lima, 1981), 25–27—i.e., the popular martyr of 1879.

campaigns for massive artisan electoral societies (as in February 1868) against the military Balta regime, which threatened, among other things, Pardo's national guano company. Of their common foe in the army, the paper confides to artisans, "The military do not protect either agriculture or industry—only themselves."[35] By then an organized Hijos del Pueblo election club was attracting hundreds to its meetings in efforts hailed by parallel publications, such as Ulloa's 1864 paper *La República*. All this ferment was doubtless part of the failed bid of Manuel Ureta, the obscure forerunner of Pardo's civilista party. In a phrase, some "sons of the nation" were looking to the "sons of the people" for aid.

One October 1866 gathering is colorfully documented in the Lima press. It followed artisan protests of their overlooked role in the patriotic *dos de mayo* defense of Callao against Spain (led by the liberal martyr José Gálvez, designed by the engineer Malinowski, and ensured by Bolognesi's artillery)—ignored in contrast to the highly publicized December 1865 popular sacking of foreign warehouses in the port. "More than 300 known and honorable artisans" met in the San Francisco convent to debate upcoming congressional elections: "a powerful social class intervening with full deliberation and knowledge," according to *El Comercio*. Protests were raised against "all the caudillos who, to climb to posts, laud the artisan, and offer a thousand promises they never think to fulfill; worse, arriving to power, they forget and deprecate the man of the people who served as their stepping stone."[36] The meeting of this renamed Club Progresista, hosted by the jurist José Gregorio Paz-Soldán (rector of San Marcos and long-time liberal kingpin), came out in favor of the presidency of Colonel Prado—the military reformist joined by would-be civilists Pardo, Gálvez, Químper, and Cisneros. Vague on other issues, Prado embraced artisan national militias (as Pardo would in 1872) and even tried to restore a sort of officially sanctioned guild system—to the dismay, no doubt, of allies Espinoza and Tejeda.[37]

The Hijo del Pueblo appears remarkably similar to the political clubs, protoparties, that had once courted artisans at the start of the export era.

---

35. "Un artesano," *Hijo del Pueblo*, 20 June 1868; Basadre, *Historia* 4:1583 (war artisans), 1718 (Ureta bid).

36. "Candidatura del Col. Prado," *Comercio*, 12 Oct. 1866; see Dean, *Cuestión de saqueo*, for contrasting event.

37. In the 1850s Paz Soldán was editor of the opposition journal *El Constitucional*, link between liberal initiatives; Mariano Prado, "Reglamento de policía municipal," pt. vii, "De los gremios," *Peruano*, 4 June 1866; also 17 Feb., report on war role of Sociedad Tipográfica de Auxilios Mutuos.

The galloping civil pretensions of elites must have inspired the artisans' own political hopes. Why this happened in the mid 1860s seems fairly clear. Apart from social changes within the artisanry (discussed below), intensified electoral competition and nationalist politics loomed central. By 1863 municipalities and municipal politics, long suppressed in Peru, had been revived and made the natural arena for Lima guild influence. The 1860 constitution, Castilla's great political compromise, gave "masters of workshops" (even if illiterate) the vote, as the system bypassed the closed elite electoral colleges of the past. Notables would now need the support of the "middle class" of guano expansion, such as it was, and just as liberals had hoped. In a still constricted and centralist regime, urban craftsmen made an indispensable constituency, and civil groupings swiftly moved to exploit them and their budding and highly mobilizable societies.[38]

Equally decisive, no doubt, were the heady political events of 1864–1866, which brought artisans into a new nationalist mainstream. Peru's "Americanist" liberals (a group with roots in official 1850s pan-Americanism), among them Ulloa, Casós, Tejeda, Pacheco, Cisneros, Lissón, and Márquez, were already activated with Maximilian's Mexican adventure and assumed a vanguard role when Spain moved against Peru in 1864. They excited a gathering wave of popular republicanism and anti-imperialism throughout the two-year affair. Liberal nationalist legitimacy only soared during the "popular and national revolution" of 1865, led by Colonel Prado against the "treasonous" president Pezet, while Peru's antirepublican conservatives offered up apologetics (or worse) to Spain. The dramatic repulsion of the Spanish fleet at Callao on 2 May 1866—during which many sons of the pueblo offered their services and lives against "European transgression"—made for patriotic links between liberals and popular nationalists.[39] The old artisan na-

38. On electoral change, Basadre, *Elecciones y centralismo*, 22–32; Vincent Peloso, "Electoral Reform and Social Conflict in Mid-Nineteenth Century Peru" (paper presented to AHA, 1989); all papers reveal enhanced electoral organizing of artisans; by the mid 1860s authorities charged activism (and corruption) was out of hand (Peloso, 14–15). For a general appreciation of artisan republican politics, see Salvatorre, "Markets and Popular Protest," 20–26.

39. Basadre, *Historia*, vol. 4, chs. 64–69 (and many links of core liberals), vol. 3, ch. 52 (Americanist liberals); see, e.g., *Hijo del Pueblo*, Apr.–May 1864; *Comercio*, 15 May 1866; Lissón, *La república en el Perú*. Propaganda on both sides was intense: liberals in emergency papers such as *El Perú* and *El Estandarte Rojo*, *El Mercurio* (1864 alone), conservatives in *El Tiempo*, *El Proceso Católico*. MacEvoy, "Manuel Pardo," ch. 3, on Pardo shift.

tional creed was enhanced, well beyond submerged economic ideals, at a moment of crunching economic pressures on Peru. One suspects that these events—along with Pardo's frustrating term as Prado's reforming minister—affected emergent civilist thinking on the social question, widening their search for real citizens.

Another critical milestone in artisan (and official) thinking was the establishment, and burgeoning visibility, of Lima's Escuela de Artes y Oficios, which also opened in 1864. Vainly promised time after time to guilds since the mid 1840s, in many respects the school reflected the most benign facets of artisan thought and official conciliation. The school's pedagogic mission harbored a built-in antiprotectionist bias, hopes for cheaper labor, the state assumption of decrepit guild training and quality-control functions, and a stress on technical skill in petty crafts, modeled on fine European training for the backward hijos del pueblo. Superseding forced craft production in Lima's panopticon penitentiary and the (now money-losing) military mechanical training at the Bellavista naval foundry, the Escuela de Artes was meant as a controlling welfare response to the social problem. It was not preparation for an industrial future.[40] But it inadvertently opened a new stage in Peru's growing scientific fascination—a move to technical populism.

Peru recruited Julio Jarrier, the eminent Chilean pioneer in technical education, to design the vocational programs of the school, which opened at an initial cost of $295,000. At a dramatic public inaugural in December 1864 Castilla himself clarified the aims: "The growing decadence of indigenous industry is making competition impossible. Resort to the protectionist system, condemned by economic principles, has no part in remedying the evils that such conditions inflict on our obreros. But one after another have had to abandon their occupations, sterile now for the individual and society."[41] Among the dignitaries present was a certain Argentine liberal, Domingo F. Sarmiento (the dean of Americanist education), who lectured on how Mexico and Peru have never "retained" their mining riches. Educated, Anglo-Saxon California and Australia, in contrast, were truly developing.

Commitments to the school proved serious. It opened with a class of

40. A. Gutiérrez de la Fuente, *Exposición que hace la h. municipalidad de Lima al supremo gobierno* (Lima, pam., 1863), 17–18 (prison crafts); Noboa, *Memoria de hacienda de 1864,* 25; "Reglamento orgánico de factoría de Bellavista," *Peruano,* 11 Jan. 1867; idea dated from the 1849 artisan campaign, and even Silva Santisteban heartily endorsed it: *Breves reflexiones sobre los sucesos con la importación,* 35, 49–50.

41. "Escuela de artes y oficios," *Comercio,* 10 Dec. 1864.

forty-seven, for seventeen annual graduates, with steam-powered workshops for mechanics, foundries, furniture makers, carpenters, cart makers and the like, using the latest in imported craft tools. In 1866 fifteen
scholarships were added for "sons of honorable artisans." An official
report glowed, "The progress this institution brings will show in the
magnificent masters of workshops that come out, who spread throughout the republic's territory, will powerfully affect the arts, now so backward in Peru."[42] In 1869 Mayor Pardo pledged even more "stimulus to
the working class," creating a parallel municipal Escuela Industrial, with
seven workshops for some four hundred students in day (and adult
evening) classes. He instituted complementary civic prizes for workshops with growing employment, the youngest masters, and highest
literacy, awarded that year at a festival presided over by Fuentes, Cisneros, and the *El Nacional* publisher Andrés Avelino Aramburú, fast
becoming the civilista point man to artisans.

By the early 1870s two campuses were necessary in the capital, and as
Cisneros had suggested, congress dictated their expansion in "every
province of Peru," a working sign of the new national imperatives.
President Pardo ordered the first workshop-school opened in Ayacucho,
as part of an innovative Indian assimilation program, along with his
fourfold multiplication of primary students nationwide. By the late
1870s the budgets of the Lima schools alone exceeded those of the
country's six universities combined.[43] By then congress was wondering
aloud whether national benefits warranted such "huge costs."

Major political figures were involved, such as General Manuel de
Mendiburu, the 1870 director (and notable republican historian), and
Carlos Lissón, volunteer teacher, publicist, and sociologist of the nation.
Each year the school mounted public exhibitions and artisan prizes. The
academy, bent on instilling pride, was virtually a barracks in its quest for
social order. Student life was fully regimented, replete with military-style
salutes and dire prohibitions on complaints, reading, obscenity, and
"jokes"—about as fun as Casanova's bygone factory. But deploying an
apt military metaphor, one enthusiast wrote in 1872, "The European
monopoly of national industry has been mortally wounded; several years

42. "Memoria de gobierno, policía y obras públicas," *Peruano*, 23 Feb. 1867 (and
10 Jan. 1866); Manuel Pardo, "Memoria en que el alcalde de municipalidad da cuenta de
sus trabajos de actual corporación," in López, *Pardo*, 461, 482, 491 (1870).
43. Hunt, "Growth and Guano," 110; *Diarios de debates*, 1876, 140–41; "Exhibiciones industriales," *Patria*, 17 Feb. 1872, speaks of foreign models in a "jardín de
aclimatación."

will be needed to abolish it completely, and extirpate a monopoly which formed under the careless shadow of our governments."[44] "Monopoly" was taking on the signification of the artisans over that of the liberal political economists.

The material impact on the Lima artisan sector is harder to detect, given the scattered, noncomparable, and often indecipherable statistics from the 1870s. At a minimum, some 734 (taxed) manufacturing workshops operated in 1873, employing (three years later) some 6,519 working artisans and workers (almost half remained in the clothing trades). These figures were still down from the late 1850s. But these data conceal substantial numbers of poorer craftsmen exempted from tax rolls and (given the sorry lack of business records from the mid 1870s) excludes the expansive impact of post-1874 currency devaluations (estimated at 40 to 70 percent), much commented on at the time. In the crisis year of 1876 unemployment remained very high, gauged at 23.4 percent in an active urban labor force of 34,000, one-third of Lima's population.[45] Therefore, a strong case cannot be made for any immediate artisanal revival linked to the school of arts, something noted by contemporary observers. However, global numbers hide significant qualitative changes in the artisanry. Occupational heterogeneity increased (in new guilds such as bookbinders and brewmasters); more specialized crafts exchanged inputs (such as processed chemicals); mechanized "first-class" shops (many of them immigrant-led) took larger shares of business; and there was a rapid adoption and spread of small machinery (sewing machines, power tools, and the like, as touted in ubiquitous newspaper ads for their sale and use). The latter was a noteworthy shift in a sector that had traditionally eschewed all technical innovation, and enhanced productivity may account for some of the labor-force stagnation (for example, given the scores of independent cigar makers made obsolete by cigarette-rolling contraptions). For the first time, middle-

44. *Reglamento interior de la escuela nacional de artes y oficios* (Lima, pam., 1867), 6–7; J. F. Ezela y Carassa, "Escuela de artes e oficios," *Patria,* 14 Apr. 1872; "Memoria leída por el Gen. Mendiburu director de la escuela de artes y oficios al abrirse los exámenes públicos del año . . . ," *Patria,* 12 Apr. 1872; *Patria,* 20 Nov. 1872; Lissón, *Sociología del Perú,* 69–74.

45. Rough calculation from 1871 "Patentes" tax (*Peruano,* Mar.–Apr. 1873); not comparable to 1830–61 patentes series in Gootenberg, "Artisans and Merchants," chs. 2, 4; Hunt, "Growth and Guano," table 13 (labor force analysis of 1876 census), 92–93; cf. later sectoral study (1885) by Bollinger, "Rise of U.S. Influence," tables 3, 5. Clarke, *Peru and Creditors,* 53–54 on exchange devaluations; or Gootenberg, "Price Levels in Peru," table 8.

class consumers were beginning to turn to nationally made goods. Moreover, craftsmen worked alongside a wholly new network of true factories, big and small.

Less material but more important, then, was the impact on artisan and public consciousness: with such visible official concern, the School of Arts helped relegitimate the "honor" of skilled trabajo in Lima and broadened imaginings of the future. It spurred other forms of worker consciousness: for example, Manuel T. Figueroa, chief *maestro* of the workshops (and himself an amateur inventor), used the post in 1878 to form the Confederación de Artesanos Unión Universal, Peru's first syndicalist confederation.[46]

By the early 1870s, indeed, a visible workers' movement was underway in Lima. Apart from its marked craft flavor, it reflected a nascent artisan proletarianization in expanding putting-out workshops (130 workers in Cohen's cigar workshop alone, for example), in the new mechanized factories (such as López Aldana's Vitarte), and in the gangs of workers formed in public works during the Balta regime. Organizationally, it evolved fitfully from Lima's earlier network of apolitical mutual aid societies; by 1873 experienced craft leaders (such as those of the Sociedad Fraternal de Artesanos) were loudly decrying political initiatives by their members, which were strictly against the canons and customs of mutual aid. Repoliticized workers soon forged their own intellectual organs, such as *El Artesano* (1873) and, revealing of the transition in consciousness, José Enrique del Campo's *El Obrero* (1875–1877), linked to the printers and the Sociedad de Artesanos (sometimes denoted as "socialist," though del Campo was also a civilista founder). Aramburú, Pardo's staunch supporter in the semiofficial civilista *El Nacional,* donated his time and services to start the artisan press.[47] The papers even worked to organize societies in Cuzco and Arequipa, well beyond the city sights of previous artisans.

A major popular concern was the galloping inflation of food and housing costs since the mid 1860s, part and parcel of Peru's larger fiscal instability. Municipal authorities, led again by Mayor Pardo, responded with a flurry of schemes, including plans for worker-organized housing projects, based on principles of mutual aid. The popular Lima Caja de

46. Basadre, *Historia* 6:2858.

47. Gabriel Corante, "Discurso pronunciado por el presidente de la sociedad fraternal de artesanos," *Patria,* 2 Jan. 1873; Basadre, *Historia* 5:2045–48; Basadre, *Peruanos,* 47; MacEvoy, "Manuel Pardo," table 1.

Ahorros, initiated as well by Pardo, was a notable success in social insurance and workers' savings. Artisans expressed civil ideals in demonstrations against the idleness that had left large numbers dependent on the revived national guards, controlled by the same civilistas, the republican alternative to a conservative and costly army. More and more, the idiom belonged to a working class and less to segregated entrepreneurial crafts.[48] A smattering of true wage strikes even occurred, starting, symbolically enough, in 1872 with the action of construction workers tearing down the ancient walls of colonial Lima; in 1875 a dock strike was reported in Callao. One opposition charge was that now President Pardo, having used the peoples' militias in the bloody days of July 1872 (resisting the Gutiérrez coup), could not put the masses down.[49] Alarm in the commercial press was matched by the elation in the workers' own.

Apart from an explosion of new mutual aid, philanthropic, savings, and educational groups, by 1871 craftsmen had patched together a makeshift confederation of trades. The significantly named La Republicano was the forerunner, by all accounts, of the syndicalist confederation of 1878—starting point of Peru's modern workers' movement in the decade after the Pacific War.[50] The ferment was international as well as local in origin. For example, Peruvian editions appeared of overseas progressive works, such as Fernando Garrido's *Historia de las asociaciones obreras*, advocating proletarian cooperativism and industry; by 1875 the stock of artisan and worker ideas had been enriched far beyond their own traditions and experience, as the syndicalist title of their union suggests. Unlike the provincial city artisans of the 1840s, and much like the civilistas themselves, the workers soon sought nationwide connections. For example, in Cuzco, Trinidad María Enríquez (the first Peruvian woman to attend university) organized the town's artisans and new working-class night schools and in 1876 instigated the election of a Cuzqueño carpenter, Francisco González, to the congress itself. In fact,

48. Giesecke, *Masas urbanas y rebelión*, chs. 3–4, on social issues; M. Pardo, "Memoria de director de Sociedad de Beneficencia Pública" (1868), in López, *Pardo,* 403–61; "La cuestión subsistencia," *Patria,* 7 Apr. 1873.

49. "La huelga de obreros," *Patria,* 3 Sept. 1872, 19 Dec. 1872; the only precedent—rumored strike of bakery peones in 1859 (in wake of artisan riots)—"Crónica de la capital," *Comercio,* 11 Feb. 1859.

50. Peter Blanchard, *The Origins of the Peruvian Labor Movement, 1883–1919* (Pittsburgh, 1982), chs. 2, 4; Rolando Pereda Torres, *Historia de las luchas sociales del movimiento obrero en el Perú republicano, 1858–1917* (Lima, 1982), 37–44; we lack solid study of associations, often mentioned in press of mid 1870s.

two civilista-supported artisans had already sat in the congress, one (the silversmith Manuel Basurto) defeating the wealthy liberal ideologue Francisco García Calderón for his post![51]

Not much is known about artisan thinking before the dislocations of the war. (Afterward, anarchism became rife, firing new nationalist-activist intellectuals such as González Prada.) What is now known is that from the top, among Pardo and his closest civil advisers, a sense of possibilities in workers' politics emerged, picked up while Pardo headed the Beneficencia and toyed with while he was mayor in the early 1870s. Historians are divided on whether this turn reincarnated a traditional coercive "clientalism" or marked a deeper shift in Pardo's thinking, toward a needed "social element" for the citizenry of a practical republic. (This ideal of popular integration, at least, is traceable to his disappointment with Prado's *militares* and the oligarchic congress that stymied his fiscal project in 1867.)[52] Whatever the root, artisans and workers came in droves. Recruited through their workshops and civilist electoral clubs, artisans figured prominently among initial civilist founders (signatories of the 1871 manifesto of the Sociedad de Independencia electoral)—including the jeweller Ignacio Albán, president of the Society of Artisans. By one count, at a critical civilista rally at the Odeón theater (May 1871) some 35 percent of those present were identifiable as "artisans," the largest social group. In August 1871, during the dramatic, fourteen-thousand-strong inaugural march on Acho by the civilista campaign—the first mass demonstration in republican history—guild banners and leaders were again out in force. Afterward Pardo lauded the way in which "the disillusionment and political indifference of the laboring classes has been replaced by a vital enthusiasm of individuals and society."[53]

Other studies show how, if in "prepolitical" fashion, artisans and street people came to defend the regime in the riots that averted and followed the military coup after Pardo's victory in July 1872. Pardo's nemesis in office, the free-trader, social conservative, and pro-army Piérola, soon also framed himself as the man of the "people," but this was not an appealing ideological blend for artisans. Surely in the 1870s (if ever)

51. Basadre, *Historia* 5:2094–95; MacEvoy, "Manuel Pardo," 223; the same García Calderón of *Diccionario de legislación*.

52. MacEvoy, "Manuel Pardo," 218–37, for this fresh perspective and superb data, esp. table 1, "Relación de los firmantes del acta de fundación de la Sociedad Independencia Electoral," and table 2, "Relación de artesanos, jornaleros y peones asistentes al Odeón."

53. Manuel Pardo, *Patria*, 7 Aug. 1871.

artisans alone could not have formed a unified "movement," given their occupational complexities and anxieties, separations, and competitions with proletarianizing workers and Lima's new factories. They were not free of elite manipulation, nor did they hold to a single economic perspective.[54] But it was a nascent politics, based on real-life artisans and stubbornly consistent with their long-standing republican ideals and sectoral hopes. By 1872 elite liberalism had ceased to represent just a teasing hypocrisy to the artisan; its liberationist promise was up for grabs.

At least in the larger realm of economic ideas, attention to artisan perspectives, interests, and potential had become respectable again by the early 1870s. The major Lima papers, such as Ulloa's *La Patria* and Aramburú's and Chacaltana's *El Nacional* (the civilista mouthpiece), routinely began to carry features catering to the literate artisan public, including manuals on technical subjects and mutualism. The race for artisan readers became so fierce that free-trade *La Patria* was forced to condemn its civilist competitor in 1872 for dangerous pandering to "vulgar, popular" ideas, such as Pardo's notion of raising tariffs to meet the fiscal emergency and, worse, to satisfy a (rumored) protectionist petition from Lima's workshops as well. "As a general rule, one can't flatter the people without being enslaved," went their swipe against *El Nacional* populists. *El Correo del Perú* (Pérez's new literary forum) called for greater public protection and vigilance over workshops and for a turn to workers' savings as development funds. Petty protectionist measures crept back in; for example, in 1873 decrees granted privileged military supply contracts to the upland Terry and Garmendia factories, a practice hotly condemned since the 1840s. An attempt was made to lower iron duties in the name of Lima machinists.[55]

The decade before an elite cult of civilizing technology and science had risen hand in hand with the railway projects, immigrant engineers, and nationalizing mechanics. In the early 1870s a perceptible shift occurred in this thinking—triggered by the living example of the school

54. Basadre, *Historia* 6:2857–59; Giesecke, *Masas urbanas y rebelión*, ch. 4 ("prepolitical" heterogeneity), ch. 5 (1872 civilist manipulations). Giesecke speaks of a civil "protección paternal" that escapes control.

55. See, e.g., *Patria* (liberal anticivilist): "Una fábrica nacional," 2 Jan. 1872; "Aumento de grávamenes aduaneros," 15 Nov.; "La cuestión social en Europa y América," 20 Nov. (quote); "La protección mutua," 28 Nov.; 19 Dic. 1872; "Economías mal entendidas," 10 Mar. 1873; "Protección a la industria nacional," 28 Mar. 1873. *Correo del Perú*, 14 Apr. 1874.

of arts, by receptive artisans, and by positivist-civilist campaigns for popular and practical education. Instead of the previous faith in magical, technological prowess from above, these prophets advocated an activist, populist, and mechanical creed, in line with artisan standards and crossing, to varying degrees, into economic heterodoxy. Technology would happen when the people got involved. Two such writers, the Jacobin positivist Mariano Amézaga and the tinkerer and pensador José Arnaldo Márquez, reveal the emerging forms of popular mechanics.

Mariano Amézaga, a San Marcos philosophy professor, is best remembered as a radical positivist and frenetic university reformer of the late 1860s and early 1870s, a promoter of national educational works, heir to the Bilbao democrats of the 1850s. Later, a fanatical anticlericalism moved Amézaga to an anticivilist stance—a González-Prada-like repudiation of the party as a "shameful financial oligarchy of guano," and one of the paradoxical founts of the Piérolist black legend of civilismo.[56] But early on, as a prolific essayist for Pardo's El Nacional, Amézaga mainly extolled the virtues of popular vocational education. His vision was both more social and more laissez-faire than the civilist center.

Amézaga vaunted popular education as a panacea for "making a nation of Peru," preaching a creed of "trabajo" for the "sons of the working class." In his initial writings he condemned the "shameless" use of guano monies; the one proper use was diversion into primary education: "Is it just disdain for the masses, for our descamisados, among our leaders of instinctive despotism, on which we pin our country's destiny?" The people were the lonely ones "working the workshops."[57] Only mass education, including women's education, would "abolish castes" and forge a real "citizenry" capable of resisting the caudillos. Here was an activist shift from the elite notion that steam engines alone would drive Peru's technical and social revolutions. At the same time, Amézaga shared in the official school-of-arts discourse of base Peruvian craftsmanship, complaining that "industry cannot prosper because our obrero lacks initiative and industriousness; he limits himself to observing the rote practices at his grasp. There isn't the lowliest foreign worker who isn't superior."[58]

56. H. Amézaga, Perú liberal, 197–99; Basadre, Historia 5:2121; Mariano Amézaga, Perú: Galería financiera (Valparaíso, pam., 1873). See also F. C. Coronel Zegarra, La educación popular en el Perú (Lima, 1872).

57. M. Amézaga, Problemas de educación, 19 (Tauro, comp.); concerns comparable to ethics explored in Safford, Ideal of Practical, ch. 2, "Learning to Work."

58. M. Amézaga, "Escuelas municipales," Nacional, 12 Apr. 1869.

By 1870, however, Amézaga was formulating a decidedly social critique of the school-of-arts' welfare formula. In a heated commentary on the institute's annual report, he blasted the idea of willy-nilly educational expansion without commensurate opportunities for work, so lacking in jobless Lima. Graduates of the school, mainly from indigent families, lacked capital to start their own workshops and were already drifting into serving as mere *oficios* (assistants). Society was losing. Amézaga's solution was a system of provincial, state-supported workshops, to employ the minted masters as technical emissaries across the Andes. A craft reversal of Silva Santisteban's forced bucolic decentralism, here was the argument that railway demonstration effects were not enough for technological dissemination.[59] "It's not necessary to examine the impact of such an industrial revolution on the country," contended Amézaga in his precocious turn to the interior, even to the Indian, as industrial material. Because Andean agriculture was only a seasonal form of employment, Amézaga metaphorically paired "the native and the craftsman" as complementary "rudimentary fellows," needful of each other's services.

Despite his plea for state-sponsored workplaces, Amézaga's critical edge began to chisel at the proto-industrial promises of the school of arts as well. In a sharp rebuke of technical policy, Amézaga deemed the entire enterprise misguided, even misguidedly protectionist. What cried for priority was Peru's new academy of scientific agriculture, both in terms of immediate funding and in Peru's long-term and logical material evolution. "The constant plaint of national artisans that imports of overseas manufactures crushes them makes in fact lucid proof that other countries have better facilities and minds for manufacturing and industry—just as we have tremendous advantages over them in exercising *la industria agrícola*."[60] Peru needed agricultural development first. Much like the theoretical liberals of the 1850s, Amézaga ardently wished to go to the people with his practical revolution, so long as they dropped their protectionist errors. But in contrast to the 1850s, a far more tangible and autonomous national artisan was taking shape in the liberal imagination. As Amézaga approvingly noted in an 1870 tract celebrating Lima's new *bibliotecas populares:* "Our artisans of today are not those of past ages.

59. M. Amézaga, "Escuela de artes y oficios," *Nacional,* 16 Mar. 1870. The unemployment critique was not unique: see "Memoria de ministro de gobierno, beneficencia y obras públicas" (1876), in *Diarios de debates,* 1876, 140–41.
60. M. Amézaga, "Instituto de agricultura," *Nacional,* 3 June 1870; and "Escuela de comercio," *Problemas de educación,* no. 16; see Luis Sada, *Bosquejo de la organización de la escuela nacional de la hacienda normal de agricultura* (Lima, pam., 1863), for goals.

New ideas ferment in their minds and very favorable movements in their activities."[61] In short, they were almost useful citizens.

In contrast to Amézaga's still ambivalent popular mechanics was the timely appearance of the 1874 periodical *El Trabajo*, directed by José Arnaldo Márquez—Peru's best-known nineteenth-century educator. Here a science for the people fully met popular aspirations and revealed the sea change that had occurred since *Zamacueca* Luddites of 1859. Márquez, a "bohemian" writer published in the *Revista de Lima*, is remembered for his translations of Shakespeare, social poetry, Americanist politics, and youthful travels in the United States (and journals thereof), which left a visible Pardo-like democratic imprint. Márquez was also (among other trades) an amateur inventor; in 1873 he patented an automated typesetting machine in New York, only to spend the rest of his life fruitlessly chasing his rights in international courts. (His saga as an innovator was matched only by that of Peru's autodidactic clockmaker of the 1860s, Colonel Pedro Ruiz Gallo, and his imaginary airplane.) Most important, Márquez, an intimate Pardo ally, was director of the 1873–1877 *El Educador Popular*, a popular and secular teaching aid central to Pardo's educational drive and a source of grave political struggle with Peru's conservative church. During the Pacific War the peripatetic Márquez crisscrossed the globe as Peru's chief diplomatic courier, later penning critical histories of guano and nitrate finance.[62] His career promoting artisan industrialism, overshadowed by the clerical controversies, is less renowned.

El Trabajo, as the name suggests, resumed the elite self-critique of unproductive reliance on guano prosperity: "We are poor" again announced the premier issue in August 1874. "The exaggerated financial speculations of the past years have made the question of *production* the one impossible to ignore. Guano does not exempt us from the obligation to produce." Indeed, guano could no longer produce any miracles, as demonstrated by the 50 percent deficits suffered since 1871 and the calamities attendant on Peru's failed 1872 European loan bid, which

---

61. M. Amézaga, "Bibliotecas populares," *Nacional*, 21 Feb. 1870; "Guttenberg" was key to "democracy."

62. Milla Batres, *Diccionario biográfico*, vol. 6, needs three separate entries; Pike, *Modern History*, 136; Basadre, *Historia* 5:2104–11, 6:2973–77, 3:1808 (Ruiz Gallo); J. A. Márquez, *Recuerdos de viaje a los Estados-Unidos de la América del Norte* (Lima, 1862). Besides getting the name right, this last work brims with invidious comparisons to "atraso" of Peru: J. A. Márquez, *La orgía financiera del Perú: El guano y el salitre* (Santiago, pam., 1888).

paralyzed the civil government, public works, and private banks.[63] But rather than address the anxious elite, whose financial apparatus was collapsing around them, the paper turned instead to Lima's lowly artisans and their production. *El Trabajo*'s masthead read, "The weekly of sciences, the arts, and the industrial classes." If inadvertently, Lima's motley industrial classes, from school of arts alumni to guild masters and migrant industrialists, were among the few beneficiaries of fiscal instability. (Peru's sinking exchange rates boosted sugar exporters, too.) In ideological terms, *El Trabajo* was a peoples' version of the nationalizing engineers' club of the 1870s.[64]

El Trabajo featured the usual array of pieces on technical and industrial education, reflecting the local boomlet at the school of arts. But it also openly extolled, in contrast to the school and Amézaga, a protectionist and interventionist line to stem the crisis. Márquez called for a "Banco Industrial," a new mortgage institution whose interest would be paid in craft goods, not profits, and a program of state-supported workshops.[65] This was a craft version of Casanova's and Cisneros's industrial idea, recast with Continental cooperativism, and was the popular antipode of the exporter elites' agrarian, mining, and nitrates mortgage banks. "We'd have a preventative measure to avoid the near future disaster that all can now clearly see." To Márquez, unemployment was a "tragic waste when the creation of workshops is where these thousands of *industriales* will find honorable bread." *El Trabajo* entertained a number of progressive causes. It vaunted feminism in the workplace ("women as an element of riches"), employment for the handicapped, and a gamut of unheard-of social services for workers. It was antimilitarist. It taught the latest and most diverse lessons of political economy (Ricardo among the favorites) along with artisans' lessons on being the good spouse.[66] Its scope was national as well as artisanal, for example when projecting the full-scale mechanization of Peruvian agriculture and the scientific exploitation of untapped Andean resources and mines.

One surprising innovation of Márquez's mouthpiece, distinct from

63. *El Trabajo* (Lima), Aug.–Dec. 1874; "Prospecto," 12 Aug. 1874, "Somos pobres," 29 Aug. 1874.

64. *Asociación de ingenieros,* discussed in ch. 4, above.

65. "Banco industrial," *Trabajo,* 5–12 Sept. 1874. This was not an entirely new idea: Silva Santisteban (*Breves relexiones sobre los sucesos con la importación,* 52) had proposed artisan "Banco de habilitación" in 1859; "Carpentería," "Costura," *Trabajo,* 5 Sept. 1874.

66. Un artesano, "Deberes de esposo," *Trabajo,* 7 Nov. 1874; Ricardo, "Diccionario de economía política," Oct. 1874; "Fomento a la industria," 6 Dec. 1874.

artisan traditionalism and Amézaga's agrarianism, was its spirited campaign to promote capital goods industries. Artisans (and Lima's prospective factories) had always counted on imported and duty-free tools,
though precedents for protection existed in the imaginary projections of
the foreign railroad contractors of the 1860s and the engineering professionals of 1872. *El Trabajo*'s editorial of October 1874 called for the
"Iron Industry of Peru": the "mother industry" that for the United
States and Britain had formed "the principle of their grandeur and
superiority."[67] Márquez conceded that although protected ironworks
would inconvenience workshops that imported all their tools, in the
long run the entire country would benefit. For this lofty aim honorable
artisans would surely sacrifice. Machines, Peru's educator proclaimed,
were the "schools" of the "niños del pueblo," a new twist on the old
technological slogan. The industry would develop using the iron ore,
coal reserves, and recently discovered La Brea petroleum deposits of the
north. In just a slight departure from Ricardo, stiff tariffs were essential
for employment as well as learning purposes: "Free importation itself
makes consumers prefer imports. But what is really preferable—that the
country spends the same or a little more on the purchase of a machine
made in the country, as new as an import; or that competition ruin our
factories, to fire our workers and apprentices, who for lack of work just
fatten the ranks of vagrancy?"[68]

Citing the ore studies of Alfredo Duval, this campaign was likely
inspired by the early 1870s expansion of several Lima-Callao foundries
and repair shops (e.g., Straton's and White's); skills spawned in the
course of railroad construction (several engineers, such as Backus and
Johnston, opened industrial shops in Lima); the long-standing example
of the state's Bellavista machine shops; or, perhaps, Márquez's own
frustrated career as tinkerer. The idea itself was not all that bizarre,
considering the wide demand for tools, machinery, and trained resident
mechanics triggered by Peru's expanding coastal plantations and haciendas of the early 1870s. Only the politics of the scheme—the sugar
planters were already Peru's most zealous free-traders—was left unre-
solved. Patriotic artisans, Márquez's target audience, were not likely to
go it alone, if at all. *El Trabajo* continued its cry for restrictions on
machinery imports.[69]

67. "La industria de hierro en el Perú," *Trabajo*, 10 Oct. 1874; "Importación de
maquinarias," 10 Oct. 1874.
68. *Trabajo*, 10 Oct. 1874.
69. See, e.g., Sánchez, *Historia de una industria*, ch. 2; papers carry many ads for these

Above all, *El Trabajo* was trying to rescue the age-old moral emblem of Lima's artisan class—*el artesano honrado* with his *amor al trabajo*—as a national ideal for breaking the spiral of Peru's crisis. Discernible here were the first inklings of a developmental politics. As contexts changed, this politics contrasts with Pardo's and Cisneros's elite "productivity" formulas of the 1860s. By the mid 1870s trabajo rhetoric had even entered the dry but now civilist *Memorias de hacienda* and was reaching far corners of the country, such as Puno (which had a paper of the same name).[70] And in *El Trabajo* one senses ever realer artisans embraced not because of their productive potential alone but because they had been the one group in urban Peru least tempted by a chimerical export bonanza. A new economic nationalism, a sense of national integrity, a productive morality, could not derive from foreign models as liberal nationalism had. "Proverbial is the love for arts and mechanics that dominates the sons of Peru." The paper awarded hardworking craftsmen with special public recognition. It appealed to the national "capitalist class" to support their "honest" productive endeavors materially. It advanced a plan to the Beneficencia Pública, Pardo's upper-crust welfare agency, to purchase large numbers of sewing machines, printing presses, and technical manuals to provide "honorable and moral work" for the destitute (presumably, these machines would be of Peruvian make and Márquez design). Proud craftsmen, rediscovered as useful citizens, wrote to the paper in glowing tones: "*El Trabajo,* which is the teacher of the artisans, should necessarily guard our interests as well."[71]

Economic Independence?

The most compelling of the 1870s diversification projects was Juan Copello and Luis Petriconi's *Estudio sobre la independencia económica del Perú* (1876).[72] This book released an extended new na-

---

shops; *Asociación de ingenieros;* an attempt registered ("Protección a la industria nacional," *Patria,* 28 Mar. 1873) to change duties for machinists.

70. See, e.g., Elguera, *Memoria de hacienda de 1874,* 15; *El Trabajo* (Puno), 1876, was an apparently unrelated "progress" oriented paper.

71. "Señores r.r. de 'El Trabajo,'" *Trabajo,* 10 Oct. 1874; "El trabajo y la industria," 21 Nov. 1874; "Enseñanza industrial," 12 Dec. 1874. This was not a wholly new idea, since the municipality had already broached it: "Casa de trabajo para mujeres pobres," *Patria,* 26 Mar. 1872.

72. Juan Copello and Luis Petriconi, *Estudio sobre la independencia económica del Perú* (Lima, 1876), rpt. 1971, with an insightful prologue by Jorge Basadre.

tionalist critique of the passing guano boom—from which historians took their normative periodization of the export age as "the fallacious prosperity." It also presented the most far-reaching and cogent plan yet for a Peruvian industrial future. First published in March 1876 as a popular-policy series in the newspaper *El Nacional*, this book, unlike other writings of its class, has enjoyed historians' rediscovery a century later. Nearly all modern historians of Peru mine Copello and Petriconi's argument for "economic independence" as the lodestone of dependency interpretations of the republican era—not a far-fetched reading. This work also inspires invidious comparisons with civilismo: that is, by sidestepping this type of thoroughgoing response to the crisis, the civil exporter elite inexorably led Peru to its multiple national catastrophes of the late 1870s.[73]

Rather than deconstruct the entire 111-page, 48-chapter book, already a classic of historiography, this section will instead reappraise its social, political, and intellectual contexts—its origins and innovations. Four facets define the originality of Copello and Petriconi's contribution: as extension—and synthesis—of developments in elite and popular thought; as direct reflection of the reality of the fiscal and commercial collapse of the mid 1870s; as expression of Lima's novel micro-industrialization; and as sociological sign of Peru's nascent immigrant "middle class." These aspects then shed light on their central industrial argument. But the major departure of *Estudio sobre la independencia económica* was its vision of a complementary and working civil politics of development.

Copello and Petriconi, first of all, were not the isolated visionaries— "voz solitaria"—usually depicted.[74] Their work shows its incubation in the milieu of Lima's emerging nationalist and popular mobilizations. Its principal themes parallel the policy ideals of Pardo's wing of civilist politicians—a firmer liberal state, national diversification, popular productivity, imagined industrialization—but with the added virtue of long vistas. Copello and Petriconi, neither politicians nor ministers, were the rare Peruvian thinkers who enjoyed the rich luxury of standing outside the nitty-gritty, quotidian politics of crisis. But their work was still

---

73. E.g., Yepes, *Perú 1820–1920,* 103–5; Bonilla, *Guano y burguesía,* 169–71; Tantaleán, *Política económico-financiera,* 150–51 (as "pre-plan de desarrollo"); Amayo, *Política británica,* 158, and so on. Bonilla finds this work utopian, as Peru had no "internal markets" to develop.
74. Yepes, *Perú 1820–1920,* 103; Macera, "Historia económica como ciencia," 39; see also weighty analyses in Basadre, *Historia* 5:2123–24; 2260–63.

steeped in policy questions. Their publisher, Aramburú's *El Nacional,* was the active civilista organ, publicizing varied defenses of Pardo's beleaguered efforts and closely engaged in the stormy national mid-1870s debates over stalled railroads, rising intervention, export monopolies, immigration, and fiscal, banking, and educational reform. The work's populism was akin to the integrative variety espoused by leading civilista publicists, such as Aramburú and Márquez, by party builders Monti and García y García, or by *El Nacional* itself. And Juan Copello probably even knew Pardo personally, having worked under him as chief physician of the main municipal orphanage during Pardo's energetic reign at the Beneficencia.[75]

Nor was this work the antithesis of civilist export promotion. Like all serious thinkers, Copello and Petriconi strongly recognized the developmental value of new exports, such as nitrates and sugar, relating their prospects to lessons gleaned from the fading guano experience. Diversification required guidance, hardly a shocking notion in writers of the times. By the 1870s economic "nationalism" belonged to no single party or faction in Peru: nationalism was the mantle of all economic discourse. The trenchant and deafening 1869–1871 debates over the Dreyfus contract, for example, revealed its universal currency. While Pardo's hijos del país emotively decried the "denationalization" of guano trade and finance and painted themselves as the true and only national interest, pro-Dreyfus forces were just as adamant in their nationalist goals and credentials: the contract would strengthen the state's freedom of action, release national "productivity," and loosen the grip of forces "enslaving" the national interest.[76] Social critiques of civilismo—even charges of "oligarchy"—were equally commonplace.

In power, Pardo's program was bound up with the contours and turns of the economic emergency and splintered and constrained by the sundry groups vying under the civilista umbrella, from sugar barons and merchants to artisans and anticlerical firebrands. Pardo placed understandable weight on short-term stabilization: budgetary gaps, credit

---

75. For sense of Aramburú's populism, see his *Asesinato de Pardo;* Stewart, *Meiggs,* chs. 5–7 (on *Nacional* debates); MacEvoy, "Manuel Pardo," ch. 4.

76. See, e.g., *Refutación de las acciones interpuestas judicialmente por los nacionales con motivo del contrato Dreyfus* (Lima, pam., 1869); Cisneros, "Negociado Dreyfus"; Amézaga, *Galería financiera;* and J. A. Torres Paz, *La oligarquía y la crisis: Disertación leída en la sociedad jurídica-literaria en la sesión del 29 de agosto de 1877* (Lima, pam., 1877). The last is a positivist polemic against Pardo's "pseudo-civils," "popular harness," and banker "oligarchy."

sources, tax collection, and bank confidence. Each improvised solution ran up against heated opposition—from planters resisting export levies, to bankers blocking emission restraints and unified currency, to foreign creditors protesting the nitrates takeover, bond default, and new guano contracts. His medium-term goals—fiscal and administrative decentralization, streamlined and modernized bureaucracy, educational expansion, military cutbacks, resolute state action in the economy—moved ahead, despite the political fireworks sparked among the church, army, and conspiring Piérolist conservatives.[77] Pardo's long-term missions— national educational and technical renovation, an enlarged participatory citizenry, the integrative communications revolution—would have taken many years to mature even without the unrelenting economic and political shocks.

The impasse was real enough, especially after the stalled 1875 Rafael contract, and was exceptionally difficult to pass in the simultaneous process of civil democratization, which exposed the regime to explosive obstructions and charges. Even the most rudimentary steps—budget deadlines, revenue tariffs, banking controls—faced uncompromising opposition from the 1872, 1874, and 1876 congresses, from within the party's motley ranks, and from Piérolist and military cliques unconstrained by the niceties of republican rules. In four years Pardo faced some thirty-six attempted uprisings. Long-term objectives were challenged from a resurgent laissez-faire lobby in agricultural and mining futures.[78] Within this maelstrom Copello and Petriconi's project marks an attempt, within the culture of civilismo, to reformulate a stable social basis for the regime. Their stated intention was to move the buffeted "government and people" from the "road of inertia" to a "road of work."[79] And moving beyond Cisneros's and Pardo's original visions, the unsaid aim was to forward a working politics of recovery, built on restored commitments to the developmental long term. This program

---

77. See MacEvoy, "Manuel Pardo," esp. 221–27, conclusions; Ulloa, Piérola; Ugarteche and San Cristóval, Mensajes de presidentes, 1872–1876; Bonilla, "Crisis de 1872."

78. Diarios de debates, Sept.–Oct. 1872; Sept. 1876; for Pardo defense in liberal idiom, Lo que se ve y lo que no se ve: Ojeada sobre los principales actos económicos del gobierno civil (Lima, pam., 1874). For new export liberalism, José Manuel Osores, Conferencias sobre materias económicas dadas en el club literario por J. M. Osores (Lima, pam., 1876): the crisis was fiscal alone, and Peru was "essentially to be agrarian, in our fathers' footsteps"; railways were a misguided waste of capital on nonexport regions. Also Casós, Minería y agricultura.

79. Copello and Petriconi, Estudio sobre la independencia económica, "Al benévolo lector," ch. 48, conclusions.

revolved around a mediating "middle class," an inclusive smallholder ideology, and an activist state. It reflected emergent realities and was certainly geared to the civil vanguard and its tentative popular organizations. Whether civil leaders fully absorbed (or could act on) Copello and Petriconi's critique is harder to say.

Second, the reality that Copello and Petriconi best fit was the dismal one of Peru's crashing economy and soaring social stresses. They open their book with a lucid declaration: the collapse of the monoexport regime by 1875—Peru can no longer import "everything"—had for the first time made its alternatives more than academic. Guano sales to Britain slid from around £2 million annually (1865–1869), to £1.75 million (1870–1874), to £1.27 million by 1875, depletion barely compensated by fitful nitrate and sugar exports. Financial panic hit harder. After three years of tenuous overseas credit and mounting insecurities in local finance markets, in 1875 Dreyfus suspended—defaulted on— Peru's mammoth £35 million foreign debt, contributing to a major international debt crisis. There were few prospects for recovery in the long depression that soon gripped the world economy. Pardo's new Rafael contract would never get off the ground, and his early stabilizing strides vanished. The pivotal native bank, Banco Nacional del Perú, collapsed; panicking bankers called in some 30 million soles from planters, paralyzing crops and investments; rail building ground to a halt; and Pardo's nitrate monopoly and tightened budgets could not close Peru's gaping fiscal deficits. Thousands of workers from abandoned public works and militias streamed into Lima, swelling city tensions.[80] The free-fall in imports drove the crisis home to well-off Limeños. In 1870 Peru (largely Lima) could consume £1 million in English textiles (and £446,000 in motley goods); by 1876 imports had fallen more than 60 percent to £360,000 (and £180,000 sundries). Visionaries were not the only ones watching the age of guano end in a bust.

The second but positive reality pressing on Copello and Petriconi was Lima's novel process of "microindustrialization"—which suggested one palpable alternative to import shortages. By the mid 1870s, with fiscal bills, a weak new silver standard, and bullion flight sending Peruvian exchange rates plunging, profit opportunities were finally, if inadver-

---

80. Elguera, *Memoria de hacienda de 1876;* Greenhill and Miller, "Peru and the Nitrate Trade," evaluate responses; Camprubí, *Historia de bancos,* pt. 3; Bonilla, "Expansión comercial británica," table 3. Maiguashca, "Reinterpretation of Guano Age," ch. 7, and Marichal, *Century of Debt Crises,* ch. 4, both suggest recovery until world crash.

tently, to be had in import substitution. Not much is known about these industries. Small mechanized workshops expanded at breakneck speed, and *fabricantes* rapidly appeared on the tax rolls. A coterie of modern factories appeared—in beer, cotton, glass, candles, soap, cigarettes, ice, soda, machinery, construction materials, noodles, confections, and all sorts of foodstuffs. By the late 1870s, apart from its ever more noticeable artisan workshops, Lima had twenty or more genuine "factories" (twelve definitively established in the decade). A savings Sociedad Industrial Peruana formed in 1873, offering 200,000 soles in small shares.[81]

Carlos López Aldana's Vitarte cloth mill, first reusing Casanova's discarded machinery, employed more than a hundred workers and specialized in agricultural sacks and coarse cottons for coolies and laborers. According to one estimate, it shaved about 600,000 soles from the import bill in 1876. (López Aldana was also a founder of the civilista party, along with Manuel Amunátegui, owner of *El Comercio*'s struggling paper works; the Cuzco industrialist Francisco Garmendia became Pardo's first vice president.)[82] "José" Cohen's automated tobacco plant (soon expanding into printing) likely employed the most workers. Two of Meiggs's engineers, Jacob Backus and J. Howard Johnston, set up soda and ice factories; before 1879 they had already opened their famous brewery, which found a conspicuous home in the La Perricholi house, vacated since the days of the Tres Amigos factory (where López Aldana had worked in 1849). All of this activity unfolded without formal promotional and tariff policies or sure shifts in Peru's terms of trade; it came by dint of new technology, new entrepreneurialisms.

Such modest successes must have inspired beliefs in industrial possibilities—just as for the generation before a few flagrant failures had paralyzed all elite interest in industrialism. The mania for companies was so legendary that Limeño literary magazines poked fun at "pequeña in-

81. Basadre coined "microindustrialización": "Prologue," Copello and Petriconi, *Estudio sobre la independencia económica*, vii–viii; see Geoffrey Bertram, "Alejandro Garland: The Ideologist of 'Desarrollo Hacia Afuera,'" typescript, Oxford University, 1974, notes (factory foundings); Bollinger, "Rise of U.S. Influence," surveys, chs. 1–2 (tables 3–5); J. Fred Rippy, "The Dawn of Manufacturing in Peru," *Pacific Historical Review* 15 (1946): 147–58. "Patentes," *Patria* Jan.–Feb. 1872, 30 Jan. 1873. Clarke, *Peru and Creditors*, 53–54, and Carlos Boloña, "Tariff Policies in Peru," D. Phil. thesis, Oxford University, 1981, 58 (devaluation).

82. Luis Esteves, *Apuntes para la historia económica del Perú* (Lima, 1882), 26; Sánchez, *Historia de una industria*, ch. 4; MacEvoy, "Manuel Pardo," table 1 (affiliations); *Patria*, 20 Mar. 1873 (Garmendia obituary).

dustrias." One budding young writer, Manuel González Prada, trained in chemistry, decided to start one himself—a starch factory—and was doing very well until the war. A manufacturing trademark law was passed, portending the complexities of competition. Civilista finance reports stopped denouncing a bogey of fictional industries; by 1876 ministers instead lauded "the considerable improvement in many national industries," noting by name their favored textile factories. A deeper sign of attitudinal shift comes from the ubiquitous newspaper ads for Lima factory products. The decade before, advertisers spoke only of the "finest products of London and Paris" and vehemently denied covert selling of any locally made counterfeits. Now merchants proudly advertised their wares from "industrias nacionales" and "peruanas." Citations at the "National Exhibitions" boosted sales.[83]

Timidly still, some factory owners were beginning to press for the political recognition and support of their sector, rekindling protectionist debates. Pardo's 1872 tariff, ostensibly for fiscal reasons, raised duties 5 percent on competing manufactures, extended their range, and then concertedly surcharged textiles. Ministerial reports became noticeably evasive about hallowed principles of free trade. One factory magnate (Cohen) publicized his cheap cigars as the consumers' best "solution" to impending tariffs.[84] In a published 1878 petition to congress the wideranging businessman Emilio Prugue called for high tariffs and technology patents for his new candle, soap, and sulfuric acid factory. Besides offering employment for a hundred female workers, a steady stream of chemical inputs for a "multitude" of budding factories, and a sophisticated accounting of effective protection, Prugue hoisted the nationalist banner: "It is only equality we seek . . . and a national industry making the republic independent in one of its necessities. Riches have been lost, and are still lost to Peru, as shown in the manipulations of guano that took our capital off to Europe—instead of distributing them among the workers and to the advantage of the government. . . . Industry is

---

83. "Pequeñas industrias," *Correo del Perú*, 10 June 1877; Elguera, *Memoria de hacienda de 1876*, 30; ads for products and machine imports found everywhere; "Exhibiciones industriales," *Patria*, 17 Feb. 1872; 17 Apr., 12 May 1873; cf. "Industria nacional," *Comercio*, 4 Jan. 1875, with earlier ad for "Almacén de Ferrai," *Comercio*, 11 June 1865, when "se garantiza además que ninguna de las crinolinas se venden en el almacén son fabricadas en el país." Kristal, *Andes from the City*, 111 (González Prada).

84. *Patria*, 21 Sept. 1872 (Pardo speech); "Aumento de gravamenes aduaneros," 15 Nov. 1872, "Fábrica de cigarros puros y de papel," 17 Apr. 1873, "Ingresos aduaneros," 26 May 1873; free-trade *Patria* follows issues religiously. For shifting 1870s "Memorias," Dancuart, *Anales de hacienda*, vol. 9.

progress, wealth, and the general welfare."[85] Industry and "independence" were already paired. However modest these strides, "industry" was no longer just a figment of imagination.

Fourth, Copello and Petriconi even reflected a novel "class" (and cultural interest) in Lima, one that civilistas were working hard to promote. At least one critic has recognized this facet in branding the pair as typical "petty bourgeois" dependency thinkers.[86] In an interesting fashion, they were. Mobile and practical thinkers, both were naturalized Italian immigrants—just like the majority of Lima's new petty industrial entrepreneurs. (Juan Copello, a Genoa-trained physician, arrived in Lima in 1846, opening a corner drugstore and practice; he became the pioneer of blood transfusion in Peru, sometime professor of history of medicine, and author of arcane medical texts. While with the Beneficencia under Pardo's directorship, Copello served in the campaign against the yellow fever epidemic and worked for the Lima orphanage, with its children's workshops—all excellent schools on the city's social disparities. His partner Petriconi leaves us no trace.)[87]

Lima's pioneer factories of the 1860s and 1870s were not founded by the *flor y nata* of Limeño society.[88] The majority of founders bore names such as Rosello, Vignolo, Prugue, Ravettino, Chiappi, Suito, Risi, Zolezzi, Kieffer, Pouchon, Freund, Schmitt, Spinckmoller, Schroeder, Malborg, Field, Ashford, White, and Cohen—middle-class, urban European immigrants all. In a country that had seen little "white" immigration, such men quickly filled the upper ranks of small commercial life in Lima. With comfortable craftsmen, they made Peru's "respectable" (if minuscule) middle class, sandwiched somewhere between the hijos del país and hijos del pueblo. Italians alone owned some 450 small enterprises in Lima-Callao by 1873, in a European community approaching 10,000. Some, who initially thrived off the superior prestige of Euro-

85. Emilio Prugue, *Protección a la industria nacional: A los honorables representantes del congreso de 1878* (Lima, pam., 1878), 4–5. Prugue shared nationalism other ways: "Fábrica de velas esterinas," *Patria*, 12 May 1873, advertises that his "candles aren't broken, like those that come from Europe."

86. Bollinger, "Bourgeois Revolution," esp. "Origins of Dependency Theory in Peru" (34–36), at least conveys long lineage of thinking in Peru.

87. Basadre, prologue to Copello and Petriconi, *Estudio sobre la independencia económica;* Milla Batres, *Diccionario biográfico,* vol. 1; "Patentes," *Peruano,* Apr. 1873, Dec. 1885; Fuentes, *Movimiento de poblaciones,* 249; Janet Worral, "Italian Immigration to Peru: 1860–1914," Ph.D. diss., Indiana University, 1972, ch. 2, p. 143.

88. Gilbert, *Oligarquía peruana;* after 1900, Prados became first major family diversifying into factories (158–61); detailed survey of foreigners in crafts and commerce is "Datos estadísticos," *Patria,* 20 Apr. 1872.

pean goods in their corner *pulperías*, moved to replace those products with locally made substitutes (likely drawing on overseas models and connections). For varied reasons, exclusionism among them, by the 1880s Peru's nascent import-substituting industrial sector had become virtually synonymous with upwardly mobile "Italians," especially those connected with the postwar industrial Banco Italiano.[89]

Copello and Petriconi clearly shared an affinity here, and not with Lima's traditional race-conscious upper class. "Juan" Copello (né Giovanni) was a committed member of the city's Sociedad Italiana de Beneficencia y Asistencia (founded in 1862), serving an Italian colony of five to seven thousand. Key chapters of their book, not surprisingly, vaunt voluntary and skilled white immigration to Peru, "quality" people, as the sine qua non of trabajo. Industrialism, they argued, enhancing mobility, would draw even more.[90] So fixated were they on European talent (in their own ethnic blinders) that Copello and Petriconi barely noticed Peru as Indian country—a turn that would occur only after the 1879 war.

In this obsession they shared the values of Pardo's wing of civilists. Immigrants were a realization of that democratic "middle-class" social category waiting to be filled since the 1850s and sought out in their political mobilizations of the early 1870s. Like Pardo since 1860, they vigorously opposed the subsidized import of low-skill forced labor (coolies or contracted agrarian colonists), the object of ongoing campaigns by coastal exporters. In 1873–1874 civilistas halted the coolie trade, at its horrific peak in the Balta years, and instituted instead their Sociedad de Inmigración Europea. Inspired by Pedro Gálvez, and with activist Aramburú on its board, this state-subsidized venture went largely after skilled artisans. By 1876 more than three thousand had arrived, mainly Italians, at the considerable expense of 600,000 soles. Despite initial hopes, though, immigration remained an overwhelmingly urban phenomenon; it was particularly worrisome for men like Copello and Petriconi, for by 1875 joblessness bedeviled new arrivals.[91]

89. Worral, "Italian Immigration," chs. 2–3, 6; for perceptions of immigrant business acumen, see A. J. Duffield, *Peru in the Guano Age* (London, 1877), chs. 1–2; Quiroz, *Domestic and Foreign Finance*, ch. 3.

90. Copello and Petriconi, *Estudio sobre la independencia económica*, chs. 18, 20, 43–45 (esp. pp. 85–87); Worral, "Italian Immigration," 142–44.

91. For hopes, see poem "A los inmigrantes," *Correo del Perú*, 1 Mar. 1874; "Inmigración europea," *Patria*, 8 Jan. 1873; Juan de Arona [Pedro Paz Soldán], *La inmigración en el Perú: Monografía histórico-crítica* (Lima, 1891), chs. 8–9, 13–14; Pardo, "Inmigración vascongada" (1860).

Copello and Petriconi also stood apart from Peru's traditional artisan class. Their proposal is steeped in European smallholder ideology, principally that of Sismondi. It adopts a popular idiom, much like Márquez's, but still harbors a bias against guild protectionism and skills. They talk above, not for, both elites and artisans. All in all, the *Estudio sobre la independencia económica* provides a unique "middle-class" perspective on Peru's changing social problem—one highlighted in the 1870s with incipient workers' organizations, civilist populism, and the new entrepreneurialism. As a politics of development or path beyond policy "inertia," it placed their imagined middle class in the middle ground of a unifying national program, one capturing at least the creole citizenry. Even a certain professional bias slips in here, for their book reads like the anatomy, diagnosis, and prescription for an ailing economy—as medicine to break its mortal addiction to imports.[92]

Copello and Petriconi's *Estudio sobre la independencia económica* introduces itself without ambiguities:

With the frankness that comes from deep conviction, we have proposed the *promotion of national industry* [their emphasis] as the only means to solve, little by little, the commercial crisis that we now face, resolve the problem of economic independence, and with it, all of the problems of our political existence. To convert this sad and agonizing present into a future full of prosperity. . . . Our ideas are not founded simply on the healthy principles of economic science. But they derive from the factual experience of all nations, including Peru itself—that the backwardness of economic activity from a fleeting and fictional wealth (unlike the industrial kind), has created a false and trying present, and a perilous future.[93]

Most of these themes sound familiar—the precariousness of guano dependence, the commercial roots of Peru's crisis, the pragmatic inspiration of imagined ways out, and even their Panglossian pledge to resolve "all" social problems. The argument, however, is taken yet further. Copello and Petriconi boldly turn timeworn liberal discourse on its head: it was commercial growth, not manufacturing, that has now proved "artificial" for Peru.[94] The involved analysis following their

92. Many notable economic and social thinkers are suspected of medical analogizing—e.g., Quesnay (and physiocracy in general) and Comte.
93. Copello and Petriconi, *Estudio sobre la independencia económica*, "Al benévolo lector," 3–4. The book is built around forty-eight pithy chapters, which we cite separately.
94. Copello and Petriconi, *Estudio sobre la independencia económica*, ch. 1; Cisneros, less absolutely, pioneered this tactic.

switch becomes part revisionist economic history, part structural stabilization program, part infant-industry argument, part protectionist formula, and part broad political vision for the productive, social, and democratic transformation of Peru.

Introductory chapters of *Estudio sobre la independencia económica* form a didactic economic history of the guano age, which is unmistakably nearing its end. For theory Copello and Petriconi cite Sismondi and Pradier-Foderé: the former, the early French social critic of laissez-faire and noted defender of independent small producers and artisans; the latter, the French legal adviser to civilista administrators, rationalizing apostle of state sovereignty and liberal social trabajo.[95] The rest, the bulk, was Peru's own experience, beginning in 1846, the decisive year when guano gained its place as the nation's dominant export (and coincidentally, the date Copello himself landed in Lima). In the time-honored way, Copello and Petriconi illustrate Peru's secularly deeper commercial imbalances, fueled by reliance on guano incomes, manufactured imports, and foreign finance. Imports quadrupled in the export age but brought only a "fictitious" commercial florescence to Lima. Every manufactured good became an imported "fictitious necessity." Greater Peru, as often observed, had barely benefited from the bonanza. Yet one point is clearer than ever: Peru's collapsing export capacity can no longer sustain such a system. Production must radically increase, overseas consumption radically decrease. To Copello and Petriconi, Peru needs to recover its lost diversity of "1846."[96]

The departure from most civilist reformers was Copello and Petriconi's tally (and political sense) of the economic and social costs of the guano boom. None of the relished improvements or resources of the country—the banks, railroads, large plantations ("latifundia"), migration, foreign loans, and so on—"served anything" when they excluded the people from work and progress. In countryside and city the boom has "destroyed small property . . . [and] left the poor and oppressed with a lack of economic life." It aggravated wealth distribution, the basis for

---

95. Copello and Petriconi, *Estudio sobre la independencia económica*, 5, 10; they "corresponded" with Pradier-Foderé and claim slogan "independencia económica" his (stress on legal protection for industry also obvious influence). Fuentes translated two of Pradier-Foderé's works; see Trazegnies, *Idea de derecho,* 224–29, for role in Peru. On Sismondi, see Winch, "Emergence of Economics," 547–48, esp. former Smithean positions and historicism.

96. Copello and Petriconi, *Estudio sobre la independencia económica*, chs. 2–4, 9, p. 101; plays on "fictitious" and 1846 comparisons recur through book.

true "pueblos prósperos," and left oppression in its wake, as in the case of coolie "slaves." The country's export saga had exposed "the thorny terrain of abstractions and theories, as a field strewn with practical facts peculiar to Peru."[97]

The foremost cost—even costlier than concentration of power—was subversion of Peru's "economic independence." Nationalist plaint more than anti-imperial slogan, to Copello and Petriconi this soon meant one thing: the loss of Peruvian manufacturing skills. Guano's "prosperity was fictitious because it has evidently been at the expense of our industry and our economic independence—to the point of imperiling even our political sovereignty."[98] Ultimately, only foreign merchants and foreign industries prospered from Peruvian wealth. Their attractive dependency motif, sounded in the title *Estudio sobre la independencia económica*, is not by itself very clear: for what industry did Peru really have to forfeit?

At heart Copello and Petriconi were imagining, stressing what Peru might have had, had it steered a different course since 1846. They meant a loss of potentialities, a "lost opportunity," to use Shane Hunt's pithy summation of the guano age. Here Copello and Petriconi set out to redraw the lessons of history. There is much talk (but little glorification) of artisans and guilds. True, they confess, Lima's artisans appear slothful, dissolute, disorderly, and ill trained. But rather than the cause of artisan misfortunes, these traits were the results of years of underemployment, official neglect, and elite condescension. Peru must immediately foster the artisans' output of shoes, clothing, furniture, and other necessities— that is, revive the languishing basic crafts, and ingrained "habits of laziness" will dissolve. They point to the advances of the school of arts, which must be "continued, completed, perfected." Likewise, Copello and Petriconi take an unorthodox slant when conjuring up the early factory experience: "Perhaps the paper factory, and the cottons factory then established would have prospered—if only they had received the decided protection of the law."[99]

For Copello and Petriconi, Casanova's foiled optimism made him, if omitted in name, the prophet of guano-age misfortunes:

Is it not a total shame that our sole factory for newsprint, started by Sr.

97. Copello and Petriconi, *Estudio sobre la independencia económica*, 9–10, 24, passim.
98. Copello and Petriconi, *Estudio sobre la independencia económica*, 16, passim.
99. Copello and Petriconi, *Estudio sobre la independencia económica*, pp. 36–37, 49, and chs. 19, 32; Hunt, "Growth and Guano," pt. 6—economic model of lost entrepreneurial potential.

Amunátegui, has failed, when with a little protection, this product whose consumption is so wide, could have supported five or six factories in Peru? Isn't it a shame that there exists only one cottons factory [Vitarte], when with modest promotion, we could sustain perhaps fifty factories for myriad textiles, as cotton is so essential to everyday life? Is it not disgraceful to export our fine wools in huge quantities, for a terrible price, and in huge quantities and inflated prices (and to the benefit of foreign industry) we buy woolen clothes, blankets, drapes etc. Is it not a shame . . .[100]

The litany of unmet industrial "shame" goes on.

What of the drives to reform economic policy since the 1860s, and the myriad proposals in play at the peak of Peru's crisis? Copello and Petriconi remain skeptical, while taking readers through several chapters' worth of outcomes from past reformist and developmental schemes. Ever larger loans, promotion of coastal plantation crops, austerity budgets, wider taxation, the nitrate monopoly, national bank projects, sales of national property, fiscal decentralization, colonization plans—none proved sufficient to ward off the present disaster. Theirs was an absolutist hindsight. Even railroads are deemed a "beautiful theoretical principle"—yet they have brought the country to its knees financially and are proving at best an uneconomical mode of transport.[101] Certainly, Peru must continue apace with its agriculture, mining, and other primary exports, which have a sure role in balancing trade. But without expanding domestic markets and drawing natural resources into manufacturing demand, the same errors will recur. Nitrates, for example, would end up as fictitiously profitable as guano (something Chileans had the historical pleasure to learn).

For Copello and Petriconi, promotion of industry was not a deduction of dogma but a conclusion arrived at from the kind of distanced, hindsight analysis unavailable to overwhelmed and politically entrenched policymakers. But they were not simple Cassandras: again and again they speak to the "immense utility of this economic and commercial crisis—that can open the eyes of thinking men, to present dangers, and future hopes."[102] They spoke to the civilist government.

The specific industrial proposal of the *Estudio sobre la independencia*

---

100. Copello and Petriconi, *Estudio sobre la independencia económica*, 32–33.

101. Copello and Petriconi, *Estudio sobre la independencia económica*, pp. 8–9, and chs. 4–8; on railways, see *Diarios de debates,* 1876 (89–90), official confirmation of long-term losses.

102. Copello and Petriconi, *Estudio sobre la independencia económica*, ch. 10; quote is chapter title.

económica builds on three cornerstones: the social "organization of work," a critical rundown of potential industries, and open protectionism. Copello and Petriconi variously term their plan the "well-organized protectionist system" or "well-understood protectionism." All three elements find clear national precedents. (Even their terminology, for example, sounds suspiciously like Cisneros's "protectionism intelligently applied.") But they could not gloss over the known flaws of indiscriminate protectionism or the predictable objections of liberal critics, confronted head-on in a gamut of contrapuntal chapters. In Peru's grave condition, free trade becomes the tried and "utopian" option.[103]

Tariffs assume a "necessary" role as justified from their reading of Peruvian as well as British, U.S., and French economic history. Theirs was basic raison d'état: "all nations strive for economic independence." Given Peru's virtual collapse, compelling examples discussed were the recent U.S. and French resort to protection as a reconstructive tool following their civil war crises.[104] As usual, Copello and Petriconi confronted the practical difficulties of any protectionist platform: contraband, price inflation, rising labor costs, forfeited public revenue and loans, foreign market retaliation, and so on. But they shed the bashful technocratic stance of Cisneros in their clearly political appeal. And like all industrial pundits, they must convince skeptical readers that Peru enjoys all the "advantages"—hidden resources and latent skills—to become a manufacturing nation. But for Copello and Petriconi the final punch, one unavailable to past thinkers, was the simple fact that Peru's once imagined commercial crisis was now ever too real. Already overseas commerce was paralyzed, export capacity sliding, inflation rampant, incomes falling, customs revenues drying up. Already Peru was defaulted, disgraced, and deprived in European credit markets.[105] In short, the "opportunity costs" for protection—the alternatives to be sacrificed—looked exceedingly low by the mid 1870s.

In this they were right. These are the difficulties (along with wars) that typically drive countries to protectionist regimes. Their utopian

---

103. Copello and Petriconi, *Estudio sobre la independencia económica,* chs. 14–22.

104. Copello and Petriconi, *Estudio sobre la independencia económica,* chs. 13, 15, 23, and pp. 32, 104; ch. 28 is titled "Conclusión: Podemos y debemos proclamar francamente el sistema proteccionista y llevarlo al cabo con decisión como lo hacen todos los gobiernos." The 1870s saw return of defensive protection worldwide: see Peter Gourevitch, "International Trade, Domestic Coalitions, and Liberty: Comparative Responses to the Crisis of 1873–1896," *Journal of Interdisciplinary History* 8 (1977): 281–313.

105. Copello and Petriconi, *Estudio sobre la independencia económica,* esp. chs. 28, 46.

strain, however, was nonrecognition that these very depression conditions were those that also typically impede protectionist successes.[106] Peruvian consumption was already compressed. But Copello and Petriconi shared in fantasies that industrialism would spell a brisk expansion, with few painful, long-term trade-offs of the sort politicians were unwilling to risk. More appealing, and more within the parameters of civilista thinking, was their array of social (and political) supports to the recovery process.

The second underpinning of Copello and Petriconi's program, the "well-organized" part, was the promotional package to complement protection. Tariffs alone would not do. These also included measures heard or seen before: enhanced technical training, modest government subsidies ("protección directa"), technology prizes, import of foreign experts (as Garmendia had done), migration of "quality workers" (their personal obsession), industrial exports, development of oil, coal, and iron reserves, and sustained public works. Agriculture and stiff agrarian protection were not overlooked in the scheme—though the Peruvian peasant (i.e., Indian) merits a single bland mention. Many of Copello and Petriconi's suggestions fall in the ambit of civilist cultural change: founding economic societies, shifting the "middle class" into scientific pursuits, establishing a periodical of Peruvian industry—since "saber es poder." "Perfecting" new civil institutions was their watchword. Here their most novel proposal was a coordinating "Ministry of Fomento" to oversee complementary economic activities and to avert chaotic promotion—the office that civil engineers would achieve in the next generation.[107] Although government officials must help orient Peru's drive to independence, the spotlight (à la Pradier-Foderé) remains on free enterprise, individual incentives, and small-scale initiatives.

At one point Copello and Petriconi summarize their imaginings as "restrictive laws as far as foreign commerce and industry are concerned: liberal laws for national commerce and industry."[108] This was another perceptive grasp of Peru's national predicament—one of excessive liber-

106. See Thorp and Bertram, *Peru 1890–1977,* for analysis of adverse policy cycles in modern "open economy."

107. Copello and Petriconi, *Estudio sobre la independencia económica,* chs. 11, 29–32, 37, 63–65; p. 64 offers the only mention of Indians, though critique of "land monopoly" throughout suggests views. Cisneros had called more vaguely for promotion board.

108. Copello and Petriconi, *Estudio sobre la independencia económica,* chs. 34–35, passim; Basadre, *Historia* 5:2260, grasps them as liberal thinkers, despite their protectionism.

alism in the external sector and of imperfect competition, shallow markets, constrained labor, concentrated wealth, and state privilege on the domestic scene. Intelligent protectionism must develop the internal markets it shelters. The authors repeatedly proclaimed this basic liberalism in promoting "association" and rejecting coercions, monopolies, and concessions. *Estudio sobre la independencia económica* is no socialist manifesto; rather, it is a fresh expression, for Peru at least, of a small-scale national capitalist ethic.

The third crucial element of "well-organized protectionism" is its selection process for prospective industries, the same thorny dilemma addressed by Cisneros. Thoughtful selection, not planning, is the chief function of Copello and Petriconi's watchdog Council of Promotion. Chapter 39 is devoted solely to Peru's motley range of existing and envisioned industries. Its new, palpable level of detail surely reflected the differentiation of Lima manufacturers around them. The *Estudio sobre la independencia económica* isolates three branches of manufacturing, each related to spheres of imports, technology, or consumption. First are sheer luxuries and capital goods, from silks and medicines to heavy agricultural machinery. These are not worth protecting since the market is puny and Peru could never perfect their production in the short run. Copello and Petriconi obviously were not of the Peruvian tinkerer persuasion. Next are the simple industries where independent producers, largely artisans, had managed to hold out—as in leather goods, beverages, alcohol, candles, soap, furniture, hats, tobacco, and clothing. Expansion here will lighten the import burden, lend employment, stimulate national agriculture, and build on and better extant local skills.[109]

The third pivotal line comprises "those new industries that we could introduce easily, and surely master, and that use gifts of our primary materials, and on a large scale." This proposal targets big and basic factories for mass consumption, using imported capital equipment, in the popular necessities that still accounted for the bulk of Peru's import bill. They discuss, for example, varied classes of cotton textiles, linens, woolens, pottery, glass, and such natural and chemical inputs as dyes, coca, plaster, and sulfates. Prugue's petitionary factory earns an exemplary citation. They also point, Pardo-like, to potential growth areas in low-wage rural zones with raw materials, riding the national current opened by

109. Copello and Petriconi, *Estudio sobre la independencia económica*, ch. 39 ("On the existing arts . . .") and passim.

"theoretical" railways.[110] Puno wools seem most amenable to industrialization. Similar promotional distinctions are drawn for agricultural and pastoral pursuits. These were the protectionist categories defined by Peruvian reformers since the lessons of the late 1840s; protectionism demanded high selectivity. A small and undeveloped country such as Peru, Copello and Petriconi conclude, "cannot make everything."[111]

Theirs was not exactly artisan protectionism and populism of the kind hailed by the *Zamacueca* or Márquez. But significantly, Copello and Petriconi were the first to include a bolstered artisan sector as a pillar of their national program. Their ideas echoed the new urban popular politics, the evident progress of vocational arts, people's productivity calls, and their own upwardly mobile backgrounds. The first generation of diversification writers, from Casanova to Cisneros, had easily written off "backward" artisans for more efficient and abstracted large-scale factories. Copello and Petriconi were not only more identified with those left behind by free trade but were alert to the self-organized production potential of workers.

This is not to find Copello and Petriconi uncritical of existing guilds. They rebuked, for example, wasteful luxury crafts and partook of creole zeal for the moral overhaul of a debased Peruvian worker. Their conceptions, too, bespoke both the implicit threat to "public peace" in Lima's economic chaos and joblessness and the civilist ideal of order.[112] They purposely attach a ghastly chapter on possible worker "revolts" (after all, this book followed the Paris Commune—as well as Lima strikes and Pardo's worker militias).

Factories per se do not spark worker unrest, they argued, but dearth of work and public recognition do. A guided "bienestar material" (material well-being) would serve a coveted "bienestar moral." The entire *Estudio sobre la independencia económica* rings with reactive Sismondian chords of a just and stable social harmony. Development was in the common good of all national classes and demanding of active social integration.[113] Here lies the advance on Cisneros's and Pardo's rarefied

110. Copello and Petriconi, *Estudio sobre la independencia económica*, 75, 68.
111. Copello and Petriconi, *Estudio sobre la independencia económica*, chs. 23, 36–37.
112. Copello and Petriconi, *Estudio sobre la independencia económica*, chs. 19, 21.
113. Copello and Petriconi, *Estudio sobre la independencia económica*, chs. 19, 21, 44–45; the Velasco regime, of course, is seen as Peru's modern activist, corporatist, integrationist, nationalist experiment. In terms of their "middle-class" developmental politics, Copello and Petriconi presaged aspects of the 1920s APRA movement.

standard of trabajo, which (at the time) lacked a unifying civic culture of development. In this proclamation urban investors, craftsmen, and immigrants could read themselves into a political scenario; Copello and Petriconi tailored what we might now call a "social pact." It was prescribed not just as an economic remedy, but also to heal the discordant class paralysis of original civil ideals.

In this vein, the chief function of their projected Council of Promotion was to act as "intermediary between the industrial classes and the executive, charged with applying the promotion laws of the congress, and enforcing their decrees." It was imagined as twelve men, chosen by the president and "notable for their enlightenment, independence, and social position." Under this directorate's apolitical investigative-selection process, planning was not left to guilds, whom experience showed inept at deciding industrial policy.[114] If the institution has a Continental corporatist ring, it was alien neither to Lima's more traditional guilds nor, for that matter, to Peruvian landed elites. Again, one senses here a response to Peru's deadlocked crisis politics.

Despite these vagaries of social control, the striking social message throughout the *Estudio sobre la independencia económica* remains its attention to small-producer participation and ideology. It reflected aversion to the large-scale projects and social marginalizations of expansive liberalism—that is, plantation mentalities. The authors dub their message "the organization of work by the initiative of the people," though a people not lacking tutelage. In the end the industrial plan rests on the decentralized activities of democratic "sociedades industriales," modeled after Italian experiments, to be formed in "every section" of Peru.

As they closed this work, Copello and Petriconi returned to emphasize these social requisites and spurs to industrialism: "We have faith in the economic plan expressed, *but with a single condition: that there exists the open, faithful, and energetic cooperation of the pueblo, who organize work, and of the public authorities called forth to protect and foster it*" (their emphasis).[115] This was the economic analogue of the social underpinnings of civil rule evinced by the regime. In the abstract, others (even Cisneros, in his own way) had assigned workers a role in renovative development; men such as Márquez were energetically addressing real workers. Copello and Petriconi pass by a range of inspirations, from the

114. Copello and Petriconi, *Estudio sobre la independencia económica*, chs. 29–30, p. 57.
115. Copello and Petriconi, *Estudio sobre la independencia económica*, 100–101; see MacEvoy, "Manuel Pardo," ch. 4, for civilist "social" turn. Infatuation with U.S. example was common; ironic (and equally common) was Chile as developing exemplar (88–89).

"good government" of the republican United States to the dreams of Continental syndicalism. (Emergent German statism and classic French *étatisme* merit no approval.) But above all was the authors' own fixation, redolent of artisan and immigrant thinking, on the principle of "honorable work." To Copello and Petriconi, unleashed human capital was the true productive solution demanded by Peru's societal crises—"la verdadera riqueza." If "a program of *trabajo humano*" were adopted, it would "not only, in a few years, bring us to our desired economic equilibrium, but to a real and progressive prosperity, that would make Peru into one of the richest and most powerful nations of America."[116]

Of course, Peru never became that. Its officials could barely confront the commercial choices of the 1870s. The escalating pressures of unremitting crisis, felt on every front, were not opportune for putting into practice any pensive policy—much less ones that implied long-term and social change. Peru's harried leaders of the late 1870s continued to bicker over the need for such elementary reforms as banking controls and export taxes, splitting into confounding rivalries between Pardistas, Pradistas, and Piérolistas, as the export economy sank beneath them. The simpler rush to nationalize and exploit the nitrates of the desert south, if a "national" policy of sorts, directly brought on the crushing 1879 war with developing Chile.[117] Peru—as a military, economic, and, most of all, national entity—was woefully unequal to the contest, and the victors would demolish or rob whatever relics remained of the "fictitious prosperity." Yet societal crisis had at least triggered deep and original currents of alternative thought—something that Peru never lacked in its age of guano.

---

116. Copello and Petriconi, *Estudio sobre la independencia económica*, 101–3. See similar official statement in Elguera, *Memoria de hacienda de 1874*, 15: the "agent" of "productivity," of even Peru's fiscal balance, is "man."

117. On late 1870s policy paralysis, see Baltazar Caravedo M., "La economía peruana y la guerra," in Basadre, *Reflexiones a la guerra de 1879*, 75–124.

6

Economic History
Esteves, the 1880s

Aftermaths

The liberal age of guano was history—or fit for economic history. The Pacific War (1879–1881) was, at heart, a bald struggle over exports among jealous Chile, Bolivia, and Peru. Despite heroic acts of Peruvian resistance, lightning Chilean armies mauled Peru for its southern nitrate fields. When occupation lifted in 1883, Peru—quite literally—had nothing to show from its half-century age of exports.

The devastation is hard to tally, and recovery ran painfully slow. Peru lost its nitrate territories and most of its dwindling guano reserves. Of the twenty plutocratic and regional banks in 1877, only one survived the invasion—the sheltered European Banco de Londrés, México y Sudamérica. Peru lost its fiscal system; inflation and depreciations hit 800 percent during the war, leaving a bewildering mountain of worthless paper bills for a national currency. Peru lost its modernizing civil-administrative state: into the mid 1880s government revenues settled at less than one-third of prewar levels, as tax farmers reverted to archaic levies.[1] Militarism and disorder revived: a new generation of rival caudillo forces and clans (Piérolistas and Cáceristas) replaced the refined

1. Boloña, "Tariff Policies," ch. 3, esp. table 3.1, "Economic Effects of the War with Chile," is the best quantifying effort.

civilian politicos. Fighting went on amid bitter recriminations over the defeat and protracted popular guerrilla movements. Peru's fragile social order cracked in savage revolts: of Asian and black laborers and—not calming with the peace—the most serious wave of Indian rebellions since the 1780s.[2]

In large part, Peru's civil elite lost its legitimacy to rule. Peru lost its vigorous international economy; imports fell to 1840s levels, and trade deficits gaped as exports bottomed out at a quarter of prewar levels. The modest 1870s gains in diversification evaporated. Chilean troops diligently razed the plantations of the northern coast, removing their gleaming refineries as prizes; sugar production dropped two-thirds. Southern wool trades suffered comparable setbacks. Soldiers pillaged and burned railroad stock and track. The brunt of rapacious foreign occupation fell on Lima; no longer a model European capital, its buildings lay in rubble. Peru lost the capitalist plutocracy and urban middle class nurtured by guano-age regimes. One contemporary ventured that of 18 "millionaire" clans of 1870, none remained in 1894; of 11,587 "ricos," only 1,725 carried on; Peru's "comfortable" middle class shrank to some 2,000. A "half million" beggars roamed the country, and famine and epidemics stalked Lima for years.[3] Chilean troops made souvenirs of revered symbols of Limeño progress: virtually all 58,000 volumes were shipped from the Biblioteca Nacional (confounding historians forever); all tools and machinery of the closed Escuela de Artes y Oficios went to uplift Chilean craftsmen. Even the Vitarte mill sold out to British buyers by 1890. And Peru lost something more elusive in the collapse: its national pride.

The two definitive legacies of the guano age were an unpayable foreign debt of £40–50 million and a web of half-completed national railways across the Andes. Soon Peru lost its control over these too, and a good measure of its sovereignty as well. If hotly resisted by some leaders as national and economic humiliation, in 1889 a desperate General Cáceres finally signed the infamous Grace contract to retire Peru's enormous debt—to somehow place Peru back on its feet. Not much economic salvation came of it, but the British "Peruvian Corporation"

2. Manrique, *Las guerrillas indígenas;* or new social history work on war in Basadre, *Reflexiones a la guerra de 1879,* and Wilson Reátegui et al., eds., *La guerra del Pacífico* (Lima, 1979).

3. José Clavero, *El tesoro del Perú* (Lima, 1896), 51, passim (figures to take with much salt); Caravedo, "Economía peruana y la guerra"; Klarén, *Modernization and Dislocation,* 5–9.

(1891) assumed long-term control of Peru's ten main trunk lines, guano commerce, customs, debt service, steam shipping, and chunks of Amazonian lands and Andean mineral rights to boot.[4] Everywhere foreign companies picked up pieces of Peru's guano patrimony, initiating a new "enclave" phase in the country's modern dependency.

In short, the nineteenth-century age of exports ended in a complete loss for Peru. It would take two decades to fumble toward a new order, though once begun, the economic reconstruction per se proceeded swiftly and widely. Such a profound national disaster was bound to propel new currents of thinking on the shape of national reconstruction, introspections eased by the breakup and disillusionment of the older oligarchy. The diversity of these ideas is too wide to capture here—from anarchosyndicalists to academic neo-free-traders—though once again, circumstances rather than imagination ultimately set Peru's course by 1900.

The "lessons" drawn from the nineteenth century crossed the spectrum of modern Latin American thought. There were lingering nineteenth-century liberals—such as José María Químper—who passionately filibustered in congress against acceding to the Grace contract—until dramatically expelled with other refuseniks in January 1889. Minister of finance at the war's outbreak, Químper penned many warnings of "absorption" by overseas interests.[5] There were hagiographers of Manuel Pardo (martyred by a political assassin on the eve of the war), who saw the civilist evolutionary road sabotaged by foreign powers (i.e., British nitrate interests) and divisive reactionary militarism at home. There was a nascent school of critical sociology at San Marcos University, blending neopositivism, nationalism, and state-guided development as Peru's way out. Among them, Joaquín Capelo surveyed the dilemmas of Lima's industrial classes, vaunted automobile roadways and mass education, protested foreign investment takeovers in Junín, and called for an activist state to uplift and regulate working conditions throughout Peru. Carlos Lissón, still kicking, rejected a return to overseas loans and investment—Peruvians must manage their own trabajo and reconstruction—and studied the public-directed civilizing of Indians, whom he, unlike most thinkers, viewed as a source of opti-

---

4. Miller, "Making of the Grace Contract"; Basadre, *Historia*, vol. 6, ch. 3 ("El contrato Grace") for full debates; Velarde, *Deuda externa y ferrocarriles*. Miller is among those now viewing Peruvian Corporation as unprofitable, less exploitive venture.

5. José María Químper, *Las propuestas de los tenedores de bonos por J. M. Q.* (Lima, pam., 1886). Químper's published speeches alone exceed 250 pages; rejoinders in *El señor J. M. Q. y el contrato Grace* (Lima, pam., 1887).

mism. Similar motifs sounded in the sociology of Cornejo, Villarán, and Manzanilla.[6]

Manuel González Prada, as is very well known, personified a new breed of iconoclastic intellectual, who at least theoretically would directly join fates with the oppressed workers and Indians of Peru. Like other men of letters, González Prada drew from the war a totalizing indictment of Peru's hopeless ruling classes and ideologies, though his positivist anarchism really erupted during his European sojourn of the early 1890s. It never interfered with his rebuilding of the Biblioteca Nacional. Less well known were González Prada's industrialist ambitions of the 1870s (as would-be starch mogul) and his stalwart Pardista loyalties until late in his career.[7] His Unión Nacional party (1891) launched a new strain of populist politics, soon practiced by respectable nationalist politicians such as Guillermo Billinghurst. Redemptive and positivist indigenismo, brewing among civilist writers before the war, emerged as a major literary and political genre. Clorinda Matto de Turner's affecting novels and the Zulén's muckraking *Asociación Pro-Indígena* were just the most renowned manifestations. The novelty here was not the urban-liberal reification of the "degraded" Indian (much like visions of artisans in earlier reformers) but the inescapable Andean lens forged by a nationwide war and the indigenous revolts that followed, as in the sanguinary events of 1885 Huaraz. Indigenismo became one idiom of the genuine provincial intellectual circles emerging after 1890. Popular movements revived and assumed new forms, from the busily reorganizing workers and artisans of Lima and Cuzco, with a rich gamut of fresh European social ideologies at their disposal, to what one historian depicts as a more indigenous postwar "peasant nationalism" of the central highlands.[8]

By the 1890s economic issues had acquired greater sophistication and

---

6. Pike, *Modern History,* 160–77, for survey; also Jesús Chavarría, *José Carlos Mariátegui and the Rise of Modern Peru, 1890–1930* (Albuquerque, 1979), ch. 1; Lissón, *Sociología del Perú;* Joaquín Capelo, *Sociología de Lima* (Lima, 1895–1902), 4 vols. After his urban studies, Senator Capelo became a leading indigenista.

7. Kristal, *Andes from the City,* p. 111, and chs. 3–4, esp. "Manuel González Prada and the Industrial Elite"—overblown in its "class" analysis and grasp of generic term "industria"; Klaiber, *Religion and Revolution,* chs. 2–4. Peter Blanchard, "A Populist Precursor: Guillermo Billinghurst," *JLAS* 9 (1977): 251–73; a fascinating figure, who started his career as nitrate investor wary of foreign capital; see G. Billinghurst, *Los capitales salitreros de Tarapacá* (Santiago, pam., 1889).

8. Thomas M. Davies, *Indian Integration in Peru: A Half Century of Experience, 1900–1948* (Lincoln, 1970), chs. 2–3; José Tamayo Herrera, *Historia social e indigenismo en el altiplano* (Lima, 1982); J. Tamayo Herrera, ed., *El pensamiento indigenista* (Lima, 1981); Blanchard, *Origins of Peruvian Labor,* chs. 2–3; Mallon, *Defense of Community,* ch. 3.

historical depth. New economic "technocrats" appeared in the leaner rebuilding administration, many reacting strenuously against the inefficiencies and excesses of nineteenth-century state builders: the liberal José Payán in banking and monetary reform; José M. Rodríguez with his sobering history of fiscal and customs development; Alejandro Garland, pioneer of modern and historical statistics; and P. Emilio Dancuart, encyclopedic collector and codifier of republican economic documents.[9] *El economista Peruano* (1896) became their house organ, the first specialized journal of its kind, and President Piérola's innovative 1895 Ministerio de Fomento their base, offshoot of the engineering movement of the 1870s. There were also more wide-ranging discussions of development aims, from, for example, "national bourgeoisie" spokesman Francisco García Calderón, whose 1907 opus appealed for national capital and nationwide free labor to restore a diversified export economy. By then, as several historians now insist, the bulk of that project, a "national" entrepreneurial experiment, was well underway.[10]

The place of manufacturing industry in this revived (but subtler) liberal order became a contested issue by the late 1890s. Import-substituting industries advanced rapidly in the aftermath of war as a response to weak currency and trade, dire consumption needs, and the fiscal-emergency tariff of 1886—protectionist in impact if not intent. By 1899 about 150 modern factories and enlarged workshops were operating in Lima alone (employing perhaps six thousand workers), and their "industrialists," including many notables, were emerging as a genuine interest, with their specialized Banco Italiano and new Sociedad Nacional de Industrias. As the new export economy boomed in the late 1890s, led by sugar, cotton, and industrial mining, protectionist–free-trade debates climaxed—this time not about fictitious factories or uncannily abstract exports.[11] The lobbyist Felipe Barreda y Osma waved a familiar

9. Macera, "Historia económica como ciencia," 39–53, for survey; J. M. Rodríguez, *Estudios económicos y financieros y ojeada sobre la hacienda pública del Perú y la necesidad de su reforma* (Lima, 1895); Dancuart, *Anales de hacienda;* Carlos Camprubí Alcázar, *José Payán y de Reina (1844–1919): Su trayectoria peruana* (Lima, 1967).

10. Thorp and Bertram, *Peru 1890–1977,* pt. 2, "The Rise and Fall of a Local Development Effort: 1890–1930"; Mallon, *Defense of Community,* chs. 4–5, for regional entrepreneurs; Alfonso Quiroz, *Banqueros en conflicto: Estructura financiera y economía peruana, 1884–1930* (Lima, 1989), for financial angles. Francisco García Calderón, *Le Pérou contemporain* (Paris, 1907). Recall Cisneros's and Copello and Petriconi's precursor "fomento" plans.

11. Julio Revilla, "Industrialización temprana y lucha ideológica en el Perú: 1890–1910," *Estudios Andinos* 17 (1981): 3–41, with Barreda in Copello and Petriconi tradition; Bertram, "Alejandro Garland"; Boloña, "Tariff Policies," ch. 3. Felipe Barreda y

protectionist banner. A new breed of academically trained free-traders (especially Garland and J. Russell Gubbins), though mired in agricultural futures, vaunted concerted use of exports as a nationally run motor of capitalist and regional development. Their victory was assured as Peru's long isolation lifted—but the "aristocratic" republic that arose was not entirely to their liking.

This chapter, the dénouement of our story here, moves back to the immediate war years, as the country's elite, state, economy, and prospects all lay in shambles. What "lessons" were absorbed from the fiasco with export liberalism? In 1880 how did intellectuals best envision Peru's reconstruction? Many answers and influences came into play, but only one didactic and retrospective economic history: Luis Esteves's pioneer *Apuntes para la historia económica del Perú*, with its regionalist echoes. It was to be forgotten in many ways.

Indians and Industries

Esteves's 157-page *Apuntes para la historia económica del Perú* (1882) marks the first formal and full economic history of Peru. To be sure, others had dabbled in history to score policy points—in the initial republic (sizing up the material costs of Spanish colonialism) or with Pardo and Cisneros (collecting statistics, grasping trends, drawing their needed lessons). Pardo worked from several crude studies of regional evolution; Copello and Petriconi forged a synthesis of the export age still relevant to historians.[12] In some sense, Esteves was extending this tradition in his highly nationalistic retrospect—which makes still another pro-industrial tract from Peruvian experience. New distinctions and directions are also pronounced: its uncompromising national scope

---

Osma, *Los derechos de aduana y las industrias nacionales* (Lima, pam., 1900); Alejandro Garland, *Las industrias en el Perú* (Lima, pam., 1896); J. R. Gubbins, *¡Más luz! Estudio económico social: Continuación de lo que se ve y lo que no se ve* (Lima, pam., 1900).

12. P. Macera, prologue to 1971 edition of Luis Esteves, *Apuntes para la historia económica del Perú* (Lima, 1971); for prior histories, see Santiago Távara, *Análisis y amplificación del manifiesto* (Lima, 1831), and Pardo, "Partido de Saña" (1860). One can compare Esteves's work to other 1880s retrospects: e.g., the overseas A. J. Duffield, *The Prospects of Peru: The End of the Guano Age and a Description Thereof* (London, 1881)— highly pro-Pardo (including verbatim conversations with Pardo). Apart from the sarcastic tone ("Guanomakers" chapter surveys bird life), Duffield is notable for emphasizing the total lack of development during the "Guano Peruvian Republic."

(a turn from Lima altogether), its explicit strand of indigenismo, its policy-making withdrawal, its most discernible positivist influence, and its baldly anti-imperialist stance.

Little is known of its lawyer author, who apparently escaped the furies of the Pacific War by retiring to his study—and to history. The book, in fact, studiously ignores the impact of the war, even though its statistics range through 1880. We know that Esteves was a close "friend" of the liberal nationalist Químper—to whom his book is dedicated— and also a staunch admirer of Pardo (the only guano-age politician to escape his wrath) and of the Cuzqueño industrialist and politico Francisco Garmendia. The decade before we find Esteves as a none too active but perennial congressional deputy; he may have brushed up on statistics on the agricultural and commerce committees.[13] In 1881, though overlooking wartime realities, Esteves was already looking to prospects of restoring the devastated country, and on very different footings.

Apuntes para la historia económica is no academic tour de force, one reason for its subsequent obscurity.[14] Its intended and actual readers— the "nation"—seem equally mysterious. Much of the text runs over predictable themes: the shape of nineteenth-century agricultural, mining, commercial, and fiscal developments, spotty attempts to splice together workable statistics on these topics, motley colonial, archaeological, and scientific background materials. Esteves surveys such mildly controversial topics as labor systems and immigration (favoring "toleration" for free or indigenous workers); the efficiency of sugar, cotton, and wine growers (lauding Peruvian innovators, scorning Spanish business mentalities); the saga of guano consignment and sales (long, disjointed polemics on foreign and caudillo perfidy); railroads (for uniting the nation in Incan fashion, from north to south); the Dreyfus contract ("perpetual swindler of the fisc and his Jew-coterie"); silver mining (key

---

13. Esteves, *Apuntes para la historia económica,* dedication, 34, and ch. 8; *Diarios de debates,* vol. 1, Congreso ordinario de 1870, Oct. 1870 (and 1872–1876); e.g., Esteves voted against Dreyfus contract, yet he was hardly outspoken on any issue. In the preface Esteves lauds Mexico and France as exemplary builders from economic and military disasters.

14. An "empiricism" noted by Macera too (prologue, 1971 reprint). Mallon, *Defense of Community,* 125, recognizes Esteves's perspective; all recent studies of indigenismo (Kristal, Davies, etc.) overlook the book. One contemporary reader was J. M. Rodríguez, citing Esteves in preface to *Estudios económicos* (1895). But this work became so lost that even César Antonio Ugarte, *Bosquejo de la historia económica del Perú* (Lima, 1926), fails to recognize it; in 1922 Ugarte became first formal Profesor de Historia Económica y Financiera del Perú.

to retiring Peru's paper bills); and nitrate policy (in support of Pardo's nationalizing course). The tone, however, remains restrained; though not as technocratic as the academic economic histories to follow (C. A. Ugarte's of the 1920s, for a dry instance). Much of the text, updated with Raimondi's discoveries, replicates that exploratory genre of Peru's boundless and untapped regional resources, as in forays into coming tropical products of the *montaña* (the Amazonian foothills of the Andes).[15] The entire country receives coverage, with extensive chapters examining coastal and ("no menos importante") sierran domestic farming and pastoralism. Only the Lima economy remains conspicuously and significantly absent. Three topics, however, excite Esteves's real passions: imperialism, manufacturing horizons, and the Indian laborer. Together they construct a novel nationalist argument.

The principal aim of Esteves's historical synthesis, revealed from start to end, is to "awaken" Peruvians from despair over their own industrial potential:

There is no people that instinctively does not aspire to make themselves industrial; if any exists, it is only due to their powerlessness. . . . Nor is there any industry alien to a country, if the primary materials are found there to make it run. For this reason, they call "barbaric" those peoples who do not know how to adapt the wealth of their soils to its intended object, content with selling abroad the raw material. And for this reason they call "civilized" those peoples who best know how to give form, color, and substance to the products of nature. . . . Is Peru a country that can hope to join the ranks of factory nations? That is what we hope to demonstrate in the best manner possible.[16]

Several idiosyncratic angles converge. First, philosophically, Esteves is turning the categories of European positivism on their heads. Instead of a dismal indictment of native or racial capacities—the usual interpretation throughout Latin America—they become here a scientistic call to evolve socially along the "industrial" path. The lingo of Comtean positivism had affected reformers since midcentury; here it was a new logic. Second, Esteves poses his industrial argument in overwhelmingly psychological rather than policy terms; he strives to disabuse the ren-

15. Such topics surveyed in three large sections: 1, "Historia y porvenir de las industrias agrícola y manufacturera"; 2, "Historia y porvenir de la industria extractiva"; 3, "El comercio, su historia y porvenir en el Perú." Chapters cited below divide in three sections.

16. Esteves, *Apuntes para la historia económica,* 35; in the preface Esteves similarly highlights "regeneration from past errors," "past *locuras,*" and the notion that "peoples are the only ones responsible for their own disasters."

tier mentality of Peru's fallen export-consumption society—the under-mining of entrepreneurial spirit and faith worked by effortless riches. Although similar motifs pervaded works by Casanova, Cisneros, and Copello and Petriconi (their shared national or Saint-Simonian cult of trabajo), here intervention, protectionism, and tariffs escape mention. The book is striking in its lack of policy recommendations.[17] Pardo-like, Esteves purposely steers clear of the stereotyped trade debates of the past, which had made no headway as industrial argument in the 1870s. Instead, the history overflows with vignettes of modest advances worked by Peruvian businessmen, farmers, industrialists—and past civilizations of "twenty millions"—when they put their minds and peoples to work. The most specific arguments are of a stark cost-benefit kind. Esteves thinks that by clearly demonstrating the profits to be had in manufactur-ing, his self-improving, self-interested Peruvians will heartily respond. Third, these psychological-positivist elements come together in Es-teves's new conception of Indians as the keystone of Peru's industrial future. Once freed from "oppression," their true industrial and civilizing instincts will rise to the fore.

Finally, Esteves offers the related critique of static comparative advan-tage—that Peru as a whole is also capable of industrial diversification. Esteves confronts, with his pragmatic psychology, that ancient and pessimistic canard of natural advantage in exports: Peru as immutable país minero y agrícola. The message of industrial revolutions, and of Peru's peculiar nineteenth-century saga, is that all civilized countries can—"must," he now insists—industrialize. With his historical and entrepreneurial exhortations, Esteves was Peru's post facto Casanova.

But Peru is constrained by an outside factor: imperialism, a theme broached openly for the first time in Peru's economic literature. By his final chapter on world trade (an extended attack on British commercial "monopoly"), Esteves lets go with a striking historical and cultural critique of overseas influence. Peru's guano specialization nourished only European industrialization; at home it starved the true spirit of progress: "They have relegated to us the subaltern post of pliers of raw material." Esteves makes Peru akin to Ireland under the political econo-mists' classic British "absentee landlords"—a country ruined by careless

17. Precursors are not mentioned. Esteves broaches protectionism once (57), claim-ing it ineffective in early wheat trade); interventionism with silver mining was also unworkable. Positivism entered Peru by the 1860s (e.g., "Estudios sociales: Faz de deca-dencia," *Revista de Lima* 3 [1861]), but it is generally regarded (e.g., in Pike, *Modern History*, ch. 6) as post-1890 current.

control from abroad. "The statesman knows how the nature of industries influences the progress of peoples, and it is shocking how for fifty years we left industries on the other side of the seas—fertilizing them with our natural products and commerce, as payment for the artifacts that our own production had made possible."[18] Latent or folkloric notions of "free-trade imperialism" (such as Copello and Petriconi's) now become overt, for in Esteves a long history of informal dominion lies behind Peru's barbaric specialization and deep sense of national impotence:

Why did England not use its cannons to take over America just as they conquered India? . . . By her moral preponderance she projected actions in the national interest, to forge more durable chains. And so it was more practical and fruitful to lend pennies to the caudillos of independence, and capture these republics after three centuries of domination, just like birds escaping from a cage. And without suffering any disturbance to her own liberty, she was able to bond them to her industries, through a commercial prowess. . . . And thus, invading with her subjects all the routes of commercial movement, she paralyzed the lax activity of the South Americans. In short shrift, our capital, shipping, and industries all fell into English hands.[19]

Apart from passionate denunciations of British and French guano speculations, Esteves cites ominous cases of imperial perfidy in Peru. These, for example, emerge when discussing hopes to regulate montaña harvests of cinchona bark and promote its more profitable local industrial refinement into sulfate of quinine. Puno businessmen had apparently once attempted such a factory—only to see it sabotaged by the studious price manipulations of British export houses at Arequipa and Tacna.[20]

Prior to the 1870s it was rare to hear such antiforeign sentiments—except in the losing cries of irate artisans—in a Peru so adoring of European ways and sway. The financial acrobatics of Dreyfus, the crash of the 1870s, and European displeasure with Pardo's reforms were awakening such elite antiforeign feelings. The Pacific War was also helping—the conflict Esteves brands a European "war of foreign interests against the guano and other riches of Peru."[21] Yet with equal might,

---

18. Esteves, *Apuntes para la historia económica*, p. 156; pt. 3, ch. 3; pp. 154–56.

19. Esteves, *Apuntes para la historia económica*, 155.

20. Esteves, *Apuntes para la historia económica*, 66; cf. pt. 3, chs. 2–8, on guano.

21. Esteves, *Apuntes para la historia económica*, 155. For British roles in Pacific War, see survey by H. Bonilla, "La dimensión internacional de la guerra del Pacífico," in Basadre, *Reflexiones a la guerra de 1879*, 415–36, or free-trade conspiracies in Amayo, *Política británica*.

the British, in their self-interested achievements, have shown the world the way to industrial society and commercial greatness. For example, Esteves's most concrete proposal is a crash program, like Elizabethan England's, to develop an independent merchant marine, out of British grasp, salvaging plans scrapped in the free-trader 1860s. But within a tradition, Esteves does not advocate autarky but greater autonomy. Unlike Químper, for example, he speaks favorably of "European or American capitalists" developing coastal irrigation and plantations, after the opening of a Panama canal that will only broadcast the benefits of world commerce.[22]

The anti-imperialist edge of this work then merits attention less for theological reasons than for its novelty. Intellectual historians assume that such outward incriminating arguments, as opposed to positivist "self-incriminating" images of development, arrived late to Latin America, in the 1920s baggage of imported Marxism.[23] But the detached comparative and social methods of positivism could assail Europe just as well. Peru, through José Carlos Mariátegui and Víctor Haya de la Torre, would excel in those "new" radical ideologies of anti-imperialism and indigenismo.

The industrialization proposal of *Apuntes para la historia económica* is singular in several ways. For Esteves, as for his predecessors, palpable experience rather than economic theory guides his sense of industrial possibilism. In one rare mention of Lima, the success of the Vitarte cotton mill in weaning Peru from British import dependence makes heady inspiration:

We ourselves are tributaries of that diligent nation to no small degree—as any look at the British imports to Peru show. . . . Thus we have paid out to England for cotton pieces alone almost double what we received for producing raw cotton. . . . The textile factory of López Aldana, in Vitarte a few miles up from Lima, is now responding to our way of doing commerce—so inconceivable and anomalous for a country of middling culture. Sr. Aldana has sparked an economic revolution in this field, which in the future will be worth many millions to Peru; in its first moments of action in 1876 it

22. Esteves, *Apuntes para la historia económica,* 6; cf. Químper, *Propuestas de los tenedores de bonos,* 5, 12, who warns of British commercial path to empire (e.g., a Peruvian East Indies Company), but was most concerned with Peru becoming "Yankee territory." Elite anti-imperialism finds a (political) counterpart only in the liberal "Americanist" (anti-Spain) agitation of the mid 1860s.

23. E.g., Hirschman, "Ideologies of Development," 4–12; Burns, *Poverty of Progress.*

provided as a practical result 108,738 pounds sterling, which before we spent on cottons imports.[24]

More salient heroes are the oft-praised highland Garmendia (Lucre) and Terry (Urcón) woolens factories. The intriguing side of Esteves's industrial utopianism is his full shift from Lima—the occupied capital then lying in ruins. Such national concerns cropped up as early as 1860 in Pardo's visions of rural industry and were glimpsed too in the 1860s railroad genre—an idea consistent with cost factors, natural protection, civilist decentralism, and the imagined decadence of Peru's Europeanized capital. By the 1870s foreign and Peruvian geographers, naturalists, and technical advisers (the Raimondis, Martinets, and Paz-Soldáns) had opened up national vistas of problems and possibilities, and helped produce the beggar-on-the-mountain Peru, just as Fuentes had done for the capital in the prior generation.[25] Now, in *Apuntes para la historia económica*, Lima's criollo or immigrant artisans merit no attention whatsoever as a source of entrepreneurial dynamism—a sharp move from the urban, middle-class industrialism of Copello and Petriconi.

There are two striking dimensions to Esteves's turn to rural industry: indigenismo and colonial precedents. Economic nativism is positivist inspired, part of his global effort to demonstrate just how indigenous to Peru are industrial capabilities and aspirations. It deepens the civilist "progressive vindication" of the Indian that we now know had begun before the war.[26] To Esteves, industry is the true—and liberating— vocation of Peru's submerged Andean majorities.

Esteves's introduction to Indian industrialism unfolds during two long discussions of wool and alpaca production and export trades. In part, the terms of trade are at issue: the 1870s dive in wool prices makes

24. Esteves, *Apuntes para la historia económica,* 26; the figures (simple fall in textile imports, 1875–1876) are doubtful for production.

25. J. B. Martinet, *La agricultura en el Perú* (1877; rpt. Lima, 1977), sticks closely to coastal realms; although not part of a critical literature, it is notable for its Continental interventionist assumptions and its agrarian critique of "unproductive" wealth, extractive "lotteries," and elite "capital" flight. Here, Indians are dismissed as "muy poco industrioso" (88).

26. Kristal, *Andes from the City,* ch. 2, which quickly deems 1870s civilist indigenismo an "exporter" ideology—not Esteves's perspective. Mexican positivism (Hale, *Transformation of Liberalism*) rarely produced indigenista variants, for that country (unlike Peru) was fast erasing "Indians" in its Porfirian commercial expansion; Hale, however, underlines the "industrial" and liberal thread of Comtean positivism, which might have gone into the redemptive posture of an Esteves.

"no more pressing necessity in Peru than utilizing this wealth in the only manner possible: manufacturing."[27] But more essential than short-term price instability is Esteves's long-term rediscovery of the "naturals'" informal weaving and spinning traditions—dating to Incan glories. A striking and patriotic reminder occurred amid the exigencies of war. During the initial Chilean blockades of southern ports, Indian artisans of Puno, Arequipa, and Moquegua rose to supply the army with their coarse cloths—*cordellates, paños, jergas,* and *frazadas;* soon enough "this demand had inspired a meticulousness of construction, to the point of comparing perfectly with the ordinary cashmeres we import from abroad at such exorbitant prices."[28] The blankets of Paucarcolla district alone were now worth eight to ten thousand soles a year, profits that stay with improving village authorities. With but a touch of European direction, this "industria naciente" will keep on advancing.

Animated by his discoveries, Esteves is set to preach on Indians:

Such fabrication with the crudest instruments prove his mechanical talent, uncultivated only for lack of example. It is no difficult task to make the Indian into an industrial being; they enjoy gifts of imitation and patience, which are enough to transform them into useful workers, and their sobriety will keep them content with the most modest of salaries. . . . The largest part of our population, he must be made into its productive element. This is the mission that, sooner or later, only the woolens manufacturing industry can fulfill.[29]

In part, this industrial indigenismo appears in dissembled contrast to the better-known creole city artisan, always shunned for lethargic work habits, high costs, and "immoral" living in general. Yet, if framed in a primitive positivist idiom, Esteves is trying to invert ingrained racist representations of the sleepy, sullen Indian (typical of earlier rail writers), who now holds the energetic answer to Peru's national reconstruction. Although Indians are obviously portrayed as simpler beings, it is not biological or cultural inferiority that isolates them from development, but white oppression: "What destroys their fine qualities, undermines their spirit, and mistreats their body are the endless persecutions by speculators during the republic's rare periods of peace and by the

---

27. Esteves, *Apuntes para la historia económica,* 41; pt. 1, chs. 7–8.

28. Esteves, *Apuntes para la historia económica,* 41; Hunt's analysis of 1876 census ("Growth and Guano," 95) finds 167,778 self-styled rural "female spinners"—part-time artisans, at best.

29. Esteves, *Apuntes para la historia económica,* 42.

militares who made them cannon fodder in the usual years of revolutions and combat."[30] To be sure, the coastal literary and political critique of *gamonal* oppressions had been voiced before, most vociferously from the late 1860s Sociedad Amiga de los Indios. But here the "naturals" become a perfect economic metaphor for Peru's own hobbled development—an anti-imperial image to stick in coming decades.

The extensive chapters in *Apuntes para la historia económica* on rural economy come laced with "antifeudal" messages, in that perplexing composite of admiration and paternalism, coveted integration and exploitation, assimilationism and autonomy typical of turn-of-the-century city indigenistas. The notion of the Indian as "worker" is the shared modernist motif. Hoary and decadent "Spanish custom" allows white landowners and merchants to exploit the indigent and innocent Indian, as detailed in the ways petty traders and mestizos managed to swindle natives during the rise of the nineteenth-century alpaca trade. Indian producers are now the wiser. Indians require secure landed property and full freedom of commerce; the government must "extend them its public administration."[31] The "naturals" must be protected from dangers of alcohol and coca. There are wider laudatory themes: admiration for the Incan agriculture, irrigation, and roads that united the whole Andes, supported its millions, and saved Europe from starvation with their "gift" of the potato. Tawantinsuyo could always inspire a distant adulation from Peruvian elites—usually in contempt of its living Indian relics—but here a thriving and ancient "industriousness" comes to the fore.[32] Modern rural industry (unlike the obraje or republican landed exporter) was to emancipate the Indian—with the helping hand of progressive capitalists like Garmendia and Terry.

Like Copello and Petriconi, then, Esteves presents another version of the popular and liberal wellsprings of progress. National events and transformations were redefining the social problem in the eyes of Peru-

30. Esteves, *Apuntes para la historia económica*, 42; cf. metaphor in Samuel Velarde, *Los antiguos contratos y el contrato Grace* (Lima, pam., 1887), which opens by comparing Peru's debt dependency to Indian "debt slavery" of Amazon rubber trade, followed by reconstruction focus on small national entrepreneurs. See also "abuse"-oriented Juan Bustamante, "Los indios en el Perú," in Tamayo, *Pensamiento indigenista*, 21–29, and documents of Sociedad Amiga, in Emilio Vásquez, *La rebelión de Juan Bustamante* (Lima, 1976), anexos.

31. Esteves, *Apuntes para la historia económica*, 31–32, 42–44, 62.

32. See Cecilia Méndez, "República sin indios: La comunidad imaginada del Perú," in H. Urbano, ed., *Tradición y modernidad en los Andes* (Cuzco, 1992), 15–41, on racist split perceptions of Incas and Indians; similarly, Walker, "Rhetorical Power."

vian elites. "Our revolts and anarchy," Esteves finally admits in that familiar refrain, "find no origin but the lack of occupation among the masses, who need work as the glue of order and morality."[33] If fundamentally more hopeful, this lost treatise was an economic analogue of the literary-political indigenismo of disillusioned postwar intellectuals.

More difficult is fathoming authentic regional echoes of Esteves's decentralist call. One notable (but equally unrecognized) contemporary voice was Luis Carranza, whose incisive "Consideraciones generales sobre los departamentos del centro" (1883) takes us on a social tour of postwar Ayacucho, Huancavelica, and Apurímac. Carranza, a Huamangan physician turned journalist, migrated to Lima in the 1860s; became a charter member of the pro-Bustamante Sociedad Amiga de los Indios; a founder of the Partido Civil (in which he served as Ayacucho party chief); a Pardista congressman (like Esteves); and by the late 1870s director of El Comercio (whose owner, Manuel Amunátegui, was also among the Indians' celebrated "friends"). After the war Carranza created and led the prestigious Sociedad Geográfica de Lima, the new scientific beacon for greater Peruvian awareness.[34] Carranza, the prototype of the provincial intellectual figures awakening almost everywhere after the 1880s, was obviously a less quirky figure than Juan Bustamante. In this essay it is the war—Carranza served as chief publicist while fighting with Cáceres's legendary Andean guerrillas—that focuses the new interior vision.

Carranza, like Esteves, undertakes a retrospective as well as spatial voyage, around what he terms the late "Kingdom of Huano." His Limeño readers must grasp the true Peru left in ruins. His aim was in another economic history: to herald "the raza indígena del Perú—no inconvenience or fetter to national progress and greatness," but, with gentle guidance, its "latent force."[35] To be sure, Carranza leaves us with distressful liberal-positivist images of the Indian—mired in "passivity," ignorance, disorder, drunkenness. But such degradation was produced

33. Esteves, Apuntes para la historia económica, 156; for how disorders at least felt to anxious elites, see Bonilla, "War of Pacific and the National Problem."

34. Luis Carranza, "Consideraciones generales sobre los departamentos del centro" (1883), in L. Carranza, Colección de artículos publicados por Luis Carranza, médico (Lima, 1885–1888), 3:48–84; other relevant essays include reviews of Raimondi's El Perú; travelogues of the United States; and varied studies of the evolution and archaeology of the Indian "race." For biography, see Tauro, Diccionario 1:283–84; Manrique, Las guerrillas indígenas, 25, 50–53; Vásquez, Bustamante, 156, 196; MacEvoy, "Manuel Pardo," table 1.

35. Carranza, "Consideraciones generales sobre el centro," 68, 84.

by Peru's nineteenth-century commercial centralism, which enervated the Indian's natural "activity" and stamina of Incan and Spanish times. Carranza, through his thick description of natal Huamanga, traces contemporary backwardness—"barbarity," in positivist lingo—to three factors: parish priests, political chaos, and, of most harm for the regions, the century's "revolución económica." In the mode of Amézaga's anticlericalism, Catholicism draws positivist fire for constraining the Indian's material wants and vision. Here priestly oppression is imaginatively conceived as the imposition of "comunismo evangélica" over vestiges of an Incan "sistema comunista," the latter suggesting the (more approving) categories of 1920s indigenista anthropology. Postindependence chaos, caudillos, and corruption had sparked endless local uprisings, devastated interior commerce, upset Indian political subordination, and—as Carranza himself could attest—hurried white flight from the sierra.[36]

"Consideraciones generales del centro" lays most blame, nonetheless, on Peru's "revolución económica"—Carranza's special term for the commercial transformations of the guano age—and its "disastrous," "decadent," and disparate impact on regional possibilities. In Esteves or Pardo fashion, the colonial period reappears as a lost golden age of regional diversity and wholeness, guided by Spain's "indirectly protectionist system." Homeland Huamanga, for example, bustled in tocuyo cottons trades, fructiferous wheat-trading haciendas, productive leather works, and mines. The pueblo of Pacaisaca "formed a singular and vast establishment of looms," with a thousand busy workers "of both sexes." Together the three provinces under study once exchanged $2 million in wares from their obrajes, farms, and mines.[37]

Provincial economies were thus wholly unprepared for the shocks of Lima's republican "libre competencia comercial." Within a few years their mainstays and markets lay abandoned to overseas competitors and factories. "For sparse populations like these, with generally poor soils, the loss of their returns (from local and coastal trades) brought sudden proportional falls in capital and population—and the provinces' intellectual and moral depression."[38] Mass poverty, lack of work, and insecurity

---

36. Carranza, "Consideraciones generales sobre el centro," 53–61.

37. Carranza, "Consideraciones generales sobre el centro," 62–63; Ayacucho examples used parallel those heard in 1845 congressional debates (ch. 3, above) and remain of uncertain origin.

38. Carranza, "Consideraciones generales sobre el centro," 64–65.

marginalized the Indian laborer; a modernizing coast schizophrenically split from Andean Peru. Such regional "disasters" amount to "the most serious that can affect a nation."

But Carranza cannot wax nostalgic for a colonial "commercial and industrial prosperity" built on "economic principles opposed to modern societies."[39] Liberalism remains his civilist creed, just as it did in Pardo's admiration of colonial culture. The problem, in practice, was that liberalism had proven perverse to regions and peoples with such modest comparative advantages; history had inverted liberalism's decentralist populating and capitalizing pledges of the 1840s. And as history, Carranza got it right, for Peru's modern dualisms and regional left-behinds did incubate in this age of guano.

Rising here is a rhetoric of interior resentment. It was the kind that 1860s technicians and regional elites had hoped to assuage with railroad integration, as had Pardo and civilismo with their later decentralist politics. To Carranza, the Spanish kingdom's intendencies had at least upheld a de facto regional balance, with multiple "foci of wealth and culture," a more "solid and vigorous national vitality." In contrast, the kingdom of Huano, by "centralizing its fiscal riches in Lima," shrank the "industrial wealth of the interior" and paralyzed their entrepreneurial prospects.[40] For with a kind of "brain drain" concept of human capital loss, Carranza tells how "all the useful and capable population fled to Lima, which quickly absorbed in its heart the most distinguished provincial families, our most enlightened men." Exaggerated commercial, credit, and agricultural development on the coast became "active cause of the rapid decadence of the rest"—a regional devolution not seen since the "fall of the Incas." Solutions, however, are but implied: will rectification of indigenous barbarity be achieved through the return of *misti* (white) entrepreneurs or through Incan-style reintegration of schools, roads, and authority?

This regionalism ends, Esteves-style, as a could-have-been postmortem on a squandered age of guano: "If only our fiscal wealth had been

39. Carranza, "Consideraciones generales sobre el centro," 67; Pardo, "Partido de Saña"; Carranza does note some gradual agricultural replacements by the 1870s.

40. Carranza, "Consideraciones generales sobre el centro," 68, 78. The sarcasm of the "kingdom" references parallels that of Duffield, *Prospects of Peru,* who contrasts the "Golden Age of the Incas" with the passing "Age of Manure"—a periodization that thankfully never caught on. For a modern take on trade, human capital, and uneven development, see Keith Griffin, *Underdevelopment in Spanish America* (London, 1969), chs. 2, 6.

used instead to create and promote great industries on our soil, the disaster would not have assumed today's crushing proportions"—that is, the national and military weakness that gave the war to Chile.[41] Lacking the bitter edge, Carranza presaged González Prada's industrial and indigenista indictment.

Esteves then did not stand alone in the 1880s, but his *Apuntes sobre la historia económica* still stands out as the first economic analysis to encompass the Indian directly. Historians have aptly deemed the nineteenth century as the age of shrinking "Andeanness" in national consciousness, though Quechua peasants hardly shrank as the country's ethnic majority nor faded in poetic imaginations.[42] Here and there Indians sparked controversies in the capital—during the 1855 abolition of tribute; in cursory and coercive ways in a scattering of railroad manifestos; in the quintessentially elite sympathies of the Sociedad Amiga de los Indios in reaction to the mid-1860s return of head taxes; in the scandalizing "terror" of Puno's 1867 Huancané uprising, which martyred Bustamante; and by the 1870s in the landed and clerical oppressions conjured up in the capital's civilist literary salons. But in the nineteenth-century economic calculus Indians were most conspicuous for their absence. Pardo himself selected a distinctive mestizo region for his exemplar of Andean developmentalism, and though he was progressively more attuned to Indians in later writings and politics, his thinking never progressed beyond the whitest of assimilationist clichés.[43]

There is a genealogy and causality of denial and memory here, related to shifting regional concerns. Above all, a strategic angst was always the mother of Peru's developmental imagination. Peru's remarkable indigenous quiescence between 1827 and 1867—a full half century without rebellions—had kept Indians off official and economic worry lists in the capital. National rediscovery must have traveled the railroad lines themselves and the tracks of the new national census-takers. And by the early 1870s localized ethnic tensions were again heating up between expansive regional elites and communities, to be fought out later by awaken-

41. Carranza, "Consideraciones generales sobre el centro," conclusions, 79.

42. Alberto Flores Galindo, "In Search of an Inca," in Steve Stern, ed., *Resistance, Rebellion, and Consciousness in the Andean Peasant World, Eighteenth to Twentieth Centuries* (Madison, 1982), 193–210; Kristal, *Andes from the City.*

43. Davies, *Indian Integration,* chs. 1–2; MacEvoy, "Manuel Pardo," 187–94, which analyzes Pardo's most focused writing, the tame 1867 essay "Algunas cuestiones sociales sobre los disturbios de Huancané"; Vásquez, *Bustamante,* anexos. However, Gen. Medina, who chaired the Sociedad Amiga, was also a leading civilist.

ing provincial intellectuals. But until the strategic and regional shocks of 1876–1881, a national amnesia prevailed. Only the ruin of the coastal economy by guano collapse and war, the frightful mobilizations of dark-hued Andeans in the conflict, and the utter white defeat (at the hands of Chile) put Indians, in varied ways, into Peru's developmental imagination. And only then could developmental thought assume its modern social and national forms.[44]

Along with economic explorations of the countryside and the Indian, *Apuntes para la historia económica* marks a milestone for rescuing the lost and related colonial obraje. Esteves's historical survey of obrajes, long scorned by liberal republicans as symbolic relics of inefficient and op-pressive colonialism, is the first positive word on their achievements in the critical tradition (and almost the only word since the initial republic). The obraje woolens plants of Cuzco and Huaraz, despite their regres-sive, forced-labor regimes, managed to clothe Peru's common folk, revealed native manufacturing predilections, and overcame both Spain's imports and capricious anti-industrial policy. To Esteves the viceroyalty "was for manufacturing industry the golden age in Peru, for during the republic these obrajes, the *embrión de fábricas,* vanished as soon as free-dom of trade in our ports brought a flood of imported textiles from the other nations of Europe."[45] To be sure, imported cloth was cheaper and appealed to Peruvian "vanities," but this history had consequences: "We buried beneath the debris of the oppressive obraje the idea of nationaliz-ing factory industry. . . . Without awareness of what was going on in the world, except needing to dress up in the latest cuts of Paris, we considered it a *locura* [folly] to bring factories to our wool-producing provinces."[46]

This remark shows insight into the liberal trivialization of industry in the early republic, which politically linked the industrial idea with retro-grade obrajes and artisans. But now Esteves brings in his most exem-plary entrepreneurs: "against the current," Garmendia and Terry estab-lished their rural factory centers, which Esteves takes us through in

44. Following trends analyzed in Gootenberg, "Population and Ethnicity," 141–53; see Jacobsen, *Mirages of Transition,* pt. 2, for finest study of conflicts; Tamayo, *Historia social e indigenismo,* for case of "awakening" regional intellectuals—in Puno as well.

45. Esteves, *Apuntes para la historia económica,* 33. His use of notion "embryo of factories," so common in the Mexican writings, is uncanny; for fine analysis of concept (and of colonial obrajes), see Richard Salvucci, *Textiles and Capitalism in Mexico: An Economic History of the Obrajes, 1539–1840* (Princeton, 1987), ch. 2, "Embrión de la Fábrica?"

46. Esteves, *Apuntes para la historia económica,* 33–34; for typical liberal view, see Távara's 1831 *Análisis y amplificación del manifiesto,* 46–49: Távara could even call for free-trade destruction of the obrajes as an Indian "emancipation" measure.

detail. (Francisco Garmendia's 1859 Lucre factory was, in fact, built literally on the debris of a defunct obraje.) These "firm patriots" proved beyond a doubt "the possibility for implanting a woolens textile industry in Peru." They sacrificed enormously for the war efforts. Here, perhaps, were the sort of notables needed back in the Andes.

In a didactic tale Esteves reveals his personal relation with the now-deceased Garmendia. Esteves had in fact served with Garmendia (and the Terrys) in congress; sometime in the early 1870s, as he tells it, the two had together presented a legal brief to Peru's supreme court itself pleading for government support. In what was surely a precocious case of the new economic legalism, the misguided judge demanded further "proof" of Peru's industrial potential—"whether Peru has the advantages for being a manufacturing country, or should continue as to now exporting its raw materials."[47] To Esteves, Garmendia's thriving mill was the living verdict on industrial possibilities.

Following these temporal and exemplary excursions, chapter 9 of *Apuntes para la historia económica*, entitled "Woolen Manufactures," simply renders the argument in its technical and capitalistic form. Harking to Casanova's intricate cost-profit calculations, the calculus has clearly tipped from coastal cottons to sierran wools. Tapping Genoese records and accounts from giant Central European factories, Esteves presents arithmetical page on page on machinery, labor, transport, and wool costs to prove the "advantageous conditions that Peru enjoys for becoming a manufacturing nation"—even without the latest technology. Using their cheap and abundant Indian workers, national capitalists could reap up to 3.3 million soles on initial investments.[48] The judge, if still around, might have been pleased.

Perhaps Esteves sensed that such felicitous cost and production conditions would outflank the contentious issue of tariff protection, fully ignored in the book. Especially during the 1870s crisis Peru's coastal elites had proved unmoving on both free trade and their clamors about costly labor shortages. Esteves's answer was to look to the forgotten highlands instead. He applauds the arrival of railroads to the "rich and productive department of Junín" (i.e., Pardo's Jauja)—spur to this "economic revolution, which will resolve if not all, then most of our current

47. Esteves, *Apuntes para la historia económica*, 35; Basadre has a fine oral biography of Garmendia's experiments (*Historia* 3:1293–95); *Diarios de debates,* 1870–1873. Garmendia, recall, was Pardo's vice president; he died in 1873 while buying new machinery in Italy.
48. Esteves, *Apuntes para la historia económica,* pt. 1, ch. 9, "Manufactura de lanas"—which taps Chemnitz.

problems and somber future." The hyperboles of the 1850s lived on. He envisages southern Indian pastoral zones of Puno (the country's poorest traditional region) as the future industrial heartland of Peru. Other discussions in *Apuntes para la historia económica* argue for the industrialization of the tropical quinine trade; new silk industries ("to give our agriculture novel sources of wealth"); the production of gin from sierran barley (though the factories must guard their product from susceptible natives); coal mining (for fantasized factories); Amazon hat and wood exports; concerted use of Moquegua clays and porcelains; and the gamut of domestic food industries. In one particularly prophetic aside, Esteves ventures that coca leaf (now mere colonial Indian "abuse") must eventually find, by the miracle of "modern chemistry," more "profitable uses."[49]

The closing pages of the *Apuntes para la historia económica* follow an unruly fiscal analysis of Peru's lost guano opportunity and an unbridled assault on British commercial hegemony. Here Esteves conjures up a veritable "new world economic order"—or at least foretells the global dissemination of consumer industry that indeed was to mark the twentieth century. Esteves rhetorically demands, "Should we continue with the commercial despotism to which we are subjected?" His answer, by now, is pat: "The progress of all nations resents the monopoly that the British have established over a third of the globe." Only industry will impart genuine and lasting value to Peru's bounteous natural treasures. Without hinting how it should come, Esteves imagines an imminent turning point in world economic history:

Then will arrive in the world a moment of economic transition—that will establish on a fair basis its commercial order. Industry, escaping the grips of its present tyranny, will go on to settle in all the corners of the globe. There will be a just and regular distribution of riches. The popular masses will be carried away by this current of work, to a society in its natural seabed of equilibrium. This is the future that belongs to us.[50]

With this retrospect of nineteenth-century experience, Peru's utopian developmental discourse had broached its modern form.

49. Esteves, *Apuntes para la historia económica,* 48, 55, 60–61, 88, 92–93, 73, 75. Silk "agro-industry" projects (dating from Sarratea's time) were common; see, e.g., Luis Sada, *Proyecto de asociación para introducir y generalizar en el Perú el cultivo de la morera y del gusano de seda* (Lima, pam., 1870), cited; Mörner, *Notas sobre Cusco,* 16, for similar 1872 Mangelsdorff beer factory and regional barley crops. Lissón, *Sociología del Perú,* 63, also lauds coca's promise: "que la ciencia moderna viene haciendo en gran artículo con sus potencias aplicaciones." Prophetic indeed.

50. Esteves, *Apuntes para la historia económica,* 156–57.

7

Conclusions
Thinking about Guano

This book has explored thinking about economic development and diversity among key members of Peru's civil elite in the age of guano—one of the most infamous export booms in the history of Latin America. This was no fringe group of intellectual mavericks but the very core of Peru's leadership class: Manuel Pardo y Lavalle (financier, president, and father icon of the civilist movement); Luis Benjamín Cisneros (legal theorist, literary light, and architect of economic reform); Manuel Anastasio Fuentes (the republic's premier social scientist and administrator); Juan Norberto Casanova (its first would-be industrialist); Luis Esteves (pioneer economic historian); José Arnaldo Márquez (the century's outstanding educator); Ernesto Malinowski (prototypical technical adviser); Juan Copello and Luis Petriconi (new-breed urban, immigrant thinkers); Luis Carranza (regional intellectual and publicist); and many others, notables and common folk alike, along the way.

These men, it now appears, harbored a complex set of ideas for turning the country's "fictitious prosperity" into a lasting development. Self-critical reflections on the official free-trade liberalism of the state, their projects stemmed from Peruvian experience and conditions and went against the grain of laissez-faire European political economy— then at the height of its international prestige. Strikingly rare were unreserved champions of free-trade development. These thinkers knew perfectly well what economic philosophy and example were telling Peru to do—specialize in primary products—but they broke with it as reservations grew on the stability and social consequences of Peru's new dependence. Laissez-faire struck them as increasingly inadequate for larger tasks of constructing a viable state and integrating a fragmented nation. They wished to avert the nation's risky reliance on overseas trade and finance while offering credible plans for transforming its social and economic structures. They spoke eloquently in terms of harnessing exports to diversify Peru, of bolstering national markets, of extending public protection, of enhancing Peru's global sovereignty, and of engaging the left-behind masses in productive, developmental, and honorable "work." In thinking about guano, they imagined no set contradiction between the country's export foundation and its domestic progress.

The most common thread was fascination with what might be called utopian industrialism.[1] Peruvians read the North Atlantic industrial revolution, particularly the North American experience, as an opportunity for their emulation. They envisioned import substitution and modern technology (especially the railroad) as indispensable answers to the country's troubling commercial, regional, and social imbalances, spelling out their industrial projects in fanciful detail. They imagined the day when production and participation would supersede Peru's fictitious prosperity. These often subtle ideas presaged elements of the formal Latin American developmental ideologies of the twentieth century.

There is even a marked genealogy, or evolution, in this thinking, revealing of its roots in Peruvian dilemmas. It began from changing perceptions of the social costs of liberalism, notably the "social problem" of ambient Lima; it followed the unfolding stages in the high fiscal and commercial crisis of guano; it ended in the discovery of a larger Peru needful of technological uplift. It found expression in a shifting locus of concern (the capital, the nation); the types of industry required (workshop or factory, urban or rural); and changing conceptions of the social groups to integrate into productive work (artisans, middle classes, Indians). In stages, it borrowed richly from Peru's popular economic nationalism as well as from overseas examples. So marked is the lineage of these schemes, and the linkages between its advocates, that we may speak of a

1. Peru's technological utopianism, one ventures, also incarnates creole aspirations for cultural subordination of Andean Peru. Adas's *Machines as Measure of Men*, pioneering study of the technological construction of colonial-racial "superiority," omits Latin America; and yet in neocolonial regions one detects the purest cultural (rather than coercive) forces at work; see also Pratt, *Imperial Eyes*. See Chandra, "Colonial Indian Views of Development," for a case of (anticolonial) utopian industrial thought; and John F. Kasson, *Civilizing the Machine: Technology and Republican Values in America, 1776–1900* (New York, 1976), for the emulated (but ambiguous) northern utopias.

Peruvian "counterliberal tradition"—even though it was forged by the country's most prominent liberals and plutocrats.[2] If comparative sociology makes sense here, their collective mentality was analogous to that normally associated with other Western national bourgeoisies.

These findings are surprisingly at odds with prevailing sociological views of Peru's guano-age elite and with conventional wisdom about nineteenth-century Latin American liberalism. In such views, elite thinking was limited by a peripheral vision: a dogmatic and derivative brand of European economic liberalism, blind to social repercussions, focused on narrow economic interests. Out of touch with national realities, civilists, as a ruling class, could only sink Peru further into ill-fated export dependence, as displayed by their railroad and foreign debt boondoggles. This view is mistaken in both its textual specifics and sociological generalities. It emerged, one assumes, from the assumption that dependence and underdevelopment can result only in backward or neocolonial thinking. It makes a strangely ad hominem form of class analysis and a strangely idealist class of dependency analysis. It misses the dialectical mentalities so evident in other spheres of postcolonial imagination.[3]

Yet a dramatic gap did persist between Peruvian ideas and practice. These thinkers were producing a Peru that never was. A few of these plans made their way selectively but effectively into policy—railway projects, rationalization and nationalization of guano finance, the early strides in vocational training. And by the 1870s Peru was amplifying its commercial, geographic, manufacturing, and political bases, before the guano collapse cut short such promising developments. But by and large Peru never escaped its monoexport dependence, much less embraced state-sponsored development. Nor did this critical tradition spawn results for the future. After the Pacific War the "lessons" recognized were selective too, as the country rapidly returned to liberal-oligarchic policies

2. "Counter" does not imply "anti" here, for these men clearly belonged to and extended nineteenth-century liberal traditions; nor does their discourse reveal clearly discernible or conflictive social interests. Our view thus differs from, e.g., Shumway's recent *Invention of Argentina* (and many analogous works, such as Burns, *Poverty of Progress*). In those analyses, similar currents are found in national mythologies but interpreted as antitheses to triumphant liberalism or as precursors of modern social schizophrenias.

3. As in the political nationalisms evoked in Anderson's *Imagined Communities*. See ch. 1, above, for sociological school. Note that apart from economic thought and policy, recent historiography is capturing new subtleties: e.g., Trazegnies, *Idea de derecho*, and MacEvoy, "Manuel Pardo" (legal and political thought); Quiroz, *Domestic and Foreign Finance* (entrepreneurialism); Kristal, *Andes from the City*, and Watson, *Cuadro de costumbres* (literary-social imaginations).

and rule, despite another generation of critical thinkers. In the twentieth century Peru became legendary as the most open of the major Latin American economies and among the most closed of its political regimes. Not until 1968, with the Velasco military revolution, and not for long, did guided diversification, Andean social integration, and import substitution become national agendas—a century after their first articulations.[4]

What could explain Peru's yawning gap between elaborate alternatives and their translation into policy? We can only speculate, in two directions, trying to add some structural sense to economic imaginings. First—in terms of policy-making cycles—Peruvian leaders of the opening decades of the guano age lived under an intoxicating "wealth illusion"—not unlike, say, Mexico's during its recent age of oil. Like petroleum, guano was a utopian export good that required concerted efforts to convert expansive consumption into broader development. Given the easy material and political rewards of guano monies, it is unlikely that much could have been done then to sway minds or switch tracks—though the initial warnings of reformers aimed precisely to unmask the "fictions" of rentier wealth and to move beyond idle riches into a productive ethic of national "work." They also held, fertilized by guano, an exaggerated faith in the transforming magic of their imagined reforms.

In contrast, during the final two decades of the guano age harried Peruvian statesmen and administrators worked under a perpetual and bewildering cloud of economic "crisis"—the worst atmosphere, truly, for effective implementation of long-term policies. Try they did, if not always facing the real-world trade-offs of delayed consumption for hopes of stabler development. But the relentless shocks, uncertainties, and penury of crisis made incubative and building responses ever so trying and muddled. Certainly it is a truism that Peruvian leaders were responsible for the errors committed. But they were also victims of adverse boom-to-bust policy cycles that still afflict Latin American struggles for development.[5]

4. Thorp and Bertram, *Peru 1890–1977*, esp. analysis in ch. 15 of Velasco as attempted "dependency" program; not coincidentally, this era saw the intellectual revival of forgotten works by Copello and Petriconi, Casanova, Esteves, and Pardo.

5. Thorp and Bertram, *Peru 1890–1977*, follows such boom-and-bust policy cycles; Rosemary Thorp, *Economic Management and Economic Development in Peru and Colombia* (Pittsburgh, 1991), addresses Peru's poor learning function. See also H. Bonilla, ed., *Las crisis económicas en la historia del Perú* (Lima, 1986), a timely foray into anatomy of crises responses. Crisis psychology may be the sorely unstudied aspect of Latin American policy-

Second—in terms of class and state formation—the Peruvian export economy and state appeared constrained, though not in the abject ways usually assumed. The rudimentary nature of guano production and the state's fast fiscal capture of its export produced a consolidating state remarkably "autonomous" of civil and regional society. Not only that, but core Peruvian elites (such as the urbanites studied here) remained unusually free themselves of fixed class interest, as their essential activities were flexible commercial, political, and ideational ones. This characteristic provides one interesting clue to their free-ranging thinking.[6] At the same time, the Castillan state could freely pursue its own interests, which lay in expansive liberalization and fiscal aggrandizement—and thus could selectively override the cries of core critics.

By the latter half of the guano age, however, more stationary and more national elite class interests began taking hold, offshoots of the diversifying developments in Peru's coastal sugar, Andean commercial, and southern nitrate zones. For this reason, civilist leaders of the crisis years appeared hamstrung by newly rooted forms of laissez-faire, which they lectured against from the now less autonomous state they inherited. As they looked around for alternative constituencies (such as urban middle sectors), they found weak actors still coming back from their initial economic and political losses of the export age. This is not to mention the deep-seated antipathies to popular protectionism and industrial possibilities embedded in elite consciousness since the 1840s, reflexes that still impeded flexible responses to export exhaustion. At any rate, both structural explanations—of adverse policy cycles and relations of class and state—merit further thinking.

Perhaps such speculations also suggest that diverse and fertile ideas simply don't matter that much—or more precisely, that causality should be reversed in explaining a gap between ideas and practice. It was the stark simplicity and dependency of the Peruvian export order that, in reaction, could spark such a rich array of utopian counterproposals. An analogous process worked itself out in twentieth-century Peru, where

---

making; some of Hirschman's early work (*Journeys Toward Progress* and *The Strategy of Economic Development*) suggests some aspects in the psychological metaphors of "unbalanced growth" and "fracasomania." In comparative politics, see Gourevitch, "International Trade and the Crisis of 1873."

6. Gootenberg, *Between Silver and Guano*, 132–37, analyzes guano-state autonomy; or autonomous politics view in Berg and Weaver, "Reinterpretation of Political Change." Guano was not unique in sparking imaginative answers; see Barbara Weinstein's incisive look at other odd "enclave" export, *The Amazon Rubber Boom, 1850–1920* (Stanford, 1983), esp. ch. 5 and Manaus merchant crisis responses.

the most socially conservative of South American societies erupted as the intellectual hotbed of social radicalism, producing such frustrated millennial thinkers as González Prada, Mariátegui, and Haya de la Torre (related or not to the pensadores before them).[7] Seen from this angle, Peruvian thinkers were not simply "failures," or if they were, they left us a vital kind of "fracasomania." From this angle, even an oddity like guano defies enclavity—by generating wide *intellectual* linkages across the larger society.

Yet this notion of imagined development does not actually spring sui generis from a Peruvian social history of ideas. In other guises, our most inspired reflections on ideology and policy in the modern world have evoked it. Keynes, one recalls, was the first to speculate on disjunctures between feasible economic reforms and business cycles—a gap that surely looms widest in "dependent" societies subject to far greater amplitudes of boom-and-bust conditions. Gerschenkron, reflecting on the spread of modernizing economic doctrines, fixed on a Toynbeean "state of tension between actualities and potentialities." The growing gap between perceived Western progress and backward national realities led to exaggerated—and often monumentally tragic—strategies of development in that (Eastern) European periphery. Hirschman, in profound ponderings of latecomer Latin American strategies, defines developmentalist "ideology" itself as a severe case of wishful thinking. Policymakers must invent ideology to dramatize and prioritize problems—especially in societies barraged by more felt problems and solutions than can be realistically handled.[8] Perhaps then the Peruvian gap between utopian

---

7. Klarén, *Modernization and Dislocation*, chs. 5–8; Chavarría, *Mariátegui and Modern Peru;* Fredrick B. Pike, *The Politics of the Miraculous in Peru: Haya de la Torre and the Spiritualist Tradition* (Lincoln, 1986): although links may go to the nineteenth century, this social nationalism was less an imagining of development than reaction to realer modernizations. For other cases of elite "fantasy" plans, see Safford, *Ideal of Practical,* or notion of "precocious" urban-industrial cultures in Véliz, *Centralist Tradition,* ch. 10, a suggestive analytic framework. Early Andean millenialism was also a mental reversal of abject oppressions (see Flores Galindo's *Buscando un inca*), but by the nineteenth century urban and Andean dreamers appeared to inhabit separate spheres of thought.

8. John Maynard Keynes, *The End of Laissez-Faire* (London, 1927), 53–54; Gerschenkron, *Economic Backwardness,* ch. 1 and esp. ch. 7, "Economic Development in Russian Intellectual History of the Nineteenth Century" (on the "curious divorce" of ideas and economic history): Russians were peculiarly struck by radical agrarianisms, a fixation rare in urban Peruvians, at least until the indigenismo of the 1920s. Albert O. Hirschman, "Problem-Solving and Policy-Making: A Latin American Style?" in Hirschman, *Journeys Toward Progress: Studies of Economic Policy-Making in Latin America* (New York, 1973), 227–50. Interestingly, both Gershenkron and Hirschman build on common links to Schumpeterian adaptive/creative responses.

yearnings and unyielding realities lies in the very nature of modernist developmental thought.

Finally, what might thinking about guano suggest about the Latin American liberal experience writ large? Comparative historians may go on from here, exploring, for example, Mexican thinking on foreign capital, Argentines' on the human kind, Brazilians' on state activism, Colombians' on agrarian innovation. I prefer to end thinking about general questions of timing and political culture. For many years now historians, gleaning the officialist rhetoric of economic liberalism, have discerned a sharp break between the exogenous "outward-oriented" thinking of the nineteenth century and the national "inward-oriented" developmentalism after 1929.[9] In the imitative nineteenth century, Latin America emerged as the purest outpost of economic liberalism in the Western world; after the 1930s, at least for the "Third World," Latin America soon became the beacon of *desarrollista* thought.

This neat divide is fast blurring. For one thing, economic historians have been discovering how nineteenth-century "liberal" states—such as Mexico, Chile, Brazil, and even Argentina—were off the record pursuing a fairly mixed bag of economic policies: creeping interventionism, a sophisticated manipulation of exchange rates and monetary tools, export-price fixing, highly effective tariff regimes. Inadvertently or advertently, some export economies developed substantial industrial and processing sectors even before they had to do so in the 1930s. In short, no clear dichotomy was felt between "outward" growth and domestic development—an idea, of course, recognized by prescient Peruvian thinkers. Many historians now identify ongoing regional statist and nationalist traditions that never quite dried up under the liberal pause and that simply assumed greater weight with the loss of world markets and finance in the Great Depression.[10]

9. E.g., Furtado, *Economic Development of Latin America;* Cardoso and Faletto, *Dependency and Development;* Hirschman, "Ideologies of Development"; Popescu, *Pensamiento económico latinoamericano;* or Joseph Love, "Structural Change and Conceptual Response in Latin America and Romania, 1860–1950," in Love and Jacobsen, *Guiding the Invisible Hand,* 1–34. Dependency theory per se fits irregularly into this scheme, since initial versions (e.g., A. G. Frank) posited extreme continuities in Latin American capitalism; see exegesis in Halperín-Donghi, "'Dependency Theory' and Historiography." But dependency also produced the extreme binaries of works such as Burns, *Poverty of Progress,* discussed in ch. 1 (introduction), above.

10. This literature is now vast; see, e.g., Stephen Haber, *Industry and Underdevelopment: The Industrialization of Mexico, 1890–1940* (Stanford, 1989); Palma, "Growth and Structure of Chilean Industry"; Henry Kirsch, *Industrial Development in a Traditional*

In the realm of economic ideas, it appears as if the recently re-furbished prestige of "neoliberalism" in the region, often of an anti-industrial and autocratic bent, also complicates simpler stage theories. More and more, Latin Americanists recognize an interplay of statism and liberalism as a permanent feature of the regional intellectual and political landscape. It seems as pointless to blame Chicago and Moscow today as to blame Manchester or Seville in the nineteenth century; evangelical messages from abroad always suffer mutation, and even growth, in such politically catholic contexts. In new thinking about political regimes, many historians (whose professional bias, of course, lies with "continuity") are also questioning 1929 watersheds.[11] The entry of middle classes and working masses into Latin American politics did not occur overnight; populist politics ran deeper, and the modern variants are heavily infused with corporatist and authoritarian—as well as democratic—traditions.

If the zealously liberal Peru of the age of guano was stirring strong subterranean currents of heterodox social thought, it looks certain that historians will find similar intellectual upwellings elsewhere, which no doubt worked a greater worldly effect. The broadest conclusion, that Latin America is constantly evolving, or devolving, in a sea of shifting social traditions, seems the best fit with a fitful reality.

Society: The Conflict of Entrepreneurship and Modernization in Chile (Gainesville, 1977); Topik, *Political Economy of Brazilian State;* Weaver, *Class, State, and Industrial Structure,* ch. 5; Quiroz, *Domestic and Foreign Finance;* and esp. Rosemary Thorp, ed., *Latin America in the 1930s: The Role of the Periphery in the World Crisis* (London, 1984).

11. See, e.g., Véliz, *Centralist Tradition;* liberal revisionisms in Love and Jacobsen, *Guiding the Invisible Hand;* Richard Morse, "Notes Toward a Fresh Ideology," in Morse, *New World Soundings* (1989), 131–66, for the guru of cultural heterogeneities; new literatures on populism, corporatism, authoritarianism and democracy are, needless to say, massive.

Bibliography

Archives and Documents Consulted

Actas del Congreso del Perú, 1822–1879. Lima: Instituto Riva Agüero.
Anales universitarios del Perú, 1862–1869. Lima: La Época.
Biblioteca Denegri Luna. "Memorias del General Manuel de Mendiburu." 3 vols. 1829–1854. (Also includes pamphlet collections.)
Colección de Manuscritos; Colección de Volantes. Biblioteca Nacional del Perú, Lima.
Correspondence Between British Diplomatic and Consular Officers in Peru and the Foreign Office. Foreign Office Series 61, vols. 1–187, 1823–1860. Public Record Office, London.
Despatches from United States Consuls in Lima. U.S. Department of State, Record Group 59, M154, vols. 1–6, 1823–1854; T52, vols. 1–16 (U.S. Ministers). National Archives, Washington, D.C.
Diarios de los Debates: Congresos Ordinarios, Cámara de Diputados. Lima: Comercio, 1862–1878.
Libros de Cabildos/Actas de la Municipalidad. Archivo Municipal de Lima. Books 45–49, 1821–1839.
Libros Manuscritos Republicanos de la Sección Hacienda. Archivo General de la Nación, Lima. Section H-4. Oficios y Comunicaciones de Hacienda, Section H-1.
Matrículas de Patentes de Lima, 1830–1885. Archivo General de la Nación, Lima. Sections H-4 and H-1, Libros Manuscritos Republicanos de la Sección Hacienda; Archivo Histórico de Hacienda. (Periodical versions also available.)
Memorias de Hacienda y Comercio, 1845–1881. E. Dancuart, comp. Lima: various pub., 1902–1904. (See also separate pamphlets cited below.)
Mensajes de los presidentes del Perú. P. Ugarte and E. San Cristóval, comps. Lima: Gil., 1943.

Tribunal del Consulado (Republicano), 1821–1860. Archivo General de la Nación, Lima. Section H-8.

Periodicals

(All Lima unless otherwise noted)
El Acento de la Justicia, Cuzco (1829)
La Actualidad (1855)
El Amigo del Pueblo (1840)
El Artesano (1873)
Los Clamores del Perú (1827)
El Comercio (1839–1880)
El Constitucional (1858)
El Correo de Lima (1851–1852)
El Correo del Perú (1874–1878)
El Eco de la Opinión del Perú (1827)
El Hijo del Pueblo (1864–1868)
Los Intereses del País, Cuzco (1848–1851)
El Intérprete del Pueblo (1852)
El Nacional (1869–1871)
La Opinión Nacional (1875)
La Patria (1870–1873)
El Perú (1864)
El Peruano (1839–1851; 1871–1873)
El Progreso (1849–1851)
El Redactor Peruano (1836–1838)
El Rejistro Oficial (1850–1853)
La República (1863–1864)
La Revista de Lima (1860–1862)
La Revista Política y Administrativa (1878)
El Telégrafo de Lima (1827–1839)
El Tiempo (1864)
El Trabajo (1874)
El Trabajo, Puno (1876)
La Zamacueca Política (1859)

Pamphlets

("Pam." in notes)
Amézaga, Mariano. *Perú: Galería financiera.* Valparaíso: Tip. J. Fierro, 1873.
Aramburú, Andrés Avelino. *El asesinato de Manuel Pardo, presidente del senado.* Lima: Imp. de la Opinión Nacional, 1878.

Artesanos. Lima: J. M. Monterola, 1859.

La asociación de ingenieros del Perú. Lima: Imp. Libertad, 1871.

Barreda y Osma, Felipe. *Los derechos de aduana y las industrias nacionales.* Lima: Sociedad Nacional de Industrias, 1900.

Barroilhet, Carlos. *Ojeada sobre la crisis política y financiera del Perú.* Paris: Imp. D'Aubusson y Kugelmann, 1859.

Basadre, Carlos. *El ferrocarril de Iquique: Observaciones jenerales sobre los benéficos resultados que esta empresa producirá en favor de las industrias salitreras y minerales de la provincia de Tarapacá.* Lima: "Comercio," 1860.

Billinghurst, Guillermo E. *Los capitales salitreros de Tarapacá.* Santiago: El Progreso, 1889.

Blume, Federico. *Observaciones sobre el proyecto del banco central.* Lima: Imp. Masías, 1876.

Cámara de Diputados, Perú. *Dictamen de la comisión de hacienda de cámara de diputados sobre las representaciones de los gremios de Lima y el Callao.* Lima: Alfaro y cía., 1859.

Carranza, Luis. "Consideraciones generales sobre los departamentos del centro." 1883. In Carranza, *Colección de artículos publicados por Luis Carranza, médico* 3:48–84. Lima: Imp. del Comercio, 1887.

Casós, Fernando. *La minería y la agricultura al punto de vista del progreso.* Lima: Imp. del Comercio, 1876.

Cisneros, Luciano Benjamín. *Apuntes sobre la comisión al sur por el ex-ministro de beneficencia.* Lima: Imp. de Estado, 1868.

Cisneros, Luis Benjamín. *Proyecto de ley presentado por el diputado de Jauja d.d. L. B. Cisneros y memoria sobre los ferrocarriles peruanos.* Lima: J. Noriega, 1868.

Cochet, Alejandro. *Disertación sobre el origen del huano de Iquique.* Lima: Monterola, 1841.

Constitución reglamentaria de la sociedad los hijos del pueblo. Lima: Tip. América, 1864.

Davelouis, Héctor. *Informe que el suscribe eleva a la consideración de los poderes legislativo y ejecutivo sobre el estado actual de la minería en el Perú.* Lima: Imp. de Huerta, 1863.

Dávila, Tomás. *Medios que se proponen al actual congreso constitucional del Perú y al gobierno supremo, para salvar de su total destrucción la casi-arruinada agricultura de la importante provincia de Moquegua.* Arequipa: F. Ibáñez y hm., 1853.

Dean, José. *Cuestión saqueo de 6 de noviembre de 1865 en el Callao ante la opinión pública.* Lima: Imp. E. Prugue, 1866.

Echenique, José Rufino. *El General José Rufino Echenique a sus compatriotas.* Lima: A. Alfaro y cía., 1858.

Elguera, Juan Ignacio. *Memoria presentada al congreso ordinario de 1876 por el ministro de hacienda y comercio.* Lima: Imp. del Teatro, 1876.

———. *Memoria presentada por el ministro de hacienda y comercio a la legislatura ordinaria de 1874.* Lima: Imp. de la Opinión Nacional, 1874.

Estudios sobre el huano, o historia de los contratos celebrados por el gobierno para su expendio exterior. Lima: J. Masías, 1851.

Exposición de los motivos para que no se lleve adelante el decreto del 10 de diciembre 1865 sobre derechos de trigos y harinas. Lima: El Progreso, 1867.

Ferrocarril de Arequipa: Informe de los empresarios. Arequipa: F. Ibáñez, 1864.

El ferrocarril de Islay a Arequipa y la posibilidad de su ejecución. Lima: E. Aranda, 1862.

Fuentes, Manuel A. *Relación sucinta de los principales hechos ocurridos en algunos pueblos del Perú, con motivo de la ingerencia de los funcionarios políticos en la renovación de los colegios electorales*. Lima: F. García, 1850.

Gálvez, Pedro. *Memoria que el ministro de hacienda y comercio presenta al congreso nacional de 1862*. Lima: La Época, 1862.

García y García, José Antonio. *Ferrocarril de Eten a Monsefú, Chiclayo, Lambayeque, y Ferreñafe*. Lima: A. Alfaro, 1867.

Garland, Alejandro. *Las industrias en el Perú*. Lima: Imp. del Estado, 1896.

Gubbins, J. Russell. *¡Más luz! Estudio económico social: Continuación de lo que se ve y lo que no se ve!* Lima: Imp. del Estado, 1900.

Huano y salitre: Publicaciones hechas por la prensa en defensa de los lejítimos intereses de la industria salitrera. Lima: El Nacional, 1874.

Inauguración del ferro-carril de Mollendo a Arequipa por A. U. G. Lima: El Comercio, 1871.

La Fuente, Antonio Gutiérrez de. *Exposición que hace la h. municipalidad de Lima al supremo gobierno*. Lima: El Comercio, 1863.

Larrañaga y Loyola, Luis. *Apuntes sobre la situación económica del Perú en 1888: editoriales de La Opinión Nacional*. Lima: Bacigalupi, 1888.

Larrea y Loredo, José de. *Principios que siguió el ciudadano José de Larrea y Loredo en el ministerio de hacienda y sección de negocios eclesiásticos de que estuve encargado*. Lima: J. M. Concha, 1827.

Lo que se ve y lo que no se ve: Ojeado sobre los principales actos económicos del gobierno civil. Lima: Imp. de la Opinión Nacional, 1874.

Malinowski, Ernesto. *Ferrocarril central transandino: Informe del ingeniero en jefe d. Ernesto Malinowski*. Lima: El Nacional, 1869.

———. [E.M.] *La Moneda en el Perú*. Lima: Tip. A. Alfaro, 1859.

Márquez, José Arnaldo. *La orgía financiera del Perú: El guano y el salitre*. Santiago, 1888.

Noboa, Ignacio. *Defensa del ex-ministro de hacienda y comercio, acusado por la cámara de diputados*. Lima: Imp. del Estado, 1864.

———. *Memoria que el ministro de hacienda y comercio presenta al congreso de 1864 en los distintos ramos de su despacho*. Lima: Imp. del Estado, 1864.

Nystrom, Juan Guillermo. *Informe al supremo gobierno del Perú sobre una espedición al interior de la república*. Lima: Imp. de Prugue, 1868.

———. *Informe al supremo gobierno sobre la espedición de Chanchamayo por J. G. Nystrom*. Lima: Imp. de Prugue, 1869.

Observaciones sobre el proyecto de reglamento de comercio presentado al congreso por la comisión de hacienda. Lima: Imp. de la Libertad, 1828.

Osores, José Manuel. *Conferencias sobre materias económicas dadas en el club literario por José Manuel Osores*. Lima: El Correo del Perú, 1876.

Pando, José María. *Memoria sobre el estado de la hacienda de la república peruana en fin de 1830 presentado al congreso por José María Pando.* Lima: José Masías, 1831.

———. *Reclamación de los vulnerables derechos de los hacendados de las provincias litorales del departamento de Lima.* Lima: J. M. Concha, 1833.

Pardo, Manuel. *Memoria que el ex-secretario de estado en el despacho de hacienda y comercio presenta al jefe supremo provisorio de la república.* Lima: Imp. del Estado, 1867.

El Perú y la influencia europea. Paris: Librería Universal, 1862.

Piérola, Nicolás de. *Memoria presentada por el ministro de hacienda y comercio a la legislatura ordinaria de 1870.* Lima: Heraldo de Lima, 1870.

Prugue, Emilio. *Protección a la industria nacional: A los honorables representantes del congreso de 1878.* Lima: El Comercio, 1878.

Químper, José María. *Las propuestas de los tenedores de bonos por J. M. Q.* Lima: La Época, 1886.

Raimondi, Antonio. *Apuntes sobre la provincia litoral de Loreto.* Lima: Tip. El Nacional, 1862.

Refutación de las acciones interpuestas judicialmente por los nacionales con motivo del contrato Dreyfus. Lima: A. Alfaro, 1869.

Reglamento de la sociedad tipográfica de auxilios mutuos. Lima: El Comercio, 1868.

Reglamento interior de la escuela nacional de artes y oficios. Lima: Tip. El Nacional, 1871.

Ribero, Francisco de. *Memoria sobre las huaneras de la república precedida de algunas ligeras observaciones sobre los abonos en general.* Lima: El Correo Peruano, 1846.

Rojas y Briones, Pedro de. *Proyectos de economía política que en favor de la república peruana ha formado el ciudadano Pedro Rojas y Briones, diputado del soberano congreso nombrado por la provincia de Cajamarca.* Lima: J. M. Concha, 1828.

Saanpperé, Tomás L. *Memoria sobre los medios de estimular a los peruanos según la situación actual de la sociedad al trabajo provechoso y más conducente al orden público.* Lima: Imp. del Estado, 1867.

Sada, Luis. *Bosquejo de la organización de la escuela nacional de la hacienda normal de agricultura.* Lima: Imp. Mercurio, 1863.

———. *Proyecto de asociación para introducir y generalizar en el Perú el cultivo de la morera y del gusano de seda.* Lima: El Comercio, 1870.

Salcedo, Juan José. *Memoria que presenta al congreso de 1860 el ministro de hacienda y comercio.* Lima: Imp. de Masías, 1860.

El señor J. M. Q. y el contrato Grace. Lima: Imp. Bacigalupi, 1887.

Silva Santisteban, José. *Breves reflexiones sobre los sucesos ocurridos en Lima y el Callao con motivo de la importación de artefactos.* Lima: José Sánchez, 1859.

[Távara, Santiago]. *Análisis y amplificación del manifiesto presentado al congreso del Perú por el honorable sr. ministro d. José María Pando.* Lima: Imp. J. Masías, 1831.

Tejeda, José Simeón. *Emancipación de la industria.* Arequipa: Imp. de F. Ibáñez, 1852.

Torres Paz, José Andrés. *La oligarquía y la crisis: Disertación leída en la sociedad jurídico-literaria en la sesión del 29 de agosto de 1877.* Lima: Imp. del Teatro, 1877.

Tribunal del Consulado. *Razones poderosas que da el comercio de esta capital por las cuales no deben permitirse los establecimientos de martillo.* Lima: Juan Ross, 1834.

Ulloa, José Casimiro. *Huano (apuntes económicos y administrativos).* Lima: A. Alfaro, 1865.

———. [Un peruano, pseud.]. *El Perú en 1853: Un año de su historia contemporánea.* Paris: Imp. de Maulde et Renou, 1854.

Velarde, Samuel. *Los antiguos contratos del Perú y el contrato Grace.* Lima: La Época, 1887.

———. *Deuda externa y ferrocarriles del Perú.* Lima: F. Masías, 1886.

Vidaurre, Manuel. *Discurso sobre la acta de navegación pronunciado por el diputado Manuel Vidaurre.* Boston: n.p., 1828.

X. Y. Z. *Reflexiones sobre la ley de prohibiciones reimpresas y aumentadas con notas.* Lima: Jose Masías, 1831.

Nineteenth-Century Monographs and Collected Works

Amézaga, Mariano. *Problemas de la educación peruana.* Alberto Tauro, comp. Lima: Universidad Nacional Mayor San Marcos, 1952.

Arona, Juan de [Pedro Paz Soldán]. *La inmigración en el Perú: Monografía histórico-crítica.* Lima: Imp. del Universo, 1891. Rpt. Lima: Academía Diplomática del Perú, 1971.

Bilbao, Francisco. *El gobierno de la libertad.* Lima: Monterola, 1855.

Bustamante, Juan. *Apuntes y observaciones civiles, políticas y religiosas con las noticias adquiridas en este segundo viaje a la Europa por el peruano d. Juan Bustamante.* Paris: Lacrange Son et cie., 1849.

Capelo, Joaquín. *Sociología de Lima.* 4 vols. Lima: Imp. Masías, 1895–1902.

Carranza, Luis. *Colección de artículos publicados por Luis Carranza, médico.* 5 vols. Lima: Imp. del Comercio, 1887.

Carrasco, Eduardo. *Calendario y guía de forasteros de la república peruana para el año de 1849.* Lima: José Masías, 1848.

Casanova, Juan Norberto. *Ensayo económico-político sobre el porvenir de la industria algodonera fabril del Perú.* Lima: Imp. de José Masías, 1849. Rpt. with a foreword by Pablo Macera. Lima: Biblioteca Peruana de Historia Económica, 1972.

Casós, Fernando. *Para la historia del Perú: Revolución de 1854.* Cuzco: Imp. Republicana, 1854.

Castilla, Ramón. *Ideología.* Ed. Alberto Tauro. Lima: Hora de Hombre, 1948.

Cisneros, Luis Benjamín. *Ensayo sobre varias cuestiones económicas del Perú.* Le Havre: Alfred Lemale, 1866.

————. *Memoria sobre ferrocarriles.* 1868. Rpt. in Cisneros, *Obras completas* 3:141–86. Lima: Imp. Gil, 1939.

————. *Obras completas.* 3 vols. Lima: Imp. Gil, 1939.

Clarke, William. *Peru and Its Creditors.* London: Ranken and Co., 1877.

Clavero, José. *El tesoro del Perú.* Lima: Imp. Torres Aguirre, 1896.

Copello, Juan, and Luis Petriconi. *Estudio sobre la independencia económica del Perú.* Lima: Imp. El Nacional, 1876. Rpt. Lima: Biblioteca Peruana de Historia Económica, 1971.

Coronel Zegarra, Félix Cipriano. *La educación popular en el Perú.* Lima: Imp. El Nacional, 1872.

Cuerpo de Ingenieros y Arquitectos del Estado (Perú). *Anales del cuerpo de ingenieros del Perú.* 2 vols. Lima: Imp. del Estado, 1874.

Dancuart, P. Emilio, comp. *Anales de la hacienda pública del Perú: Historia y legislación fiscal de la república.* Lima: various publishers, 1902–1926. 24 vols.

Duffield, A. J. *Peru in the Guano Age.* London: Richard Bentley and Son, 1877.

————. *The Prospects of Peru: The End of the Guano Age and a Description Thereof.* London: Newman and Co., 1881.

Espinoza, Juan. *Diccionario para el pueblo: Republicano democrático, moral, político y filosófico.* Lima: José Masías, 1855.

Esteves, Luis. *Apuntes para la historia económica del Perú.* Lima: Imp. Huallaga, 1882. Rpt. Lima: Centro de Estudios de Población y Desarrollo, 1971.

Extracto de las sesiones de la cámara de diputados publicados en el "Comercio" de Lima. Lima: Imp. del Comercio, 1845.

Fuentes, Manuel Anastasio. *Aletazos del murciélago: Colección de artículos publicados en varios periódicos.* 3 vols. Paris: Laine et Havard, 1866.

————. *Estadística del movimiento de la población de la provincia de Lima en un período de cinco años y en el año de 1877.* Lima: Imp. del Estado, 1878.

————. *Estadística general de Lima.* Lima: Tip. Nacional, 1858.

————. *Guía histórico-descriptiva, administrativa, judicial y de domicilios de Lima.* Lima, 1860.

————. *Lima: Apuntes históricos, descriptivos, estadísticos y de costumbres.* Paris: Didot et Escolar, 1866–67.

García Calderón, Francisco. *Diccionario de la legislación peruana.* Lima: Imp. del Estado, 1879.

————. *Estudios sobre el banco de crédito hipotecario y las leyes de hipoteca.* Lima: Imp. Noriega, 1868.

García Calderón R., Francisco. *Le Pérou contemporain.* Paris: Dujarrig, 1907.

Garrido, A., trans. *Principios jenerales de economía política por P. H. Suzanne, traducidos libremente al español y aumentados con notas por A. Garrido, oficial mayor y tesorero interno de departamento de Ayacucho.* Ayacucho: Imp. de B. Cárdenas, 1832.

Herndon, William Lewis. *Exploration of the Valley of the Amazon,* 1854. Rpt. Hamilton Basso, ed. New York: McGraw-Hill, 1952.

Herrera, Bartolomé. *Escritos y discursos.* J. Leguía, comp. 2 vols. Lima: Biblioteca de la República, 1929.

Ledos, Carlos. *Consideraciones sobre la agricultura*. Lima: José Masías, 1847.

Leubel, Alfredo G. *El Perú en 1860 o sea anuario nacional*. Lima: Imp. del Comercio, 1861.

Lima, Consejo Provincial. *Datos e informes sobre las causas que han producido el alza de precios de los artículos de primera necesidad que se consumen en la capital*. Lima: Consejo Provincial, 1870.

Lissón, Carlos. *Breves apuntes sobre la sociología del Perú en 1886*. Lima: Imp. Gil, 1887.

———. *La república en el Perú y la cuestión peruano-española*. Lima: Imp. del Comercio, 1865.

Márquez, José Arnaldo. *Recuerdos de viaje a los Estados-Unidos de la América del Norte*. Lima: Comercio, 1862.

Martinet, J. B. *La agricultura en el Perú*. 1877. Rpt. Lima: Centro Peruano de Historia Económica, 1977.

Masías, Felipe. *Curso elemental de economía política por Felipe Masías*. Lima: J. Masías, 1860.

Mendiburu, Manuel de. *Diccionario histórico-biográfico del Perú*. 24 vols. Lima: Imp. de Palacios, 1931–1934.

Menéndez, Baldomero. *Manuel de geografía y estadística del Perú*. Paris: Lacrange, 1861.

Pacheco, Toribio. *Dissertation sur les instruments qui concourent à la formation de la richesse*. Thesis, Faculty of Law, University of Brussels, 1852. Brussels: Imp. J. Vanbuggenhouldt, 1852.

Pardo, Manuel. *Estudios sobre la provincia de Jauja*. Lima: La Época, 1862.

———. *Manuel Pardo*. Jacinto López, comp. Prologue by E. San Cristóval. Lima: Imp. Gil, 1947.

Pérez, Trinidad Manuel. *La industria y el poder*. 3d ed. Lima: El Nacional, 1876.

Perú, Congreso. *La protección y la libertad: Debates del senado y otros documentos*. Lima: Imp. El Nacional, 1868.

Perú, Convención Nacional. *Documentos legislativos sobre el establecimiento y la mejora de las vías de comunicaciones en el Perú*. Lima: Imp. del Estado, 1856.

Perú, Dirección de Estadística. *Resumen del censo general de habitantes del Perú hecho en 1876*. M. A. Fuentes, ed. 7 vols. Lima: Imp. del Estado, 1878.

Químper, José María. *Derecho político: El liberalismo*. Lima: Imp. de Buscher, 1886.

———. *El principio de libertad*. Rpt. Alberto Tauro, ed. Lima: Ediciones Hora del Hombre, 1948.

Radiguet, Max. *Lima y la sociedad peruana*. 1856. Lima: Biblioteca Nacional del Perú, 1971.

Raimondi, Antonio. *El Perú*. 3 vols. Lima: Imp. del Estado, 1874–1879.

Ribero, Francisco de. *Memoria o sea apuntamientos sobre la industria agrícola del Perú y sobre algunos medios que pudieron adoptarse para remediar su decadencia*. Lima: Imp. del Comercio, 1845.

Riva Agüero, José de la [Pruvonena, pseud.]. *Memorias y documentos para la historia de la independencia del Perú y causas del mal éxito que ha tenido ésta*. 2 vols. Paris: Garner hms., 1858.

Rivero y Ustariz, Mariano Eduardo de. *Colección de memorias científicas, agrícolas e industriales publicadas en distintas épocas.* 2 vols. Brussels: H. Goemaere, 1857.

Rodríguez, José M. *Estudios económicos y financieros y ojeada sobre la hacienda pública del Perú y la necesidad de su reforma.* Lima: Imp. Gil, 1895.

Rodríguez, Pedro Manuel. *Elementos de economía política.* Lima: La Opinión Nacional, 1876.

Schutz, C. Damián, and Juan Moller. *Guía de domicilios de Lima y Callao para el año de 1853.* Lima: Imp. del Estado, 1854.

Tauro, Alberto, ed. *Viajeros en el Perú republicano.* Lima: Universidad Nacional Mayor San Marcos, 1967.

Valdivia, Juan Gualberto. *Memorias sobre las revoluciones de Arequipa desde 1834 hasta 1866.* Lima: La Opinión Nacional, 1874.

Vigil, Francisco de Paula González. *Importancia de la educación popular.* 1858. Lima: Biblioteca de Pensamiento Peruano, 1948.

———. *Importancia de las asociaciones.* 1858. Lima: Biblioteca de Pensamiento Peruano, 1948.

Secondary Literature: Peru

Adrianzén, Alberto, ed. *Pensamiento político peruano.* Lima: DESCO, 1987.

Aguirre, Carlos, and Charles Walker, eds. *Bandoleros, abigeos y montoneros: Criminalidad y violencia en el Perú, siglos xviii–xx.* Lima: Instituto de Apoyo Agrario, 1990.

Albert, Bill. *South America and the World Economy from Independence to 1930.* London: Macmillan, for the Economic History Society, 1983.

Amayo, Enrique. *La política británica en la guerra del Pacífico.* Lima: Editorial Horizonte, 1988.

Amézaga, Hugo Garavito. *El Perú liberal: Partidos e ideas de la ilustración a la república aristocrática.* Lima: Ediciones el Virrey, 1989.

Ballon Lozada, Héctor. *Las ideas socio-políticas en Arequipa.* Arequipa: Publi-Unsa, 1986.

Basadre, Jorge. *Elecciones y centralismo en el Perú: Apuntes para un esquema histórico.* Lima: Universidad del Pacífico, 1980.

———. *Historia de la república del Perú.* 5th ed. 11 vols. Lima: Editorial Peruamérica, 1963.

———. *La multitud, la ciudad y el campo en la historia del Perú.* Lima: Imprenta A. J. Rivas, 1929.

———. *Peruanos del siglo xix.* Lima: Editorial Richay Perú, 1981.

———. *Perú: Problema y posibilidad.* Lima: F. y E. Rosay, 1931.

———. Prologue to Juan Copello and Luis Petriconi, *Estudio sobre la independencia económica del Perú,* i–viii. Lima: Biblioteca Peruana de Historia Económica, 1971.

Basadre, Jorge, et al., eds. *Reflexiones en torno a la guerra de 1879*. Lima: Centro de Investigación y Capacitación, 1979.

Berg, Mary. "Writing Biography of Nineteenth-Century Women: The Lives of Manuela Gorriti and Clorinda Matto de Turner." Paper presented to the Latin American Studies Association, Miami, 1989.

Berg, Ronald, and Frederick S. Weaver. "Toward a Reinterpretation of Political Change in Peru During the First Century of Independence." *Journal of Interamerican Studies and World Affairs* 20, no. 1 (1978): 69–84.

Bernales, Enrique. "La instauración del estado liberal en el Perú." In Bernales, ed., *Burguesía y estado liberal*, 231–75. Lima: DESCO, 1979.

Bertram, Geoffrey. "Alejandro Garland: The Ideologist of 'Desarrollo Hacia Afuera.'" Typescript, Oxford University, 1974.

Blanchard, Peter. *The Origins of the Peruvian Labor Movement, 1883–1919*. Pittsburgh: University of Pittsburgh Press, 1982.

———. "A Populist Precursor: Guillermo Billinghurst." *Journal of Latin American Studies* 9, no. 2 (1977): 251–73.

Bollinger, William S. "The Bourgeois Revolution in Peru: A Conception of Peruvian History." *Latin American Perspectives* 4, no. 3 (1977): 18–57.

———. "The Rise of United States Influence in the Peruvian Economy, 1869–1921." M.A. thesis, University of California, Los Angeles, 1971.

Boloña, Carlos. "Tariff Policies in Peru, 1880–1980." D.Phil. thesis, Oxford University, 1981.

Bonilla, Heraclio. "Continuidad y cambio en la organización política del estado en el Perú independiente." In I. Buisson et al., eds., *Problemas de la formación del estado y de la nación en Hispanoamérica*, 481–98. Cologne: Böhlau Verlag, 1984.

———. "La coyuntura comercial del siglo xix en el Perú." *Desarrollo Económico* 46 (1972): 305–31.

———. "La crisis de 1872 en el Perú." In Bonilla, ed., *Las crisis económicas en la historia del Perú*, 167–88. Lima: Centro Latinoamericano de Historia Económica y Social, 1986.

———. "La dimensión internacional de la guerra del Pacífico." In J. Basadre et al., eds., *Reflexiones en torno a la guerra de 1879*, 415–36. Lima: Centro de Investigación y Capacitación, 1979.

———. "La expansión comercial británica en el Perú." *Revista del Museo Nacional* 40 (1974): 253–75.

———. *Guano y burguesía en el Perú*. Lima: Instituto de Estudios Peruanos, 1974.

———. "Guano y crisis en el Perú del xix." In C. Araníbar and H. Bonilla, eds., *Nueva historia general del Perú*, 123–37. Lima: Mosca Azul Editores, 1979.

———. "El impacto de los ferrocarriles: Algunas proposiciones." *Historia y Cultura* 6 (1972): 93–120.

———. "Peru and Bolivia from Independence to 1870." In Leslie Bethell, ed., *The Cambridge History of Latin America* 3:539–72. Cambridge: Cambridge University Press, 1985.

————. "The War of the Pacific and the National and Colonial Problem in Peru." *Past and Present* 81, no. 4 (1978): 92–119.

Bonilla, Heraclio, comp. *Un siglo a la deriva: Ensayos sobre el Perú, Bolivia y la guerra.* Lima: Instituto de Estudios Peruanos, 1980.

Bonilla, Heraclio, ed. *Las crisis económicas en la historia del Perú.* Lima: Centro Latinoamericano de Historia Económica y Social, 1986.

Bonilla, Heraclio, and Karen Spalding. "La independencia en el Perú: Las palabras y los hechos." In H. Bonilla et al., eds., *La independencia en el Perú,* 15–65. Lima: Instituto de Estudios Peruanos, 1972.

Burga, Manuel. *De la encomienda a la hacienda capitalista: El valle de Jequetepeque del siglo xvi al xx.* Lima: Instituto de Estudios Peruanos, 1976.

Camprubí Alcázar, Carlos. "Los bancos en el Perú en el siglo xix: Antecedentes y primeras realizaciones." *Revista Histórica* 21 (1954): 102–37.

————. *Historia de los bancos en el Perú (1860–1879).* Lima: Editorial Lumen, 1957.

————. *José Payán y de Reina (1844–1919): Su trayectoria peruana.* Lima: P. L. Villanueva, 1967.

Caravedo Molinari, Baltazar. "La economía peruana y la guerra." In J. Basadre et al., eds., *Reflexiones en torno a la guerra de 1879,* 75–124. Lima: Centro de Investigación y Capacitación, 1979.

Castañón, Emilio. "Esquema de nuestra historia económica en el siglo xix." *El Comercio* (Lima), 28 July 1957 (supplement).

Chavarría, Jesús. "La desaparación del Perú colonial (1870–1930)." *Aportes* (Paris) 23 (1972): 121–53.

————. *José Carlos Mariátegui and the Rise of Modern Peru, 1890–1930.* Albuquerque: University of New Mexico Press, 1979.

Conaghan, Catherine, James M. Malloy, and Luis A. Abugattás. "Business and the 'Boys': The Politics of Neoliberalism in the Central Andes." *Latin American Research Review* 25, no. 2 (1990): 3–30.

Contreras, Carlos. *Mineros y campesinos en los Andes: Mercado laboral y economía campesina en la sierra central, siglo xix.* Lima: Instituto de Estudios Peruanos, 1987.

————. "Perú y el liberalismo." MS., Lima, 1989.

Cornejo Foronda, David. *Don Manuel Pardo y la educación nacional.* Lima: Pontificia Universidad Católica del Perú, 1953.

Cotler, Julio. *Clases, estado y nación en el Perú.* Lima: Instituto de Estudios Peruanos, 1978.

————. *Democracia e integración nacional.* Lima: Instituto de Estudios Peruanos, 1980.

Davies, Thomas M. *Indian Integration in Peru: A Half Century of Experience, 1900–1948.* Lincoln: University of Nebraska Press, 1970.

Demelas, Marie-Danielle. "¿Un libro o un autor a la deriva?" *Allpanchis* 18, no. 21 (1983): 205–11.

Engelsen, Juan Rolf. "Social Aspects of Agricultural Expansion in Coastal Peru, 1825–1878." Ph.D. diss., University of California, Los Angeles, 1977.

Ferrero Rebagliati, Raúl. *El liberalismo peruano: Contribución a una historia de ideas*. Lima: Biblioteca de Escritores Peruanos, 1958.

Flores Galindo, Alberto. *Arequipa y el sur andino: Ensayo de historia regional, siglos xviii–xx*. Lima: Editorial Horizonte, 1977.

———. *Buscando un inca: Identidad y utopía en los Andes*. Lima: Instituto de Apoyo Agrario, 1987.

———. "In Search of an Inca." In Steve Stern, ed., *Resistance, Rebellion, and Consciousness in the Andean Peasant World, Eighteenth to Twentieth Centuries*, 193–210. Madison: University of Wisconsin Press, 1982.

———. "El militarismo y la dominación británica (1825–1845)." In C. Araníbar and H. Bonilla, eds., *Nueva historia general del Perú*, 107–23. Lima: Mosca Azul Editores, 1979.

Friedman, Douglas. *The State and Underdevelopment in Spanish America: The Political Roots of Dependency in Peru and Argentina*. Boulder: Westview Press, 1984.

Giesecke, Margarita. "Las clases sociales y los grupos del poder." In J. Basadre et al., eds., *Reflexiones en torno a la guerra de 1879*, 43–74. Lima: Centro de Investigación y Capacitación, 1979.

———. *Masas urbanas y rebelión en la historia: Golpe de estado, Lima, 1872*. Lima: CEDHIP, 1978.

Gilbert, Dennis. *La oligarquía peruana: Historia de tres familias*. Trans. Mariana Moulde de Pease. Lima: Editorial Horizonte, 1982.

Gleason, Daniel M. "Ideological Cleavages in Early Republican Peru, 1821–1872." Ph.D. diss., University of Notre Dame, 1974.

Gonzales, Michael J. *Plantation Agriculture and Social Control in Northern Peru, 1875–1933*. Austin: University of Texas Press, 1985.

Gootenberg, Paul. "Artisans and Merchants: The Making of an Open Economy in Lima, Peru, 1830 to 1860." M.Phil. thesis, Oxford University, 1981.

———. "Beleaguered Liberals: The Failed First Generation of Free Traders in Peru." In J. Love and N. Jacobsen, eds., *Guiding the Invisible Hand: Economic Liberalism and the State in Latin American History*, 63–97. New York: Praeger, 1988.

———. *Between Silver and Guano: Commercial Policy and the State in Postindependence Peru*. Princeton: Princeton University Press, 1989.

———. "*Carneros y Chuño*: Price Levels in Nineteenth-Century Peru." *Hispanic American Historical Review* 70, no. 1 (1990): 1–56.

———. "Guilty Guilds? Artisans and the 'Monopoly' Problem in Nineteenth-Century Peru." Typescript, State University of New York, Stony Brook, 1992.

———. "Merchants, Foreigners, and the State: The Origins of Trade Policy in Post-Independence Peru." Ph.D. diss., University of Chicago, 1985.

———. "North–South: Trade Policy, Regionalism, and *Caudillismo* in Post-Independence Peru." *Journal of Latin American Studies* 23, no. 2 (1991): 1–36.

———. "Population and Ethnicity in Early Republican Peru: Some Revisions." *Latin American Research Review* 26, no. 3 (1991): 109–57.

———. "The Social Origins of Protectionism and Free Trade in Nineteenth-

Century Lima." *Journal of Latin American Studies* 14, no. 2 (1982): 329–58.

———. *Tejidos y harinas, corazones y mentes: El imperialismo norteamericano del libre comercio en el Perú, 1825–1840.* Lima: Instituto de Estudios Peruanos, 1989.

Gorman, Stephen M. "The State, Elite, and Export in Nineteenth-Century Peru: Toward an Alternative Reinterpretation of Political Change." *Journal of Interamerican Studies and World Affairs* 21, no. 3 (1979): 395–418.

Greenhill, Robert, and Rory Miller. "The Peruvian Government and the Nitrate Trade, 1873–1879." *Journal of Latin American Studies* 5, no. 1 (1973): 107–31.

Grieve M., Jorge. "El desarrollo de las industrias mecánicas en el Perú entre 1800 y 1880." *Historia y Cultura* 15 (1982): 23–69.

Harth-Terré, Emilio, and Alberto Márquez Abanto. "Las bellas artes en el virreinato del Perú: perspectiva social y económica del artesano virreinal en Lima." *Revista del Archivo Nacional del Perú* 26 (1962): 352–446.

Hünefeldt, Christine. "Los negros de Lima: 1800–1830." *Histórica* 3, no. 1 (1979): 17–51.

———. "Viejos y nuevos temas de la historia económica del siglo xix." In H. Bonilla, ed., *Las crisis económicas en la historia del Perú,* 33–60. Lima: Centro Latinoamericano de Historia Económica y Social, 1986.

Hunt, Shane J. "Growth and Guano in Nineteenth-Century Peru." Discussion Paper 34, Research Program in Economic Development, Woodrow Wilson School, Princeton, 1973.

———. "Growth and Guano in Nineteenth-Century Peru." In Roberto Cortés Conde and Shane J. Hunt, eds., *The Latin American Economies: Growth and the Export Sector, 1830–1930,* 255–319. New York: Holmes and Meier, 1985.

———. "Peru: Interpretive Essay." In Roberto Cortés Conde and Stanley J. Stein, eds., *Latin America: A Guide to Economic History, 1830–1930,* 547–71. Berkeley and Los Angeles: University of California Press, 1977.

———. "Price and Quantum Estimates of Peruvian Exports, 1830–1962." Discussion Paper 33, Research Program in Economic Development," Woodrow Wilson School, Princeton, 1973.

Jacobsen, Nils. "Civilization and Its Barbarism: The Inevitability of Juan Bustamante's Failure." In Judith Ewell and William Beezley, eds., *The Human Tradition in Latin America: The Nineteenth Century,* 82–102. Wilmington, Del.: Scholarly Resources, 1989.

———. "Desarrollo económico y relaciones de clase en el sur andino (1780–1920): Una réplica a Karen Spalding." *Análisis* 5 (1979): 67–82.

———. "Free Trade, Regional Elites, and the Internal Market in Southern Peru, 1895–1932." In J. Love and N. Jacobsen, eds., *Guiding the Invisible Hand: Economic Liberalism and the State in Latin American History,* 145–76. New York: Praeger, 1988.

———. *Mirages of Transition: The Peruvian Altiplano Between Colonialism and the World Market, 1780–1930.* Berkeley and Los Angeles: University of California Press, 1993.

Kapsoli, Wilfredo. "La crisis de la sociedad peruana en el contexto de la guerra." In J. Basadre et al., eds., *Reflexiones en torno a la guerra de 1879*, 333–58. Lima: Centro de Investigación y Capacitación, 1979.

Klaiber, Jeffrey. *La iglesia en el Perú: Su historia social desde la independencia.* Lima: Pontificia Universidad Católica del Perú, 1988.

———. *Religion and Revolution in Peru, 1824–1976.* Notre Dame: University of Notre Dame Press, 1977.

Klarén, Peter. *Modernization, Dislocation, and Aprismo: Origins of the Peruvian Aprista Party, 1870–1932.* Austin: University of Texas Press, 1973.

Kristal, Efraín. *The Andes Viewed from the City: Literary and Political Discourse on the Indian in Peru, 1848–1930.* New York: Peter Lang, 1987.

Leguía, Jorge G. "Las ideas de 1848 en el Perú." In Leguía, *Estudios históricos,* 113–54. Santiago: Ediciones Ercilla, 1939.

Levin, Jonathan V. *The Export Economies: Their Pattern of Development in Historical Perspective.* Cambridge: Harvard University Press, 1960.

López, Jacinto. *Manuel Pardo.* Lima: Imprenta Gil, 1947.

Macera, Pablo. "Algodón y comercio exterior peruano en el siglo xix." In Macera, *Trabajos de historia* 3:275–96. Lima: Instituto Nacional de Cultura, 1977.

———. "Bibliotecas peruanas del siglo xviii." In Macera, *Trabajos de historia* 1:283–312. Lima: Instituto Nacional de Cultura, 1977.

———. "La historia económica como ciencia en el Perú." In Macera, *Trabajos de historia* 2:21–71. Lima: Instituto Nacional de Cultura, 1977.

———. "Las plantaciones azucareras andinas (1821–1875)." In Macera, *Trabajos de historia* 4:9–310. Lima: Instituto Nacional de Cultura, 1977.

MacEvoy, Carmen. "Manuel Pardo, pensamiento y proyecto político: Aproximación a un intento de modernización en el Perú." Tesis de Postgrado, Pontificia Universidad Católica del Perú, 1989.

Maiguashca, Juan. "A Reinterpretation of the Guano Age, 1840–1880." D.Phil. thesis, Oxford University, 1967.

Mallon, Florencia E. *The Defense of Community in Peru's Central Highlands: Peasant Struggle and Capitalist Transition, 1860–1940.* Princeton: Princeton University Press, 1983.

Manrique, Nelson. "Los arrieros de la sierra central durante el siglo xix." *Allpanchis* 18, no. 21 (1983): 27–46.

———. *Las guerrillas indígenas en la guerra con Chile.* Lima: Centro de Investigación y Capacitación and Editorial Ital Peru, 1981.

———. *Mercado interno y región: La sierra central, 1820–1930.* Lima: DESCO, 1987.

Mariátegui, José Carlos. *Seven Interpretive Essays on Peruvian Reality.* Trans. M. Urquidi. Austin: University of Texas Press, 1971.

Mathew, W. M. "Antony Gibbs and Sons, the Guano Trade, and the Peruvian Government, 1842–1861." In D. C. M. Platt, ed., *Business Imperialism, 1840–1930: An Inquiry Based on British Experience in Latin America,* 337–70. Oxford: Oxford University Press, 1977.

———. *The House of Gibbs and the Peruvian Guano Monopoly.* London: Royal Historical Society, 1981.

———. "The Imperialism of Free Trade: Peru, 1820–1870." *Economic History Review,* ser. 2, 21, no. 4 (1968): 562–86.

————. "A Primitive Export Sector: Guano Production in Mid-Nineteenth Century Peru." *Journal of Latin American Studies* 9, no. 1 (1977): 35–57.

Méndez, Cecilia. "Importaciones de lujo y clases populares: Un motín limeño." *Cielo Abierto* 29, no. 10 (Sept. 1984).

————. "República sin indios: La comunidad imaginada del Perú." In Henrique Urbano, ed., *Tradición y modernidad en los Andes*, 15–41. Cuzco: Centro de Estudios Regionales Andinos Bartolomé de las Casas, 1992.

Milla Batres, Carlos, ed. *Diccionario histórico y biográfico del Perú: Siglos xv–xx.* Barcelona: Editorial Milla Batres, 1986.

Miller, Rory. "The Making of the Grace Contract: British Bondholders and the Peruvian Government, 1885–1890." *Journal of Latin American Studies* 8, no. 1 (1976): 73–100.

————. "The Population Problem of Late Nineteenth-Century Lima." Paper presented to International Congress of Americanists, Amsterdam, 1988.

————. "Railways and Economic Development in Central Peru, 1890–1930." In R. Miller, C. Smith, and J. Fisher, eds., *Social and Economic Change in Modern Peru*, 27–52. Monograph 6. Liverpool: Center for Latin American Studies, 1975.

Moreyra y Paz Soldán, Carlos. *Bibliografía regional peruana.* Lima: P. L. Villanueva, 1976.

Mörner, Magnus. *Notas sobre el comercio y los comerciantes del Cusco desde fines de la colonia hasta 1930.* Lima: Instituto de Estudios Peruanos, 1979.

Morse, Richard M., and Joaquín Capelo. *Lima en 1900: Estudio crítico y antología.* Lima: Instituto de Estudios Peruanos, 1973.

Orrego Penagos, Juan Luis. "Domingo Elías y el club progresista: Los civiles y el poder hacia 1850." *Histórica* 14, no. 2 (1990): 317–53.

Palacios Moreyra, Carlos. *La deuda anglo-peruana, 1822–1890.* Lima: Librería Studium, 1983.

Pásara, Luis. "El guano y la penetración inglesa." In J. Basadre et al., eds., *Reflexiones en torno a la guerra de 1879*, 15–42. Lima: Centro de Investigación y Capacitación, 1979.

————. "El rol de derecho en la época del guano." *Derecho* 28 (1970): 11–33.

Peloso, Vincent C. "Electoral Reform and Social Conflict in Mid-Nineteenth Century Peru." Paper presented to the American Historical Association, San Francisco, 1989.

————. "Entrepreneurs and Survivors in Rural Peru: Planters, Peasants, and Cotton in the Pisco Valley, 1840–1940." Typescript, Howard University, Washington, D.C., 1991.

————. "Succulence and Sustenance: Region, Class, and Diet in Nineteenth-Century Peru." In John Super and Thomas Wright, eds., *Food, Politics, and Society in Latin America*, 46–64. Lincoln: University of Nebraska Press, 1985.

Pennano, Guido. "Desarrollo regional y ferrocarriles en el Perú." *Apuntes* 5, no. 9 (1979): 131–51.

Pereda Torres, Rolando. *Historia de las luchas sociales del movimiento obrero en el Perú republicano, 1858–1917.* Lima: Universidad Nacional Federico Villarreal, 1982.

Piel, Jean. "The Place of the Peasantry in the National Life of Peru in the Nineteenth Century." *Past and Present* 46, no. 1 (1970): 108–33.

Pike, Fredrick B. *The Modern History of Peru*. New York: Frederick A. Praeger, 1967.

———. *The Politics of the Miraculous in Peru: Haya de la Torre and the Spiritualist Tradition*. Lincoln: University of Nebraska Press, 1986.

Podestá, Bruno. *Pensamiento político de González Prada*. Lima: Universidad del Pacífico, 1975.

Portocarrero M., Gonzalo. "Conservadurismo, liberalismo y democracia en el Perú del siglo xix." In Alberto Adrianzén, ed., *Pensamiento político peruano*, 85–98. Lima: DESCO, 1987.

———. "Ideologías, funciones del estado y políticas económicas. Perú: 1900–1980." *Debates en Sociología* 9 (1983): 7–30.

Quiroz, Alfonso W. *Banqueros en conflicto: Estructura financiera y economía peruana, 1884–1930*. Lima: Universidad del Pacífico, CIUP, 1989.

———. *La deuda defraudada: Consolidación de 1850 y dominio económico en el Perú*. Lima: Instituto Nacional de Cultura, 1987.

———. *Domestic and Foreign Finance in Modern Peru, 1850–1950: Financing Visions of Development*. London: Macmillan and St. Antony's, 1992.

———. "Estructura económica y desarrollos regionales de la clase dominante, 1821–1850." In, A. Flores Galindo, ed., *Independencia y revolución* 2:201–68. Lima: Instituto Nacional de Cultura, 1987.

Quiroz Chueca, Francisco. *La protesta de los artesanos: Lima-Callao, 1858*. Lima: Universidad Nacional Mayor de San Marcos, 1988.

Reátegui, Wilson, et al., eds. *La guerra del Pacífico*. Vol. 1. Lima: Universidad Nacional Mayor de San Marcos, 1979.

Regal, Alberto. *Castilla constructor*. Lima: Instituto Libertador Ramón Castilla, 1967.

———. *Historia de los ferrocarriles de Lima*. Lima: Instituto de Vías de Transporte, 1965.

Reinaga, César Augusto. *Esbozo de una historia del pensamiento económico del Perú*. Cuzco: Editorial Garcilaso, 1969.

Revilla, Julio E. "Industrialización temprana y lucha ideológica en el Perú: 1890–1910." *Estudios Andinos* 17, no. 18 (1981): 3–41.

———. "Loan Frenzy and Sovereign Default: The Case of Peru in the Nineteenth Century." Typescript, Boston University, Boston, 1990.

———. "The Peruvian State and Its Economic Policies: From the Guano Age to the Beginning of the Twentieth Century." M.A. thesis, University of Texas, Austin, 1987.

Revoredo, Alejandro. "La obra nacionalista y democrática del partido civil." In *Centenario de Manuel Pardo, 1834–1934*, 79–127. Lima: Imprenta Gil, 1931.

Rippy, J. Fred. "The Dawn of Manufacturing in Peru." *Pacific Historical Review* 15, no. 2 (1946): 147–58.

Rochabrún, Guillermo. "La visión del Perú de Julio Cotler." *Análisis* 4 (1978): 69–85.

Romero, Emilio. *Historia económica del Perú*. Buenos Aires: Editorial Sudamericana, 1949.

————. "Perú." In Luis Roque Gondra et al., eds., *El pensamiento económico latinoamericano*, 274–324. Mexico: Fondo de Cultura Económica, 1945.

Sánchez, Luis Alberto. *Historia de una industria peruana: Cervecería Backus y Johnston S.A.* Lima: Backus y Johnston, 1978.

San Cristóval, Evaristo. *Manuel Pardo y Lavalle: Su vida y su obra.* Lima: Imprenta Gil, 1945.

Stein, Steve. *Populism in Peru: The Emergence of the Masses and the Politics of Social Control.* Madison: University of Wisconsin Press, 1980.

Stewart, Watt. *Henry Meiggs: Yankee Pizarro.* Durham: Duke University Press, 1946.

Tamayo Herrera, José. *Historia social e indigenismo en el altiplano.* Lima: Ediciones Treintaitrés, 1982.

————, comp. *El pensamiento indigenista.* Lima: Biblioteca del Pensamiento Peruano, 1981.

Tantaleán Arbulú, Javier. *Política económico-financiera y la formación del estado: Siglo xix.* Lima: CEDEP, 1983.

————. "Politícas, técnicas e instrumentos económicos del estado: Perú 1821–1879." *Economía* 6, no. 11 (1983): 47–112.

Tauro, Alberto, ed. *Diccionario enciclopédico del Perú ilustrado.* 4 vols. Lima: Editorial Mejía Baca, 1975.

Thorp, Rosemary. *Economic Management and Economic Development in Peru and Colombia.* Pittsburgh: University of Pittsburgh Press, 1991.

Thorp, Rosemary, and Geoffrey Bertram. *Peru 1890–1977: Growth and Policy in an Open Economy.* London: Macmillan, 1978.

Trazegnies, Fernando de. "La genealogía del derecho peruano: Los juegos de trueques y préstamos." In Alberto Adrianzén, ed., *Pensamiento político peruano*, 99–133. Lima: DESCO, 1987.

————. *La idea de derecho en el Perú republicano del siglo xix.* Lima: Pontificia Universidad Católica del Perú, 1980.

Trelles, Efraín. "Modernidad signo cruel: Curso y discurso de modernizantes peruanos (s. xvii–xix)." In Henrique Urbano, ed. *Modernidad en los Andes*, 135–60. Cuzco: Centro de Estudios Regionales Andinos Bartolomé de las Casas, 1991.

Ugarte, César Antonio. *Bosquejo de la historia económica del Perú.* Lima: Imprenta Cabieses, 1926.

Ulloa, Alberto. *Don Nicolás de Piérola: Una época en la historia del Perú.* Lima: Imprenta Santa María, 1949.

Vásquez, Emilio. *La rebelión de Juan Bustamante.* Lima: Editorial Juan Mejía Baca, 1976.

Villanueva, Víctor. *El CAEM y la revolución de las fuerzas armadas.* Lima: Instituto de Estudios Peruanos, 1973.

————. *Ejército peruano: Del caudillaje anárquico al militarismo reformista.* Lima: Instituto de Estudios Peruanos, 1973.

Walker, Charles. "Rhetorical Power: Early Republican Discourse on the Indian in Cusco." Paper presented to the American Historical Association, Chicago, 1991.

Watson Espener, Maida Isabel. *El cuadro de costumbres en el Perú decimonónico.* Lima: Pontificia Universidad Católica del Perú, 1979.

Wibel, John Frederick. "The Evolution of a Regional Community Within the Spanish Empire and Peruvian Nation: Arequipa, 1780–1845." Ph.D. diss., Stanford University, 1975.

Wilson, Fiona. "The Conflict Between Indigenous and Immigrant Commercial Systems in the Peruvian Central Sierra, 1900–1940." In Rory Miller, ed., *Region and Class in Modern Peruvian History*, 125–61. Liverpool: Institute of Latin American Studies, 1987.

Worral, Janet E. "Italian Immigration to Peru: 1860–1914." Ph.D. diss., Indiana University, 1972.

Yeager, Gertrude M. "Women and the Intellectual Life of Nineteenth-Century Lima." *InterAmerican Review of Bibliography* 40, no. 3 (1990): 361–93.

Yepes del Castillo, Ernesto. *Perú 1820–1920: Un siglo de desarrollo capitalista.* Lima: Instituto de Estudios Peruanos, 1972.

Secondary Literature: General

Adas, Michael. *Machines as the Measure of Men: Science, Technology, and Ideologies of Western Dominance.* Ithaca: Cornell University Press, 1989.

Albert, Bill. *South America and the World Economy from Independence to 1930.* London: Macmillan, for The Economic History Society, 1983.

Alcalde, J. G. *The Idea of Third-World Development: Emerging Perspectives in the United States and Britain, 1900–1950.* Lanham, Md.: University Press of America, 1987.

Anderson, Benedict. *Imagined Communities: Reflections on the Origins and Spread of Nationalism.* London: Verso, 1983.

Arndt, H. W. *The Rise and Fall of Economic Growth: A Study in Contemporary Thought.* Melbourne: Longman, Cheshire Pry, 1978.

Baroch, Paul. "Agriculture and the Industrial Revolution." In C. Cipolla, ed., *The Fontana Economic History of Europe*, vol. 3, *The Industrial Revolution*, 452–506. Glasgow: Fontana, 1973.

Batou, Jean, ed. *Between Development and Underdevelopment: The Precocious Attempts at Industrialization on the Periphery, 1800–1870.* Geneva: Librairie Droz, 1991.

Berg, Maxine. *The Machinery Question and the Making of Political Economy, 1815–1848.* Cambridge: Cambridge University Press, 1980.

Bernhard, Virginia, ed. *Elites, Masses and Modernization in Latin America, 1850–1930.* Austin: University of Texas Press, 1979.

Bitar Letayf, Marcelo. *Economistas españoles del siglo xviii: Sus ideas sobre la libertad de comercio con Indias.* Madrid: Ediciones Cultura Hispánica, 1968.

Bloomfield, Arthur I. "British Thought on the Influence of Foreign Trade and Investment on Growth, 1830–1880." *History of Political Economy* 13, no. 1 (1981): 95–120.

Brading, David A. *The First America: The Spanish Monarchy, Creole Patriots, and the Liberal State, 1492–1867.* Cambridge: Cambridge University Press, 1991.

———. *The Origins of Mexican Nationalism.* Latin American Miniatures. Cambridge: Centre of American Studies, 1985.

Burns, E. Bradford. *The Poverty of Progress: Latin America in the Nineteenth Century.* Berkeley and Los Angeles: University of California Press, 1980.

Bushnell, David, and Neill Macaulay. *The Emergence of Latin America in the Nineteenth Century.* New York: Oxford University Press, 1988.

Calderón, Francisco. "El pensamiento económico de Lucas Alamán." *Historia Mexicana* 34, no. 3 (1985): 435–59.

Cardoso, Fernando Henrique. "The Originality of the Copy: The Economic Commission for Latin America and the Idea of Development." In Rothko Chapel Colloquium, *Toward a New Strategy for Development,* 53–72. New York: Pergamon, 1979.

Cardoso, Fernando Henrique, and Enzo Faletto. *Dependency and Development in Latin America.* Trans. M. Urquidi. Berkeley and Los Angeles: University of California Press, 1979.

Carr, Raymond. *Spain 1808–1939.* Oxford: Oxford University Press, 1966.

Chandra, Bipan. "Colonial India: British Versus Indian Views of Development." *Review* 14, no. 1 (1991): 81–167.

Chartier, Roger. *Cultural History.* Ithaca: Cornell University Press, 1988.

———. "Intellectual History or Sociocultural History? The French Trajectories." In D. LaCapra and S. Kaplan, eds., *Modern European Intellectual History: Reappraisals and New Perspectives,* 13–46. Ithaca: Cornell University Press, 1982.

Coats, A. W., and David Colander, eds. *The Spread of Economic Ideas.* Cambridge: Cambridge University Press, 1989.

Coatsworth, John H. *Growth Against Development: The Economic Impact of Railroads in Porfirian Mexico.* De Kalb: Northern Illinois University Press, 1981.

———. "Obstacles to Economic Growth in Nineteenth-Century Mexico." *American Historical Review* 83, no. 1 (1978): 80–100.

Conaghan, Catherine, James M. Malloy, and Luis A. Abugattás. "Business and the 'Boys': The Politics of Neoliberalism in the Central Andes." *Latin American Research Review* 25, no. 2 (1990): 3–30.

Corden, W. M. "Booming Sector and Dutch Disease Economics: Survey and Consolidation." *Oxford Economic Papers* 36, no. 3 (1984): 359–80.

Correo Calderón, Evarista. *Registro de arbitristas, economistas y reformistas españoles (1500–1936).* Madrid: Fundación Universitaria Española, 1981.

Cortés Conde, Roberto. *The First Stages of Modernization in Spanish America.* New York: Harper and Row, 1974.

da Costa, Emília Viotti. "Liberalism: Theory and Practice." In da Costa, *The Brazilian Empire: Myths and Histories,* 53–77. Chicago: Dorsey, 1988.

Darton, Robert. "In Search of the Enlightenment: Recent Attempts to Create a Social History of Ideas." *Journal of Modern History* 43, no. 1 (1971): 113–32.

Davis, Harold Eugene. *Latin American Social Thought: The History of Its De-*

velopment since Independence. Washington, D.C.: University Press of Washington, 1966.

Dawson, Alexander. "Mexico—The Treasure House of the World: Perceptions of Economic Development in Porfirian Mexico." M.A. thesis, University of Calgary, 1991.

Deane, Phyllis. *The State and the Economic System: An Introduction to the History of Political Economy*. Oxford: Oxford University Press, 1989.

Dumont, Louis. *From Mandeville to Marx: The Genesis and Triumph of Economic Ideology*. Chicago: University of Chicago Press, 1977.

Fei, John, and Gustav Ranis. "Economic Development in Historical Perspective." *American Economic Review* 59, no. 2 (1969): 386–460.

Felix, David. "De Gustibus Disputandum Est: Changing Consumer Preferences in Economic Growth." *Explorations in Economic History* 16 (1979): 260–96.

Friedman, Douglas. *The State and Underdevelopment in Spanish America: The Political Roots of Dependency in Peru and Argentina*. Boulder: Westview Press, 1984.

Furtado, Celso. *Economic Development of Latin America: A Survey from Colonial Times to the Cuban Revolution*. Trans. S. Maceda. Cambridge: Cambridge University Press, 1970.

———. "Subdesarrollo y dependencia: Las conexiones fundamentales." In Furtado, *El desarrollo económico: Un mito*, 92–114. Mexico: Siglo Veintiuno, 1978.

Gallo, Ezequiel. "Agrarian Expansion and Industrial Development in Argentina, 1880–1930." In Raymond Carr, ed., *Latin American Affairs*, 45–61. St. Antony's Papers no. 22. Oxford: Oxford University Press, 1970.

Gerschenkron, Alexander. *Economic Backwardness in Historical Perspective*. Cambridge: Harvard University Press, 1962.

———. "History of Economic Doctrines and Economic History." *American Economic Review* 59, no. 2 (1969): 1–17.

Gilmore, Robert L. "Nueva Granada's Socialist Mirage." *Hispanic American Historical Review* 36, no. 2 (1956): 190–210.

Glade, William P. "Latin America and the International Economy, 1870–1914." In Leslie Bethell, ed., *The Cambridge History of Latin America* 4:1–56. Cambridge: Cambridge University Press, 1986.

Gourevitch, Peter. "International Trade, Domestic Coalitions, and Liberty: Comparative Responses to the Crisis of 1873–1896." *Journal of Interdisciplinary History* 8, no. 2 (1977): 281–313.

Graham, Richard. *Independence in Latin America: A Comparative Approach*. New York: Knopf, 1972.

Grenier, Jean-Yves. "La notion de croissance dans la pensée économique française au 18ᵉ siècle (1715–1789)." *Review* 13, no. 4 (1990): 499–550.

Griffin, Keith. *Underdevelopment in Spanish America*. London: Allen and Unwin, 1969.

Haber, Stephen. "Assessing the Obstacles to Industrialization: The Mexican Economy, 1830–1940." *Journal of Latin American Studies* 24, no. 1 (1992): 1–33.

————. *Industry and Underdevelopment: The Industrialization of Mexico, 1890–1940*. Stanford: Stanford University Press, 1989.

Hahner, June. *Poverty and Politics: The Urban Poor in Brazil, 1870–1920*. Albuquerque: University of New Mexico Press, 1986.

Hale, Charles A. *Mexican Liberalism in the Age of Mora, 1821–1853*. New Haven: Yale University Press, 1968.

————. "Political and Social Ideas in Latin America, 1870–1930." In Leslie Bethell, ed., *The Cambridge History of Latin America* 4:367–441. Cambridge: Cambridge University Press, 1986.

————. "The Reconstruction of Nineteenth-Century Politics in Spanish America: A Case for the History of Ideas." *Latin American Research Review* 8, no. 2 (1973): 53–73.

————. *The Transformation of Liberalism in Late Nineteenth-Century Mexico*. Princeton: Princeton University Press, 1989.

Halperín-Donghi, Tulio. "Argentina: Liberalism in a Country Born Liberal." In Joseph Love and Nils Jacobsen, eds., *Guiding the Invisible Hand: Economic Liberalism and the State in Latin American History*, 99–116. New York: Praeger, 1988.

————. "'Dependency Theory' and Latin American Historiography." *Latin American Research Review* 17, no. 1 (1982): 115–30.

————. *Historia contemporánea de América Latina*. Madrid: Alianza Editorial, 1969.

Higonnet, Patrice, David S. Landes, and Henry Rosovsky, eds. *Favorites of Fortune: Technology, Growth, and Economic Development Since the Industrial Revolution*. Cambridge: Harvard University Press, 1991.

Himmelfarb, Gertrude. *The Idea of Poverty: England in the Early Industrial Age*. New York: Random, Vintage Books, 1985.

Hirschman, Albert O. "The Concept of Interest: From Euphemism to Tautology." In Hirschman, *Rival Views of Market Society and Other Recent Essays*, 35–55. New York: Viking, 1986.

————. *Essays in Trespassing: Economics to Politics and Beyond*. Cambridge: Cambridge University Press, 1981.

————. "Ideologies of Economic Development in Latin America." In Hirschman, ed., *Latin American Issues: Essays and Comments*, 3–42. New York: Twentieth Century Fund, 1961.

————. *Journeys Toward Progress: Studies of Economic Policy-Making in Latin America*. New York: Norton, 1973.

————. *The Passions and the Interests: Political Arguments for Capitalism Before Its Triumph*. Princeton: Princeton University Press, 1977.

————. "The Political Economy of Import-Substituting Industrialization in Latin America." *Quarterly Journal of Economics* 82 (1968): 2–32.

————. "A Prototypical Economic Adviser: Jean Gustave Courcelle-Seneuil." In Hirschman, *Rival Views of Market Society and Other Recent Essays*, 183–86. New York: Viking, 1986.

————. "The Rise and Decline of Development Economics." In Hirschman, *Essays in Trespassing: Economics to Politics and Beyond*, 1–24. Cambridge: Cambridge University Press, 1981.

———. *The Strategy of Economic Development.* New Haven: Yale University Press, 1958.

Hobsbawm, E. J. *The Age of Capital, 1848–1875.* New York: New American Library, 1975.

Hoselitz, Bert F., ed. *Theories of Economic Growth.* New York: Free Press, 1989.

Hunt, Lynn, ed. *The New Cultural History.* Berkeley and Los Angeles: University of California Press, 1989.

Jones, Garth Stedman. *Languages of Class: Studies in English Working Class History, 1832–1982.* Cambridge: Cambridge University Press, 1983.

Kasson, John F. *Civilizing the Machine: Technology and Republican Values in America, 1776–1900.* New York: Grossman, 1976.

Keynes, John Maynard. *The End of Laissez-Faire.* London: Hogarth, 1927.

Kirsch, Henry. *Industrial Development in a Traditional Society: The Conflict of Entrepreneurship and Modernization in Chile.* Gainesville: University of Florida Press, 1977.

LaCapra, Dominick. "Rethinking Intellectual History and Reading Texts." In *Modern European Intellectual History: Reappraisals and New Perspectives,* 47–85. Edited by D. LaCapra and S. L. Kaplan. Ithaca: Cornell University Press, 1982.

LaCapra, Dominick, and Stephen L. Kaplan, eds. *Modern European Intellectual History: Reappraisals and New Perspectives.* Ithaca: Cornell University Press, 1982.

Lazonick, William. "What Happened to the Theory of Economic Development?" in P. Higonnet et al., eds., *Favorites of Fortune: Technology, Growth and Economic Development Since the Industrial Revolution,* 267–96. Cambridge: Harvard University Press, 1991.

Lindo-Fuentes, Héctor. *Weak Foundations: The Economy of El Salvador in the Nineteenth Century, 1821–1898.* Berkeley and Los Angeles: University of California Press, 1990.

Love, Joseph L. "Raul Prebisch and the Origins of the Doctrine of Unequal Exchange." *Latin American Research Review* 15, no. 3 (1980): 45–72.

———. "Structural Change and Conceptual Response in Latin America and Romania, 1860–1950." In Joseph Love and Nils Jacobsen, eds., *Guiding the Invisible Hand: Economic Liberalism and the State in Latin American History,* 1–34. New York: Praeger, 1988.

Love, Joseph L., and Nils Jacobsen, eds. *Guiding the Invisible Hand: Economic Liberalism and the State in Latin American History.* New York: Praeger, 1988.

McClosky, Donald N. *The Rhetoric of Economics.* Madison: University of Wisconsin Press, 1985.

McKinley, Erskine. "The Theory of Economic Growth in the English Classical School." In Bert F. Hoselitz, ed., *Theories of Economic Growth,* 89–112. New York: Free Press, 1960.

Mallon Florencia E. "Economic Liberalism: Where We Are and Where We Need to Go." In Joseph Love and Nils Jacobsen, eds., *Guiding the Invisible Hand: Economic Liberalism and the State in Latin American History,* 177–86. New York: Praeger, 1988.

Marichal, Carlos. *A Century of Debt Crises in Latin America: From Independence to the Great Depression, 1820–1930.* Princeton: Princeton University Press, 1989.

Matossian, Mary. "Ideologies of Delayed Industrialization." *Economic Development and Cultural Change* 6, no. 3 (1955): 217–29.

Merrill, Michael. "The Anticapitalist Origins of the United States." *Review* 13, no. 4 (1990): 465–97.

Morse, Richard M. *New World Soundings: Culture and Ideology in the Americas.* Baltimore: Johns Hopkins University Press, 1989.

———. "Toward a Theory of Spanish-American Government." *Journal of the History of Ideas* 15, no. 1 (1954): 71–93.

Myrdal, Gunnar. *The Political Element in the Development of Economic Theory.* Trans. P. Streeten. 1929. New Brunswick: Transaction, 1990.

Ospina Vásquez, Luis. *La industria y protección en Colombia 1810–1930.* Medellín: Editorial Santa Fe, 1955.

Pael, Ellen Frankel. *Moral Reform and Economic Science: The Demise of Laissez-Faire in Nineteenth-Century British Political Economy.* Westport: Greenwood, 1979.

Palma, José Gabriel. "Growth and Structure of Chilean Manufacturing Industry from 1830–1935: Origins and Development of a Process of Industrialization in an Export Economy." D.Phil. thesis, Oxford University, 1979.

Popescu, Oreste. *Estudios en la historia del pensamiento económico latinoamericano.* Bogotá: Plaza y James, 1986.

Potash, Robert A. *The Mexican Government and Industrial Development in the Early Republic: The Banco de Avío.* Amherst: University of Massachusetts Press, 1983.

Pratt, Mary Louise. *Imperial Eyes: Travel Writing and Transculturation.* London: Routledge, 1992.

Reddy, William M. *Money and Liberty in Modern Europe: A Critique of Historical Understanding.* Cambridge: Cambridge University Press, 1987.

Romero, Luis Alberto. *La Sociedad de la Igualdad: Los artesanos de Santiago de Chile y sus primeras experiencias políticas.* Buenos Aires: Instituto Torcuato DiTella, 1978.

Roque Gondra, Luis, et al. eds. *El pensamiento económico latinoamericano.* Mexico: Fondo de Cultura Económica, 1945.

Roseberry, William. *Anthropologies and Histories: Essays in Culture, History, and Political Economy.* New Brunswick: Rutgers University Press, 1987.

Safford, Frank. *The Ideal of the Practical: Colombia's Struggle to Form a Technical Elite.* Austin: University of Texas Press, 1976.

———. "Politics, Ideology, and Society in Post-Independence Spanish America, 1821–1870." In Leslie Bethell, ed., *The Cambridge History of Latin America* 3:347–421. Cambridge: Cambridge University Press, 1985.

Salvatorre, Ricardo. "Markets, Social Discipline, and Popular Protest: Latin America from Charles III to the IMF." Paper presented to the Social Science History Association, New Orleans, 1991.

Salvucci, Richard. *Textiles and Capitalism in Mexico: An Economic History of the Obrajes, 1539–1840.* Princeton: Princeton University Press, 1987.

Scitovsky, Tibor. "Two Concepts of External Economies." *Journal of Political Economy* 52, no. 2 (1954): 143–52.

Scott, Joan W. *Gender and the Politics of History.* New York: Columbia University Press, 1988.

Semmel, Bernard. *The Rise of Free Trade Imperialism: Classical Political Economy and the Empire of Free Trade and Imperialism, 1750–1850.* Cambridge: Cambridge University Press, 1970.

Senghaas, Dieter. "Friedrich List and the Basic Problems of Modern Development." *Review* 14, no. 3 (1991): 451–67.

Shafer, Robert James. *The Economic Societies in the Spanish World, 1763–1821.* Syracuse: Syracuse University Press, 1958.

Sheahan, John. *Patterns of Development in Latin America: Poverty, Repression, and Economic Strategy.* Princeton: Princeton University Press, 1987.

Shumway, Nicolas. *The Invention of Argentina.* Berkeley and Los Angeles: University of California Press, 1991.

Skidmore, Thomas E., and Peter H. Smith. *Modern Latin America.* New York: Oxford University Press, 1984.

Smith, Robert S. "The Wealth of Nations in Spain and Spanish America, 1780–1930." *Journal of Political Economy* 55, no. 2 (1957): 104–26.

Spengler, Joseph J. "Notes on the International Transmission of Economic Ideas." *History of Political Economy* 2, no. 1 (1970): 133–51.

Spiegel, Henry William. *The Growth of Economic Thought.* Durham: Duke University Press, 1983.

Staley, Charles E. *A History of Economic Thought: From Aristotle to Arrow.* Cambridge: Basil Blackwell, 1989.

Stein, Stanley J., and Barbara Stein. *The Colonial Heritage of Latin America: Essays on Economic Dependence in Perspective.* New York: Oxford University Press, 1970.

Streeten, Paul. "Development Ideas in Historical Perspective." In Rothko Chapel Colloquium, *Toward a New Strategy for Development,* 21–52. New York: Pergamon, 1979.

Taylor, Arthur J. *Laissez-faire and State Intervention in Nineteenth-Century Britain.* Studies in Economic and Social History. London: Macmillan, 1972.

Taylor, William B. "Between Global Process and Local Knowledge: An Inquiry into Early Latin American Social History, 1500–1900." In O. Zunz, ed., *Reliving the Past: The Worlds of Social History,* 115–90. Chapel Hill: University of North Carolina Press, 1985.

Thompson, E. P. "The Moral Economy of the English Crowd in the Eighteenth Century." *Past and Present* 50, no. 1 (1971): 76–136.

Thompson, Noel W. *The People's Science: The Popular Political Economy of Exploitation and Crisis, 1816–1834.* Cambridge: Cambridge University Press, 1984.

Thomson, Guy P. C. *Puebla de los Ángeles: Industry and Society in a Mexican City, 1700–1850.* Boulder: Westview Press, 1988.

Thorp, Rosemary. "Latin America and the International Economy from the First World War to the World Depression." In Leslie Bethell, ed., *The*

Cambridge History of Latin America 4:57–81. Cambridge: Cambridge University Press, 1986.

Thorp, Rosemary, ed. *Latin America in the 1930s: The Role of the Periphery in the World Crisis*. London: Macmillan, 1984.

Topik, Steven. *The Political Economy of the Brazilian State, 1889–1930*. Austin: University of Texas Press, 1987.

———. "State Interventionism in a Liberal Regime: Brazil, 1889–1930." *Hispanic American Historical Review* 60, no. 4 (1980): 593–616.

Véliz, Claudio. *The Centralist Tradition in Latin America*. Princeton: Princeton University Press, 1980.

———. "La mesa de tres patas." *Desarrollo Económico* 3 (1963): 231–47.

Versiani, Flavio Rabelo. "Industrial Investment in an 'Export' Economy: The Brazilian Experience Before 1914." Working Paper 2. London: Institute of Latin American Studies, 1974.

Wallerstein, Immanuel, and Ignacy Sachs, eds. "Developmentalist Theory Before 1945." *Review* 8–9 (1990–1991).

Weaver, Frederick S. *Class, State, and Industrial Structure: The Historical Experience of South American Industrial Growth*. Westport, Conn.: Greenwood Press, 1980.

Weinstein, Barbara. *The Amazon Rubber Boom, 1850–1920*. Stanford: Stanford University Press, 1983.

Whigham, Thomas L. "The Iron Works of Ibycui: Paraguayan Industrial Development in the Mid-Nineteenth Century." *Americas* 35, no. 2 (1978): 201–18.

Will, Robert M. "The Introduction of Classical Economics into Chile." *Hispanic American Historical Review* 44, no. 1 (1964): 1–21.

Winch, Donald. "The Emergence of Economics as a Science, 1750–1870." In C. Cipolla, ed., *The Fontana Economic History of Europe*, vol. 3, *The Industrial Revolution*, 507–73. Glasgow: Fontana, 1973.

Zea, Leopoldo. *The Latin American Mind*. Norman: University of Oklahoma Press, 1963.

Zeitlin, Maurice. *The Civil Wars in Chile, or, the Bourgeois Revolutions That Never Were*. Princeton: Princeton University Press, 1984.

Index

Compositor:	Keystone Typesetting, Inc.
Text:	10/13 Galliard
Display:	Galliard
Printer and Binder:	Maple-Vail Book Mfg. Group, Inc.